TRANSPORTATION AND THE AMERICAN PEOPLE

Railroads Past & Present

H. ROGER GRANT AND THOMAS HOBACK, EDITORS

H. ROGER GRANT

TRANSPORTATION AND THE AMERICAN PEOPLE

INDIANA UNIVERSITY PRESS

This book is a publication of

Indiana University Press
Office of Scholarly Publishing
Herman B Wells Library 350
1320 East 10th Street
Bloomington, Indiana 47405 USA

iupress.indiana.edu

Library of Congress Cataloging-
in-Publication Data

Names: Grant, H. Roger, [date] author.
Title: Transportation and the American
people / H. Roger Grant.
Description: Bloomington : Indiana
University Press, [2019] | Series:
Railroads past and present | Includes
bibliographical references and
index.
Identifiers: LCCN 2018049665 (print) |
LCCN 2018051099 (ebook) | ISBN
9780253043344 (e-book) | ISBN
9780253043306 (cl : alk. paper)
Subjects: LCSH: Transportation—United
States—History.
Classification: LCC HE203 (ebook) | LCC
HE203 .G693 2019 (print) | DDC
388.0973—dc23
LC record available at https://
lccn.loc.gov/2018049665

1 2 3 4 5 24 23 22 21 20 19

FOR MY BROTHER:

Richard D. Grant (1933–2004)

CONTENTS

Preface   ix

Acknowledgments   xi

1   Steady but Uncomfortable: Stagecoaches and the American People   1

2   Waterways and the American People   23

3   Slow and Steady: Canals and the American People   63

4   Railways and the American People   95

5   Buses and the American People   149

6   Airplanes and the American People   183

Notes   219

Index   241

PREFACE

Transportation and the American People is designed as the third book in my specialized social history series. The previous studies, both published by Indiana University Press, include *Railroads and the American People* (2012) and *Electric Interurbans and the American People* (2016). The present work partially came about because of what I saw as a void in the published literature. For years I have taught an upper-division undergraduate course on the history of American transportation, and early on I realized the need for a more inclusive and available work on the topic. Although there are studies that explore aspects of the social history of travel, none are comprehensive and up-to-date. Bus passengers, most of all, have been marginalized, having never been covered in any depth. Through its coverage of six commercial travel experiences, ranging from those on stagecoaches to airplanes, *Transportation and the American People* hopefully addresses these shortcomings.

A challenging dimension of writing the present volume involved its connection to my previous two works. Obviously, I cannot examine steam and electric interurban railways to the same degree here, needing in this study to reduce coverage and to provide fresh narrative materials. Those readers who wish for more specialized information on such topics as town building, regulatory reform, and railroaders' personalities should consult these earlier books.

There is no question that historians of all types should pay more attention to the nonrailroad topics found in this study. It makes sense for further work to examine in greater detail the social history of airlines, buses, canals, stagecoaches, and waterways. Nor should we ignore noncommercial transport, including travel by foot, horseback, bicycle, motorcycle, and automobile. Each topic might easily become one or perhaps multiple full-length studies. Through additional research and by asking imaginative questions, a more comprehensive social history of American transportation can be achieved.

When one considers the sweep of the American experience, it becomes clear that the movement of people has been a vital and ongoing part of molding the national character. Historian Frederick Jackson Turner proposed his famed frontier hypothesis in 1893—that American democracy was rooted in the frontier—when he saw correctly that mobility contributed to such recognizable traits as individualism, materialism, nationalism, and optimism, as well as democratic thought.

ACKNOWLEDGMENTS

As with every book project, there are individuals and institutions to acknowledge that have made contributions. Various contacts that I have made through my longtime association with members of the Lexington Group in Transportation History have allowed me to tap the insights of knowledgeable people and have provided suggestions for source materials. One person stands out: John (Jack) W. White Jr., former curator of transportation at the Smithsonian Institution. Even though recovering from a stroke, he kindly commented on several chapters of the manuscript. Others, too, have assisted, notably William (Bill) Howes and Art Peterson. Kay Crocker, IT specialist at Clemson University, repeatedly gave me much-needed technical support, and Alan Burns likewise aided with production. A variety of institutions have helped. These include the Booth Western Art Museum, Cartersville, Georgia; Main Street Blytheville, Blytheville, Arkansas; Indiana Historical Society, Indianapolis; Library of Congress, Washington, DC; Library of Virginia, Richmond; Mercantile Library at the University of Missouri–Saint Louis; Minnesota Discovery Center, Chisholm, Minnesota; Toledo-Lucas County Public Library, Toledo, Ohio; Wells Fargo Museum, San Francisco; and the Clemson interlibrary loan department. Once again I have received continued support from the talented and dedicated staff of Indiana University Press.

Since 2006 I have benefited from being the Kathryn and Calhoun Lemon Professor of History at Clemson. This academic chair has provided research funds and allowed for a reduced teaching load, just as it aided with my two previous social history works in this three-part series, *Railroads and the American People* and *Electric Interurbans and the American People*.

As with more than thirty previous academic books, my wife, Martha Farrington Grant, read the manuscript and made valuable suggestions, which is devotion above and beyond our marriage contract that we made in 1966.

TRANSPORTATION AND THE AMERICAN PEOPLE

Steady but Uncomfortable   1

Stagecoaches and the American People

From colonial times until the steam-car civilization took hold with the coming of the Gilded Age, the stagecoach was often the primary form of commercial domestic travel and essential where water options were unavailable. "Stagecoaches were the symbol of rapid transportation in 1815," observed economic historian George Rogers Taylor. "Though coastwise voyages were less expensive and certainly more comfortable, travelers in a hurry took the stages, whose speed was being considerably increased as a result of the rapid spread of turnpikes." On poor roads and trails, coaches were slower than most river, coastal, and lake vessels. But compared with trips on the nation's emerging network of canal packets, stagecoaches usually traveled at speeds that were two, three, or more times greater. Time certainly mattered, but there was widespread agreement among patrons that the stagecoach was frequently an uncomfortable form of public transportation, most of all when they were riding overnight.[1]

Although Americans would reveal their proclivity for innovations, the modern stagecoach originated in Great Britain or possibly France. It is impossible to determine when the prototype of this land vehicle appeared, but the "Staging Era" dates from at least the sixteenth century. Within a hundred years or so, great advances took place with coaches, roads, and infrastructure both in Great Britain and Europe. Originally these small, horse-drawn contraptions lacked springs, but eventually they became strongly sprung, greatly enhancing passenger comfort.

In Great Britain, as more turnpikes opened, initially radiating out of London, other large population centers also became coach hubs. Roadside public houses likewise became commonplace, and they facilitated and enhanced travel. After all, the stagecoach derived its name from how this transport was structured: trips were made in a series of short-distance stages between stops at taverns and inns. Such places might be substantial

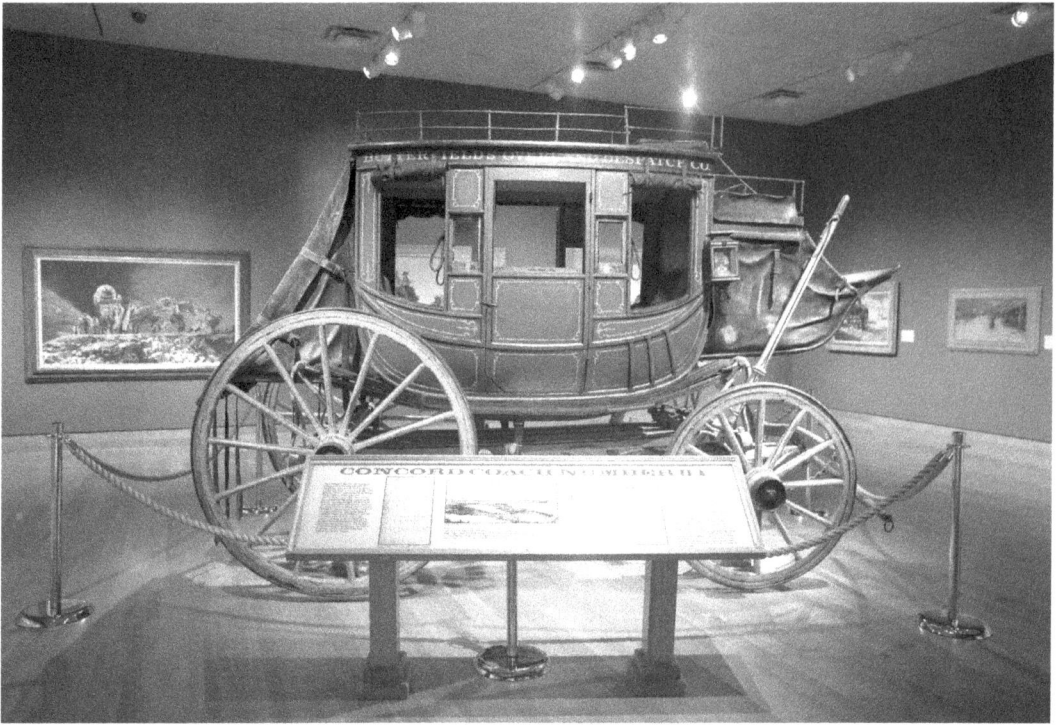

A well-preserved Concord stagecoach, built in 1864 for the Butterfield Overland Despatch Company, is on permanent exhibit at the Booth Western Art Museum in Cartersville, Georgia.

Booth Western Art Museum

structures, providing support services for both passengers and operators. Travelers could acquire food and drink, and likely a bed for the night. At designated stops the horses, usually a spirited team of four, would be exchanged for fresh ones.

Stagecoaches appeared in pre–Revolutionary War America, although the exact date of the first service is not known. The initial stage route, which may date from 1706, linked Burlington and Port Amboy, New Jersey. It created a land-water route between the two largest colonial cities, New York and Philadelphia. Within a decade a line connected Boston and Newport, Rhode Island, and by the 1730s a mostly direct land service linked Philadelphia with New York. Additional routes opened before the revolution, including one between Boston and Portsmouth, New Hampshire, and two on Long Island, New York. Stages commonly operated in conjunction with connecting water transport, just as they had in that pioneer Burlington-Port Amboy operation.[2]

During the early national period, an explosion in stage routes occurred. A rapidly growing population and an accelerating turnpike movement attracted scores of stagecoach operators, many inspired by the profitable Lancaster Turnpike, which opened in the mid-1790s between Philadelphia and Lancaster, Pennsylvania. These newly established lines were concentrated in New England and the Middle Atlantic states, where generally passable roads served popular destinations.

By 1801 Boston, for one, claimed extensive access to stagecoaches. One hundred and sixteen coaches arrived and departed weekly. There were twenty-six separate lines to as many destinations. Notably, all of these operations came about before the turnpike craze peaked. A quarter of a century later, turnpikes and other improved roads made Albany, New York, a premier stagecoach center. "Probably there is no point in the United States where so many public stages meet and find employment as at Albany," commented a writer in 1827. "They issue thence upon every point in the compass and it has become a business in which a large amount of capital is invested, and much enterprise and competition enlisted." As had been the established practice, these stages commonly connected with area water transport, linking landlocked communities with steamboats on Lake Champlain and the Hudson River and packets on the Erie Canal.[3]

Primitive stage wagons or stagecoaches also rolled along roads (or trails) in the southlands. Take Georgia. The first line began in 1786 between Savannah and Augusta, but it failed because of financial troubles after only a year. A decade later a second attempt to connect the two growing cities succeeded. Then in 1797 another stage line operated out of Savannah, connecting with Charleston, South Carolina. As settlements developed westward from the Savannah River valley, additional stage routes opened.[4]

As the nineteenth century progressed, a vast network of stage lines covered the settled or mostly settled areas of the East and South. When pioneers migrated westward into the Old Northwest and Old Southwest, stagecoaches followed. For a time stagecoaches were able to compete successfully with some of the early steamboats that served ports on the Great Lakes and places along the Ohio-Mississippi river system and other streams, largely because land travel was less dangerous than water navigation. It did not take long for the citizenry of the larger towns and cities to have a good chance of accessing a stage line, and they might have had multiple options.

Ohio is but one state that experienced a transportation revolution. By the 1840s residents in the north were taking advantage of their access to new Great Lakes steam vessels, and those in the south commonly relied on Ohio and Muskingum riverboats. Buckeye State residents who lived in interior sections found Ohio's shallow rivers of little or no value, however, although some could take advantage of an expanding lake-to-river and lateral canal network. A few miles of railroad had also opened, and more were either under construction or planned. Nevertheless, early on stagecoaches played a vital role in how people moved about the state and beyond its borders.

Ohio's capital city of Columbus illustrates the importance of commercial stages. Although it was located on a feeder canal of the

Ohio & Erie Canal, its citizens mostly depended on land transport. In the early 1820s William Neil, a local banker, entered the stagecoach business, and by the early 1840s his Ohio Stage Company operated a system of about 1,500 miles, including service that extended into nearby states. Neil and other operators benefited from a series of improved roads, but most of all from the famed National Road or Cumberland Road. This well-built "Appian Way of America," or the "Grand Portage" between the Atlantic Seaboard and the trans-Allegheny West, was federally financed and begun in 1811, reached Columbus in 1833 from Cumberland, Maryland, and soon entered Indianapolis. Modest construction efforts continued into Illinois before railroads made the road largely obsolete in the 1850s. According to *Mitchell's Travel Guide through the United States*, published in 1837, it is hardly surprising that fourteen of the Buckeye State's thirty-two stage routes connected with this grand pike, and others used it exclusively or in part.[5]

By the time workers pushed the National Road beyond Indianapolis, stage routes had emerged in the trans-Mississippi West. Most were modest in length, usually connecting major settlements with lake and river transportation. Later, though, several claimed great length, extending from Missouri and Tennessee terminals across the prairies, mountains, and deserts to California, a US possession since the Mexican War and the center of developing gold fields.

Even before the California gold rush got under way, an increasing network of mail and passenger stage runs appeared in the western portions of the Old Northwest and in trans-Mississippi states and territories. By mid-century the firm of Frink & Walker of Chicago dominated staging operations in Illinois, Indiana, Iowa, Michigan, Missouri, and Wisconsin. Like so many lines, Frink & Walker coaches connected with water transport, including Lake Michigan boats and Illinois & Michigan canal packets. They also served Galena & Chicago Union passenger trains and soon those of other gestating railroads as well.[6]

The stage routes that caught the public's greatest attention involved what were arguably the longest in the world, namely those from the nation's midsection to the Pacific coast. In the late 1850s veteran stagecoach owner John Butterfield and his partners took advantage of a lucrative US mail contract to launch mail and passenger service between Saint Louis (stages left from Tipton, Missouri, western terminus of the Pacific Rail Road, which connected to Saint Louis) and San Francisco, via a southern route: Fort Smith, El Paso, Tucson, and Los Angeles. The distance on this "Oxbow Route" was an astonishing 2,795 miles. A connecting line from Memphis to Fort Smith was also established. With the coming of sectional strife a central route emerged, one that provided a similar mail and passenger service and that was also operated by Butterfield. Starting in

Saint Joseph, Missouri, it crossed the present states of Kansas, Nebraska, Wyoming, Utah, and Nevada before reaching California. Lengthy connecting lines also appeared, including one from Utah through Idaho to Oregon. Also of importance was the Leavenworth & Pikes Peak Express, organized by William Russell and launched in 1859. This mail and passenger service linked the Missouri River with the gold-mining boomtown of Denver, a distance of nearly seven hundred miles.[7]

The coming of more railroads during the immediate post–Civil War years, highlighted by completion of the transcontinental Union Pacific-Central Pacific in 1869, made long-distance Midwest to West Coast stage operations unnecessary. Travelers found steamcars to be much faster, more comfortable, and less expensive. The stagecoach nevertheless remained an important transportation component in parts of the West; not until the early twentieth century did rail lines finally dominate. The mining frontier moved about, a process that continued long after the forty-niners made their way to California. Stage operations became essential for the movement of people, mail, and express to and from these often remote diggings. Assuming that there were passable trails and roads, stagecoaches offered flexible routing patterns. Operators became adept at providing new service to these mineral locales and then abandoning them when business waned or disappeared altogether. Even with the coming of the iron horse, a mining settlement might not last for more than a few years, making construction of an expensive rail outlet impractical.[8]

Stagecoaches commonly served places that lacked direct railroad service. That made them wanted and financially viable. One example comes from Arizona Territory. Although several stagecoach routes had appeared by the time of the Civil War, mineral discoveries in the 1870s and later led to new mining centers. In 1877 the opening of the isolated Tip Top silver mines in the Black Canyon area north of Phoenix prompted formation of the Patterson, Caldwell & Company Stage Line between Phoenix and Prescott, and for several years passenger, mail, and express traffic sustained it. The petering out of deposits and subsequent railroad building through the region explain the firm's demise and the dissolution of similar operations.[9]

Even in the heavily settled East, stagecoaches continued to serve locations until alternative forms of transportation, usually automobiles and buses, made them unnecessary. The Jameson's Stage Line, based in Sandwich, New Hampshire, is representative. Although a summer operation, the company provided convenient connections with the Concord & Montreal Railroad at Nashua Junction, New Hampshire, and with the Boston & Lowell Railroad at Weirs, New Hampshire, for Centre Harbor, New Hampshire, and for the Lake Winnipesaukee steamer *Lady of the Lake*. This operation lasted until the early years of the twentieth century.[10]

All transportation forms—stagecoaches included—change over time. Yet after introduction of the well-built and practical Concord coach in the 1820s, only modest upgrades and refinements to stagecoaches followed. Initially domestic stagecoaches were not much more than wagons with backless benches. This seating provided capacity for a dozen passengers, and there was room for the driver or reinsman who managed the team of horses or perhaps mules. Still, these primitive conveyances were stages; they required a change of animals at regular intervals along a set route.

The American stagecoach responded well to the generally poor conditions of roads, including some turnpikes. Unlike contemporary foreign coaches, domestic ones lacked metal springs. Metal-spring suspension worked well on Europe's smooth roadways, making for a reasonably comfortable ride. But in the American environment, springs were vulnerable to breaking, potentially leaving the driver and passengers stranded in a remote location. Springs, furthermore, made for a lateral rigidity, causing top-heavy coaches to overturn if rounding a sharp curve at a brisk clip. In the early nineteenth century, carriage makers explored better designs. They sought to build a light but sturdy enclosed coach that could be easily pulled by a team of horses and was flexible enough to provide a safe and endurable ride over difficult roads.

As with the plethora of automobile makers in the early twentieth century, a number of small manufacturers (in reality woodworking shops) built stagecoaches, these "wooden machines." Although a true General Motors equivalent never appeared, the two firms that came the closest to dominating the business were Abbot, Downing & Company of Concord, New Hampshire (its geographical location gave the coach its popular name—the Concord stage), and the Eaton & Gilbert Company of Troy, New York (likewise, because of its origin, it became known as the Troy stage). By the mid-1820s the latter firm gained fame for a multitude of products: "chariotees, razees, gigs, sulkeys, coach wagons, and pleasure wagons." Later on Eaton & Gilbert manufactured railway cars.[11]

The Concord stage best typifies the American stagecoach, and no wonder competitors modeled their coaches after this successful New Hampshire product. Although built in several sizes, all Concords shared similar characteristics. The body, commonly fashioned from white oak, white ash, and other hardwoods and braced with iron bands, was oval or "egg-shaped" and flattened on top to provide extra room for passengers and baggage. This exposed area had iron railings to secure luggage and any riders. A raised open front seat served the driver and a passenger or two, and there was a footboard for their feet. Also included were a leather-covered front boot and a larger covered, triangular-shaped rear boot designed for mail and express storage. The suspension system featured two leather thoroughbraces that extended lengthwise under the coach and were attached at each end to a standard that protruded up from the axle. The thoroughbraces themselves consisted of leather straps placed on top of each other to a thickness of about three inches, and they permitted the coach to rock slightly forward and back. The wheel sets stood at different heights: the rear ones were sixty inches high, and those at the front were forty-five inches, permitting sharp turns and allowing the stage to clear road obstacles. In the West, especially, manufacturers modified the wheels, namely widening them to better negotiate mud and sand. The body was usually painted in glossy, bright colors like green, red, and yellow and protected with several coats of varnish. Paintings of landscapes or of noted historical or contemporary figures decorated the side panels. Some coaches were named. The Western Stage Company, which served communities in the Midwest, had coaches stenciled with names such as "Councillor O'Neil," "Judge Hammon," and "Yankee." These names, like those on some contemporary canal packets, often appeared in fancy gold-leaf script. And at each side of the coach a square brass-and-glass candle lamp was mounted, but they really were more for ornamentation than illumination.[12]

A Concord stage interior might best be described as a "cozy nook." It was outfitted with three passenger seats. Those at the front and back were upholstered in cloth or leather; these faced each other, and the one in the center faced forward. This middle seat had its center fabric-covered segment bolted to the floor and an extension hinged to each end. The two sections folded up to allow passageways between the two doors and rear seat. A British traveler provided this description of the distinct seating component: "The three passengers who sit upon it, rest their backs against a stuffed leathern strap, permanently buckled to one side of the carriage, and attached to the other side by means of a stout iron hook." Passengers usually had barely fifteen inches of seat space. The normal inside capacity was nine, but several more might crowd in, squeezing into the corners. Leather straps on the sidewalls helped adjacent riders to hold on over bumpy roads. During wet or cold weather, leather or oilcloth curtains could be rolled down over the windows. The coach interiors, too, were usually attractively decorated. "The inside of coaches were all handsomely and artistically painted and ornamented," a traveler said about the Concord stages that operated over the National Road.[13] The Concord stage left the factory a well-designed and well-made vehicle, a wonderful illustration of Yankee ingenuity and craftsmanship. Moreover, these coaches were exceptionally durable. Some remained in regular service over poor roads for a half century or longer.

The coaches were not self-propelled; animals provided locomotion. Most were horses, and they were the common work or carriage horses of the day rather than fast Arabians or thoroughbreds. Mules, which were often employed in desert locales and at times in the hot and humid southlands, likewise pulled plows, carts, and wagons. When compared to horses, mules were cheaper to acquire and to maintain.

The costs of a 2,500- to 3,000-pound stagecoach and its animal power were not excessively prohibitive for an individual operator. Some operators had the personal wherewithal to enter the business, but many acquired a partner or two. New stages ranged in price from $1,000 to $2,500 or more, and good road horses might cost from $250 to $500 each. These entry costs were somewhat comparable to those of a canal packet boat and animal team.

DRIVERS

While the Concord-type coach epitomized staging equipment, the driver, reinsman, or "Knight of the Reins" best represented the human component. This was the man (and in rare instances the woman[14]) who was in charge. The public came to greatly admire the driver, who was known for his steady nerves, determination, resourcefulness, and love for the job. Following the death of a beloved local driver, the Portland *Oregonian* editorialized, "Pride of craftsmanship was the rule among them—it would be a fine thing for the country if every man took such joy in his job as the *old stage drivers* [italics in original]." Mark Twain, who in 1861 traveled by stage on the Central Overland Route from Saint Joseph, Missouri, to Carson City, Nevada Territory, remarked: "The stage-driver was a hero—a great and shining dignitary, the world's favorite son, the envy of the people, the observed of the nations." This often-dashing individual frequently wore the finest, yet most practical, of clothing. When bringing his stage to a scheduled stop with a smart trot of his team, he might put on a stylish top hat. A surely apt contemporary description: "Handsome, dressy, and a perfect lady's man."[15]

What was the driver's background? He commonly hailed from a farming past. Perhaps, too, he had been a stable boy or had worked in similar jobs; he likely had firsthand experience with horses. A fondness for these animals may have gotten the future driver involved in amateur racing: driving a fast Morgan trotter over tortuous country roads would have made him an ideal person to manage a team. Other backgrounds were represented, including clerks, mechanics, and canal boatmen. Then, as railroad competition eliminated staging operations in the East, an unemployed driver could move west to continue his profession. Once employed by a stagecoach company or even a stagecoach owner, he might establish a family tradition, having sons, nephews, or cousins who became drivers. These offspring and relatives would learn the art of reinsmanship from early boyhood. Stage driving was a respected, albeit demanding, occupation.[16]

No one questioned the skills required of a stagecoach driver. He needed to know how to control his horses or mules. "The Driver's skill with his whip was great as Robin Hood's with the bow and arrow," said one source. "It was the expression of his will to his champing team, and from it they knew their duty better than if they could have understood his spoken word. Concentration and long use had ground and polished the experienced Driver's skill with his long whip to a rapier's point." One contemporary went so far as to divide drivers into four distinct classes (numerical divisions added):

> (1) Awkward, slovenly, careless drivers, such as handled the whip and "ribbons" so clumsily, and kept their teams so unseemly together, up hill, down grades and on the level; (2) Cruel men—their cruelty amounting almost to brutality. This class seemed to take a fiendish delight in whipping, lashing and gashing horses; (3) Careful, easy-going, common, every day kind of drivers—men who never made pretensions to fancy styles; (4) Well dressed drivers, clean and neat in person, and men who regarded sitting down to a meal in shirt sleeves as *contra bonos mores* [contrary to good manners]. This class manipulated the whip and "ribbons" scientifically, and sat on the box in a way that showed they were masters of the situation.

Operating the coach itself meant mastering its primitive and temperamental braking system. "A real reinsman could perform on the brake with the skill of a musician manipulating pipe-organ pedals." Furthermore, drivers had to know the roads they traveled intimately and had to understand how to meet the public and how to cope with emergencies.[17]

Being exposed to the adversities of the road required proper preparation and physical toughness. Reinsmen had to dress appropriately for inclement weather, whether cloudbursts, hail, sleet, or snow. In winter months, assuming the stage operated during heavy snows or at all, they bundled up with coats, scarves, gloves, and boots, but still they might be miserable. In the summer a blazing sun, wind, and blowing dust, especially on desert or semi-humid prairie runs, hardly made for a comfortable trip.

Firsthand descriptions of drivers abound. Typical of reinsmen in the East and also likely in other regions, this description explains why they were admired. "Imposing in bearskin caps, in vast greatcoats, and with their teams covered with ivory rings, with fine horses and clean coaches, they and their surroundings were pleasant to the eyes." There was more. "They acquired characteristic modes of speaking, of thinking. They were terse and sententious in expression, had what is termed horse sense." When traveling in Ohio in 1842, Charles Dickens made these sharp comments: "The frequent change of coachmen [drivers] works no change or variety in the coachman's character. If he be capable of smartness of any kind, moral or physical, he has a faculty of concealing it which is truly marvelous. He never speaks to you as you sit beside him on the box, and if you speak to him, he answers (if at all) in monosyllables." His expanded commentary: "He always chews and always spits, and never encumbers himself with a pocket-handkerchief. The consequences to the box passenger, especially when the wind blows towards him, are not agreeable."[18]

Regular drivers were usually well known in places along their regular routes. They knew their territory and often its citizenry. "Drivers carried from country to town, from house to house, news of the health of loved ones, or of sickness when weary nurses were too tired to write. A kindly driver would stop his horses or walk them past a lane corner where an anxious mother or sister waited, dreading; and passenger in the coach would hear him call out to her, 'John's better, fever's all gone.'" Some did errands and other favors for residents. In the less populated trans-Mississippi West there developed a pronounced informality, and it was not uncommon for these drivers to acquire colorful nicknames, some of which surely sounded strange to outsiders: Fiddler Jim, Fish Creek Bill, Happy Jack, Rowdy Peter, Rattlesnake Peter, and Whisky Jack.[19]

Whisky Jack may have enjoyed a stiff drink or two before or after his time on the stage. Some contemporaries suggested that when facing a challenging route under not-so-ideal conditions, a driver might turn to alcohol to steady his nerves, and others remarked that "drivers were few who passed up a free drink or two at the stations." Yet heavy drinking or perhaps drinking at all may not have been the norm among reinsmen. A knowledgeable source about drivers in the West stated: "Passengers riding on the seat with the driver was supposed to treat the driver to drinks and cigars on the road. Drinks was free to drivers at all stations but it was seldom that [the] driver drank on the road."[20]

Unlike later railroads with their rigid book of rules, which included the "Rule G" that prohibited the use of alcohol while on duty, stagecoaches usually enjoyed freedom from outside controls. The driver was the man in charge of his stage—totally in charge. Admittedly attempts were made to provide rules of conduct, but they really amounted only to the employment of moral suasion. In the 1820s a group of New York State drivers, owners, and other interested parties drew up guidelines that sought to control the number of glasses of spirituous drinks an employee might be allowed to consume in a day. Their efforts also produced these resolutions: "No Stage Driver shall leave his team untied unless he has two men to hold them," and "No Stage Driver shall drive his team faster, nor allow it to be driven faster than a trot."[21]

Drivers made a decent living. Salaries were comparable to those earned on other contemporary forms of travel, perhaps with the exception of steamboat pilots, locomotive engineers, and some railroad conductors. Unlike British stagecoach drivers, Americans did not expect tipping, although it occurred. Some reinsmen saved; others did not. After retiring from a hectic career, a driver with enough accumulated savings might open a small business, establish a farm or ranch, or simply enjoy a comfortable home life during his golden years.

HAPPY TRAILS

Americans have always sought better transportation, whether for their own travel or for movement of agricultural products, manufactured goods, US mail, or something else. In parts of the nation, most of all in New England and the Middle Atlantic states, residents frequently backed efforts to construct investor-owned turnpikes, and they urged governmental bodies to build and improve public roads. Better roads meant better connectivity.

Citizens welcomed the establishment of regular stagecoach operations. The arrival of the first coach, paralleling that of the first canal boat, first steam train, or first electric interurban car, might have been recognized by the community in a celebratory way. A good example comes from Montrose, seat of Susquehanna County, Pennsylvania. Early in the nineteenth century, investor, community, and political support backed the Milford and Owego Turnpike, Bridgewater and Wilkes-Barre Turnpike, and other area roadway betterments. With improved roads in northeastern Pennsylvania and in neighboring New York, it became practical for a stage company to serve the isolated town of Montrose. The red-letter day for this regular overland connection to the outside world came in January 1824. "Huzza! huzza! for the new stage *via* Milford and Owego turnpike," wrote resident Jerre Lyons in his diary. "This evening about 7 o'clock, the new stage direct from New York. O what a shouting! It was saluted by the drum and fife, and by the cheers of the populace. A number of buildings were brilliantly illuminated." He added, "The stage was forty-one hours coming from the city, but might have got in less than forty hours, but stayed at Dundaff [Pennsylvania] unnecessarily; six persons aboard."[22]

As with all domestic transportation, stagecoach patrons encountered diverse travel experiences, good and bad. Although negative reactions predominated, there were positive commentaries. If roads were smooth, weather nice, equipment operable, and driver and support personnel accommodating, a trip could be pleasant, on schedule, relatively comfortable, and often faster and more convenient than alternative forms of commercial travel. Specific pleasures varied. Some stage passengers relished the company of their fellow riders. Seating was democratic; rich and not-so-rich, young and old, male and female, and native and foreign-born rode together. This mixture allowed for a range of talk, including the latest political news and debate, economic opportunities in business and real estate, matters of health and disease, and the questioning of any faraway traveler. Also common on a trip, whether long or short, were commentaries about the passing landscape. A driver might indicate points of interest. One reinsman in New England liked to show off "the biggest ellum [*sic*] in the county," and "the best grove of sugar-maples in the state." And riders might enjoy a breathtaking vista as a coach traveled along a ridgetop or some other elevated location. A traveler from Louisville to Frankfort, Kentucky, had a "generally pleasant journey because the region between the two cities is very romantic and the continual change between mountain and valley offered the eye many a beautiful picture." Even sprawling prairies pleased some. "The rugged, hard, sublime mountain scenery has its charms, but to me the softened, genial, finished, smooth outlines of a cooling sea of land, sinking in the horizon, and colored by the different hues of the atmosphere, awakens sentiments of a different and far more agreeable character." There might be singing, telling of tall tales, a friendly game of cards, or a practical joke or two. Historian Philip Jordan made these comments about stagecoach travel along the National Road: "When travelers wearied of talk and when all good stories had been told, they sometimes amused themselves by opening mailbags." (Although such actions were against federal law, apparently no one faced legal consequences.) "They then would hold a letter at arm's length from the coach window and beckon to a villager. The excited rustic, thinking the missive was for him, might sprint after the stage for a mile or so before realizing he was duped." And female passengers might encounter deferential males. In the late 1830s a woman stage rider from the German states observed pleasantly that "Americans reserve the first place to all ladies without distinction of class, which you seek in vain in Germany.[23]

For many patrons there was the excitement of taking a stagecoach, especially for the first time. They surely anticipated that an adventure would follow. Merely watching a stage coming into a stop had its appeal. In the smaller communities, the arrival and departure of this physical contact with the greater world became a highlight of a typical day. Even in the twilight years of staging, there remained that pleasant sensation of an arriving coach. An itinerant laborer recalled the following events, which had occurred in 1900:

> What a wonderful country [Wyoming] I thought to myself, as I sat there [on the hotel porch] and looked on mountain peaks, further south over in Colorado, and pretty soon, I caught sight of a small black moving object away out there among the sagebrush and greasewood bushes, and wondered what it could be. After watching it for a while, first losing sight of it, and then picking it up again, as it swung around the point of a hill, or a pile of rocks, on the trail, ever coming nearer and nearer, until I finally made it out as the overland stagecoach, drawn by six horses, and on its daily run between Rawlins [Wyoming] and the mining country, which lay a hundred miles or more south of there.

Then came the most exciting moments.

> Pretty soon here they come, clipping right along up Front street, the six horses in a long swinging trot, that did not slacken until the driver pulled them up and swung them around the corner and up to the stage station, and stopped just a little ways from where I was watching, and it sure was some pretty sight to see, the six fine, rangy horses, the big heavy stage coach, with the driver sitting upon the box, with his long whip, and big white stetson hat, and a six-shooter strapped around the his waist, and the express guard, who sat beside him, with two big six-shooters strapped on him, and a winchester rifle held across his lap, gee, it all gave me a thrill that I cannot explain.[24]

If passengers stopped overnight at an inn or tavern, they might find accommodations to their liking. This was generally true along turnpikes and roads in the East, where by the 1830s business and support facilities had matured. Usually food was good and plentiful, beds clean and comfortable, hosts pleasant and knowledgeable, and prices reasonable. There was a renowned stagecoach stop on the well-traveled Boston to Providence road in the village of Wrentham, Massachusetts, a place that sported two hotels, Fuller's and Polley's. Dinner were always "a superb creation," and "many a traveler would say that although he had dined sumptuously in other places he had never tasted dinners like those he obtained at Wrentham."

Travelers in the poorly developed regions, particularly the West, usually did not find such fare, though occasionally they seemed pleased with their scheduled stops. "At the Green river station we had breakfast—hot biscuits, fresh antelope steaks, and coffee," remarked Mark Twain about his 1861 trip to Nevada Territory. He added that it was "the only decent meal we tasted between the United States and the Great Salt Lake City, and the only one we were ever really thankful for."[25]

"TRAVAIL BY STAGECOACH"

The list of travel discomforts and complaints became long and varied. "Those outlandish vehicles, the American stage coach!" exclaimed one Englishman. For many it was "travail by stagecoach." Even before a departure, passengers might become upset because of rigid, albeit necessary, luggage-weight limitations. Mark Twain commented about such restrictions in his description of his western trip: "Then an inconvenience presented itself which we had not properly appreciated before, namely, that one cannot make a heavy traveling trunk stand for twenty-five pounds of baggage—because it weighs a good deal more." Twain and a companion responded accordingly. "So we had to snatch our trunks open, and make a selection in a good deal of a hurry. We put our lawful twenty-five pounds apiece all in one valise, and shipped the trunks back to St. Louis."[26]

Lack of reasonable speed bothered some riders. A stage might dash along good roads at eight to ten miles an hour, but on poorer ones, or because of company policy, a coach might travel at only a few miles an hour. Take a June 1827 trip from New York State into nearby Massachusetts. "The journey was only 38 miles, but owing to the rough and hilly roads, the dilatory mode of changing horses, and the eternal stopping to water them, it cost us eight hours and a half of very hard work; rendered still more disagreeable by the heat and the dust, and by the stage being crammed quite full." When New Yorker Henry Benjamin Whipple traveled by stage in Florida in early 1844, he found that the trip seemingly went on forever. He complained that it took four and a half hours to make the eighteen miles from Saint Augustine to Picolata, Florida. "No danger being apprehended from rapid driving, & the caution appended to the head of the way bill, 'all running of horses strictly prohibited on this line,' seemed to me quite a farce. Jog, jog along more like an old scow than a northern stage coach." A 210-mile trip between the North Carolina towns of Goldsboro and Charlotte taken in summer 1849 by David Swain, president of the University of North Carolina, consumed three and a half days, or eighty-four hours, producing an average speed of about two and a half miles per hour.[27]

Stagecoach patrons faced other and more disturbing aspects of their journeys. A ride over poor or virtually impassable roads produced predictable complaints. At times the roads created up-and-down bouncing and considerable side-to-side movements, leading to jostled and stage-bruised passengers. Even the highly regarded National Road became known as the "Shake-Guts" route. "The great object was to prevent our heads coming in contact with the roof of the carriage, when any particularly violent jolt threw us into the air," remarked a traveler on this popular road. "It was difficult to imagine any poor human beings more in the situation of shuttle-cocks."[28]

Roads outside most sections of the East were nearly always dreadful. A foreign traveler opined in 1839, "I must say that very few macadamized roads or built roads are to be found in America. They are much readier to lay railroad rails instead." These poor conditions occurred largely because of a modest population and a general unwillingness of voters to tax themselves so that roadways could be built or properly maintained. Existing arteries were nothing more than muddy or dusty trails with a variety of obstructions. In the 1830s an Englishman described the public-road situation in the Old Northwest this way: "Where there *were* [italics in original] roads, they were execrable, such as a European could have no conception of. If a man were to set about describing bad roads and were to draw on the powers of the liveliest imagination, he would fall far short of the realities which I experienced." Another disgusted mid-century stagecoach rider said, "Heaven speed the building of rail roads until stages are no longer needed, and until that time arrives I would advise those who have occasion to travel on the route between Louisville and St. Louis to employ a road maker to take them through on a wheelbarrow. The journey would be about as quick, about as cheap, and with far less irritation to the passengers, especially if the gentleman of the wheelbarrow acts as his own agent." Charles Dickens did not even care for road betterments that had been made by the early 1840s in northern Ohio. "A great portion of the way was over what is called a corduroy road, which is made by throwing trunks of trees into a marsh, and leaving them settle there. The very slightest of the jolts with which the ponderous carriage [coach] fell from log to log was enough, it seemed, to have dislocated all the bones in the human body."[29]

Travel became slow, difficult, and occasionally dangerous. In the mid-1850s Charles Murray, a wealthy British subject who traveled through the rural South, provided this description of what he encountered: "The stage was driven by six good nags, and driven by a lively fellow; but the road bade difiance [sic] to all these advantages—it was indeed, such as to compell [sic] me to laugh outright, not-withstanding the constant and severe bumping to which it subjected both the intellectual and sedentary parts of my person." As for the roads: "I had before tasted the sweets of mudholes, huge stones, and remnants of pine-trees, standing and cut down; but here was something new, namely, a bed of reddish-coloured clay, from one to two feet deep, so adhesive that the wheels were at times literally not visible in any one spot from the box to the tire, and the poor horses' feet sounded, when they drew them out (as a fellow-traveler observed), like the report of a pistol." In 1855 a Georgia traveler on his way to a railroad connection offered these observations: "Early in the morning I took the stage for Double Wells, on the Georgia Railroad. A ride in an inferior vehicle, with horses the worse for wear, prepared us to appreciate the speed and comfort of the rail. Farewell to hacks and horses; and if ever, still be it so. Too slow for the 'progress,' and too rough for the luxury of the age—farewell." About the same time, a woman recalled her springtime journey from the Mississippi River town of Keokuk, Iowa, to the central part of the Hawkeye State. "The mud was a yard deep in some places; many of the large creeks were not bridged, and the old fashioned sloughs were very much in evidence, and at their worst we thought that Skunk Bottom [adjoining the Skunk River] ought to be named Skunk 'Bottomless.'" Her description continued.

> Father walked most of the way. The stage coach was a few rods ahead of us, and kept us informed as to the depth of the mud. [Male passengers] both paid for and worked their passage, for they walked miles every day, carrying rails on their shoulders to pry the coach wheels out of the mud, while the driver unmercifully lashed his four horses. Sometimes a horse lunged, sunk in the mud to his body; that frightened the other horses, and then the men at the end of the rails dropped them and sprang for the horses. So it went every day.

That travel-delaying Midwest gumbo was described this way: "a sort of thick composite of clay and mud that clings to the feet in huge lumps."

The experiences of legendary New York City journalist Horace Greeley echoed so many others. In his 1859 trip to the West, he and fellow travelers encountered the crossing of Turkey Creek in eastern Kansas Territory. "The passengers were turned out (as once or twice before), to lighten the coach, which was then driven cautiously through the steep-banked ford, while the passengers severally let themselves down a perpendicular bank by clinging to a tree, and crossed a deep and whirling place above the ford, on the vilest log I ever attempted to walk—twisty, sharp-backed, and every way detestable." Greeley mentioned that one passenger was not about to use the log walkway "but hired one of the lazy Indians loafing on the further bank to bring over a pony, and let him ride across the ford." And crossing streams and rivers might result in baggage and other personal possessions becoming waterlogged or ruined.[30]

Poor roads or careless driving could cause the feared stagecoach "upset" or "turnover." In the parlance of the day, an upset referred to an accident in which the coach remained where it fell, although passengers might be pitched headlong to the ground, and with a turnover the coach "rolls over and over again down a declivity." Death or serious injuries seldom resulted from either an upset or a more serious turnover. The most common inflictions suffered were contusions, lacerations, or maybe broken limbs. Take the case of passengers in a stagecoach that experienced a turnover between the Iowa towns of Davenport and Muscatine in 1855: "One got a bloody gash in his head another his collar bone broken and torn loose from his shoulder blade, and Judge [James] Grant was severely injured in the shoulder, some of the muscles being probably jerked from their sockets. Another was got out raving like a maniac, ignorant of whence he came from or whither he was going, or the name of his friend." Fortunately their injuries received attention. "A German named Hetzell was kind enough to take care of the wounded. Dr. Fountain, a skillful physician, of Davenport, attended to the wants of the invalids." These non-life-threatening conditions can be explained by the relatively slow speed that most stages traveled. Passengers, usually in the trans-Mississippi West, commonly believed that a raging prairie fire, blinding blizzard, or Indian attack might lead to their demise. In reality, stagecoach travel was more disagreeable than deadly.[31]

Interior stagecoach conditions varied, whether because of season, weather, or maintenance. During the hot summer months, the sun beat down on the coach and heated the inside like an oven, and the choking dust kicked up by the animals' hooves and the large wheels made things worse. With freezing temperatures, the only ways for passengers to keep warm were to wear heavy clothing and close the window curtains, blinds, or folding shutters. They might also obtain hot bricks for foot warmers. Then, worsening the travel experience, some operators failed to maintain their coaches properly. A traveler in Ohio in 1849 was less than happy with his stage. "The door was an inch too small on every side for the aperture it was designed to close. This, however, was not considered important, as the four panes of glass which formed the upper half were broken. During the previous night it had rained, and the vehicle having been exposed without cover to the storm, the seats were soaked with water and were now dripping like a wet sponge." To make matters more unpleasant, "The wind being high and squally the curtain flapped in our faces every moment, literally giving us gratis a shower bath."[32]

Fellow passengers could cause problems. Just being squeezed together in tight quarters—"tortured confinement" was one description—could become a constant annoyance. This crowding might force a passenger to travel topside even in poor weather conditions. "The stage was so crowded that I had to ride outside most of the time and I thought sure I would freeze to death," remarked a Kansas rider in the 1880s. "During the 10-hour trip, it rained, hailed and snowed." An obese passenger was always unwelcomed; a rider usually had no more than fifteen inches of dedicated seating. When US Congressman and later US Senator Dixon Hall Lewis of Alabama boarded a stagecoach, fellow passengers might have been horrified. Since the renowned states'-rights politician weighed about 450 pounds, stage companies usually demanded that he pay for two or three seats. Especially irritating were loquacious persons who babbled constantly. It might be a preacher who endlessly quoted Scriptures, a lawyer who addressed an imaginary jury, or a Spiritualist who repeatedly communicated with those individuals who had passed beyond. Women, especially, were accused of "chattering like magpies." Thomas Hamilton, an English visitor who traveled through Georgia in 1831, did not care for the level of passenger conversation "to which I was condemned to listen during this journey," considering it more debased than what one could hear in the confines of London's Newgate Prison. A political debate could turn nasty, particularly when the burning issue of the expansion of slavery into new territories dominated the national conversation during the 1850s. Interestingly, an English female traveler was somewhat amused or perhaps annoyed that "Americans are too little susceptible of petty annoyances, and not sufficiently alive to the delicacies of life, to find a carriage crowded with promiscuous company at all disagreeable." Native folks, though, likely found that fellow travelers who had had too much to drink, who were sick, or who had not bathed for days hardly contributed to a pleasant passage. Rambunctious children and crying and fussing babies nearly always caused aggravation.[33]

A universal complaint of passengers involved their overnight journeys. There was no such thing as a good night's sleep either in coaches or in

One can easily imag-
ine how close and
unpleasant travel-
ing by stagecoach
could be. Especially
uncomfortable were
those middle seats
that lacked even a
wall to aid in napping
or sleeping. And no
passenger had much
dedicated seating
space or leg room.

Author's Photographs

some primitive inns. Some companies dispatched stagecoaches that were designed to run continuously between terminals, except for brief stops to change horses or drivers and to allow passengers short rest and toilet breaks and hastily served refreshments. Firms seeking to meet what might be cutthroat competition often demanded the fastest possible schedules. Since western operators faced contractual limits on the length of time to deliver the US mail between Missouri and California or other far-flung destinations, these coaches rolled along day and night. If a traveler opted to stay overnight at on-route stations, the quality of these accommodations might be dreadful. Stagecoach traveler Demas Barnes told of his journey through the West in an 1866 account. "Stop over nights? No you wouldn't. To sleep on the sand floor of a one-story sod house or adobe hut, without a chance to wash, with miserable food, uncongenial companionship, loss of a seat in a coach until one comes empty, etc., won't work."[34]

Riding in a stagecoach frequently induced drowsiness, and travelers responded to this physical state as best they could. The most attractive situation was to stretch out on the middle seat if that were an option. In a crowded stage only those riders seated in the corners could lean their heads back against the walls, and for others this meant dozing in a sitting position. As passenger Barnes related, "A through-ticket and fifteen inches of seat, with a fat man on one side, a poor widow on the other, a baby in your lap, a bandbox over your head, and three or four persons immediately in front, leaning against your knees, makes the picture, as well as your sleeping place for the trip." He opined: "I have just finished six days and nights of this thing; and I am free to say, until I forget a great many things now very visible to me, I shall not undertake it again." A traveler in the Pacific Northwest commented that, based on his own long-distance stagecoach ride, this "experience made me understand the stories I heard of the stage passengers who could not sleep, coming in after long journey downright sick and even actually demented." On those exceptionally long trips, passengers might become inured to their loss of sleep, hopefully catching short periods of real rest at stops when the animals were being changed.[35]

Repeated complaints focused on poor food and accommodations along stagecoach routes. A good illustration of an unattractive meal comes from commentary made by Henry Whipple. When traveling by stage in Florida, he encountered a most unpleasant inn-prepared fare:

> Hotel! no! tavern! no but to the frame or skeleton of the building where weary wayfarers wait impatiently for a boat to remove them from this dreary hole. A few moments after we arrived dinner (?) [sic] was announced and our appetite as well as curiosity prompted us to inspect the fare. But oh! what a downfall to all our hopes when we came in sight of the table. A mass of smoke not smoking substances covered the table and one might very reasonably doubt whether they were intended for food or were in reality charred fuel from the fire place.

In 1889 a photographer captured two crowded stagecoaches that presumably were headed to Deadwood, Dakota Territory. Multiple horses provided ample power to carry passengers, luggage, and possibly mail and express. The road and bridge were primitive but far superior to most roadways of the nineteenth century.

Library of Congress

But Whipple and his party did eat while awaiting a connecting riverboat. "We managed half sick to knaw [*sic*] at sundry bones and crusts of bread and wash them down with dirty brackish water and our only wish was the arrival of the boat might save us from another & a similar infliction."[36]

Inns, taverns, and those private homes that took in passengers not only might serve monotonous, albeit pricey, food in unappetizing surroundings but offered sleeping accommodations that often caused discontent. Travelers' concerns: beds public and dirty; mattresses either missing or lumpy; bathing lacking; smells stifling; and bedbugs, fleas, flies, lice, and ticks abundant. To make matters worse, proprietors sometimes set rates for these venues at exorbitant levels. Small town inns and taverns in antebellum Georgia, for instance, commonly drew the repeated wrath of guests. One scholar quoted travelers as calling them "offensive, vile, abominable, wretched, dirty, horrible, filthy, miserable, disgusting, and revolting."[37]

Overnight and long-distance travel, most of all in the trans-Missouri West, could produce a situation akin to sleep deprivation—the anguish of a potential or actual robbery. Graphically portrayed by Hollywood filmmakers, particularly in the B-grade movies produced by Republic Studios in the 1940s and 1950s, road bandits did occasionally stop coaches and rob passengers of their money, watches, and other valuables. These men probably were more interested in taking express shipments of gold dust and bullion from the mines or specie destined for payrolls at these diggings. From the mid-nineteenth century until these valuables went by rail, the driver might have at his side not a passenger but a "shotgun messenger" who with his loaded shotgun or rifle was there to protect. While holdups occurred throughout the mining West, highwaymen were especially active in the Black Hills of Dakota Territory during the late 1870s. Finally, better security practices and law enforcement mostly ended this threat.[38]

Whether the stagecoach trip was enjoyable, miserable, or frightening, there could be the sting of high ticket prices. Where competition did not exist, an operator could charge what the traffic would bear. Rates, too, might rise on a seasonal basis because of operational costs. But the greatest price changes were usually decreases caused by actual or threatened competition over the same route. Fares might range from ten to fifteen cents per mile on the high end to five cents a mile on the low end. The mid-nineteenth-century ticket price between Saint Louis or Memphis and San Francisco was initially set at $200 westbound and $100 eastbound, or ten cents per mile for shorter distances. The cost of a journey from Atchison, Kansas, to Salt Lake City in 1866 amounted to a whopping $350 and meals en route were extra, ranging from one to two dollars each. When compared to the mileage costs levied by a steamer, canal boat, or railroad, the expensiveness of stage travel is evident. In fact, many citizens could not afford to take a stage at all, and instead they traveled on foot or horseback. Wealthy travelers commonly relied on their own horse-drawn vehicles, or they might charter a stagecoach for themselves or their family members and servants at the cost of multiple regular fares.[39]

The era of the stagecoach helped to bind the American republic, and it would have lasted longer if it had not been for the advent and spread of railroads. Before that occurred, the widespread stagecoach network delivered people, mail, and express. In the process it created a sense of connectedness among the towns and villages that appeared along the earliest trails and roads. Likewise, the stage routes contributed to urban growth, making these places logical ones for future rail service.

Differing from other forms of public transportation, the stagecoach has virtually disappeared from the American scene. There are no stagecoach hobby organizations, except for such a nonacademic organization as the Westerners International, which focuses on elements of the "Old West." There are surviving stages in private and museum collections, with the best known being a Concord stage that resides in the Wells Fargo Museum in downtown San Francisco. Not surprisingly, the stagecoach and a team of spirited horses serve as the corporate logo of the Wells Fargo

The icon of the Wells Fargo Bank is this Concord stage that graces the company's museum in San Francisco, California.

Photo used with permission from Wells Fargo Bank, N. A.

Bank. Then there are the scattered physical remains of the stagecoach era, including the Inn (now the Old Stagecoach Inn) in Waterbury, Vermont; Stacy's Tavern in Glen Ellyn, Illinois; and the Butterfield station at Warner's Ranch in San Diego County, California. The "real" contact, however, comes from Hollywood films, with the most memorable being the 1939 epic *Stagecoach*, "A Powerful Story of 9 Strange People," starring Donald Meek, Thomas Mitchell, and Claire Trevor and directed by John Ford.[40] Over the decades, stages have been used in Wild West shows and rodeos, often racing each other. But in more recent times, chuck wagon races have become the common rodeo spectacle. Nevertheless, the stagecoach itself is readily recognizable by virtually every adult and by most children.

Waterways and the American People

2

WONDROUS WATERWAYS

Americans have long benefited from their extensive network of oceans and navigable lakes and rivers. By the formative decades of the nineteenth century, various bodies of water offered practical and often convenient avenues for commercial travel and performed an inestimable service to national development. Not only did the Atlantic Ocean and the Gulf of Mexico and later the Pacific Ocean allow travelers access to coastal vessels, but the Great Lakes also facilitated deep-water transport. These five large inland seas, which measured about 1,500 miles from east to west, became more valuable with completion of the Welland Canal between Lake Ontario and Lake Erie in 1829 (rebuilt in 1848) and the Saint Mary's Falls Ship Canal, opened in 1855, which connected Lake Superior and the lower lakes of Erie, Huron, Michigan, and Ontario. French traveler Guillaume Tell Poussin commented in 1834: "One of the most curious circumstances is, no doubt, the abundance of its [America's] vast and navigable rivers, its great bays, straits, and lakes, all of which contribute to a coherent interior navigation system incomparable to that of any other continent."[1]

There were thousands of miles of boat-friendly rivers awaiting an expanding American population. Residents of the eastern and southern regions used such streams as the Connecticut, Hudson, Delaware, James, Savannah, Altamaha (and tributaries Ocmulgee and Oconee), Chattahoochee-Apalachicola, Saint Johns, and Coosa-Alabama. Those who inhabited large sections of the trans-Allegheny West relied heavily on the massive Ohio-Missouri-Mississippi river drainage system, including such navigable tributaries as the Allegheny, Monongahela, Kanawha, Green, Cumberland, Tennessee, Kentucky, Muskingum, Wabash, Illinois, Des Moines, Wisconsin, Minnesota, Kansas (or Kaw), Arkansas, Red, and Yazoo. An astounding feature of the Mississippi system was that it measured some four thousand miles from the headwaters of the Missouri to the Gulf of Mexico. As late as 1890 there was navigation of some kind

"The Lorena" on Muskingum River, Malta, Ohio

The paddle-wheeler *Lorena*, built for freight and passenger service between Pittsburgh, Pennsylvania, and Zanesville, Ohio, steams along the Muskingum River near Malta, Ohio. This waterway had been "canalized" with a series of locks and dams from Marietta, Ohio, located at the mouth of the Muskingum on the Ohio River, to Dresden, Ohio, north of Zanesville, situated on the Ohio & Erie Canal.

Author's Collection

on forty-five rivers that were part of this system, making for a total of slightly more than sixteen thousand miles. No wonder *Harper's Magazine* proclaimed that "the basin of the Mississippi is the Body of the Nation." Those residents and travelers in the West found useful the Colorado, Sacramento-American, San Joaquin, Willamette, Yamhill, and Columbia-Snake Rivers. There was also the Red River of the North that flowed from present-day South Dakota into Canada and emptied into Hudson Bay. Smaller streams, including the Santee in South Carolina, White in Indiana, Gasconade in Missouri, Fox in Wisconsin, James (Big Jim) in South Dakota, Yellowstone in Montana, and Spokane in Washington, at times served as commercial freight and passenger arteries.[2]

It would be the "Mighty Mississippi" river system that experienced the greatest volume of passenger traffic. This natural superhighway directly linked a number of rapidly growing urban centers: Pittsburgh, Wheeling, Cincinnati, Louisville, Paducah, Saint Louis, Saint Paul, Memphis, and New Orleans. Its navigable tributaries also served places of increasing importance, ranging from Charleston, Virginia (West Virginia), to Shreveport, Louisiana. Unfortunately, not all of these streams flowed in the most convenient directions. Take the Tennessee River, largest tributary to the Ohio River and formed by the confluence of the French Broad and Holston Rivers near Knoxville, Tennessee. The Tennessee rolled for more than 650 miles in a loop-like fashion through Tennessee, Alabama, and Kentucky before emptying into the Ohio near Paducah.

Unfortunately for those who lived in the Lower South, this major stream did not run directly into the Mississippi, resulting in an excruciatingly long travel route. "If only the tenn. [*sic*] went as the crow flies from e. tenn. to Mobile or directly to the Miss," lamented a Tennessee merchant. Other residents of the region heartedly agreed.[3]

Navigable rivers did not mean that boat passage would be without difficulties. Smaller streams commonly lacked enough water to allow extended periods of travel even for the smallest boats, and only during times of high water was passage possible. Low water also haunted the Ohio, the Missouri, and the upper stretches of the Mississippi; in fact, all rivers periodically suffered from inadequate rates of flow, halting traffic for possibly weeks or even months. This usually occurred between mid-summer and late fall. When a water famine turned to a water feast with snowmelts and heavy rains, floods occurred. Raging currents made river travel either impossible or dangerous. Periodic high waters could cause a river to change course, cutting across oxbow necks and altering the main channel by thousands of feet. The Missouri River, the "Big Muddy," became notorious for changing course. "She's a bad actor, that old river: you can't tell what tricks she'll play," said one riverman. "Arn't never been controlled yet and never will." Eddies and whirlpools plagued streams. The famed "Suck" on the Tennessee River near Chattanooga became a constant threat to navigation. And river debris might hinder or prevent transit. The upper region of the Red River became notorious for the "Great Raft," an accumulation of driftwood that blocked the channel for many miles near Fulton, Arkansas. "This barrier was so solid in places that a man could ride across it on horseback." While steamboats plied the river below this obstruction, above the Great Raft only small boats were useable. Then in colder climes rivers froze, and the spring breakup of moving ice threat-ened watercraft. Always concerning to boats on nearly all rivers were snags and sawyers. The former were trees that had fallen into the water by the constantly crumbling banks, and their trunks, sans branches, eventu-ally became embedded on the bottom and likely moved with the current, appearing and disappearing at intervals. These submerged obstacles could damage or sink a boat. "I soon learned that the logs which keep their heads above water and lie parallel with the current are not dreaded much," com-mented a riverboat passenger, "but those which lie on the bottom across the river are the great difficulty." The sawyers were trees in the stream with soil still clinging to their roots. When forced by the current, they made an up-and-down bobbing motion. Usually only aggravating occurrences, sawyers could block the best navigable portions of a channel and force boats into shallower and more dangerous waters. Sandbars, submerged or partially submerged, posed still another threat. Similarly, silt—mud and sand—caused trouble; waterways over time might become much more shallow and treacherous. The Sacramento River, for one, suffered from the effects of tons of debris produced by extensive hydraulic gold mining. Some streams had falls or rapids that hindered or blocked some or all boats. The Ohio River had a well-known obstacle, the Falls of the Ohio, located near Louisville. But in 1830 the Louisville & Portland Canal opened around these rapids, and later it would be enlarged, helping to make the Ohio River a premier water highway. Still, the Ohio required boat pilots to have skill and use caution; it had fifty-three islands, for example, between Pittsburgh and Cincinnati.[4]

STEAMBOATS

Rivers throughout America had been traveled long before the appearance of steam-powered craft in the early nineteenth century. From time immemorial boats plied these streams. The canoe age involved a variety of mostly small and crudely built craft. American Indians, later joined by explorers, missionaries, fur trappers and traders, and then settlers, found dugout and birch-bark canoes practical ways to exploit waterways for their personal use. Some of these primitive canoes became larger and hence more valuable. Take pirogues: these impressive canoe-like crafts measured thirty-five to forty feet in length, featured square sterns, and contained space for as many as fifteen occupants and several thousand pounds of cargo. Sometimes these oversized canoes sported sails.[5]

By the early nineteenth century, the flatboat and keelboat dominated river travel. Numbering in the thousands, these wooden craft were easy and relatively inexpensive to construct. Immigrants usually opted for the one-directional flatboats, being a cheap—fifteen to twenty dollars on average—and practical way to reach downstream destinations. Farmers and merchants used flatboats to transport their products—animals, bacon, flour, fruit, lard, lumber, pork, whiskey, and the like—to market. The sizes of these simple vessels varied, although they usually measured about thirty or forty feet in length and a dozen feet in width. Upon drifting downstream to their destinations on both minor and major streams, owners likely sold the wood to local lumber dealers. Individuals wishing to travel on flatboats might pay to accompany the owner and his associates or exchange their labor for the ride. With the coming of steamboats, flatboats still appeared on most rivers, and often in large numbers. But they frequently offered connecting service from the smaller streams and nearly always served as cargo carriers. "It is ironic that the Steamboat Age nurtured so primitive and preindustrial a craft as the flatboat," observed historian Michael Allen. "Although the years 1815–1861 are known for the 'transportation revolution,' it is important to remember that this revolution occurred in stages, and that steamboats, canal boats, and railroads did not instantly replace cruder, pre-industrial modes of transport."[6]

Unlike the flatboat, the keelboat (or poleboat) was a more sophisticated and versatile river craft. It was able to ascend as well as descend a principal stream. This cigar-shaped vessel was built on a keel and had ribs like a ship. The keel itself consisted of a heavy timber to withstand contacts with rocks and snags. Being long and narrow, the vessel commonly measured about forty to eighty-five feet in length and seven to ten feet in width, and it contained pointed prows and running boards on each side from end to end to facilitate poling upstream. Often a roof covered much of the structure to shelter the twenty to forty tons of freight and the Spartan living quarters. A keelboat might have a dozen crew members, one of whom was the helmsman who controlled the long-handled rudder. There might be as many as twenty-five or more passengers on board, some or all paying for their trip. Downstream speeds varied with the strength of the water flow, but upstream rates were far less, usually less than several miles per hour. Crews employed various types of propulsion: poling, rowing, sailing, and towing from the riverbank. Moving a keelboat against the current was slow and difficult, especially during bad weather, and expensive with a hired crew.[7]

One danger early on for crew members and passengers who traveled by flatboats and keelboats was the presence of river bandits. Along remote areas of waterways, these gangs might ambush and then rob their victims, physically removing or killing those on board, taking command of the craft, and ultimately selling the boat and its contents. A late-eighteenth-century keelboat packet company that operated between Pittsburgh and Cincinnati sought to calm the fears of any shippers and passengers with this announcement: "A large crew, skillful in the use of arms, a plentiful supply of muskets and ammunition, an equipment on each boat of six one-pound cannon, and a loop-hole, rifle-proof cabin for passengers." As populations grew and law-enforcement expanded, piracy on the principal rivers largely ended by the 1820s and 1830s.[8]

At last the steamboat appeared, ending dependence on human or animal power. This transportation revolution was pioneered in part by such tinkerers/inventors as John Fitch, William Henry, and James Rumsey. When compared to its main predecessor—the keelboat—the steamboat was an impressive advancement in water travel and somewhat the equivalent of the later railroad locomotive. A red-letter day in navigation took place on August 17, 1807, when the 150-foot-long *Steam Boat*—a most unimaginative name—churned its way up the Hudson River at the rate of five miles per hour, much faster than any keelboat could manage the fast-flowing stream. This triumph by Robert Fulton allowed the inventor-entrepreneur to become the first American to operate steamboats commercially. It did not take long before steam-powered vessels appeared on more major rivers, the Great Lakes, and coastal waters. In October 1811 a notable journey took place between Pittsburgh and New Orleans when the Fulton steamboat *New Orleans* made a successful downstream trip via the Ohio and Mississippi Rivers. Four years later the steamboat *Enterprise* succeeded in making two round trips from Pittsburgh to Louisville, terminating there because of low water. Not long thereafter it proceeded under its own power from Pittsburgh to the Crescent City.[9]

The steamboat age was at hand. Not long after the inaugural trips of the *Enterprise*, western waters saw a growing number of steamers, and by the 1830s hundreds of these wooden vessels of various sizes served navigable waterways, with the highest proportion operating on the Mississippi River system. On the Tennessee River, a tributary of the Ohio, high water during the spring of 1828 permitted the *Atlas* to steam past numerous obstacles, including the treacherous currents near Chattanooga, to become the first steamboat to reach Knoxville, the upper limit of commercial steam navigation. Arrival of the little *Atlas* triggered a community celebration, and its owners received a cash prize from local businessmen for their noble accomplishment. Soon steamboats called seasonally at the Knoxville dock, delighting merchants and travelers alike.[10]

Even in the remote Pacific Northwest, the appearance of the first steamboat gladdened the population. That was the case in summer 1851 when the little *Lot Whitcomb* made its maiden trip along the upper reaches of the Willamette River of Oregon. The event prompted the mother of Edwin Markham, the famed American poet, to pen this verse for the *Oregon Spectator*:

> Lot Whitcomb is coming!
> Her banners are flying—
> She walks up the rapids with speed;
> She ploughs through the water,
> Her steps never falter—
> Oh! that's independence indeed.
> Old and young rush to meet her,
> And waves lash the shore as they pass.
>
> Oh! She's welcome, thrice welcome
> To Oregon City;
> Lot Whitcomb is with us at last.
> Success to the Steamer
> Her Captain and crew.
> She has our best wishes attained.[11]

Prototypes of American river steamboats readily took shape, being the result of extensive experimentation to find better and faster two-directional vessels. The initial Fulton-type boats featured deep and narrow hulls and bulky low-pressure engines, and by the 1820s these mostly eastern river and coastal boats had become eye-catching monsters. An example was the *Ariel*, which operated between New York City and Albany. A passenger in the late 1820s recalled, "Exactly as the clock struck eight, the [side] paddle-wheels began to stir, and away sallied the fairy ship with her gay flags and snow-white awnings, like a huge swan, on the broad bosom of the magnificent Hudson."[12]

Soon a steamboat developed by New Jersey–born inventor and river boatman Henry Shreve became the "western" prototype. In 1817 his 140-foot *Washington* demonstrated that a flat-bottom and shallow-draft vessel could speed along on a stream's surface either up- or downstream and navigate waters barely four feet deep. Boilers and engines occupied the deck between the paddle wheels, and the high-pressure propulsion weighed much less than Fulton's machinery and consumed about three-fifths of the amount of cordwood. The *Washington*, a side-wheeler, also possessed good maneuvering abilities. "Where the single up-right steamship engine compelled all ships to describe a circle in order to turn around, the steamboat's double high-pressure unconnected engines at once demonstrated their superiority. For, by reversing one wheel and running the other forward, the steamboat could turn around in her own length." These new hoarse, cough-chug-sounding western riverboats were powered by engines that were more compact and cheaper to build, operate, and maintain. Still, Fulton-type vessels worked well in deep water, whether on the Hudson River, Long Island Sound, or the Great Lakes.[13]

Western steamboats had distinct characteristics. Their main decks were about five feet above the waterline but varied greatly in length, ranging from 75 to 350 feet. Usually these vessels contained more than a single deck; upper ones became their signature features. "[They] looked like a cheaply constructed, ornate white wooden castle floating on a raft," according to one apt contemporary description. "These boats are more like the work of carpenters and house builders," opined another. "It is as if their model had been slowly developed from that of a house-boat, or barge with a roof over it." Still another commented, "The vast number of vessels on the western waters, the peculiarity of their construction, and the singular nature of the navigation of which they are employed, make them objects of considerable interest to the traveler." This 1838 commentary continued, "We must not expect to find, however, in that class of vessels the same display of good workmanship, and the attainment of the high velocities which characterize the vessels on the eastern waters." One feature of these boats was their "guards." These wooden extensions of the main deck protruded from the hull line to become flush with the outer edges of the side paddle wheels. They were designed to extend the main deck and to protect the moving wheels from floating objects. The upper deck (or decks) contained space dedicated to passengers, including private cabins for sleeping and public places for eating and lounging. Officers' quarters were usually found on the second deck. This was the Texas deck, a name derived from the tradition of identifying the various staterooms, of which the officers' were the largest, after the states in the union according to their size. The Texas deck might contain the pilothouse, but its location varied, being at times placed above that deck. There was usually a passenger-accessible area popularly known as the hurricane deck because it was open to the wind and elements. Here one could see the double, smoke-belching stacks; the river; and the passing scenery. For decades side-wheelers predominated, but there were also stern-wheelers, the latter being more popular on the lesser streams since they were less prone to damage from river debris. Yet as transportation historian John White observed, "This general plan [of river steamboats], for all of its peculiarities, proved very successful and was never greatly altered during the history of the riverboat." In this way these craft resembled the persistence in the basic design of contemporary canal packets and stagecoaches.[14]

As the steamboat age matured on inland rivers, especially the major ones, accommodations improved for travelers. These "moving hotels" developed from somewhat plain eating, sleeping, and public spaces to often garish, albeit for the times stylish, surroundings. Meals became more lavish, and they were served by accommodating waiters and enjoyed at well-appointed tables. Gender-segregated open berths gave way to much more pleasing cabins and private spaces for males, single females, and married couples. The stateroom on a Mississippi steamboat of the 1830s was described this way: "In our stateroom we [husband and wife] had two beds, a mirror, a small table and two small chairs," and it adjoined a fancy ladies' parlor. Common areas followed suit. On the best boats, these "floating palaces" that dominated the New Orleans or "lower river" trade, first-class passengers found saloons that offered impressive elegance. "Rich carpets, preferably Brussels, ornamental paintings, lustrous draperies, gleaming mirrors, ornate chandeliers, furniture of mahogany or rosewood upholstered with velvet or plush came to be regarded as necessary saloon furnishing in steamboats of the first class." In the ladies' parlor there would be fashionable furniture and floor coverings, but "above all, that touchstone of refined elegance in the ante-bellum years, a piano." The ceiling was commonly raised above the hurricane deck to allow side skylights, which might be of colored or etched glass. Steamboats, whether large or small, also were equipped with wood-burning or coal stoves, which provided much-appreciated heat during damp, chilly, or cold weather.

Individuals may have been amazed by the pleasant-smelling lavatories that might be found in the main public space and the women's cabins. On one Columbia River vessel, constant jets of water moved through these facilities while the boat was moving, "so that no offensive effluvia taints these sumptuous cabins."[15] Such a floating environment surely dazzled the eye of the rustic inlander.

Even those riverboats that plied the lesser streams could possess a certain elegance. In an 1858 newspaper advertisement, the captain of the *Time and Tide*, which operated on the Minnesota River, claimed that his vessel "combined all the latest and most modern improvements that could add to the safety, comfort and pleasure of passengers. Nothing will be found wanting in any of her appointments, which belong to those of a first-class passenger steamer." In another instance of how a small firm, which operated on a backwater stream, sought to make a vessel attractive involved the *Manitoba*. Merchants International owned and operated this unpretentious craft on the Red River of the North. Then in 1875 it sank. But the boat came back to life; it received the necessary mechanical repairs and important upgrades. Most noticeably, the passenger quarters were gussied up. "The Sky-light has been renewed by a handsome one, a crowning roof sets off the upper part of the deck. The inner cabin has been greatly improved, painted and decorated and at the rear end of the ladies' cabin is the name Manitoba, the letters being in gold and shaded," reported a local newspaper. "Immediately underneath is painted a badger, in a green leaf as a background, and on either side are the ensigns of England and America supported by the Lion and Eagle. Everything within has a fresh, pleasant appearance." Neither was the exterior ignored. "[It] has received many additions, among which is gingerbread work about the upper rail of the boiler deck and gilded knobs and a sign immediately over the fore part of the hurricane deck."[16]

Notably, because of explosions, fires, and wrecks, the life expectancy for the typical antebellum western-type steamboat was not long. While eastern steamers on average lasted a dozen years or more, those in the West might operate for only a few years. When contrasted to whaling and ocean sailing ships, differences in longevity were striking. The former might be in service for fifty years or longer, and the latter might be used for twenty to twenty-five years.

STEAMBOAT CREWS

Resembling other forms of water transport, steamboats, no matter their size or routes, were labor intensive. Obviously, the larger craft, whether in the eastern or western rivers or on Great Lakes or coastal waters, had more workers than boats that operated on minor streams. By way of example is the *Diana*, a popular riverboat launched in 1838 that ran on the busy Ohio-Mississippi corridor between Louisville and New Orleans. Its crew consisted of thirty-six paid personnel and two who were not. There was the captain, a clerk, a carpenter, a steward, and a chambermaid. Then there were two pilots, two mates, two engineers, two African American cooks, three waiters, eight deckhands, and twelve firemen. The one barber was unpaid because he was an independent agent who charged his customers and kept the proceeds. And the lone bartender actually paid a monthly fee of fifty dollars to the boat's owner to practice his trade and had "to provide the crew with hard liquor at no cost." On smaller vessels the owner might serve as the captain and pilot, and his crew size might resemble that employed on a large canal packet boat.[17]

Some generalizations can be made about steamboat workers. Most were recruited locally, namely in river towns and cities. These employees, though, often had a farming background and were of native stock. Some had experience working on flatboats and keelboats. The deck crew was a mixture of unskilled individuals—men, youngsters, and a few women. Freed or surplus slaves (their wages mostly went to their owners) worked usually on southern rivers as deckhands, roustabouts, cooks, and attendants. Boat captains, pilots, clerks, engineers, and mates enjoyed greater job security and had better pay, often staying with the same vessel for multiple years or seasons. Other workers tended to move about—from boat to boat and from river to river. Or they might take jobs on Great Lakes or coastal vessels. They were boomers, indeed, and often they lacked home responsibilities. While generalizations about their personalities are speculative, some undoubtedly were "wild roistering, devil-may-care fellows, hard drinkers, fighters-at-the-drop-of-a-hat and impatient of interference." These men probably sought adventure and the chance to eke out a living wage. There were also those who had no use for these "Alligator Horses." Recalling his Ohio and Mississippi River experiences in 1849 and 1850, a boatman said: "I did not drink a drop of liquor or ever taste it then, and never learned or knew how to play a single game of cards, or have anything whatever to do with prostitutes, although I was surrounded by Drinking, gambling, prostitution and every form of vice." He added, "It all disgusted and repelled me." Some boatmen had ambitions, wanting to learn the steamboat business and hoping to become pilots, captains, or owners.[18]

Although it might be thought that the steamboat captain was the most admired member of the onboard crew, that usually would be incorrect. Yes, the captain had power and responsibilities. He was in command while the boat was entering and leaving a dock or levee, and he could order the boat to land for repairs and in case of an emergency. The remainder of the time the pilot, who possessed far greater skills than the captain, was in charge. "[Pilots] were the accepted aristocrats of the steamboat business," observed regional writer Herbert Quick. "For pilots were treated with a great deal respect by every one aboard a steamboat: captains, waiters, deck hands, clerks, engineers, firemen and passengers. They never asked any one for anything: on all occasions they gave orders. Ashore they were envied for the pay they drew." Added Quick, "Quite naturally they developed a grand air of authority, a heavy swagger."[19]

The lives of deckhands and roustabouts, however, lacked much attractiveness. The formers' assignments called for maintaining the deck, measuring the depth of the stream, and serving as watchmen. The latter had the laborious job of taking freight on and off the boat. These were grueling occupations. "The work on those Steamers and Steamboating is the hardest in the world," remembered a mid-nineteenth-century deckhand. "Work night and day with only short spells of sleep, and roused up at any minute to load or unload freight and at Wood Piles." To make matters worse, "Fed like pigs out of pans on deck & Sleeping in bunks, every man having his own 'Dunnage' or bedding, and carrying it with him from one Steamer to another." And treatment by fellow crew members could be brutal. "Those Steamboat Mates knocked and kicked the men about like brutes. Many knocked overboard with handpikes and abused liked dogs." Getting ahead financially was difficult, if not hopeless. "I had not saved a cent. It was impossible to work long enough to earn anything. No one could stand the work of over one trip, it was so hard, working night and day. It was the want of sleep that prevented it. After every trip there was a necessary rest and it took all the earning to pay for the board. Then again it was sometimes hard to get work, and to be 'hard up' or 'dead broke' was the common lot of most Boatmen."[20]

Labor unrest became much more common on riverboats than on either canal boats or stagecoaches. Deck crews had power. In order to force concessions from management—more pay or the redress of some other grievance—these unhappy workers turned to the tactic of "jumping the boat." As the vessel docked, the deck crew merely walked off, knowing that their demands would likely be met or that they could hire out to another captain. Their work action could cause extended delays in the operation of a boat, resulting in a loss of business and hence income for the owner. Then in the early 1850s the US Supreme Court ruled that federal admiralty jurisdiction extended to navigable rivers and lakes. This victory for management meant that a strike became a mutiny and jumping a vessel became desertion and subject to heavy penalties. Even though as seamen these deckhands won some legal protections, labor relations at times remained tense.[21]

Whether happy or not, steamboat crews had an impact on river communities. The crews included cooks, deckhands, firemen, porters, and stewards. Frequently these boatmen patronized saloons, brothels, gambling joints or "poker rooms," and the occasional opium den. After too much alcohol, it was not uncommon for them to engage in brawls and other disturbances. They were not alone; some passengers also helped to make areas around public docks rowdy and sinful. Shadowy figures often came to town, including professional gamblers, confidence men, robbers, and thugs.

RIVERBOAT TRAVEL

When compared to overland or canal travel, river steamboats offered superior speed. Times varied, but generally they moved about ten to twelve miles per hour downstream and four or five miles per hour less upstream. Within a decade after their debut, steamboats made on average about a hundred miles a day. By way of example, faster boats in the 1850s made the trip from Cincinnati to Louisville in eight and a half hours and the upstream ascent in eleven to twelve hours. As engines became more powerful and reliable and as government snag boats removed hazardous obstacles speeds increased, reaching on occasions an average of twenty miles per hour or slightly more. In the 1880s the *Albany* covered the 145 miles between New York City and Albany in less than seven hours and operated faster for the 124 miles that were in "good, deep water" but slowed down for the final twenty miles into the New York capital because of "intricate and difficult navigation." When a race between riverboats occurred, short-distance speeds increased considerably. Stagecoaches, on the other hand, might roll at a clip of five or six miles per hour, and canal packets poked along at three or four miles per hour or less.[22]

Americans loved speed, but travelers in the nineteenth century also relished comfort. On a steamboat, passengers—both cabin and deck— had the opportunity to stretch their legs. They were not confined to the stuffiness of a stagecoach interior or the limited space on its top or to the closeness of a canal-boat cabin. The open deck space these packets provided came with an element of danger, however, if there were low bridges over the waterway. Then there was the matter of sleep: steamboat passengers could usually find a place to recline horizontally. First-class passengers had assigned cabins or staterooms that over time became more inviting on the larger, better-appointed boats. In contrast, deck passengers had to sleep on a hard plank surface amid an assortment of freight and provide their own bedding, an indication that America was hardly a classless society. Occasionally, this deck space might be limited because of excessive amounts of cargo or passenger overcrowding. If deck passengers were lucky, on the other hand, they might be provided with hammocks. In the earlier steamboats, those who were quartered above the main deck might have only bunks with cheap straw mattresses in tiny compartments, but in time some boats provided quality mattresses in full-size beds, larger rooms, and much less Spartan accessories. Cabin patrons often enjoyed access to a spacious and elegant saloon. Even smaller, less pretentious craft might please patrons. Traveling to the lead-mining region of the Upper Mississippi River in 1834, businessman Theodore Rodolf made these observations: "The cabin was plainly but substantially furnished, and kept very clean. There were no state rooms; but two tiers of bunks, containing the beds, ran along the side of the boat and were separated at night from the saloon by curtains." Unlike a bumpy, bone-jarring stage-coach ride, river travel was relatively smooth, although there were noises coming from the engines and paddle wheels, crews working freight and fuel, and occasional blasts of the steam whistle.[23]

Comfort also involved food. Unlike the fare found in some inns and taverns, and especially at most western stops on the transcontinental stagecoach routes, or on many canal packets, steamboat offerings generally involved greater choice and better quality. During the golden age of steamboating, the premier boats gave passengers an amazing assortment of tasty options for their cabin passengers. (The cost was included in the ticket price.) Breakfast might consist of eggs, ham, bacon, sausage, hotcakes, bread, milk, tea, and coffee. For the noontime dinner meal, there were likely beefsteaks or pork, or possibly chicken, turkey, duck or other fowl, potatoes, rice, corn, rice pudding, and tarts. Fruits and nuts were commonly offered. The supper resembled breakfast. Milk and butter, however, were often missing from the table. If it were available, it might be of poor quality and perhaps rancid.

A positive assessment of food served to cabin passengers came from a letter penned in June 1845 by a young Presbyterian minister during his trip on the Ohio River steamboat *Constellation*. "We have just risen from our dinner table and the passengers are lounging and picking their teeth. We fare altogether too sumptuously on these boats." And the offerings: "I have seldom sat down to a dinner where there has not been on the table some six or eight kinds of meat, e.g. roast pig, beef, boiled ham, corned beef, tongue, roast turkey. All of these and more were on our table to day, which with the condiments, and three or four kinds of pie ought to satisfy an alderman. This is the style on all these western boats, and when you have paid your passage you are at liberty to gormandize as much as you please." As he concluded, "I have little relish for these rich dinners. Something more simple would better suit my palate." Food choices resembled what later in the century would become available on premier intercity passenger trains.[24]

On better boats additional amenities existed. It was customary for the grand saloon to have a bar that served various alcoholic drinks. While many passengers appreciated the service, there was by mid-century a growing temperance movement. After all, America was considered by many to be an alcoholic republic, and the cold water brigade sought change. Similarly, there were gambling tables. Again, there were mixed reactions, but for some travelers this was a pleasant way to pass time and perhaps to benefit financially from one or more winning hands of cards.

Deck passengers usually did not partake of either quality food or drink. They normally brought their own food or bought it at stops where crews loaded and unloaded freight and passengers or took on wood or coal and other supplies. Some boats provided small stoves for meal preparation. Perhaps, too, these steerage-like patrons brought on board their water and other beverages, but more likely they drank dirty river water. At times deck passengers, if they were allowed and they paid for the privilege, ate and drank on an upper deck. It was not uncommon, however, for the captain to order a burly fellow to stand guard at the head of the stairs to the second deck to keep deck people in their proper place.[25]

Whether traveling in a cabin or on the deck, everyone appreciated the reasonable cost of a steamboat ticket. Fares generally declined as competition increased and boats became larger. By way of illustration, cabin passengers initially paid between $100 and $125 to travel the nearly 1,400 miles from New Orleans to Louisville, but within a decade or so charges ranged from $25 to $30. Somewhat later they dropped even more, becoming as low as $10. An Austrian civil engineer, Franz Anton Ritter von Gerstner, who visited America's network of canals, railroads, and waterways between 1838 and 1840, estimated that the actual fare for transportation on the Mississippi River system was about 2.5 cents a mile. Fares rose following the Civil War, yet they remained attractive. Admittedly, costs for all classes of passengers on steamboats that plied the lesser streams were higher, but not outlandishly so. Deck passengers paid much less. "Even the poorest man could find the few dollars—at times it was as little as two dollars—necessary for deck passage," remarked one student of river travel. At one point the price of a deck ticket from Pittsburgh to Cincinnati was only one dollar. It cost a deck passenger in 1850 as little as three dollars to travel between New Orleans and Saint Louis or Louisville. On some boats if passengers helped with loading fuel their transit costs decreased further, perhaps by as much as 25 to 30 percent of regular fares. Even for the time, these were incredible transportation bargains. No wonder water accommodations became a boon for settlers. "On account of the universality and cheapness of steamboat and canal passage and transport, more than half of the immigrants now arrive in the West by water," noted an 1832 commentary. "They no longer experience the incessant altercations with landlords, mutual charges of dishonesty, discomfort from new modes of speech and reckoning money, from breaking down carriages and wearing out horses."[26]

No matter how much a steamboat trip cost or whether passage involved first-class or deck accommodations, passengers frequently enjoyed the company of others. There might be that foreign visitor, cotton planter, land speculator, community booster, prominent businessman, military officer, rising politician, or professional gambler; in fact, there was a cross section of the population, or what one traveler called "a medley of people." From these folks it was possible to learn the current gossip about the economy, politics, or prominent personalities; to hear the latest jokes and stories; and to listen to the most popular songs and poetry. Travelers also mentioned that they appreciated the singing and chanting of deck crews, especially by those of color.

Viewing the passing scenery, particularly on a pleasant day from the vantage point of the hurricane or upper decks, pleased countless passengers. There were new and exciting vistas. An Englishman going upstream on the Hudson River in May 1827 wrote:

> We proceeded to West Point, some thirty miles farther up the glorious Hudson, the beauties of which increased as we went onwards, till at the place we had now reached, the scenery had acquired all the grandeur of the finest Highland lochs of Scotland, as far as altitude or form are concerned, with the additional embellishment of a rich coating of foliage, reaching from the tops of the highest mountains, in some places nearly to the water's edge. As the steam-boat glided across from one landing-place to another, we had the enjoyment of much variety of the landscape; and, upon the whole, I have seldom, if ever, seen a more beautiful line of river scenery.

Notably, the Ohio River at times was equally scenic. After all, it was often referred to as the "beautiful river" or "Labelle Riviere." Darkness also produced viewing delights. "By night the scene is one of startling interest and magical splendor," observed a passenger who traveled on a riverboat along the lower Mississippi. "Hundreds of lights are glancing in different directions from villages and plantations on shore, and from the magnificent floating palaces of steamers that frequently look like mountains of light and flame, so brilliantly are these enormous leviathans illuminated outside and inside. Indeed the spectacle presented is like a dream of enchantment."[27]

There were travel complaints. Some passengers fussed about noise. It might have come from the machinery, paddle wheels, working cargoes, or other sources. John C. Calhoun, the prominent South Carolina politician, for one, disliked the "tremor from the machinery, the puffing of the waste pipe," and the "endless thumping of the billets of wood on their way to the furnace." There were objections about smells, most of all when animals were part of the consist. Some objected to the recurring push of the hungry to the tables for meals. "As the dinner hour drew near, the doors of the saloon were besieged very much as those of an opera-house are at a popular singer's benefit," recalled one disgusted passenger, "and upon their being opened, a rush took place, succeeded by a hot contest for seats." More likely passengers did not care for "tramp" riverboats that might not make any real efforts to please them. The naturalist John James Audubon was irritated with his trip in 1843 on such a vessel from Louisville to Saint Louis. "A crazy, dirty little craft, which was provided with but twelve berths or sleeping shelves, furnished with scanty and dirty bedding. The food was detestable—salty meats, rancid butter, coffee and tea without milk." Charles Francis Adams, lawyer, politician, diplomat, and son of president John Quincy Adams, did not care for the *Alhambra* on a trip in 1860 to Saint Paul, Minnesota. "Old and bad at the best," he called this riverboat, and the berths were "so dubious that I deemed it most prudent not to risk the reception of vermin. Hence I was awake most of the night." There were those who disliked conditions on the hurricane deck. A female passenger complained that it was impossible to be on the top level "without being covered with black sparks, or greased by some horrid invention in the neighborhood of the funnels." There were passengers who actually became horribly bored with their journeys. "Traveling by water to me grows irksome after a day or two," wrote the roving George Foster Pierce, a Methodist bishop, who in 1855 traveled on the Cumberland River. "Three meals a day—reading a little, talking a little, walking a little, and all the while paddle, paddle, puff, puff and the first step on solid ground brings a thrill of pleasure." Passengers might not find the passing scenery entrancing, particularly on the lower Mississippi River. "The journey from St. Louis to the mouth of the Mississippi is one of singularly little interest," wrote a well-to-do Australian passenger. Another traveler, who in 1839 headed north from New Orleans, agreed: "So far as the grandiose scenery on the Mississippi goes, I could not find it at all, for the banks are mostly flat and covered with forest, seldom rising to a significant height." Inevitably passengers did not like trips that missed their anticipated departure times. In 1839 a woman and her husband, who took the *Farmer* from Montgomery to Mobile, were scheduled to leave on May 8, "but, against our will, we had to be patient and wait another day because the captain delayed departure for lack of passengers. In the hottest sun, accompanied by a Negro who carried our bags, we appeared at the boat at the appointed hour, 4:00 P.M., only to suffer another delay: passengers were expected off the stagecoach, which was not to arrive until later." Some complained about when boats left. Those who took steamboats from Portland, Oregon, to points up the Columbia River needed to arrive in ample time before the regularly set departures at 5:00 a.m. Most travelers did not care for a policy established in the mid-1840s by Captain Gilbert Blue, who operated the steamboat *Putnam* between Pittsburgh and Zanesville, Ohio, on the Ohio and Muskingum Rivers.

Being a devout Sabbatarian, he refused to run on Sundays. Moreover, he forbade card playing and expected passengers to behave as ladies and gentlemen. Captain Blue did not last long on the route. "It was too strict a boat for the patrons of the days." Still, Blue's anti-card-playing policy pleased some. When Bishop Pierce traveled on the lower Mississippi River, he offered this account of card-playing gamblers: "Among the party were some who during the day affected to be sober, sedate gentlemen, and who, I learned, at home contrived to maintain the character of praiseworthy citizens. Yet here they were midnight gamblers, fleecing the green boys who amid smoke and liquor were wasting the substance of their fathers' life-long industry." The bishop closed with these thoughts: "Heaven save young men of the land from the wiles of their seniors in depravity!"[28]

In the 1830s a young, well-educated Englishman provided a good example of the feelings of those who complained about their fellow passengers. "One meets with a very strange collection of people in a Western steamer. On board the Pittsburgh were about 300 passengers, some of whom were very curious specimens of their kind, such scrambling for places as there was at meal times, such unaccommodating, take-care-of-myself spirit characterized every individual that in self defense we were obliged to be as rude and rough as our neighbors." His negativity continued. "The *Gentlemen* [italics in original] passed most of their time in gambling, and while they were engaged in this occupation, the wanton imprecations and shocking blasphemy that were bandied round the tables were absolutely disgusting. The whole scene appeared to me to realize the idea of 'Hell afloat.' The morals of the Southern and Western people seem to be at a very low ebb. As far as I have had an opportunity of judging, they are a gambling, drinking, swearing set of profligates."[29]

Clergy and others who sought to uphold "village virtues" applauded the early steamboat practice of sexual segregation in cabins, which served to minimize inappropriate male-female contacts. Apparently prostitutes traveled the rivers, but they were not that common. "Two or three veiled allusions to the subject by travelers and several accounts of *nymphes du fleuve* ejected from steamboats or prevented from boarding them are the only references to this form of immorality which have come to the writer's attention," concluded historian Louis Hunter. Interesting, too, is that unmarried couples who traveled together ran the chance of being put ashore if they were discovered. Surely they were unhappy or even distraught.[30]

An annoyance that involved bodily risks to crew and passengers alike occurred when a steamboat became lodged on a sandbar. Just as a stagecoach might become stuck on a muddy road, forcing riders either to push or to watch, a similar occurrence plagued steamboat passengers during times of low water. Thomas Low Nichols, who traveled down the Ohio

River on the *Fort Wayne* before the Civil War, described events when this vessel became wedged on a sandbar near the mouths of the Cumberland and Tennessee Rivers. The large tributaries continually deposited huge quantities of sand and silt into the Ohio, and when that river became shallow during an extended dry period, this became a navigation trouble spot. "Our captain determined to take every precaution. He hired a flat boat, lashed her alongside, and loaded into her many tons of whisky and butter. This done, just as breakfast was ready, all the male passengers were summoned to go on board the flat boat, so as to lighten the steamer as much as possible, and when we were all aboard we started; but the current carried the [*Fort Wayne*] a few feet out of her proper course, and she stuck fast." The captain's response? "It was time now to go to work in earnest. More freight was discharged into our lighter and all the passengers, except women with children, were sent on board of her." The strategy worked, and after a considerable delay, the *Fort Wayne*, with its passengers, crew, and freight, proceeded down the Ohio.[31]

Even without the interference of annoying sandbars, rapids and low water levels might prevent free-moving travel. On the Upper Mississippi River, for example, the "Lower Rapids," which extended between the Iowa communities of Montrose and Keokuk, meant that, during the frequently dry periods that occurred in fall and early winter, passengers needed to take carriages or wagons around the obstacle. Freight, too, was forced to move by public roads. This delay took hours, and passengers often grumbled.[32]

Travel dangers by steamboat overshadowed any passenger unhappiness about a relatively uneventful trip. The public, though, mostly realized potential dangers. "The cabin of a Mississippi riverboat is strangely contrasted with the scenes of wretchedness on the lower decks, and its splendor serves in some measure to distract the attention of the unthinking inmates from the dangers that lie below," observed an astute water traveler. "But no one who is at all acquainted with the steam engine can examine the machinery of one of these boats without shuddering at the great risk to which all on board are exposed." A similar commentary came from the pen of Theresa Yelverton, who took passage on a riverboat that plied the Savannah River between Savannah and Augusta, Georgia:

> The curious little steamer upon which we made this voyage was called "The Swan." She bore no resemblance to that majestic bird in the symmetry of her proportions, for she was a long flat boat, or barge, with a hurricane deck hoisted up on poles, and looking anything but solid or safe. Upon that the cabin was perched, and around it was a little balcony on which to sit and enjoy the *dolce far niente* [pleasant idleness] of life—always provided you had no foolish fears of being tipped over into the water from the breaking of said poles, of being launched into the air by the bursting boiler, or that the engine—which keeps

repeating in hoarse vulcanic roars, "Going, going, going, gone"—means that you and he are going to your last home, and that his next agonized puff will be the end.

She closed with these thoughts: "If you can disregard all these tokens, then I say you may travel very pleasantly."[33]

Journeys created risks. Yet a steamboat trip was far more dangerous than one by stagecoach, canal boat, or, usually, a train. In fact, western riverboats developed an appalling accident record. Death rates on inland rivers and other bodies of water were not insignificant. A railroad trade publication reported that for the ten-year period between 1853 and 1863, steamboat accidents accounted for 3,545 deaths but railroads for only 1,699, and there were many more injuries involving both forms of travel. When the signature disasters of each transportation type are considered, the deadly nature of water transport is borne out. For riverboats it was the explosion, fire, and sinking of the *Sultana* near Memphis, Tennessee, on April 27, 1865. About 1,700 of the estimated 2,400 passengers and crew on board died. For Great Lakes steamers it was the capsizing in the Chicago River of the *Eastland* on July 24, 1915, drowning 844 passengers and crew members. But catastrophic deaths for steam and electric interurban railroads have been much fewer. For the former, the head-on crash on July 9, 1918, outside Nashville, Tennessee, of two speeding Nashville, Chattanooga & St. Louis Railway passenger trains killed 101 passengers and crew, and for the latter it was the collision on September 21, 1910, of two interurban cars near Kingsland, Indiana, killing 41.[34]

The greatest dangers to steamboat passengers involved sinkings, collisions, explosions, and fires. These factors mostly explain why these craft had relatively limited life spans, although their boilers and engines might be salvaged and find renewed life in other vessels. "Without luck, a steamboat lived on borrowed time," observed a historian of the riverboat era in the Pacific Northwest. "If no reef, rock, or snag drove a hole in her hull, if no wandering bark ran her down and cut her in two, if her engine did not blow up, if she kept away from fire, if the weather was kind, she had a fair chance of survival."[35]

Snags caused the greatest number of riverboat accidents. Based on an 1852 survey, which covered the forty-year period between 1811 and 1851, 57.5 percent of the 995 wrecks identified were caused by this type of waterway obstruction. Yet when a boat sank, the loss of property might be high, but the loss of passenger lives was likely relatively low. The reason, according to John White, was "because the boat was often beached on the riverbank before the sinking occurred." As he further notes, "At times of low water only the first deck was submerged and the passenger deck remained above the river. In such cases it was safe for the travelers to remain aboard until rescued."[36]

A snag could cause a major tragedy, however. A memorable one took place in the early morning hours of Friday, December 19, 1845, when the steamboat *Belle Zane*, steaming downstream on the Mississippi River to New Orleans, hit a snag that ripped through its hull about fourteen miles above the mouth of the Arkansas River. It did not take long before the boilers rolled into the water, and the hull separated from the cabin. This wooden structure drifted toward the hamlet of Napoleon, Arkansas, and landed on a sandbar. More pieces of debris made their way to an island, where they ran aground. Some passengers managed to cling to that portion of the wreckage and were saved.[37]

In a letter to his brother, one passenger described the sinking of the *Bell Zane* and the immediate aftermath:

> Lying about half asleep, I heard a hollow crash somewhere forward, when I immediately sprang out of the upper berth in my room on the starboard side, calling at the same time to my fellow passenger, Clyde, that we "had got it now." I opened the inner door and perceived that she was careening over on her larboard [port] bow. I immediately sprang back, put my purse and watch in my pantaloons pocket, (they being on,) by that time Clyde had got up, seized his cap, when we found we were sliding out the outside door (the boat having held on the snag,) and were compelled to spring for our lives into the Mississippi; at the same moment two or three hundred empty molasses barrels and forty of fifty coops of turkeys came thundering (if I may so speak) off the skylight and hurricane deck around us, two of them, the barrels, striking C. on the head and nearly killing him.

The writer was luckier. "Fortunately none of them hit me, and one of them I caught hold of and held on to it, while C. caught hold of coop, and each of us held to our respective articles until we could make out to get on the [floating] hurricane deck, which had come off, and from that on her larboard side, while there were about 70 souls—some with pants on—some with drawers on—some with a bed comforter around them and so on." This survivor was one of 64 passengers who reached shore safety. The remainder of the 125 passengers perished, either downing or dying from exposure on that cold December day.[38]

According to that 1852 report, the remainder of accidents involved boiler explosions (21 percent) or fires and collisions (21.5 percent). Interestingly, boiler explosions occurred only occasionally on steam railroads. The most deadly one, which happened at the Southern Pacific shops in San Antonio, Texas, on March 18, 1912, killed twenty-six workers but of course no travelers.

One monumental and significant explosion and fire during the riverboat era involved the magnificent *Ben Sherrod* and took place on the lower Mississippi early on the morning of May 8, 1837. This boat, which carried about three hundred passengers and cargo, was headed toward Saint Louis from New Orleans. About the time that the *Ben Sherrod* left the public dock in the Crescent City, the *Prairie* also departed. It did not take long before some passengers on both vessels sought a race, and their respective captains agreed. On the *Ben Sherrod* passengers urged crew members to create as much steam pressure as possible, and their reward was a barrel of whiskey. The dash commenced. Disastrously for the *Ben Sherrod*, the soon drunken crew overfed the boilers with wood and highly combustible pine knots and rosin. Near Fort Adams in Wilkinson County, Mississippi, the overheated boilers set fire to sixty cords of fuel, which erupted into a nearly instant and rapidly spreading inferno. During the conflagration eight explosions ensued, initially barrels of whiskey and brandy, then boilers, and lastly forty barrels of gunpowder. The boat, which collapsed on itself, quickly sank. Passengers who were sleeping either on the deck or in upper cabins had little time to escape, if, in fact, escape was possible. Many, including those who had been excited race spectators, jumped overboard and clung to the floating debris. It was alleged that the captain failed either to alert passengers when the fire was discovered or to steer the vessel toward shore.[39]

The fire and explosions created a nightmare scene. "The screams of the men, women and children pierced the air for miles around," reported a New Orleans newspaper. A witness said, "Poor wretches clung convulsively to the burning sides of the boat" and "struck the deepest anguish into the heart of the spectators." There was more to this calamity. The *Prairie*, which was a few miles ahead, failed to come to the rescue of survivors, and the passing *Alton* also did not lend assistance. Even a man in a nearby canoe refused to save any victims unless they agreed to "pay him handsomely for his services." Fortunately two steamboats, the *Columbus* and the *Statesmen*, provided aid, saving numerous lives. When the death count was taken, about 150 bodies were identified.[40]

It would not be unjust to say that passengers on the *Ben Sherrod* contributed to this awful loss of life. Many aboard enjoyed steamboat racing, and so they demanded speed at any cost. A meeting of steam boatmen held in Cincinnati in 1838 concluded that "the public have, themselves, contributed in no inconsiderable degree, to increase the evil [of disasters] by the constant desire which a large portion of those who travel on steamboats, manifest 'to go the fastest' and even to urge an increase of speed." These men asked, "Is it wonderful then that under such circumstances some commanders should be induced to force their boats beyond the bounds of safety, when great patronage and applause are the rewards for risk incurred? This morbid appetite among travelers for 'going ahead' is probably one of the greatest causes of the evils."[41]

The *Ben Sherrod* calamity led to a formal inquest in Natchez, Mississippi. But more importantly, because of this tragedy and several others, the US Congress in 1838 passed a measure for steamboat boiler, hull, and equipment inspections. In 1852 stronger regulations came about, including provisions for the prevention of fires and collisions. This act also created administrative machinery and led to the hiring of competent government inspectors. Safety generally improved, at least in terms of boiler explosions.[42]

Even without a precipitating boiler explosion, the potential of a devastating fire was always present. These wooden riverboats were nothing more than floating tinderboxes. "Boats on the Western waters are all built very light and dry, and there is a good deal of paint and varnish on them, which makes them burn almost like shavings," remarked a pilot who worked on the Ohio and lower Mississippi Rivers. A deadly conflagration could start in a variety of ways. A slight collision with a snag or another vessel could tip over cooking and heating stoves, spilling hot coals. Candles and oil lamps in the staterooms became an ever-present hazard. A careless smoker could also ignite flammable material, or something else might start an uncontrollable blaze.[43]

Head-on collisions also took their toll. One of the deadliest occurred on October 31, 1837, on the lower Mississippi near Baton Rouge, Louisiana. The *Monmouth*—a small steamboat heading northward with more than 900 passengers packed on board, nearly all of whom were Creek Indians being relocated to government lands in present-day Oklahoma—struck the southbound sailboat *Trenton*, which was being towed by the steamboat *Warren*. Of the 611 Creeks on board, only about 300 were rescued. As for the officers and crew, "the bar-keepers and a fireman were the only persons attached to the Monmouth who lost their lives." The *Monmouth* was traveling in the wrong part of the river channel; the *Warren* did not expect to encounter a forward-moving vessel in its prescribed path. "The disaster was chiefly owing to the neglect of the officers of the Monmouth," concluded a chronicler of this tragedy.[44]

Another real fear involved catching the highly infectious and potentially deadly Asiatic cholera bacterial disease or some other communicable affliction. Cholera, most of all, took a heavy toll on the American population, especially during a pandemic that raged in North America between 1827 and 1835. Steamboat passengers, just as those who took stagecoaches or canal packets, might contract and then spread the disease. Infected individuals might board the vessel, and onboard sanitation, poor or virtually nonexistent, could start a cholera outbreak. Some travelers believed that a variety of nostrums could save them. A popular one in the antebellum period consisted of the following ingredients: "a little nutmeg or essence of peppermint and water added to some burnt cork poured in a teaspoonful of brandy and mashed with loaf sugar." Nostrums or not, deaths reigned on board scores of vessels during several serious regional outbreaks. A passenger on the *Excelsior*, which operated on the Upper

HUDSON RIVER DAY LINE

STEAMERS
WASHINGTON IRVING   ROBERT FULTON
HENDRICK HUDSON   AND ALBANY

1915   DAILY, EXCEPT SUNDAY   1915

NORTH BOUND	A. M.	A. M.	P. M.
New York			
Desbrosses St.	8 40	9 40	1 45
West 42d St.	9 00	10 00	2 00
West 129th St.	9 20	10 20	2 20
Yonkers	9 45	10 50	*2 45
Bear Mountain		12 30	*4 30
Highland Falls			4 45
West Point	11 50	1 00	5 00
Cornwall		1 25	5 25
Newburgh	12 25	1 45	5 45
New Hamburgh			6 15
Milton			6 30
Poughkeepsie	1 15	2 35	6 45
Kingston Point	2 10		
Kingston			7 45
Catskill	3 25		
Hudson	3 40		
Albany	6 10		

Column notes (North Bound): May 14 to Nov. 1 · June 19 to Sept. 18 · June 1 to Sept. 18 · *Yonkers and Bear Mt. Stop from July 7 to Sept. 4

SOUTH BOUND	A. M.	A. M.	P. M.
Albany		8 30	
Hudson		10 40	
Catskill		11 00	
Kingston	7 00		
Kingston Point		12 25	
Poughkeepsie	8 00	1 20	4 10
Milton	8 15		
New Hamburgh	8 30		
Newburgh	9 00	2 15	5 05
Cornwall	9 15		5 20
West Point	9 35	2 50	5 50
Highland Falls	9 40		
Bear Mountain			6 00
Yonkers		4 30	7 35
New York			
West 129th St.	11 55	5 10	8 10
West 42d St.	12 15	5 30	8 40
Desbrosses St.	12 45	6 00	

Column notes (South Bound): June 2 to Sept. 18 · May 15 to Nov. 2 · June 19 to Sept. 18 · This Steamer will run one-half hour later on Saturdays

☞ Over for Rates and Important Notes.

Although railroad competition dramatically reduced passenger traffic on the Hudson River between New York City and Albany, the excursion business remained popular for decades. Early in the twentieth century, the Hudson River Day Line dominated this market with its four large steamboats.

Author's Collection

Mississippi, commented in 1851 about this scourge. "The first intimation I received of the presence of death in our midst was the tolling of the bell & the mooring of the boat at the foot of a high bluff on the Illinois shore. Soon some hands jumped ashore, a grave was speedily dug & as the last rays of the setting sun glided from the waters face, a bird sent up a joyful note over the grave of the infant which an hour before had breathed its last." But that was not the sole death. "We proceeded on our way an[d] 'ere two days had passed we had buried *five* [italics in original] deck passengers, I fear some of them victims of cholera no doubt aggravated or induced by filthiness, exposure, fatigue & improper diet." The writer also commented on a cholera outbreak on another steamboat. "Nine cases, some of them fatal, broke out on the *Galena* while on her way upstream to St. Paul. One of the victims lay in a canoe on the St. Paul levee surrounded by some fellow passengers who vainly strove to revive him."[45]

Public concerns about possibilities of deadly or serious accidents or a potentially fatal disease did not kill off the riverboat passenger business. It was railroad competition, especially during the post–Civil War era, that continually caused owners either to exit the passenger trade or to abandon their operations altogether. What happened on the Missouri River is representative. About the time of World War I, the *Chester* became the last boat to offer passenger accommodations between Saint Louis and Kansas City. Although the favored Saint Louis to Kansas City passenger railroads—Missouri Pacific and Wabash—had been in business for decades, water travel had continued, usually because it was cheaper and served communities that lacked a railroad or had poor connecting rail service. The *Chester* remained in service, becoming in the early 1920s a short-lived Kansas City–based seasonal excursion boat.[46]

GREAT LAKES TRAVEL

Passenger-carrying vessels on the Great Lakes shared similarities with those that served the numerous ports along the Atlantic and Pacific Oceans and the Gulf of Mexico, and they also might resemble the finest boats that operated on inland streams. "The steamboats used on the lakes are much more durable and sturdy than those that only ply the rivers," observed the Austrian transportation expert Franz Anton Ritter von Gerstner, "and in fact they bear a greater resemblance to the ships that travel the high seas." Although small craft and later sailboats of various types—barks, brigs, and schooners—were for decades the only option for both passengers and freight, the steam era dawned early in the nineteenth century. In 1816 the steamboat *Fontenac* appeared on Lake Ontario, and two years later *Walk-in-the Water*, which was designed for passenger service, made its debut on Lake Erie. The *Cleaveland Gazette* heralded its arrival: "A passage between this place [Cleveland] and Buffalo is now not merely tolerable, but truly pleasant." It did not take long before scores of steam-powered boats became part of the brisk Great Lakes passenger trade. For a half century or so, these lake steamers dominated passenger travel while faithful sailing boats handled the bulk freight.[47]

Just as the lower Mississippi became the epicenter for steamboat travel, Lake Erie claimed much the same honor on the Great Lakes. Steam vessels rapidly dominated the routes that linked Buffalo, Cleveland, Toledo, and Detroit. By the 1840s Chicago and Milwaukee also emerged as busy ports of call. After steam's formative years in operation, auxiliary sails on these Great Lakes boats largely disappeared; the low-pressure steam engines became more powerful and dependable. On the eve of the Civil War, there were 106 side-wheel steamers and 135 propeller-driven ones on these fresh water seas and more than a thousand sailing vessels of various types. Even though boats under sail were freight haulers, some accepted paying passengers. Steam-powered lake boats evolved slowly from wooden, to iron, to steel hulls, and they grew larger and more elegant. They became grander than anything afloat on the nation's rivers.[48]

The accommodations provided by developing Great Lakes boats varied. Some that operated during the antebellum period were designed not only to favor cabin passengers but also to cater to steerage patrons, who were often some of the thousands of immigrants who were headed to destinations throughout the Midwest and beyond. Men, women, and children who hailed from western Europe, the British Isles, British North America, and the United States made up the mix of nationalities. With passengers such as these in mind, the "steerage hold" of the early steamer *Superior* contained bunk beds, cooking stoves, tables, pantries, and baggage bins, and there was space for farm implements, animals, and other personal possessions.[49]

The contemporary *May Flower* represented the best of these antebellum passenger vessels. An English woman traveler claimed that this railroad-owned steamer, which operated between Buffalo and Detroit, was the most splendid one that she had seen, being grander than the palaces of her native land. John White aptly described this most stunning boat: "The main cabin, or saloon, was 300 feet long. The ceiling rose up in a gothic arcade festooned with gilded grapes and vines, panels, and rich moldings. It had eighty-five staterooms that offered space to 300 first-class patrons. Space was provided for 350 immigrants. The floor of the great cabin was covered in velvet pile carpet decorated with brilliant flowers. The walnut furniture was covered in green velvet." And to add to the attractiveness of the *May Flower*, "a handsome piano, eight chandeliers, and huge mirrors at the ends of the [great cabin] space completed the decor."[50]

Before the Civil War another stunning passenger steamer appeared on Lake Erie: the 348-foot-long and 72.5-foot-wide *Western World*. Costing more than $250,000 ($6.5 million in current dollars) and belonging to the Michigan Central Railroad, this "mammoth" paddle wheeler claimed a capacity of 1,500 passengers. Resembling the *May Flower* and several other first-class vessels of the period, the *Western World* epitomized the new standard of luxury that had become available and appreciated by the fussiest travelers. This steamer featured two handsome bridal chambers, resembling other first-class cabins and being tastefully furnished with marble-topped washstands, embroidered lounging chairs, and other distinguishing appointments. The food served to cabin passengers, which was included in the price of the ticket, was equally impressive. The *Western World* and similar vessels were unquestionably the equals of any of the finest boats that plied eastern waters. As with riverboats, desk or steerage passengers needed to provide their own food or to pay for their meals "at the second table."[51]

With Great Lakes vessels, especially the largest, it was necessary to employ a sizable crew. In addition to the many sailors or deckhands, cooks, waiters, porters, and maids, these boats had a captain, first and second mate, steward, engineers, wheelsmen, stokers, and a clerk or bookkeeper. Their pay typically equaled or was greater than that of their counterparts on inland rivers. These boats probably also had freelance barbers and barkeepers. Most crew members were native born, and some had worked previously on oceangoing ships, canal packets, and riverboats.[52]

As with all forms of transportation, Great Lakes vessels were not immune from disasters. Although there is no complete record of the number of passenger-carrying boats that went down on the lakes, the shallow and storm-prone Lake Erie became the most littered with the sunken remains of hundreds of ill-fated craft. The majority of sinkings occurred because of gales and squalls that produced disastrously high waves and the general absence of protective harbors where boats could find safety. Furthermore, the dangerous rocky shores went unlighted for years. Then there were deadly onboard fires and occasional collisions, the latter frequently caused by heavy fogs. Ice, too, could trap a vessel. The winter of 1884–1885, which was exceptionally severe, resulted in the ice-capture of several passenger-carrying boats on Lake Michigan, yet there were no deaths or serious injuries. Fortunately, the average loss of life on the Great Lakes was considerably less than during the peak years of riverboat travel, and over time more sinkings involved freight rather than passenger vessels. Nevertheless, a colossal accident occurred on July 24, 1915, when the excursion boat *Eastland* capsized while moored in the Chicago River. This accident was due to its top-heaviness and not to a storm, collision, or fire. Of the 2,573 merry-goers on board, most were employees of the Hawthorn

THE SUMMER TIME TABLE OF

SEASON OF 1893

COLUMBIAN NAVIGATION 1492

THE GOODRICH LINE.

S.S. VIRGINIA.

GOODRICH TRANSPORTATION COMPANY

TO THE PRINCIPAL PORTS ON LAKE MICHIGAN.

...OFFICERS

A. W. GOODRICH, Pres't, Chicago.
G. HURSON, Gen'l Traffic Mgr., Milwaukee.
J. W. GILLMAN, Sup't, Chicago.
JNO. SINGLETON, Gen. Pass. Agt., Chicago.

THE GRAZEO DESIGNERS,
315 Dearborn St. Chi.

OFFICES AND DOCKS
. Foot of Michigan Avenue, Chicago .

STROMBERG, ALLEN & CO., PRINTERS, 337-339 DEARBORN ST., CHICAGO.

Even after the golden age of passenger travel ended on the Great Lakes, business and pleasure travelers continued to board lake vessels. The Goodrich Line, for example, operated the *Virginia* on Lake Michigan.

Author's Collection

CITY OF CLEVELAND

plant of Western Electric in Cicero, Illinois, and 844 men, women, and children drowned, "trapped like rats in a cellar."[53]

The 1850s marked the golden age of Great Lakes passenger travel. But by the end of the Civil War, the expanding railroad network, notably through routes between New York, Buffalo, Cleveland, Toledo, Detroit, and Chicago, cut into patronage. These ironways offered speed and dependability, and they were more direct, especially for trips from Chicago and other Lake Michigan ports to destinations in the East. Rates also became more competitive, and at times "homeseekers'" rail fares were less than those charged by lake boats. Although time-conscious businessmen and immigrant travelers had largely abandoned the lakes, passenger traffic did not evaporate.[54]

Unlike the disappearing riverboat markets, important and profitable passenger transport operations continued on the Great Lakes for generations. Owners survived financially because their boats provided a more relaxed way to travel between several major and rapidly growing population centers. And their vessels generally provided good food and service, attractive accommodations, refreshingly cool breezes during the summer months, and some pleasant scenery. Moreover, unlike most rivers, the Great Lakes' seasonal fluctuations in water levels have little effect on water transportation.

In the 1890s James J. Hill, famed "Empire Builder" and founder of the recently completed Great Northern Railway between Minnesota

and Washington State, decided to take advantage of Great Lakes water transit to make his crack passenger trains more attractive to easterners. In 1894 his Northern Steamship Company subsidiary placed in service the twin-screw *North West*, "the last word in fresh water transportation." This luxury boat could cruise at twenty miles per hour with a top speed of twenty-seven miles per hour, and it had a capacity of 758 passengers, 544 in first class and 214 in second class. A year later the companion *Northland* became the firm's second passenger vessel. Both boats were magnificent; in reality they were medium-sized ocean liners. A contemporary description revealed that their interiors had "a rich mahogany finish, spirited carving, soft coloring, and a judicious use of gold, producing a symphony of brown, bronze-green and gold with the delicate carving and relief work repeated through an imposing length of space." Some staterooms featured private baths, and electric dynamos supplied safe, bright lighting. The exteriors were white with cream smokestacks; the center one featured a red star lit by floodlights at night. President William McKinley proclaimed the craft to be "a veritable floating palace." Even with the best of equipment and semiweekly service between Buffalo and Duluth, however, the operation failed to become a smashing success, in part because of the catastrophic depression of 1893 to 1897 and months of

Shown steaming out of Toledo harbor in 1894, the *Idlewild*, a passenger and packet freight vessel, operated for years between Port Huron, Detroit, and Toledo. Originally the *Grace McMillan*, built in 1879 by the Detroit Dry Dock Company in Wyandotte, Michigan, it belonged to the Detroit & Cleveland Steam Navigation Company.

Photograph of Idlewild, *ca. 1894, courtesy of the Toledo-Lucas County Public Library, obtained from http://images2 .toledolibrary.org/*

ice blockage. In a change of strategy, the *Northland* later steamed between Buffalo and Chicago, making connections with passenger trains of the Chicago, Burlington & Quincy Railroad, another Hill property. Although the two vessels rarely showed a profit, they generated traffic for the Hill Lines, and they created a positive public image. These boats continued in service only through the season of 1910, and the following year the *North West* sank while at the Buffalo docks, being fitted for a season that would never begin.[55]

By the early years of the twentieth century, several companies dominated the Great Lakes passenger sector, and on the traditionally busy Lake Erie, two carriers held sway: the Detroit & Cleveland Steam Navigation Company (D&C) and the Cleveland & Buffalo Transit Company (C&B). The former, which began in 1868, proclaimed early on to be "The Daily Line between Detroit and Cleveland." By the immediate post–World War I years, the D&C operated what were allegedly the largest side-wheelers in the world, the *Greater Detroit* and the *Greater Cleveland*. The latter carrier, started in 1892, focused on the Cleveland to Buffalo route and began with two small side-wheelers. Then in 1913 the C&B introduced its impressive *Seeanbee*. "She marks the last word in marine architecture," crowed one commentator. Yet he wrongly predicted, "and it is not likely that there will be built in the future anything of her type exceeding her proportions." Still, the *Seeanbee* was gigantic: its five-hundred-foot, four-deck, all-steel structure accommodated 1,500 passengers and tons of freight, mail, and express.[56]

Until increased automobile usage and the Great Depression crippled passenger traffic, Lake Erie boat operators attracted substantial patronage, mostly capitalizing on pleasure seekers. Passengers enjoyed good accommodations, with even a touch of luxury typified by decorative woodwork, Wilton carpets, and potted plants. Many appreciated the freedom to roam a much larger area, not being confined to a railroad consist. There were also attractive scheduling features: tourists, businessmen, or shoppers could board a C&B boat in the early evening; dine leisurely; enjoy clean, comfortable staterooms; and arrive at their destination the next morning. "Spacious staterooms and parlors combined with the quietness with which the boats are operated insures refreshing sleep," boomed the C&B in the 1920s. Yet attractive boats and convenient schedules could not save either the C&B or D&C. The former liquidated in 1939, and the latter lasted somewhat longer. However, there have been attempts to revive excursion trips. In 1957 the nine-deck *Aquarama*, a streamlined, single-screw, oil-fired, and turbine-powered converted World War II troop carrier, sought to exploit that once profitable business. But operations of this largest passenger vessel to sail the lakes ended in 1962, a victim of unprofitability. In more recent years, several much smaller craft have offered

pleasure cruises on the Great Lakes, often promoting evening dinner and dance experiences.[57]

COASTAL VOYAGES

The history of coastal passenger transport largely parallels that on the American Great Lakes. Sailing vessels gave way to boats powered by steam and auxiliary sails and then to low-pressure steam engines that initially burned cordwood and later anthracite coal. Boat hulls saw a similar progression, going from wood to iron to steel, and in the process boats became larger, faster, and more dependable. Likewise these vessels were more elegant and comfortable. As with other areas where water travel developed popularity, including the lower Mississippi River system and Lake Erie, Long Island Sound, the "Mediterranean of the Western hemisphere," emerged as the most active corridor for intercity water travel.[58]

Early in the saga of passenger service on Long Island Sound, a body of water that is about one hundred miles long and thirty miles wide, sailing sloops initially provided transport between the rapidly growing port of New York and points along the southern coast of New England. In 1815 steam appeared, and it did not take long before scores of ever-better boats followed. One notable vessel, the *Lexington*, the handiwork of the innovative and hard-driving Cornelius Vanderbilt, made its maiden voyage in June 1836. This paddle wheeler, which claimed to be the "fastest boat in the world," cut through frequently choppy waters on its 210-mile trip from

New York City to Providence, Rhode Island and took only twelve hours, being about six hours faster than any previous water voyage between the two cities. At first there were connecting stagecoaches between Boston and Providence, the former city being a major source of passenger traffic, but about the time the *Lexington* entered service, the Boston & Providence Railroad made the Boston leg faster and more comfortable.[59]

In order to capture the brisk and lucrative Long Island Sound trade, a host of steamboat firms appeared. Understandably, the traveling public benefited from this fierce competition, gaining access to more garish appointments and elaborate services provided by scores of boatmen. These coastal carriers often became true floating palaces. Ticket prices were relatively inexpensive, especially for those who were willing to accept fewer amenities. There also might be the excitement of boat racing between rival lines, and by the era of the Civil War, faster craft might move at a clip of twenty miles an hour or better.[60]

Although most trips were uneventful, dangers always lurked on Long Island Sound and the neighboring waters. Whirlpools and rocks at the entrance of the East River to Long Island Sound in New York created hazards, as did strong currents at Point Judith near the entrance to Narragansett Bay. Gales, fog, and other weather features might cause boats to sink or collide. While fewer in number than those disastrous fires that seemingly plagued riverboats, such calamities did occur.

One of the deadliest accidents took place on January 13, 1840, when Commodore Vanderbilt's *Lexington* caught fire off Eaton's Neck, Long Island, on its way to Stonington, Rhode Island, and a direct rail connection for Boston. The wood casing of the boiler stack erupted into flames, and a strong wind whipped the fire, which soon engulfed the vessel. In his contemporary book *Steamboat Disasters and Railroad Accidents in the United States,* S. A. Howland graphically pictured in his own Victorian style the horrors of that fiery disaster. "The lurid light of the blazing wreck shone far over the cold and dreary waste of waters, showing with fearful directness the dreadful scene in its immediate vicinity. Human beings were floating around in every direction—some were yet living, but more had ceased to be—some were struggling to gain a fragment or bale of cotton, while others in happy unconsciousness, were sinking into the cold flood of death." He added to his morbid description: "Here was heard the last wild shriek of despair—husbands, wives, fathers, mothers and children were plunging into eternity, with the heart-breaking cry of agony dying on their lips." One hundred and fifty people perished, and only one passenger and three crew members survived. Soon colored prints of the burning *Lexington* became popular, the handiwork of printmaker Nathaniel Currier, future partner of James Ives.[61]

Although the memories of the *Lexington* disaster lingered in the public imagination, most travelers thought about (and remembered) the classy vessels that served the sound. Those boats were operated by the Fall River Line between New York City and Fall River, Massachusetts, with connecting boat trains to Boston. This long-enduring, profitable, and largely accident-free steamboat company represented the best of everything that could be found on these waters. The *Priscilla* belonged to its luxury fleet. Not long after entering service in 1894, Scottish author David Christie Murray waxed enthusiastic about what he had experienced on that magnificent boat. "It is a thing built in stories, about as high as the Pyramids, more or less. You walk from the dock into an entrance hall. There is room here for a pair of tennis courts. You don't believe it but you are 'on board.' You go up a huge, great staircase and find yourself in a concert hall in which there is ample room to seat a thousand people." There was more:

> You go up another magnificent staircase, and you lose yourself in hundreds of yards of lordly corridor. There is plush velvet enough to upholster several theaters. There are more staircases and more stories and a restaurant like a football field in its dimensions, and you laugh at the ridiculous Aladdin who made his genii build such a city of a vessel under the impression that it is in the power of any machinery made by man to make the "derned" thing move. It begins to move, and away you glide, majestic, impossible, and before you know it you are doing three and twenty miles an hour.[62]

Murray could have mentioned the presence of the *Priscilla* orchestra, a popular feature of the better boats on the sound. In a commentary about the earlier *Providence* and *Bristol* were these remarks: "To add to the pleasure of the lovely ride up the Sound, a fine band of music accompanies each steamer and delights the passengers with sweet strains of choice music through the first four hours of the trip."[63]

Other commercial ships, although not the equal to the *Priscilla*, handled passengers along the Atlantic and Gulf coasts. Traffic developed between Boston and Portland, Maine; New York City and Norfolk; and Newport News, Virginia, and New York City, Charleston, Savannah, Mobile, and Galveston. Take service from Gotham to Virginia ports. By the early twentieth century, the Old Dominion Line, the dominant carrier, operated five vessels on its Main Line Division between New York City and Norfolk and several more, albeit smaller, ones on its Virginia Division between Norfolk, Richmond, and other Old Dominion State destinations. The company proclaimed its staterooms to be "spacious, airy and comfortable" and catered to travelers who preferred a more leisurely means of transportation than on competing railroads and vacationers who sought "attractive short sea trips."[64]

No matter the location of a coastal voyage or the weather facing a sailing vessel or steamer, seasickness became the recurring complaint, mitigating for the sufferer any attractiveness of a comfortable stateroom, excellent food, or superb services. When cleric Henry Benjamin Whipple journeyed under sail from New York City to Jacksonville, Florida, he made this diary entry for October 20, 1843: "This is to me as unlucky a day as ever a Friday was to man for here I am suffering all the horrors of seasickness. I would not wish an enemy's dog a sorer punishment than this deadly seasickness. This turning a man wrong side out is anything but pleasant, to say nothing of the disagreeable appearance of such an operation." But, of course, he recovered. "As my seasickness wears away I find a great deal of amusement in watching the porpoises dance about our good ship." In 1906 when a young railroader took the *Denver*, a medium-size vessel owned by the New York and Texas Steamship Company, the "Mallory Line," from Galveston to New York City, he, too, experienced seasickness. He later graphically recalled:

> Now everything went fine and dandy, until the second day out of Galveston, when we were away out there in the Gulf of Mexico, we run into a bad storm, and boy, I began to think my time had come. At first I was scared almost stiff, for I was afraid that the old tub was going to sink, but after a short time I got so deathly seasick that I just layed [sic] in my bunk and heaved up my insides, and just about that time I did not give a dang if the old scow did sink, for boy, I had never felt such a sickly sickness before in my whole life, and just the thought of something to eat made me feed the fishes all the more.

Unfortunately, a rapid recovery did not occur. "Well the next day after the storm had passed I was up on the promenade deck, and I was feeling pretty tough too, for my stomach was so weak and felt so funny, that I did not care much about anything." Then he became the victim of a practical jokester.

> While I was standing by the rail looking down into the blue, blue water, another passenger came up to me and asked me how I felt, and I says oh I feel pretty rotten, and then he says to me do you know what would be good to settle your stomach and make you feel better, and I says no, what is it, then he says, why a nice big piece of good fat bacon, and man oh man, I thought my stomach would turn inside out. Oh boy, but I sure was sick, and this fellow beat it away from me and joined his friends, and they got a big kick and a good laugh out of it, but I'll tell the cockeyed world it was no laughing matter to me, for the kick in my stomach right then had just about kicked me out. Gee, what a funny feeling seasickness is.

By the time the *Denver* reached Key West, he had recovered, and the remainder of his voyage went well.[65]

Most trips along the Pacific coast were uneventful. The deadly hurricanes that plagued the Atlantic and the Gulf of Mexico were far less a threat for vessels that served Seattle, Portland, San Francisco, and other

JANUARY AND FEBRUARY, 1909.

MALLORY STEAMSHIP LINES

MALLORY S.S. COMPANY

BETWEEN

NEW YORK

AND

KEY WEST, FLORIDA
TAMPA, FLORIDA
MOBILE, ALABAMA
GALVESTON, TEXAS

WITH THROUGH SERVICE
TO AND FROM ALL POINTS IN
TEXAS,
FLORIDA, ALABAMA,
MISSISSIPPI, ARIZONA,
LOUISIANA, OKLAHOMA,
COLORADO, NEW & OLD
MEXICO AND CALIFORNIA

MALLORY STEAMSHIP COMPANY
GENERAL OFFICES
80 SOUTH STREET
NEW YORK

While passengers on ships operated by the Mallory Steamship Lines might have expressed displeasure with travel conditions—namely those caused by stormy weather—this New York City–based company provided good service between Gotham and various ports on the Gulf of Mexico.

Author's Collection

West Coast ports. Gales were more likely to make a voyage along the Pacific Ocean uncomfortable and potentially dangerous. And as with all vessels there were the occasional collisions, especially during storms and periods of dense fog.[66]

For all practical purposes, Pacific coast service dated from the time of the famed California gold rush that began with the forty-niners and continued for years to come. With strong demand for passage, scores of vessels, both sail and steamer, either traveled around Cape Horn or operated to and from the Panamanian ports of Colón and Panama City. Soon the Nicaragua Route passage via the San Juan River and Lake Nicaragua became a feasible option, being about 750 miles shorter than the Panamanian route. Initially connections on the Pacific coast were unpredictable, often forcing long delays. Most passengers eventually arrived at their destination of San Francisco, yet few had a pleasant journey. In 1851 one who had booked the *Pacific*, which connected Nicaragua with San Francisco, wrote: "The accommodations, or in fact the want of them on the steamer, beggars all description. The potatoes gave out in three days; no fresh bread; the ship's biscuit was old, rotten and wormy, and was put in the oven every day to drive out and kill the insects; the fish stunk; the oranges instead of coming to the table, were sold at the bar for 12 ½ cents per piece; soda water at fifty cents a glass." But over time ocean service became better organized and more stable, and equipment and accommodations improved. What became the popular route for argonauts and others—Panama and the forty-seven-mile trans-isthmus Panama Railroad—made sea travel more enjoyable than during the trying days at mid-century.[67]

Toward the latter part of the nineteenth century, wholly coastal operations also became significant. Improved steamship technology, harbor improvements, and strong public patronage led to the possibility of dependable and comfortable travel. In 1883 Sir Charles Russell, a British traveler, took the *Queen of the Pacific* from Seattle to San Francisco, and this vessel of the Pacific Coast Steamship Company delighted him. "The Queen [underlining in original] is a very fine and a very fast ship; and it is no exaggeration to say that expense and ingenuity have not been spared in making her the most luxurious boat I ever saw." Yet other contemporary ships were described as proverbial "old tubs." Since for decades rail service between California and the Pacific Northwest was slower than water options, the coastal passenger business remained brisk well into the twentieth century. For years the Southern Pacific Railroad—the transportation "octopus" of Frank Norris's popular novel of that name—largely monopolized service between San Diego, Los Angeles, San Francisco, and Seattle with its Pacific Coast Steamship Company and its San Francisco and Portland Steamship Company. Early in the twentieth century, the latter firm crowed that it provided "elegantly equipped steamships with the latest appliances for comfort and safety" between San Francisco and Portland and between San Francisco and San Pedro (Los Angeles). For years the company's San Francisco to San Pedro route had the fast *Harvard* and *Yale* steamships, offering an overnight schedule that made the nineteen-hour voyage attractive. This Southern Pacific affiliate also offered additional service between San Francisco and Coos Bay, Oregon, and later between Portland and Coos Bay. Still, additional companies challenged the Pacific Coast Steamship Company; for example, in 1914 eleven steamship firms competed for this coastal passenger trade.[68]

The Southern Pacific was not the sole railroad that entered the Pacific coastal passenger trade. In June 1915 the Great Northern and Northern Pacific Railroads, the Hill Lines, began operations with two magnificent and appropriately named vessels, *Great Northern* and *Northern Pacific*. Under the control of the railroads' subsidiary Great Northern Pacific Steamship Company, these boats provided a luxuriousness that appealed to those who wished to travel between San Francisco and Portland. At Astoria (Flavel), Oregon, passengers boarded an awaiting train on another Hill property, the Spokane, Portland & Seattle Railway, which took them directly to downtown Portland. These two ships, the company believed, could compete effectively with the Southern Pacific for the coastal trade. "The journey from San Francisco to Portland, via this new route, consumes approximately thirty hours, equaling the time of the trains between these two points and the expense of the trip is less, as all meals and stateroom accommodations are included in your fare, except in the case of special accommodations, such as parlor rooms, rooms with private bath, etc.," proclaimed the inaugural brochure/timetable. "Fast steamer trains between Portland and Astoria, at the mouth of the Columbia River, run directly to the side of waiting steamers, and passengers may step from the train directly to the largest and most magnificent ships in the Pacific waters." Alas, the Great Northern Pacific Steamship Company found that quality did not guarantee profitability, and it sold the vessels to the US government during World War I for use as trans-Atlantic troop transports.[69]

Much less impressive in overall quality but always in demand by travelers were the ships that connected Seattle, Tacoma, and other coastal ports with the District of Alaska (after 1912 the Territory of Alaska). Although vessels, including those of the Pacific Steamship Company, had operated over this route before the gold rush to the Klondike region from 1897 to 1899, business burgeoned when a "footloose fraternity of adventurers" clamored to reach diggings in the Yukon of Canada and along the Yukon River in Alaska. A popular way to travel to these coveted destinations was to patronize the Alaska Steamship Company, operating since 1895 between Seattle and Skagway, located in the panhandle of southeastern Alaska. Soon the surge in business promoted the acquisition of additional vessels, and in 1900 the powerful Guggenheim business interests bought both the Alaska Steamship Company and the competing Northwest Steamship Company, and service for both freight and passengers improved.[70]

During those frantic years of the Klondike gold rush, accommodations on the various vessels were hardly luxurious. If a prospector or anyone else on board got a comfortable place to sleep or a decent amount of good food, that person considered himself pampered. Deck space frequently became overcrowded and poorly served. The goal was not to enjoy a pleasant voyage through the inland passage, but rather to find as quickly as possible that pot of gold at the rainbow's end. Nevertheless, "Klondikers" did their best to spend their six or seven days at sea in the most agreeable way possible. "The time passes between boxing-bouts on deck, singing to the accompaniment of the piano, inspecting one another's outfits, and poker, five-cent limit."[71]

As with commercial passenger boat transportation on rivers, lakes, and coastal waterways, the automobile, bus, and airplane had their negative impact. Alaska was unusual in that no direct rail service ever connected the future forty-ninth state with the lower forty-eight, although the Alaska or Alcan Highway, constructed during World War II and opened to the public in 1948, linked the contiguous United States with its remote northern territory. It would be air service, however, that would effectively bind Alaska to the rest of the states.

ENTHUSIASTS

Although fewer in number than those enthusiasts for steam and interurban railroads and perhaps those for aviation, there are individuals who have fallen in love with the history of boats and ships. Over time a number of historical groups have formed, and historical research collections and museums have appeared. Tangentially related are art museums whose holdings depict watercraft and travel, and, more recently, tourist cruise lines that offer trips on inland rivers, namely the Ohio, Mississippi, and Columbia; the Great Lakes; and coastal waters.

One of the largest waterways-enthusiast groups is the Steamship Historical Society of America, headquartered in Warwick, Rhode Island, and devoted to the history of engine-powered vessels. Organized in 1935 by several steamship historians and collectors, the society has developed an impressive collection of books, photographs, paintings, brochures, advertisements, and other ephemera. And it publishes *PowerShips*, a quarterly magazine for its hundreds of member-subscribers.

For individuals interested in river transportation, there exists a variety of research opportunities and museums. Arguably the foremost one for historical materials is the Herman T. Pott National Inland Waterways Library, a unit of the Saint Louis Mercantile Library at the University of Missouri–Saint Louis. But there are numerous river-related museums. Two that focus on the Mississippi River are the Cape River Heritage Museum in Cape Girardeau, Missouri, and the National Mississippi River Museum and Aquarium in Dubuque, Iowa.

Even greater opportunities abound for conducting research and enjoying artifacts associated with the American Great Lakes. These include such facilities as the Historical Collections of the Great Lakes located on the campus of Bowling Green State University in Bowling Green, Ohio, and the Dossin Great Lakes Museum in Detroit, Michigan, an arm of the Detroit Historical Society.

Not to be overlooked are coastal maritime research facilities and museums. One that focuses on Pacific coastal travel and shipping is found in San Francisco, the San Francisco National Historical Park. In 1978 this facility, then the San Francisco Maritime Museum, joined the National Park Service. One notable part of its holdings is an extensive number of oral histories with employees, passengers, and others.

Non-enthusiasts have long been exposed to the heritage of America's waterways through literature and other media. Likely the best-known literary works are those by Mark Twain. In several of his popular and perpetually in-print books, he celebrated steamboats and rivermen. The prime example is his *Life on the Mississippi*, first published in 1883.

A variety of art museums, including some of the nation's finest—Metropolitan Museum of Art, National Gallery of Art, and the Fine Arts Museum of San Francisco—own paintings, prints, and photographs of watercraft and the people who used and were employed on them. The works of the regional painter George Caleb Bingham (1811–1879) are representative. This Missouri native, who superbly exemplifies the luminist style of Joshua Shaw and certain other important nineteenth-century painters, produced several masterpieces that depict boats and boatmen on the Missouri River. Bingham had a real feel for the steamboat era and the ongoing presence of flatboats and keelboats. Interestingly, the early Bingham paintings of scenes of river craft represented confidence, optimism, and enterprise, but his pro-Whig political sentiments caused him to alter the spirit of his river art. The vetoes of river and harbor improvement bills by President James K. Polk, a limited-government Democrat, infuriated Bingham, a strong proponent of federally financed waterway betterments. In 1847 this led him to paint *Lighter Relieving a Steamboat Aground*, which graphically suggests that the riverboat being stranded on a sandbar and also being threatened by a snag was a needless occurrence. That former conveyance of happiness and self-confidence had evaporated. Contemporaries likely recognized why Bingham's artwork changed. But today that recognition has largely been lost, just like nearly all commercial passenger travel on the nation's waterways.[72]

Slow and Steady

Canals and the American People

3

Canals have long been part of the human transportation experience, dating back to ancient Egypt and the Grand Canal in premodern China. But it would be in the late seventeenth and eighteenth centuries that continental European countries, especially France and the Netherlands, together with Great Britain, embarked on extensive "ditch digging," thus ushering in the modern canal era and fostering the industrial revolution. Agricultural America took note of this time-tested transportation. It was widely understood that canals, with their low-level technology, would be a good fit for a nonindustrialized nation. Toward the close of the eighteenth century and the first decades of the nineteenth century, much "canal talk" took place. Benjamin Franklin, for one, sensed canals' value. "Rivers are ungovernable Things, especially in Hilly Countries: Canals are quiet and very manageable." Yet only modest construction occurred. In 1793 the first major canal project, the Middlesex Canal, designed to link Boston with Lowell, Massachusetts, and specifically Boston Harbor with the Merrimack River, saw the start of survey work. A decade later this 28-mile waterway opened up the lower Merrimack River valley to freight and passenger service and in the process began to inspire canal advocates. But when the 363-mile Erie Canal burst on the scene, being completed in autumn 1825, it sparked a domestic canal-building craze. Even before this trans–New York State waterway united the Hudson River near Albany with Lake Erie at Buffalo, this state-owned public work had already become an impressive revenue maker. Critics had initially blasted the undertaking as "Clinton's Folly," a reference to the pivotal role played by its foremost champion, Governor DeWitt Clinton. Former president Thomas Jefferson went so far as to say that the building of the Erie Canal was a century too early. Once this engineering marvel was in operation, however, no knowledgeable observer challenged the conclusion that it diffused "wealth, activity and vigor throughout vast parts of the Empire State." All recognized that this "Grand Canal" or "Grand Western Canal" had become the glue that bound New York City and its deep-water harbor with large sections of the interior, being the path of thousands of settlers and traders to the frontier. It did not take long for this ditch to become the "canal that made America." The overwhelming commercial success convinced canal advocates elsewhere that they must have their own artificial waterways, whether they lived in Ohio or Virginia. Few seemed concerned about slow speeds, high construction and maintenance costs, or water and weather disruptions.[1]

A construction blitz followed. About 1830 this mania reached its peak, with nearly forty canals either under construction or in operation. Prior to the Panic of 1837 and the ensuing depression, state governments willingly backed a variety of projects. This was, in fact, the era of state power. Fortunately these public bodies were well positioned to turn plans into realities. Most enjoyed high credit ratings and low levels of debt. Lawmakers realized that investments of taxpayer funds in canals were politically smart and potentially well spent. Popular thinking held that the monetary gains from the canals themselves coupled with economic development and land appreciation were blueprints for prosperity; ditches would be prudent paths to riches. There also existed a widespread feeling among policymakers that artificial waterways would increase the bonds of healthy social intercourse by allowing common citizens ready access to this superior alternative to road usage.[2]

Reasons for canal fever were readily apparent. Americans sought mobility; spatial barriers needed to be shattered. An early student of canals offered this explanation: "[Canal enthusiasm] was brought about by the lack of proper means of transportation. The roads were primitive. The wagons that traversed them were inadequate to transport products and needed goods, and a universal sentiment was aroused for building [canals]." When the Indiana House of Representatives in 1834–1835 debated the $13 million Mammoth Internal Improvements Bill, these advantages of canals were listed: "First—Cheapness of construction, when compared with their utility and durability. Second—The cheapness, safety, and indeed facility, with which the heavy productions of the soil, as well as all other bulky articles, may be conveyed upon them, and the advantages they afford to farmers to use their own means of conveyance. Third—Their permanency. There are canals now in use, that have been channels of extensive commerce for centuries, and which, with trifling repairs, will remain as useful for centuries to come. Fourth—The money that is expended in their construction, is circulated among us." This yearning for improved transportation frequently sparked "canal conventions," where projects were planned and backers energized, not unlike the somewhat later and more numerous railroad conventions. Public or private funding ideally followed.[3]

During the golden age of canals, much was accomplished. By 1840 the total reached 3,326 miles, and two decades later 4,254 miles were in operation in twenty states. But by that time about 350 miles had been abandoned, including a section, between Terre Haute, Indiana, and the Ohio River at Evansville, of the nation's longest "artificial river," the 458-mile Wabash & Erie Canal. These arteries created a revolution in internal commerce, allowing goods to flow between the eastern seaboard and interior points. Residents of the Old Northwest (west of Appalachia and north of the Ohio River) heartily agreed, seeing "a viable transportation system as the *sine qua non* for the perfecting of a market for commodities between the West and other regions." Heretofore, the principal way to move goods and people had been by the Ohio and Mississippi River systems to and from the distant port of New Orleans. With the opening of the Erie Canal and also the Pennsylvania State Works and major canals in Ohio, Indiana, and Illinois, the directional flow of freight and passenger traffic became more east-west rather than north-south. This explains the developing economic, political, and social bonds between the states of New England and the Middle Atlantic and those of the Old Northwest. Subsequent (and faster, more reliable) railroads followed most canal corridors, further strengthening these ties. Collectively canals and railroads helped to ensure the preservation of the Union after the Civil War erupted in 1861.[4]

CANAL BUILDERS AND OPERATORS

Although state governments spearheaded canal building, the federal government also became involved, albeit somewhat modestly. Even though Jeffersonian Republicans, led by the "Virginia Dynasty" of presidents— Thomas Jefferson, James Monroe, and James Madison—worried about the central government gaining too much power, politicians expressed interest and support for the gestating canal era. In 1807 Congress directed Albert Gallatin, Jefferson's secretary of treasury, to prepare a national plan for internal improvements. In 1808 he did just that, presenting his much-discussed *Report of the Secretary of the Treasury on the Subject of Roads and Canals,* "one of the great planning documents in American history." Gallatin called for a federally aided transportation system to cover the nation, including canals that linked the "four great Atlantic rivers" with the Mississippi River basin. He also proposed another four major canals that would offer uninterrupted navigation along the Atlantic seaboard. The secretary optimistically believed that it would take about a decade to complete his plan and cost about $20 million ($331 million in current dollars). Not only did the states'-rights mentality of Jeffersonians delay

Gallatin's multiple projects, but tensions with Great Britain, which led to the War of 1812, further postponed action. Then in 1817 the cause of canal building received another setback when President Madison vetoed a bill that would have funded internal improvements from revenues generated by the Second Bank of the United States. In time, however, Washington came to support canal building; the Monroe administration agreed to make land grants to several states and to subscribe to stock subscriptions in scattered companies. It would be James Monroe's secretary of war, John C. Calhoun, who would help convince the president of the strategic importance of improved transportation for national defense.[5]

A federal statute that involved locating and constructing canals came in 1824. This was the General Survey Act, a measure suggested by Gallatin and endorsed by Calhoun. It permitted US Army personnel, namely graduates from the United States Military Academy at West Point, to survey and prepare cost estimates for canal routes. It did not take long for these trained civil engineers to help make possible a variety of projects, including the Chesapeake & Ohio and James River & Kanawha waterways.

Not only did the General Survey Act aid canal construction, but the establishment of several engineering-oriented schools, most importantly Rensselaer Polytechnic Institute in Troy, New York, also increased the body of experts. Yet there was an initial shortage of civil engineers. Fortunately this void was filled largely by self-trained individuals. Americans embraced pragmatism, believing that an idea means what an idea does. Even before educators came to the rescue, a number of men took advantage of these employment opportunities. Several individuals who conducted the engineering work on the Erie Canal, including James Geddes, John Jervis, and Benjamin Wright, lacked formal training. Soon, though, they learned how to locate a canal, prepare the corridor, and construct locks, aqueducts, and other components, functioning as surveyors, designers, and contractors. This harbinger of the canal era became a training ground for engineers who were involved in more canal building, later railroads, and other construction projects. Simply put, the Erie Canal trained a generation of engineers. In the early 1820s Geddes, for one, left New York to assume the position of chief engineer for the Ohio & Erie Canal, and he also worked on the Pennsylvania Main Line, Chesapeake & Ohio Canal, and additional waterways. From all accounts the peripatetic Geddes did excellent work.[6]

It would be construction workers who as a group became much more remembered than canal engineers, even though these common laborers lacked individual distinction and left few written accounts. Canal building relied heavily on the unskilled, requiring these men to use axes, mattocks, picks, shovels, wheelbarrows, and other simple tools to remove trees, rock, and dirt. At times they were aided by workers who used black blasting powder to penetrate dense rock formations, a skilled but danger-ous job. The result was that it took an army of diggers toiling hour after hour, month after month, and year after year to create the waterways. How many men were involved? A precise number cannot be determined, in part because subcontractors who worked for a general contractor com-monly kept incomplete records. On the Erie Canal perhaps as many as nine thousand men were employed, and between 1825 and 1832 a similar number labored on the Ohio & Erie Canal. By 1826 two thousand men toiled on the Delaware & Hudson Canal. This frequently was a "floating" workforce; thousands migrated from project to project, and many joined future railroad construction gangs.[7]

Who were these laborers? In the South slaves were used extensively and at times almost exclusively, but nationally the workers were pre-dominantly Euro-Americans. During the 1790s, female slaves played a role in the construction of the Santee Canal in South Carolina, the only American waterway in which women participated in a substantial way. Elsewhere during the formative construction period, a large number of the white male workers, who were native born, came from nearby farms. They learned about these jobs by word of mouth or through newspaper advertisements and posted broadsides. In particular, farm lads willingly accepted employment on canal excavations. After all, they were accus-tomed to strenuous outdoor work, whether plowing, planting, or harvest-ing, and they had blocks of time away from the fields. The great attraction was the chance to earn cash money; families needed specie and currency to pay taxes and for other expenses. For many diggers, especially the young, this would be their first wage-earning experience.[8]

By the 1830s the composition of the canal workforce had changed dramatically. Thousands of men from the Old World, who encountered limited employment opportunities at home, faced the possibilities of lingering hunger and disease, or felt the sting of political and religious oppression, learned of these distant jobs. Not surprisingly, they decided to seek the promise of American life by immigrating to New York and other canal-building states. Some came from Great Britain and the Germanys, but more hailed from an impoverished Ireland, where famines in 1817 and 1822 drove away thousands. Some of these Irishmen, however, arrived in the United States from British North America (Canada). In the mid-1820s a Cleveland newspaper reported that every lake vessel from Buf-falo "brings more hardy sons of Erin seeking employment on the canal," and by 1826 hundreds of Irishmen, coming either directly or indirectly from their homeland, had made this northern terminus of the emerging Ohio & Erie Canal their temporary residence. These men often had been common laborers in their native Ireland and likely had been involved with the Erie Canal or other construction projects, being accustomed to hard, tedious work. Observed Catherine Tobin, who studied Irish workers on the Illinois & Michigan Canal: "Although not all the Irish on canals were unskilled, the overwhelming majority did engage in unskilled work." She added, "On the I and M, the surnames listed in the 'Statistics of laborers' indicate that the vast majority of diggers were Irish. Scarcely any who had recognizable Irish surnames were carpenters, blacksmiths and masons."[9]

Not to be overlooked were those skilled workers. These included the native born and those from continental Europe and the British Isles who knew how to cut and set stone. Some had gained their construction experience on the expansive and magnificently built canal networks in Britain. This talent pool was invaluable for lock, aqueduct, culvert, sluice, waste weir, and related undertakings. Experienced carpenters and blacksmiths likewise contributed mightily to the building process.

Others participated. There were instances of convict labor being used. In 1817 New York passed a measure that permitted employment of prisoners on the Erie Canal. The contractor for the Rochester aqueduct, for one, took advantage of this labor pool, placing 150 convicts to work on that massive project. Inmates from the Ohio State Penitentiary in Columbus (guarded by deputies) dug part of the Columbus Lateral (or feeder) Canal, which connected the capital city with the Ohio & Erie Canal. Also in the Buckeye State, members of the Separatist Society of Zoar in Tuscarawas County, a struggling religious utopia of approximately 350 members who lived along the recently surveyed Ohio & Erie Canal, gained state approval to build a portion of that waterway. These communitarians earned more than $20,000 for their efforts. This dollar infusion allowed them to pay off a pressing $16,000 real estate mortgage, saving the colony from financial ruin. Since Zoarites at the time practiced celibacy, women lacked young children to tend, and so they could participate in the building. These hardworking women did just that, "carrying the dirt from the excavation in baskets on their heads and in their aprons."[10]

Terms of employment for construction workers typically lacked complexities. Contractors and subcontractors expected their men to work from sunup to sundown. For that commitment they commonly offered single males room and board, providing space for sleeping and eating in a temporary dormitory or shelter along the canal route. When the Chesapeake & Delaware Canal was being dug in the mid-1820s, the *American Watchman* commented, "The workmen live in companies of fifteen to twenty in *Shanties* [italics in original]—frame buildings along the canal, provided with a cook, or board in more private houses erected for the purpose." A Chicago newspaper offered this description of dwelling places along the developing Illinois & Michigan Canal: "[Consisting of] all sizes, shapes and materials, sod and straw; shingled or boarded sheds being in great demand. Some of these habitations, if they can be dignified with the title, are wretched looking tenements." As a canal progressed, these structures might be moved from camp to camp. Overcrowding became common. In the late 1830s, during construction of the Walhonding Canal, a feeder to the Ohio & Erie Canal, nine people lived together in a one-room log cabin provided by the contractor. Employers usually provided cooks, laundresses, and clothing menders. Married men and their families lived in simple wooden housing without amenities; they did their own cooking and other household chores. On occasions these residencies became permanent. Even though canal builders were people on the move, some elected to remain in their new abodes after having completed their immediate work assignments. They might take jobs in canal maintenance or find other employment, creating lasting shanty towns in these new or developing canal communities, including such places as Akron, Ohio; Fort Wayne, Indiana; and Joliet, Illinois.[11]

Then there was the matter of wages. Money was the attraction; construction workers frequently liked little about their jobs except for their compensation. Pay varied. Skilled workers—for example, masons and carpenters—always received more than unskilled laborers. Yet diggers' pay was comparable to that earned in agriculture and textiles. If a contractor encountered a labor shortage, wages rose. In 1837, for example, canal work on the Miami Canal in Ohio suffered from a lack of laborers because the Indiana public works offered better pay. If there was a glut of available labor, wages dropped. When hard times struck, wages were slashed. And if the employer provided food and lodging, downward adjustments were made. "I am working on the canal with Englishmen but with no Welsh for thirteen dollars a month. Many of the Welsh are doing the same for twenty-two dollars a month and their own food, but I get my food, drink, and washing as well," reported an Erie Canal laborer in an 1818 letter to his family in Wales. This advertisement appeared in a Chicago newspaper in 1840: "WANTED—Fifty Laborers on sections 54 and 55 of the summit division of the Illinois and Michigan [Canal]. Seventeen Dollars per month and good board will be given for industrious and sober men."[12]

But "sober men" might be in short supply. A majority of these laborers spurned the "cold water brigade." Whiskey was demanded, especially by the Irish, and nearly always provided. The amount, though, was not uniform. One digger indicated that he received a daily ration of a half pint, likely average for the time. Some states prohibited these men from using "ardent spirits" while on the job, but enforcement was lax, if present at all. The American culture was alcoholic. Farmers, townspeople, and others typically consumed drink, at times in excessive quantities; America was that alcoholic republic. Whiskey was inexpensive, readily available, and used as a medium of exchange. Not until the growth of the industrial sector and the rise of temperance organizations did drinking become less ensconced in the workplace.[13]

Workers and their bosses had disagreements, and occasionally they turned nasty. Money was usually the bone of contention, more so than the quality of food and lodging or the quantity of drink. There were contractors who absconded, leaving employees unpaid, or they were slow to provide the agreed-upon wages. If paid on time and for the correct amount, workers who did not get specie might not receive the face value of the paper currency. Notes, most of all from wildcat banks, were commonly discounted by merchants and others. Furthermore, IOUs given by employers might not be readily accepted. Diggers toiled for only part of the year, and even during the construction season, their work might be interrupted by material shortages, weather, or something else, reducing their income and making financial survival an ongoing struggle.[14]

Just as with toll-road, railroad, and electric interurban construction, there were schemers who exploited men who wished to better themselves through canal building. In 1842 the *Fort Wayne Sentinel* related this story of hoodwinked laborers:

> A number of stone-cutters and many with their families have arrived here the past week, from New York on their way to Lafayette to work on the [Wabash & Erie] canal. They were engaged by G. M. Nash who advertised in the New York papers and by bills posted that he was authorized by Messrs. Moorehead & Co. of Lafayette to engage them to work on the canal. Nash got $6.50 from each and gave them passage to Toledo. From Toledo, their fare would be returned. The Company denies all knowledge of Nash and needs no stone-cutters since the locks are made of wood. These families are to be pitied. Induced by high wages, now no money and no jobs.[15]

Irrespective of wages, food, and accommodations, laboring on canal projects—whether clearing the corridor of trees, brush, and rocks; blasting; plowing and digging the bed; shaping the towpath; or constructing locks and aqueducts—was never easy and in some localities was extremely demanding. Take the case of workers who built the "Great Cut" on the Ohio & Erie Canal in Licking County. Hundreds of these men encountered a dense clay that was difficult to handle. Yet they did. "It was a sight to see fifty of these barrow-men in line, wheeling out their heavy loads, following a leader who always kept them on a run." There also were those life-threatening or fatal dangers: using black powder, transporting borrow and fill with primitive equipment, and penetrating swampy areas. A digger might feel the kick of an angry mule that pulled the iron plows, scoops, and dredges. Then throughout parts of the construction season, there were pesky mosquitoes, occasionally an abundance of rattlesnakes, and always unpredictable weather. There might be infectious diseases. Cases of dysentery were common, as were outbreaks of malaria, commonly referred to as the "ague" or "autumnal fever." In 1825 typhoid fever swept through Cleveland, causing nearly a score of deaths among workers building that city's canal basin and extending the waterway southward into the Cuyahoga River valley. Somewhat later a cholera epidemic swept several major projects, including the Chesapeake & Ohio Canal, and hundreds died. Sometimes religious folks saw these outbreaks as God's punishment of canallers for "getting drunk all the time, their riots, their fights and homicides." Instances existed where medical doctors refused to treat sick and dying diggers and their family members. In 1838 as work progressed on the Walhonding Canal, the daughter of a construction worker fell ill with the flux. A physician was summoned but "refused to treat 'those canawlers' and the young girl grew worse, died, and was buried by her infant sister's side."[16]

If working conditions were not difficult and dangerous enough, troubles, which sometimes became deadly, erupted among the builders themselves. The Irish gained a reputation for fighting and drunkenness. "Canal laborers were notorious combatants," explained historian William Rorabaugh. "Deadly fights and brawls usually originated in petty disputes that escalated when laborers unleashed against each other rage engendered by this situation. More frequently, they reduced their tensions with strong drink, which they consumed exuberantly and in large quantity." Conflicts might erupt between Protestants and Roman Catholics or between rival regional groups. In 1838 a pitched battle broke out between Fardowners (or "Leinster men") and Corkonians—namely those from the North and South of Ireland—near Ottawa, Illinois, on the Illinois & Michigan Canal, and it led to the death of between ten and fifteen Corkonians. These religious and ethnic tensions would later spill over to other construction projects, most famously on antebellum railroads.[17]

Paralleling later transportation forms, most often railroads, a canal project frequently began, and ended, with a celebration. Examples abound. On July 4, 1825, the most patriotic day on the calendar, Ohio officially launched the Ohio & Erie Canal, part of an aggressive state-funded canal-building program. An enthusiastic and well-attended ground breaking took place south of Newark at Licking Summit, situated near the center of the state. The dignitaries included the father of the Erie Canal, New York governor DeWitt Clinton; Ohio governor Jeremiah Morrow; former Ohio governor and canal promoter Ethan Allen Brown; and New Yorkers Eleazar Lord and John Rathbone, who helped with financing. There were also the expected events: a military procession, a discharge of artillery pieces, prayers, and speeches. Lancaster lawyer Thomas Ewing, a future US secretary of the treasury and the first secretary of the interior, received the honor of presenting the keynote address. His themes were direct: prosperity and national unity. "As a channel of commerce—as a stimulus to manufactures—as a source of revenue—as an encouragement to agriculture—[the canal] will excite into activity all kinds of productive activity. It will also consummate the prosperity of the American people, and further exalt our national character in the estimation of the civilized world. The union of states will be as firm as the everlasting hills; and from this great epoch in our history, we may dismiss all fears of dismemberment of the American republic." His remarks were well received by the estimated ten thousand spectators and by those who read his reprinted speech. Governor Clinton claimed the other coveted role: he turned the first spadeful of earth. If there was a climactic event, it was the food and drink enjoyed by a thousand or so invited guests at a nearby grove.[18]

Just as DeWitt Clinton took the limelight at Licking Summit, he would shortly do so again in his home state. On November 4, 1825, a grand celebration, which had been ongoing since it began in Buffalo on the evening of October 25, concluded in New York harbor. This event completed the official opening of "Clinton's Ditch," or what by that time was frequently called the "Big Ditch," a term more of awe than contempt. The format of individual events that had taken place in Ohio was largely repeated. But in this case a functioning canal allowed water from Lake Erie, which celebrants placed in "two elegant kegs" painted with patriot designs, to be dumped into the Atlantic Ocean off the southern entrance of Lower New York Bay near Sandy Hook. (Later a keg of Atlantic seawater would be poured into Lake Erie, discharging "brackish Atlantic water into the fine indigo blue of Lake Erie.") This dramatic harbor happening was a symbolic act that Clinton and canal supporters savored and "one of the most spectacular events of the early national period."[19]

In an account commissioned by the Common Council of New York City, Cadwallader Colden provided this firsthand description of the "Wedding of the Waters":

> The Aquatic display transcended all anticipations, twenty-nine steam-boats, gorgeously dressed, with barges, ships, pilot-boats, canal-boats, and the boats of the Whitehall firemen, conveying thousands of ladies and gentlemen, presented a scene which cannot be described. Add to this, the reflections which arise from the extent and beauty of our Bay—the unusual calmness and mildness of the day—the splendid manner in which all the shipping in the harbour were dressed, and the movement of the whole flotilla. Regulated by previously arranged signals, the fleet were thrown at pleasure, into squadron or line, into curves or circles. The whole appeared to move as by magic.[20]

CANAL TRAVEL

Just as an army of men and boys physically created the American canal network, a comparable labor force made possible freight and passenger operations. Most positions that facilitated day-to-day commercial service involved individuals who needed only limited training. What skills were demanded usually could be learned on the job, being classified mostly as unskilled or semiskilled. The exception might be the helmsman (sometimes called a steersman), who required good judgment and considerable experience.

Resembling the steamboats, canal boats had their own captains. These men in command often owned their own craft, whether a packet (passenger), line boat (hauler of both freight and passengers), or freighter. Although their job was far less complicated than that of a maritime captain, some thought of themselves as such and dressed in full seaman's regalia. "If he were especially sporting in his attire," noted a student of the canal era, "the Erie [Canal] captain might be called a *ship-shape macaroni* [italics in original], a nautical dandy in the most romantic tradition." In 1839 a British Navy officer made these related comments: "An American packet captain is in his own opinion no small affair, he puffs and swells until he looks larger than his boat." No wonder youngsters who lived along a canal or had traveled on one might dream of becoming such a distinguished person.[21]

It would be the independent owner-operator who hired his crew. On a fully staffed packet boat, a complement of six to ten workers would be aboard. In addition to the captain, the cabin crew included a steward, cook, and cabin boy or girl, and each worked a twelve-hour shift. They would be joined by two helmsmen, bowmen, and drivers, and their work also involved two twelve-hour stints. It would be the helmsman who controlled the tiller bar to steer the craft. He also called out approaching bridges, signaled lock tenders with his brass horn or bugle, and navigated in and out of locks and around approaching boats. The bowman took charge of the ropes, making certain that the critical tow rope did not get tangled up with passing boats or in lock gates. In reality he was a general deckhand. In what might be considered a typical complement of onboard personnel, the Reed Line, which operated on the Beaver & Lake Erie Canal in northwestern Pennsylvania, provided a captain, two helmsmen, two bowmen, a chambermaid, a cook, a steward, and a helper. Some packet captains, perhaps for economy, did not employ a steward or cabin attendant, instead making one person, who also likely cooked, do the work of these crew members. The wife of the captain might be so assigned. It has been suggested that captains often hired their hands more for their fighting prowess than for other skills they might possess or learn. After all, boat crews regularly battled for the right to pass first through locks and other traffic choke points.[22]

Although the boat captain had authority and might be widely known and respected along the canal corridor, it would be the drivers, or hoggees or towboys—almost always teenage males (occasionally a few girls disguised as boys)—who became the most talked about crew members. These youngsters rode or walked beside the horses or mules (rarely oxen) that pulled boats along the level and at times winding towpath. Frequently poorly paid, overworked, shabbily clothed, and occasionally abused by boat captains and other canallers, these lads gained a reputation for drinking, fighting, and swearing. "The 'drive,' who looked like a bundle of old clothes, was as smart as a whip, and profane as 'our army in Flanders,'" observed one traveler. But they adapted to conditions and generally provided good service. These towboys, when they could, commonly left for better jobs. "Soon I came to realize that canal driving can be wearisome and footsore work," recalled a former driver, "and I was glad when I could hand over the reins to another." He further reflected: "Oh, yes; a steersman can git about $40 a month. That's the place the driver is allus fishin' for. It takes about four or five years drivin' to git there, though."[23]

Here's an illustration of the wants and actions of these drivers, who numbered in the thousands, from the comments about one who worked on the west end of the Erie Canal: "When the saloon fronted proudly on the tow path and a few feet from the canal, many a thirsty driver, as he neared the swinging doors, dropped the reins of his mule team, ran into the tavern, grabbed his schoopper of beer, gulped it down, slapped his money on the bar, dashed out and caught up with his well-trained mules as they continued to walk driverless toward Canal Street and the Buffalo harbor."[24]

It would be Horatio Alger Jr., the popular Gilded Age author of juvenile books, who helped immortalize the nameless driver. Shortly after the death of the assassinated James A. Garfield in 1881, he quickly produced a breezy account of the late president's life, naming it with his trademark rags-to-riches theme, *From Canal Boy to President*. While technically correct, the title is misleading. In 1848 Garfield did take a job as the driver on the *Eastern Star*, a boat captained by his cousin, and he traveled between Cleveland and Pittsburgh on the Ohio & Erie and Pennsylvania & Ohio canals. But he did so for only *one* trip; he then assumed the duties of a bowman. Yet his canal days were limited. After six weeks Garfield fell sick with the ague and quit.[25]

Who were these canallers (sometimes spelled with one *l*) or "canawlers"? Generally, captains came from the ranks of merchants, farmers, and ambitious boatmen. It was common for the captain of a packet boat to be native born, but over time an immigrant, perhaps an Irishman, might take command, usually on a line or freight vessel, suggesting upward mobility along the canal corridor. Others on boats might be men who had previously worked on canal construction or maintenance. They could have rural or urban backgrounds and be black or white. Newly arrived immigrants, including teenagers, might take a position, expecting to rise in the ranks of the employed or move on to non-canal jobs. A high percentage of drivers consisted of the disadvantaged and homeless. "These boys usually had few occupational skills and came from poor families," observed Erie Canal scholar Carol Sheriff. "Reformers estimated, moreover, that half the drivers were orphans." Some of them might earlier have found employment during the construction period as water boys and wished to remain part of canal life. Travelers who recorded or wrote about their canal trips inevitably commented on these lads. "A single horse pulls our vessel, and the loutish boy who manages him has hair that is as white as tow," remarked a woman who crossed Indiana and Ohio in the early 1850s. "It looks as though he had never combed it. He chews tobacco and swears at his horse; but yet he seems good-natured, and he sings between oaths some very doleful hymns, alternating with love songs of a lively cast." These youngsters might take up driving to earn wages, to free themselves from family supervision and restraints, or to enjoy the sheer adventure of being independent. Possibly they hired out for all these reasons. Some canallers—drivers, helmsmen, and the like— also moved to other canals, perhaps leaving the Erie and Pennsylvania Main Line networks for comparable or better jobs in Ohio, Indiana, or Illinois. As with steam and electric railroads, "boomers" were hardly a rare breed.[26]

Although it is risky to categorize individuals who worked the boats, it is probably not too far off the mark to say that they were a lively bunch. Some were true Christians—honest, hardworking, and God fearing; others not so much. In the late 1840s a representative of the Western Seaman's Friend Society, an Ohio-chartered organization designed "to promote the Intellectual, Social, Moral, and Spiritual condition of Sailors and Boatmen employed on the Western Waters," spent four months among canallers on the Wabash & Erie waterway. His report indicated that "profane swearing, drinking, and card playing are allowed and indulged in to any extent on board. And we here heard what reminded us of the Old Erie ten years ago men swearing just to hear themselves swear." He added, "There is more out-breaking wickedness here than on any other thoroughfare of equal magnitude in the Union [and] not one boat in ten had either a Bible or testament on board." A Protestant missionary believed that he knew why a boatman "cannot be a consistent Christian." His explanation: "Their occupation withdraws them from the salutary influences of the sanctuary and the restrains of female society, and brings them in daily contact with men who are perhaps more careless and wicked than themselves."[27]

Others, God fearing or not, made canal travel possible. There were lock tenders, toll collectors, general repairmen, canal walkers who trudged along the towpath to check for leaks and other problems, and the

"Fog-gang" who cleaned out the canal. State authorities hired the majority, while others owed their jobs to private operators. As for public employees, it was said that "lock tenders needed no special qualifications beyond a strong back and the ability to guess right on Election Day." Then there were those individuals who built and repaired boats, usually living in the larger canal towns. By way of example, several boat companies located in Akron, Ohio, the self-proclaimed "Venice of the West," being on both the Ohio & Erie and Pennsylvania & Ohio canals, employed several hundred workers by the 1840s. Also there were animal and equipment suppliers at or near canal side. In Lafayette, Indiana, boat captains who worked the Wabash & Erie Canal had convenient access to Johnson's livery stable for horses. And they could buy from Lauman and Bansemer "1/2, 5/8, 3/4 and 7/8 plain [rope] and hawser laid Tow Lines" along with "Manila cordage suitable for bow and stern lines and cables."[28]

CANAL TRAVEL EXPERIENCES

With the infrastructure and work and support forces in place, travel by canal proceeded. As with other contemporary forms of public transportation—stagecoaches and coastal, lake, and river vessels—travelers had their positive and negative experiences. These involved equipment, service, and fellow passengers.

Take the packet boat, which a contemporary traveler thought "looked like an elongated floating house, the height of which had been decreased by some great pressure." As might be expected, some passenger vessels were attractive and well maintained and others not. Although hardly the works of gifted nautical architects, they could be visually pleasing. Usually these wooden boats were brightly painted and often in white with a band of blue, orange, or red added above the waterline. Their names, frequently in elegant lettering, were displayed prominently on their sterns. But as canal travel faded by mid-century because of railroad competition, boats often took on a shabby appearance.[29]

In the late 1820s a well-regarded travel guide gave this favorable description of the interior of "A Canal Packet Boat":

> The length is 60 to 70 feet, a large part of which is devoted to the dining room, where two rows of tables are set. At night, mattresses are spread on the seat each side, and another row above them on cots suspended from the roof. The ladies are accommodated with births [sic] in the cabin, which is usually carpeted, hung with curtains, and in other respects more handsomely furnished. The kitchen and bar are conveniently situated; and the tables are spread with an abundance, and often a delicacy, which may well surprise those not accustomed to the cheapness of travelling in this part of the country [New York].
>
> A small library, a number of newspapers, &c. will serve to make the time pass agreeable, even if the traveler be a stranger, or the weather not inviting. In many places, the view from the deck is highly interesting. . . .[30]

Packet boats might be grander, but that was exceptional. In order to compete with newly opened nearby railroads, the Red Bird Line, which plied the Erie Canal in the mid-1840s, offered stellar accommodations. The company's *Niagara* exuded luxury. "She had a cedar hull and measured 100 feet long," noted transportation historian John H. White Jr. "There were separate men's and ladies' cabins. Large picture windows, a smoking room, a library and writing desks, and a bar and refreshment counter were provided. Best of all there was a washroom. The cabins were elegantly decorated, and the table was set with fine china and silver-plated eating uten-

THE LOCK.

sils." The early packets on the Middlesex Canal, for one, also had ample room for passengers, who enjoyed such appointments as an airy lounge and comfortable, upholstered seats. Since these twenty-eight-mile trips between Boston and Lowell took place in daylight, there was no need for sleeping accommodations.[31]

Even though packet boats were constructed to simple designs, being inspired by those "long boats" found in Great Britain, interior spaces varied. The not-so-elegant ones offered less privacy and fewer amenities. Yet sexes were segregated just as they would be on many Victorian era passenger trains. Usually quarters for "ladies"—women, girls, and infants—were more attractive and private. An Englishman who in 1851 traveled with his family on the Wabash & Erie Canal from Terre Haute to Toledo observed, "It was a rule in these boats that no gentleman should go into the ladies' saloon without express invitation from the ladies." Their section nearly always occupied a smaller space than that provided their male counterparts. After all, it was most likely that of the twenty-five to fifty or more passengers, the majority would be men and boys, and their numbers required much of the forty to fifty feet of the dormitory area.[32]

Packet crews had their own private section. "In the bow, carefully cut off from the rest of the boat, is a tiny cuddy for the crew," noted one source. This was a sensible allotment of space. Personnel were on and off duty throughout the day and night, and they required suitable sleeping accommodations and a place to store their belongings.[33]

While packet boats operated on most canals before railroads caused their steady demise by the 1870s, another common craft that carried passengers was the line boat (a vessel operated by a transportation company—a "line"—and hence the name). These boats handled freight and passengers, not unlike railroads with their "mixed" trains, hauling

All canals, whether long or short, had multiple locks. These features required good engineering and craftsmanship. A packet boat is being "locked in" on the Erie Canal.

Marco Paul's Voyages & Travels, 1852

THE PACKET BOAT.

This mid-nineteenth-century drawing depicts a common packet boat traveling on that harbinger of the American canal era, the famed Erie Canal.

Marco Paul's Voyages & Travels, 1852

both "hogs and humans." In some ways line boats resembled their sister vessels, but their configurations differed noticeably. Freight was stored in the middle of the boat, and rooms for passengers were placed at the front and those for the crew in the rear. And nearly always they offered less luxury in accommodations. Moreover, line boats were slower. Not only would freight have to be "worked," but these craft usually used only one or two animals for power; packets might utilize two or possibly three horses or mules.[34]

All passenger-carrying boats provided public deck space. There were small open decks at both ends of these usually fourteen-foot-wide packet and line boats. A much larger open upper deck, either flat or turtleback, extended over the cabin (and freight hold of a line boat) and usually was reached by a stairway at the stern. This area ran about three-quarters of the length of the craft.

Passengers usually had their most pleasant canal experiences from the decks. In daylight hours and during good weather, they could view the country, at times taking pleasure in the beauty of woods and fields and the occasional grand views. In June 1827 a British seaman thoroughly enjoyed traveling on the Erie Canal west of Schenectady. "The canal for a distance of 26 miles winds along the base of a low and prettily wooded bank on the south side of the Mohawk river. Our perpendicular height above the stream may have been 30 or 40 feet, by which elevation we commanded a range of prospect, both up and down, of great extent and variety." He continued, "The vigour of the spring tints had not yet yielded to the withering effect of the fierce summer. I cannot conceive a more beautiful combination of verdure; and as the windings of the canal brought us in sight of fresh vistas, new cultivation, new villages, new bridges, new aqueducts, rose at every moment mingled up with scattered dwellings, mills, churches, all span new. The scene looked really one of enchantment."

In the late 1830s a packet passenger on the Pennsylvania Main Line made these observations: "As uncomfortable as travel on a canal boat is, you forget this entirely as a result of the continual change of the most beautiful scenery. They valley of the Kiskiminites [Kiskiminetas River east of Pittsburgh] is like a splendidly blooming park; we see some salt works and coal mines, continually enclosed by a row of hills crowned with trees, and often we traveled for a while through the river." There was more. "We then traveled over a very beautiful aqueduct setting us across the Conemaugh river and then through a tunnel. In the evening,

8968 Along the Ohio Canal,
Bolivar, Ohio

Travelers along the Ohio & Erie Canal near Bolivar, Ohio, likely found the hill and dale scenery to their liking. The slow speeds of canal boats allowed opportunities to savor the countryside; nothing ever flashed by.

Author's Collection

when we had to pass locks, we often stepped ashore and went a bit ahead of the boat, enjoying nature." A few years later a traveler on the James River & Kanawha Canal, the South's premier artificial waterway, reminisced: "With a lively jerk as the horses fell into a trot, away we went, the cut-water throwing up the spray as we rounded the Penitentiary hill, and the passenger lingering on the deck to get a last look at the fair city of Richmond, lighted by the late rays of the setting sun." Meeting passing boats made impressions; those on deck might flutter their handkerchiefs

or hats in salute or extend a wave or hearty shout. Nightfall could be even more memorable. "In the evening there were many lovely scenes with shadows stealing across the placid water rippled by the boat's passage," remembered a canal passenger. Charles Dickens, who used canals extensively during his 1842 American tour, enjoyed the sounds of frogs, "whose noise in these parts is almost incredible as though a million of fairy teams with bells were traveling through the air and keeping pace with us." He experienced additional pleasures. "The gliding on at night so noiselessly, past frowning hills sullen with dark trees and sometimes angry in one red, burning spot high up, where unseen men lay crouching round a fire; the shining out of the bright stars undisturbed by any noise of wheels or stream or any other sound than limpid rippling of the water as the boat went on; all these pure delights."[35]

While the deck was a popular venue for packet passengers, there existed an inherent danger—low bridges. In order to allow regular commerce and farmers to move back and forth on property sliced by a canal, bridges were erected but often not much higher than a moving boat. And they were ubiquitous. On the Erie Canal, for example, between Albany and Utica, a distance of about ninety miles, approximately three hundred bridges crossed the waterway. Charles Dickens thought, "It was somewhat embarrassing at first to duck nimbly every five minutes whenever the man at the helm cried 'Low Bridge,' to lie down nearly flat." He wrote, however, "It took a very short time to get used to this." A passenger on his journey to Mackinac Island, Michigan, who traveled by packet from Rochester to Buffalo, recorded these remarks in his diary for October 14, 1830: "The only apparent danger to be apprehended is when passing the brigges [*sic*] which are numerous and so low that often the boat will but just pass under. As passengers are fond of walking on deck, it is necessary to keep a good look out, for the brigges [*sic*]." He further noted: "The general practice is, of course, to go below on such an occasion, but when the bridge is sufficiently high all that is necessary is to be flat on the deck till the brigge [*sic*] is past." Unfortunately, not everyone heeded the cry of the helmsman or other crew members of "Bridge!" or "Low Bridge!" or kept an eye out for such approaching danger. There were unthinking (or inebriated) souls who were injured or killed by these recurring obstructions. A traveler wrote that an Erie Canal boat captain "informs me that six persons have lost their lives by being crushed under the bridges, which is a greater number than have been killed during the same time by the bursting of steam engines in the [river] waters of the middle or eastern States."[36]

While the passenger on that James River & Kanawha packet suggested speed in his commentary, he could have noted that contemporary stagecoaches and steamboats regularly operated at a much faster clip. A canal boat moved at only a few miles an hour and nearly always less than four miles per hour. "Surely there never was a sleepier mode of travel," remarked a canal patron. James Brownlee, who immigrated to Iowa from Canada in 1838, found that traveling on the Ohio & Erie Canal from Lake Erie to the Ohio River was painfully slow. Reflecting on that trip in 1882, he tersely wrote, "We were nine days on the canal crossing the State of Ohio—rather a slow way of traveling now-a-days." Unlike other forms of public transportation, if passengers missed the boat, they could on occasion run ahead to the next bridge and drop aboard when the vessel passed or briskly walk to an approaching lock. Packets made better time than line and freight boats, in part because they did not make long stops to wait for or to work their cargoes. Faster speeds of five or more miles per hour caused bank erosion, and canal authorities placed speed restrictions on all craft. Furthermore, horses could only maintain a speed of three to four miles per hour for normal travel distances. There were exceptions. A packet boat pulled by a team of three horses might reach a sustained speed of more than four miles per hour—that, for example, being the claim of the Reed Line on the Beaver & Lake Erie Canal. When a boat approached or entered a lock or series of locks, speeds dropped to virtually zero or zero. In 1829 a Pennsylvanian who traveled the Erie Canal made an appropriate response to the well-known delays caused by lockage. "I had contemplated taking my passage at Albany, on board a canal boat; but was disuaded [*sic*] therefrom in consequence of the tediousness of the passage, to *Schenectady* [italics in original], having to surmount an elevation of

GOING TO BED.

A captain makes berth assignments in a good representation of the sleeping experience on a canal packet. In the background is the "Ladies Cabin," which a curtain separates from the men's quarters.

Marco Paul's Voyages & Travels, 1852

forty [italics in original] locks, in a distance of twenty-eight miles, and occupying twenty-four hours. I therefore took my seat [in a stagecoach] for Schenectady, distance fifteen miles by turnpike." Once in Schenectady, riders could enjoy a comfortable overnight stay at Given's Hotel and a leisurely breakfast before their scheduled boats arrived, or they could book passage on packets that awaited them at the Schenectady landing. Others in a hurry might break up their canal trip by opting for stagecoaches so as to avoid stretches of a canal with concentrations of locks. Additional delays, sometimes lengthy, occurred. There could be navigational problems, including disabled boats, breached banks, and low water. An example of the latter came from a Champlain Canal boat captain. His diary entry for May 28, 1861, read: "In the canal and ground near all day—water very low in the canal. Boats got jammed so we could not go by nor they either for a long time—got about 3 miles till near night—got under way again—got along pretty well during the night." And a captain sometimes waited for more passengers or cargo, delaying departure by hours or perhaps days. Nevertheless, canal packets usually operated around the clock, compensating somewhat for their low sustained speeds.[37]

While boat speeds were rather constant and delays expected, passengers expressed mixed verdicts about the quality of onboard food. Surely a majority of canal travelers agreed that food was usually plentiful; few went hungry. In the late 1820s a packet that plied the Erie Canal offered these items for breakfast: "The meal may consist of a pike or bass, fresh caught upon [an] overnight trawl line, a steak, bacon, sausage, and ham; a platter of scrambled eggs, baked pritties, boiled cabbage and squash, bread, both corn and white, pancakes, both wheat and buckwheat, with sorghum, maple or honey to choice; and, to wash all down, coffee, tea, milk, skimmagig, and cider."[38]

When Charles Dickens traveled on the Pennsylvania Main Line, he, too, encountered an assortment of food. His evening meal consisted of ham chops, liver, salmon, sausages, shad, steak, potatoes, pickles, bread and butter, black pudding, coffee, and tea. Notwithstanding this extensive fare, he complained that all meals were the same except for the midday "feed." It lacked coffee and tea.[39]

As for other meals, including dinner (or supper), the menu might be largely one and the same, and this became monotonous after a multiday journey. Still travelers often expressed pleasure with the food offerings.

"I brought to the table—an excellent one it was—a school boy's appetite, sharpened by travel, and thought it was 'just splendid,'" commented a James River & Kanawha Canal packet passenger. In a similar vein, well-managed packets on the Wabash & Erie Canal offered good, ample fare that might be varied with seasonally grown vegetables, especially sweet corn, acquired from farmers along the route. "No exotic dishes on the table, but meals plain and solid, served family style."[40]

Yet there were those not-so-rare remarks about bad meals. A woman from Louisville, Kentucky, who journeyed on the Wabash & Erie Canal found nothing to her liking about either the dining area or the food on her line boat:

> You know how I like good things to eat. Well, just imagine the dining room on one of our river packets, and then turn to my canal-boat *salle a manger* [dining room]. To get to it from the cabin I have to climb up a ladder through a hole to the top of the boat, then go down through another hole into a suffocating box. The table is horrid, so is the cooking. Pork and bread, bread and pork, then some greasy fish, mackerel, and bitter coffee lukewarm three times each day. I am raving hungry all the time, and nothing fit to eat. It makes me violently angry to see [brother] Tom gorge like a pig and pretend that stewed beans and catfish are delicious.[41]

Another traveler and his family on the Wabash canal were also less than pleased. "We were summoned to tea. [We] all complained bitterly of the bad tea and coffee, of the heavy hot corn bread, and of the raw beef steaks."[42]

If passengers disapproved of the food, there were options. They could bring along their own "eats." If a limited travel budget was not a concern, food and drink could be purchased at stops along the way. A traveler on the Erie Canal happily observed that "the passenger can supply himself with provisions and grog at all the lockhouses along the line."[43]

A general consensus developed that sleeping was the least attractive part of any overnight canal trip, being far less so than any meals served. Reports about sleeping accommodations undermine any wholly romantic aura of canal travel. In a contemporary juvenile-oriented book about the Erie Canal, the author accurately described the seeming chaos that occurred on a crowded packet as male passengers settled down for the night.

> "I wish I had a string to tie round my hat and hang it up; for there is no place to put it down anywhere."—"Captain, what are you going to do with the rest of us that have not got any berths?"—"Oh, what a pillow! 'tisn't bigger than my hand."—"Do you kick, sir, in your sleep?"—"Kick! yes, sir."—"For if you do, I don't want you *over* head."—"Mr. Belden!"—"Here"—"Choose your berth, sir;—they're all taken but that one."—"Gentlemen, don't make such a noise,—I want to go to sleep."—"My pillow is so thin, captain, that it makes my head lower than my heels."[44]

Negative commentaries continue. One passenger on the Ohio & Erie Canal offered this description: "During the day the beds, consisting of mattresses, sheets, pillows, and cotton quilts, were piled one above another." And much to his dislike, "The smell of animal effluvia, when they were unpacked, was truly horrid. They were saturated with the perspiration of every individual who had used them since the commencement of the season." A German tourist who took an Erie Canal packet awoke one night with "a dreadful feeling of suffocation," sensing a "weight like lead" on his midsection. He explained: "A stout heavy man, who slept in the upper frame without a mattress, was too much for the well-worn canvas; during his sleep it had given way under the weightiest part of his form, which descended till it found support on my chest." This disturbed traveler responded accordingly: "The thrust of the breastpin gave me that opportunity of making my escape I so gladly seized." If a passenger opted for an upper berth and avoided any poking from below, conditions might not be all that conducive for a good night's rest. "The first night I tried an Upper berth, but the air was so foul that I found myself sick when I awoke. Afterwards I choose an under berth and found no ill effects from the air." A British aristocrat who in 1850 traveled on the Illinois & Michigan Canal from Chicago to La Salle, Illinois, discovered that windows on his packet had been nailed shut for fear that malaria would creep in from the surrounding lowlands, and this lack of ventilation trapped "nauseous vapors," causing him to awake with an acute headache. In this description of an overnight passage taken in the mid-1830s on Champlain Canal from Lake Champlain to Troy, New York, a traveler said:

> I selected one of the lower tier [of berths], preferring to run the chance of my two upper neighbours breaking down on me to being suffocated by the heated air and unsavory smells which would naturally ascend. There was so little space between these comical berths that it was no easy matter to get into them. Once you had affected a location, you might be said literally to be laid on a shelf. You were obliged to make yourself as small as possible and to lie still for if you lifted your head three inches from the pallet it struck against the berth above.

This canal passenger related in his diary: "Arrived at Lockport at 6, & took passage in Packet canal Boat for Rochester. Oh! Such a night [underling in original]. Some 70 crowded men & women into a canal boat!! Preserve me from ever getting on one again." What bothered Dickens on one trip was nighttime spitting. "All night long, and every night, on this canal, there was a perfect storm and tempest of spitting, and once my coat, being in the very centre of a hurricane sustained by five gentlemen, I was fain the next morning to lay it on the deck, and rub it down with fair water before it was in a condition to be worn again." For some, if not many, sleeping was hopeless or nearly so. Passengers who took stagecoaches overnight may have reached a similar conclusion.[45]

A female traveler on the Wabash & Erie Canal complained about her nighttime, if not nightmare, experiences:

> It seemed that all of the heat spent by the sun during the day had settled down into the hot and stuffy little room, and that all the mosquitoes ever hatched in the mud puddles of Indiana were condensed into one humming, ravenous swarm right around my hard little bed. Tom [her brother] went up into the open air on top of the boat and spent the night. How I did wish I was a boy! All night I lay there under a smothering mosquito bar and listened to the buzzing of the insects, perspiring as I never supposed that anybody could. It was awful, horrid! It seemed that daylight was never going to come again.[46]

Such conditions may explain why one woman made these suggestions: "I would never advise ladies to travel by canal unless the boats are quite new and clean; or at least, far better kept than any that I saw or heard of on this canal."[47]

Then there was noise. It might be swarming mosquitoes or croaking frogs and other creatures of the night. It might be crew members talking or the helmsman's horn or bugle being blown as the boat approached a lock, fellow passengers snoring or moving about to use chamber pots, or babies crying in the ladies' quarters, and "women who babbled all night in Gaelic, German, Swedish, French or Swiss." Sleep might be interrupted when the craft entered a lock, bumping against the gate or side wall, or rocked because of a passing boat. Canal side businesses—taverns most likely—might have boisterous employees and patrons.[48]

When groggy or grumpy passengers awoke between five and six in the morning or were roused "when we are told," they needed to vacate their sleeping quarters. Cabin attendants hurriedly turned this space into an eating area. Those who wished to conduct their morning toilet often found less than ideal facilities. "The washing accommodations were primitive," remarked Charles Dickens. "There was a tin ladle chained to the deck, with which every gentleman who thought it necessary to cleanse himself fished the dirty water out of the canal and poured it into a tin basin, secured in like manner. And hanging up before a little looking glass in the bar, in the immediate vicinity of the bread and cheese and biscuits, was a public comb and brush."[49]

Although the unhappiness associated with meals and particularly sleeping might be anticipated by a would-be canal traveler, the choice of boats could cause apprehension and surprise. In May 1829 a would-be passenger on the Erie Canal discovered that such a decision might not be as easy as he had previously thought:

> We arrived at Schenectady about one o'clock. As all the passengers in our stage were bound to Utica, one of the number proposed that he be appointed to bargain for our passage in one boat. As soon as the stage stopped at the Hotel, even before the driver with all his activity to do undid the door, up stepped a large

muscular fellow, and bawled out at the highest pitch of polite etiquette, "Gentle-men, do you go to the West?" "We do." "The packet starts at 2 o'clock, gentlemen; you had better take your passages and secure your births; only 3 ½ cents a mile, gentlemen, and two shillings a meal, with best accommodations, and a very superior boat, gentlemen." "Hang his boat gentlemen, don't take passenger in her," said a second fellow. "I'll take you for less than half the money in a devilish fine boat, and charge you but a shilling for a meal." By this time there were at least a half a dozen more, all anxious for us to engage our passage with them at almost any price we pleased. But our Contractor very properly remarked, that he must see the boats himself before he would take passage in any. We therefore all sallied forth to the canal which passes at right angles through the town. We selected a very superior boat of the Clinton Line, calculated to accommodate thirty persons. The Captain actually engaged to take us to Utica, a distance of 89 miles, for one cent and a quarter mile! A York shilling of each meal extra, and to make no charge for births [*sic*], which are a very necessary accommodation, as the boats run day and night.[50]

Throughout commentaries about canal travel, there were indications that feelings of comradery might develop among passengers, as suggested by the group who collectively decided on what boat to take from Schenect-ady. In the 1870s a canal passenger shared these memories about a much earlier trip: "It was a merry, care-free party. We were clustered in the little forward cabin. We ran over the deck to the after-cabin for meals. We sat upon our baggage, and took something more than a bird's-eye view of the country. We told stories and sang songs and dreamed dreams." Then there were those moments of excitement: "We sat on the deck and watched the steersman's intonations. When he cried, 'Low *bridge!*' [italics in original] we merely ducked our heads; but when he said, '*Low* bridge!' [italics in original] down we went flat upon the floor like a parcel of undis-covered idolaters." After a trip on the Erie Canal in 1835, Philip Hone, a New York City politician and inveterate diary keeper, offered these com-ments: "The boat was not crowded, the weather was cool and pleasant, the accommodations good, the Captain polite, our fellow-passengers well-behaved, and altogether, I do not remember to have ever had so pleas-ant a ride on the Canal." Others enjoyed meeting interesting people and learning the freshest gossip about business conditions, politics, and other matters.[51]

There were those individuals who grumbled about their fellow travel-ers. Some passengers, particularly women, objected to the coarseness of men who drank, swore, smoked, and spit. In 1840 a Campbellite minister, who took passage on the Cincinnati & Whitewater Canal from Milton, Indiana, to Cincinnati, caught the essence of such complaints. "All of the miserable stenches from chewing, snuffing, smoking and spitting tobacco, we were ever compelled to witness, this is the nearest beyond the possi-bility of exaggeration. A good portion of the time, some one is sawing on an old fiddle, while others are whacking down their cards, amid the most horrible profanity imaginable." Another man of the cloth found "heathens" reprehensible. "Our company consists of about 30 passengers and as usual, there are but few among them who seem to regard the interest of their souls and those few have not courage to say much in behalf of Christ," complained this Presbyterian missionary. "I have left in the cabin the *Memoirs of Mr. Judson* [a missionary to Burma], and a few tracts which have arrested the attention of some—while others resort of *card playing* [italics in original], as their chief occupation while on board."[52]

JUMP! JUMP!

Although canal patrons realized that travel speeds were slow, they appreciated that boats moved methodically and safely, day and night. When compared to stagecoaches, canal service was much more frequent. Travelers might have to wait a day or longer for a coach, but packets and line boats left most places several times or more daily, including Sundays. Of course, canal travel was mostly smooth, with none of the jarring and passenger crowding (except at night) that commonly occurred on a stage and no tip-overs or robberies either.

The cost of transportation often determined the choice of a particular mode. Canal charges were usually lower or at least competitive with alternative forms of public travel, especially stagecoaches and later railroads. As early as 1824 a New York State editor indicated that fares on the Erie Canal were "so low that no man who consults economy *can afford to go on foot!* [italics in original]" In 1840 another Empire State journalist opined in this fashion: "If a man feels lazy, and wishes to lounge a day or so, get aboard of the *Red Bird* [Line] and go to Rochester one day, and back the next, it is altogether cheaper than staying at home."[53]

A recurring commentary on attractive canal fares can be found beyond newspaper reports. A personal account of an 1827 trip on the Erie Canal indicated that "passengers are carried in freight [line] boats for 1½ cents, exclusive of board. In the canal packets the fare, including all expenses, is generally four cents per mile." Toward the end of the canal packet age, a diarist who traveled from New York City to Cincinnati, Ohio, made this entry for August 22, 1844:

> Last evening toward eight o'clock I went by train from Troy to Schenectady, which we reached after an hour and where our luggage was taken to a canal packet boat which was ready to depart and had waited only for us. I thought I would find only a few passengers here because many prefer to travel by train to

Low bridges might allow passengers who had missed their boat the chance to take the plunge to the packet deck. But there was always a risk of injury, so this was not an action for the faint of heart.

Marco Paul's Voyages & Travels, 1852

Buffalo, which takes only 40 hours, while the packet boats need 75 to 76 hours. I was very much mistaken, however, because when we arrived the boat was so full of passengers that there was hardly a seat left for us. The reason might be the cheapness of the canal trip, for while the journey on the train with subsistence costs about $13.50, the one on the canal is only $7.75.[54]

Later this long-distance traveler seemed especially pleased that his six-day trip on the Ohio & Erie Canal from Cleveland to Portsmouth on the Ohio River cost a reasonable $6.50 "and no tips for the entire journey."[55]

Attractive fares helped to sustain passenger traffic on most canals into the railway age. Travelers with modest pocketbooks tended to patronize canals, just as bus riders in the twentieth century might use this highway transit rather than railroads. Immigrants and settlers, most of all, appreciated line and freight boats, which offered fares that were even cheaper than those costs associated with packets. They obtained passage for themselves and their household possessions, and for farmers this often included animals and agricultural implements. Except for canals in the Southlands, most "ditches" shut down during the winter months, and this forced the price conscious either to pay higher railroad fares or to wait for the spring thaw.

PUBLIC CONTACTS

There were canal users who did not fuss much about transportation costs. In some cases they owned and operated their own boats, although admittedly facing outlays for labor, tolls, and maintenance. A variety of groups and individuals took advantage of these waterways for business, not to ship freight but to practice their trades or professions.

It was common for communities along canals to welcome circuses, medicine shows, and theatrical companies. Their arrival became a highlight in the lives of eager ticket buyers, helping to liven daily routines. A popular attraction on the Wabash & Erie Canal was the Spalding & Rodgers Circus Company, which employed its specially constructed "Floating Palace." In an April 1853 broadside, promoters announced that this circus—in reality a traveling menagerie—would perform in Mount Carmel, Vincennes, Russellville, Hudsonville, and Darwin before reaching Terre Haute. Then there were the medicine shows. One that operated on the Miami & Erie Canal featured a boat with a side that could be lowered to create a performance platform. "The company invariably consisted of a pair of agile young Negroes who could sing, dance and hit fancy notes on a banjo, a tenor to jerk a tear with a soggy ballad and a blonde soubrette, usually the 'doctor's' wife or mistress." The profit motive for the "doctor" involved the sale of some nostrum that was cheap to produce but pricey to buy; after all, medicine shows sold medicines. On the Ohio & Erie Canal, the public encountered "a theater pulled by mules." Theatrical troupes of actors and musicians together with support personnel—deckhands, stewards, and drivers—visited community after community on board small flotillas. Their boats served as a place to live and to store paraphernalia, and one vessel became the stage. These thespians conducted a local advertising blitz, sold tickets, and presented one or more performances. "We had comedies and dramas," remembered a participant, "and just about everything the people wanted."[56]

Individuals who did not own canal boats still relied on them to conduct their trades or activities. Some were "drummers," itinerant salesmen who traveled from place to place to offer an assortment of oddments and related items. There were book dealers who sold the latest fiction, nonfiction, and religious tracts as well as used titles at dockside or in adjoining commercial areas. Ministers and lay preachers also joined the mix. Some were associated with the "Second Great Awakening," which swept much of America during the antebellum decades. Others were millennialists who expected Christ's imminent return, missionaries who sought to spread the Mormon faith, and spiritualists who appeared after the amazing revelations of "the coming of the spirits" by the Fox sisters in Hydesville, New York. There also were political reformers who consisted of abolitionists, Anti-Masonic Party activists, advocates of women's rights, and supporters of the xenophobic Know-Nothing movement. While much of this religious and reform zeal became part of everyday life along the Erie Canal, or what revivalist Charles Finney christened the "Burned-Over District," similar happenings took place along other canal corridors. Even the short-lived Sandy & Beaver Canal in Ohio facilitated the presence of these men of business, religion, and uplift. The corridor attracted not only peddlers but also proponents of a variety of nontraditional world views, including Adventism, spiritualism, and free thought. The canal environment fostered a cultural milieu that later gave birth to the Spirit Fruit Society, a metaphysical utopia launched in the 1890s. And abolitionists became frequent passengers in this heavily Quaker region.[57]

Canals made the unusual movement possible. In 1826 one such event took place along the Erie Canal. Amos Eaton, founder and professor at the Rensselaer School in Troy, New York, used canal boats to create the "Rensselaer School Flotilla" for students and others who sought to explore the natural wonders that could be found along or near this trans–New York waterway. These vessels contained all the necessities for an educational adventure, ranging from cooking equipment to scientific paraphernalia. The flotilla traveled leisurely, covering about fifteen to twenty miles per day, pausing to examine rock formations and to collect specimens of minerals, plants, and insects.[58]

The Eaton expedition probably caused limited or no interest along the canal corridor, but public docks often became a beehive of activities, attracting not only canal workers and customers but townspeople as well. "The stir and bustle of our wharves makes Fort Wayne appear like quite a seaport town," opined a Fort Wayne, Indiana, editor in 1841. Paralleling wharves on natural navigable bodies of water, arrival of a packet, line, or freight boat might well be a welcomed event in the daily routine of the citizenry. For one thing, captains of the faster craft commonly received contracts to handle the US mail, and residents desired this connection with the outside world. There were also personal contacts and observations. A courthouse, store, or tavern functioned as a community center, and so did the canal front.[59]

Although the general public welcomed the canal era, tensions did erupt between canal towns and more remote or inland communities and farms. Even though there was general agreement that canals made personal travel more pleasant and less expensive and also enhanced commerce and economic growth, there were complaints.

During the construction phase, residents reported various problems. Rowdy diggers caused repeated disturbances and mischief along emerging waterways. It might be excessive drinking and fighting or the thief of chickens, pigs, fruit, and produce. Land owners might have their trees chopped down or their fences dismembered. One farmer, who lived near a canal, lost three hundred fence rails; diggers seemed to be always seeking free fuel. In some localities the building process necessitated the damming of streams, and this caused flooding on surrounding properties and contributed to unhealthful conditions, mainly during the insect season. And agrarians usually didn't want to have their field severed by the waterways. Still, some farmers, villagers, and townspeople appreciated the chance to use those sturdy towpaths as a walkway to a destination for business or pleasure, just as many later would do along railroad rights-of-way.[60]

Once construction ended, friction did not evaporate between the canal people and corridor residents. Canal towns, especially those that appeared at the time of construction or soon thereafter and those places at or near canal side in established communities, usually lacked a dominant culture that vigorously defended prudish "village virtues." They became the subject of scorn of those individuals who embraced such a conservative or traditional outlook, and those individuals might take legal and political action against disruptive elements. Usually tensions centered on the numerous "dram shops," or taverns, located at or near locks. These establishments were frequented by boat people and others who liked such watering spots. At Pancake Lock on the Ohio & Erie Canal in Canal Fulton, a resident recalled this about a group of tough characters: "One of the saloons these 'rats' frequented was run by a one-armed man, who

avoided trouble with them by non-interference. They did as they pleased; drank his liquor, smoked his cigars, and chased out all his customers. Bad men infesting the saloons at the locks were unfit for jobs, they lived by theft and gambling." These "dens of iniquity" might become venues for sexual improprieties. Canal Fulton required a town marshal and a jail to maintain law and order on "Canal Row," creating a burden to taxpayers and angering the religious faithful and everyone who wished to have a somnolent community.[61]

There were other concerns. A recurring one was the fear of disease, most of all cholera, that canal travelers seemingly spread. After all, the population was vulnerable and helpless against outbreaks of an unpredictable infectious disease. When a community received reports that this dreaded and potentially deadly ailment was in the vicinity, frightened residents sometimes prevented boats from landing, or in a few cases they severed the waterway. The canal itself caused parents to worry about their children playing nearby or swimming in its not-so-pristine waters. Youngsters might be injured when they jumped, perhaps on a dare, from bridges onto moving boats. And contact with the unsavory elements associated with canal life also prompted concern. No one wanted the youth of a

During the twilight years of the Miami & Erie Canal near Maumee, Ohio, a mule team under supervision of a young driver pulls a boat typical of this transport form. To the far left is the mainline of the Toledo, St. Louis & Kansas City Railroad, better known as the Clover Leaf Route.

Photograph of the Miami & Erie Canal, *ca. 1900, courtesy of the Toledo-Lucas County Public Library, obtained from http://images2. toledolibrary.org/*

community to be tempted from the straight and narrow. Non-liturgical Protestants, often in sizable numbers, were not thrilled to have "Romans" in their midst. These Roman Catholics may have become permanent rather than temporary residents. Unmistakably, a strong anti-Catholic and anti-immigrant movement had taken hold in the country by the 1840s, and large numbers of canal builders and workers helped to trigger that phenomenon. Canals themselves came to be considered nuisances or worse. At a public meeting held in Lisbon, Ohio, in 1852, citizens expressed displeasure toward the owners of the faltering Sandy Creek & Beaver Canal. "Committee of Safety to be appointed and whereas the Sandy & Beaver Canal and its Reservoirs greatly obstructed the intercourse and business of the community by obstructing roads, and by breaking or dividing our school districts, injuring farms it passes through by flooding, for which no compensation can be obtained, said company being bankrupt, further it is a great expense to our country by causing the need to build bridges across the Canal which the company refuses to maintain."[62]

REMEMBERING CANALS

All types of transportation have engendered interest long after their halcyon days have passed or the form itself has disappeared. Canals are no exception. There exists a rich mix of literary works, music, and historical studies. These range from the once popular novels of Walter Edmonds, which include *Rome Haul, Erie Water*, and *Mostly Canallers*, to the enduring "Low Bridge, Everybody Down!" that generations of grade-school children have cheerfully sung. Academic and amateur historians have examined every canal in the United States and Canada, and there are several overarching publications, best exemplified by Ronald Shaw's *Canals for a Nation: The Canal Era in the United States, 1790–1860*.

As with most transport forms, public interest in the past remains strong, and in the case of canals, it focuses on these nearly always cast-off ditches. In recent years with support from public agencies, including the National Park Service, several linear canal parks have appeared. Representative of this phenomenon is the Illinois & Michigan Canal Heritage Corridor, which Congress established in 1984. Centered on the long-abandoned Illinois & Michigan Canal, this approximately hundred-mile swath of land includes remains of the waterway, highlighted by the restoration of much of the original towpath.

Supporting canal preservation and interpretation is the American Canal Society. This organization, launched in 1972, promotes the history of the nation's artificial waterways through programs of research, education, and preservation. Local groups, too, have developed; the Canal Society of Ohio is a good example. Paralleling enthusiasts who focus on other transport, most notably railroads, knowledgeable canal buffs continue to make lasting contributions to commemorating the canal era. Larry Tise, former director of the American Association for State and Local History, attests to their value in preserving the past:

> The extent to which American history has become the possession and pursuit of American people came through most vividly to me some years ago when I chanced upon the remains of a canal that had been built along the Yakin River in North Carolina. A beautiful stone wall more than a thousand feet long simply existed in the middle of nowhere, miles from any road and wholly unknown to local residents. Suspecting that it was part of an early failed canal operation, I went to the local library and found virtually nothing about canals. The same was true at two major university libraries. Finally, I turned up a little book on Pennsylvania canals published by the American Canal Society and wrote to the Society for more information. I soon found myself in receipt of a monthly newsletter, forms for the recording of canals, and a spate of pamphlets on all facets of American and international canal history. I was next recruited to help survey all the early canal remains in North Carolina and was visited by two utterly knowledgeable members of the society to provide instruction and helpful guidance on the project. Among the members of that society are more knowledge and understanding of American's largely forgotten canal history than all of the libraries and professional historians put together in the rest of world.[63]

Possibly it is this interest in the mysteries of abandoned canals that fascinates. "The Canal Era created canals of drama and beauty," observed historian Ronald Shaw, "which can be only partially glimpsed today." Less excitement exists about those artificial waterways that continue to accommodate freight vessels and pleasure craft, whether it be the Chesapeake & Delaware Canal or the New York State Barge Canal, the twentieth-century successor to the Erie Canal.[64]

Railways and the American People

4

THE RAIL NETWORK

If the nineteenth century was the age of steam, it was also the railway age. From the close of the 1820s to the Panic of 1893, thousands of miles of iron and ultimately steel rails laced the nation. Route mileage soared from a paltry 23 miles in 1830 to an impressive 163,597 in 1890, with more than 71,000 miles being completed during the boom years of the 1880s. By that time Americans claimed to have about half of all railroad mileage in the world. Following the crushing depression of 1893–1897, building again heightened. Although the *Railroad Gazette* in 1900 believed that the new railroad mileage, except in frontier areas, had "gained its full growth extensively," considerable additional trackage nevertheless appeared, with 1906 being a banner year. "More miles of railway have been constructed in the United States during the year 1906 than have been built during any year since the wonderful era of railway construction in the later eighties." Two years later *Harper's Monthly* made these appropriate remarks: "The railroad dominates. Its spreads a web across the land and holds men and cities in its meshes. Across the country the railroad stretches its embankments. It cleaves the mountain and throws trestles above the gorge. It fills the cities with its roar." Finally in 1916 the network peaked. A cobweb of 254,251 miles blanketed the forty-eight states, with Texas, Illinois, and Pennsylvania claiming the greatest totals. Although trackage remained stable during the 1920s, the Great Depression and the post–World War II explosion in motor vehicle ownership and highway construction caused a noticeable shrinkage. In 1930 mileage stood at 249,884, and by 1955 it had dropped to 220,670. Yet this was only a modest retrenchment. "The pace was glacial because regulation made abandonment difficult and because railroaders were slow to grasp the fact the world had changed," explained industry planner James (Jim) McClellan. Passage of the Transportation Act of 1958 allowed the Interstate Commerce Commission (ICC) to be more receptive towards line-abandonment petitions. Then beginning about 1960 several waves of corporate mergers—"merger madness"—took place, producing trackage redundancies. Bankruptcies, too, promoted retrenchments. In 1970 the financial failure of the 1968 merger between the New York Central; Pennsylvania; and New York, New Haven & Hartford (New Haven) Railroads, which created Penn Central Transportation Company, led to extensive pruning of this sprawling 19,000-mile system. By the twenty-first century, national route mileage had plummeted to about 140,000, but it has since stabilized. The railway age, though, had long passed; all ages are transitory.[1]

At times the iron horse appeared ahead of major settlements. When construction crews of the Central Pacific and Union Pacific, builders of the first transcontinental rail link, joined dignitaries and others to celebrate the "wedding of the rails" at Promontory, Utah Territory, on May 10, 1869, they met in a nearly unpopulated area. In fact, much of the route between Omaha, Nebraska, and Sacramento, California, was inhabited only by roaming Native Americans and prospectors and scattered farmers and ranchers. Mormons, who belonged to Brigham Young's Church of Jesus Christ of Latter-Day Saints, were the notable exception. Their settlements were located primarily in the greater Salt Lake basin of the intermountain West, and most members preferred their "splendid isolation."[2]

For much of the period prior to the Civil War, railroad projects usually involved relatively short distances, being best described as "tap roads." These little pikes connected interior places with navigable bodies of water. But after the Civil War, spurred on by a burgeoning population, stronger economy, and federal government land grants, the focus became creation of regional and interregional carriers. "System building" of the Gilded Age and after, spearheaded by investment bankers like J. P. Morgan Sr., did much to bring about these impressive networks through construction, leases, and mergers.

Long before the American railroad network was completed, the public enjoyed options for their journeys near and far. If they wished to travel between America's two largest cities, New York and Chicago, they could choose trains that operated on the Baltimore & Ohio, Erie, New York Central, or Pennsylvania Railroads. If they desired to continue from Chicago to Los Angeles, they might select ones that ran over the Atchison; Topeka & Santa Fe (Santa Fe); Chicago & North Western-Union Pacific; or Chicago, Rock Island & Pacific-Southern Pacific. For lesser distances multiple choices usually existed. Take Chicago to Minneapolis. A traveler could opt for one of these carriers: Chicago & North Western (North Western); Chicago, Burlington & Quincy (Burlington); Chicago Great Western (Great Western); Chicago, Milwaukee & St. Paul (Milwaukee Road); Illinois Central-Minneapolis & St. Louis; or Minneapolis, St. Paul

NEW ROUTE.

PASSENGERS

GOING WEST

VIA

Hannibal & St. Joseph & Platte Country R. Rs.

Will go by STEAMER from WESTON and LEAVEN-
WORTH, connecting at WYANDOTTE and
KANSAS CITY with the

UNION PACIFIC RAILWAY

For LAWRENCE, and all Central, Southern and Western

KANSAS, NEW MEXICO AND COLORADO.

PASSENGERS VIA

Missouri Pacific R.R. & Missouri River

Going WEST, will connect as above, at WYANDOTTE
AND KANSAS CITY.

Time and Distance from the following Cities

TO WYANDOTTE AND KANSAS CITY.

Miles	From	Hours	Miles	From	Hours
1692	Quebec	83	1514	New York	74
1560	Boston	76	835	Detroit	46
1399	Montreal	72	551	Chicago (via St. Joe)	35
1080	Buffalo	59	565	Chicago (Via St. L.)	31
1096	Toronto	56	283	St. Louis(via P. R. R.)	16

Constant Employment for a large number of Laborers and
Mechanics, on the Union Pacific Railway, E. D.

UNION PACIFIC

E PLURIBUS UNUM

RY & LOCO
HIST. SOC.

RAILWAY

EASTERN DIVISION.

New Route by Steamer and Railway,

TO

LAWRENCE

AND ALL

CENTRAL, SOUTHERN AND

WESTERN KANSAS

New Mexico and Colorado.

C. WOOD DAVIS,   W. H. VAN TASSEL,
General Ticket Agent.   Traveling Agent.

E. M. BARTHOLOW, Supt., Wyandotte, Kansas.

& Sault Ste. Marie (Soo Line). Even smaller places—towns and villages—often had more than a single carrier. Residents of the farming community of Lohrville, Iowa, located in the north-central part of the state, could board trains of the North Western, Great Western, and Milwaukee Road Railroads. Some states, including Iowa, by World War I developed networks that covered their political boundaries like the proverbial morning dew. Fewer and fewer places could be described as "inland communities." Without question railroads continued to satisfy the public's "relentless and roaming spirit," and as with earlier and later forms of intercity travel, they served to develop that taste for more travel.

Throughout the railway age, Americans knew that rails, being that proverbial magic carpet, were their lifelines for economic prosperity and greater mobility. Understandably, townspeople, farmers, ranchers, miners, and others did all that they could to achieve railroad service. While carriers themselves or affiliated or independent promotional companies laid out thousands of town sites, citizens who were not residents of such places did not want to be left at an inconvenient distance from the rails. In order to join the national network, hundreds of towns, villages, counties, and townships repeatedly subsidized line construction. They might have

As the iron rail network spread westward, owners of recently completed lines ballyhooed fresh travel options. In the early 1870s the Union Pacific, Eastern Division, which was originally known as the Leavenworth, Pawnee & Western and was later renamed the Kansas Pacific, offered a "NEW ROUTE GOING WEST" and listed rail and water connections.

Author's Collection

offered cash, purchase of securities, or land donations, or some combination of these inducements. Individuals, both urban and rural, might have made their own money or in-kind commitments. During the antebellum years, a few states, most notably Michigan and North Carolina, built one or more railroads.

Examples abound of this public eagerness to support railroad construction. In their desperate desire for the iron horse, residents of the southwestern Wisconsin town of Ettrick, earlier bypassed by the Green Bay & Western Railroad (GB&W) to the north and by a North Western branchline to the south, voted to finance their own outlet, the Ettrick & Northern Railroad. This shortline was designed to forge a ten-mile connection with the GB&W at Blair, Wisconsin. On September 20, 1915, voters of Ettrick Township went to the polls in a special election to consider a $75,000, 5 percent construction bond issue. This tax proposal carried by a substantial margin, 298–148, with the bulk of the negative votes coming from conservative Scandinavian farmers. Yet the victory created no hard feelings. "Those who were not in favor of the bond issue have gracefully submitted to the verdict of the majority and will be numbered among the enthusiastic boosters for the road," said a happy local journalist. After several years of some challenging construction work, the hometown railroad carried its first passengers and freight.[3]

While the Ettrick & Northern was gestating, excitement was building on the north Texas plains for still another steam railroad. A proposal to extend a tiny tap road, the Acme, Red River & Northern Railway, under the corporate banner of the Quanah, Acme & Pacific Railway (QA&P), prompted residents of several counties to consider how to make this enticing plan a reality. Scores of individuals and businesses in Quanah, soon to become the QA&P nerve center, quickly raised $40,000, constituting 222 individual donations and testifying to the strong support for this project. Communities along the projected route also promised their financial assistance. A spokesperson from Floydada, Texas, told the road's principal promoter that his town "would be very glad to have you submit us a proposition as to what you will require of us in order to secure said railroad." It would be largely through local financing that the "Quanah Route" developed into a 119-mile carrier that linked the Red River near Carnes, Texas, and a vital connection with the St. Louis-San Francisco Railway (Frisco), with Floydada and a tie-in with the Santa Fe. Places that failed to become stations on the QA&P also promised aid. Crosbyton, Texas, for one, offered a large bonus. As with so many nineteenth- and early-twentieth-century railroad projects, the prospect of rail service galvanized local boosters to pledge financial backing, at times in substantial amounts.[4]

In the case of another twilight era railroad, townspeople of inland Treynor, Iowa, and neighboring farmers showed determination both to

Farmers' Railroad Meetings

Meetings will be held at the places designated below at two p. m. on the dates given. At these meetings the Farmers Railroad project will be fully explained. It is your interests at stake. Be there and take part in the meetings.

Veblen, Mon.	Jan. 6
Foss Sc.house, NORWAY Twp.	Jan. 7
Eddy P. O., Wed.	Jan. 8
Effington, Thurs.	" 9
Crawford, Fri.	" 10
Vernon, Sat.	" 11

Boost for the Farmer's Line

Veblen, S. Dak.

A successful twilight-era railroad project was the Fairmount & Veblen Railway, which opened in 1913. Two years later the Soo Line acquired this eighty-seven-mile line, which linked Fairmount, North Dakota, with Grenville, South Dakota. This short line began as a bootstrap "farmers' railroad" scheme, promoted by local boosters who contributed their labor and materials to create a dependable and economical outlet for agricultural products and other commerce.

Author's Collection

build and to make certain the success of their fifteen-mile Iowa & Omaha Short Line Railway (I&OSL). In June 1911 this road opened between Treynor and a connection with the Wabash Railroad at Neoga, Iowa, with considerable fanfare, being financed through local stock subscriptions. Unfortunately, though, it immediately encountered economic difficulties. In order to save the I&OSL, an area livestock raiser, Henry Saar, who had initially purchased a substantial block of stock, agreed to put more money into the faltering railroad, raising most of it through a real estate mortgage. In all Saar contributed $98,000 ($2.1 million in current dollars), but alas, the I&OSL failed. In June 1916 a mixed train, carrying cattle, several empty freight cars, and a few passengers in the road's battered coach, made its farewell trip to the Neoga station, where riders gained direct rail access to Council Bluffs. This trip brought to a close almost exactly five years of operations. Investors lost everything, and for backer Saar, his family also forfeited a 160-acre farm.[5]

Enthusiasm for the I&OSL and for scores of other railroads might have proved to be a costly personal affair. Throughout the construction cycles, investments in railroads did not always have happy endings. If a road were built and continued in operation, a bankruptcy usually meant a loss in stock and perhaps bond investments. The thought of valorized money probably did not enter the minds of most backers of the iron horse, especially when work began or when parts or all of the project were completed.

One of the most remembered opening-of-construction ceremonies occurred at the dawn of the railway age. The company was the Baltimore & Ohio Railroad (B&O), the place was Baltimore, Maryland, and the date was July 4, 1828, the most patriotic day of the year. The B&O officials were not about to break with an established national transportation tradition; after all, construction of the Erie Canal commenced on July 4, 1817, the Ohio & Erie Canal on July 4, 1825, and the Pennsylvania Grand Canal or State Works on July 4, 1826.

For days B&O celebrants prepared for the big blowout. Buildings were decorated, marching units organized, and floats assembled. The first public event was the memorable 2.5-mile-long parade that stretched along Baltimore Street to the west end of the city, complete with bands; fraternal, military, trade, and association groups; railroad officials and assorted dignitaries; and floats. As for the latter, the consensus judged the best one to be the twenty-seven-foot miniature of the frigate USS *Union*. And tens of thousands of festive spectators swarmed along the parade route. Then there was that not-to-be-forgotten formal ceremony, consisting of prayer, oratory, and fanfare. Charles Carroll of Carrollton, Maryland, the venerable ninety-year-old sole surviving signer of the Declaration of Independence, delegate to the first Continental Congress, and B&O director, took center stage when he turned the first spadeful of soil for the new railroad. This revered statesman allegedly told friends, "I consider this among the most important acts of my life, second only to my signing the Declaration of Independence, if even it be second to that." Following Carroll's symbolic act, the Masons conducted their ceremonial work by laying a large granite block, appropriately inscribed with these words: "FIRST STONE Balt. & Ohio Rail Road." It was an exciting day for Baltimore and an important day in the evolution of American transportation.[6]

Throughout the railway age, other less dramatic start-of-construction ceremonies took place. Still they were meaningful to participants. One such event occurred on November 11, 1878, when ground was formally broken at Newfane, Vermont, for the narrow-gauge Brattleboro & Whitehall

Rail Road. After the customary speeches, the railroad president turned a shovelful of dirt, and then a "wildly" enthusiastic crowd followed his example. "Old and young, lame and infirm, men and women—all stepped forward to throw dirt in the air. Even some implacable opponents were carried away and joined the shoveling **fest** [*sic*]." Construction resulted in a somewhat woebegone pike that linked Brattleboro with South Londonderry, Vermont, a distance of thirty-six miles.[7]

While several formal dedications of completed rail lines stand out—most famously the driving of ceremonial spikes at Promontory—a lesser known but hardly insignificant one took place on July 4, 1854, at New Albany, Indiana. This gala commemorated completion of the 288-mile New Albany & Salem Rail Road (NA&S), which connected the Ohio River at New Albany with Lake Michigan at Michigan City, Indiana. Although the last spike in this north-south Hoosier State line (future Monon Railroad) was driven near Greencastle on June 24, festivities were held at New Albany. It was an exciting day for company officials, politicians, and the attending public. According to the *New Albany Ledger*, the railroad claimed these distinctions: "the first direct railroad connection between that lake [Lake Michigan] and the [Ohio] river and the first, if we mistake not, between either of the Great Lakes and the Ohio by any one company."[8]

The Fourth of July in New Albany was a day to remember. "On the morning of the Fourth we found the tide of pleasure and sight seeing individuals setting in a strong current toward the neighboring borough of New Albany," reported a correspondent from the neighboring *Louisville Weekly Courier*. "It is said that there the excitement commenced early in the evening previous and that when the first train of cars from Lake Michigan reached the depot on Monday night the entire city was hilarious with joy. And well might the brave little city exult." This report continued: "Upon entering the town, between eight and nine o'clock, we found its streets literally black with people, the majority evidently from the country. No matter in what direction we turned there was the living crowd presenting a perfect panorama of human faces and forms. In the place of business and residence the town people were quietly enjoying the interesting spectacle, while the strangers wandered hither and thither looking on and drinking, by way of recreation, vast quantities of mead, soda-water and other mild potatives."[9]

Special excursion trains from online communities to the north swelled the ranks of well-wishers, estimated at between twelve thousand and twenty thousand. By midmorning on the Fourth, "it became evident that the largest assemblage of persons ever seen in New Albany would be present on this occasion." What followed was predictable: a series of afternoon speeches (perhaps too many and too long) by assorted dignitaries,

including the governors of Indiana and Kentucky. After that portion of
the ceremonies, the notables, along with a multitude of onlookers, led
by military units and fire companies, proceeded to the NA&S depot,
"tastefully festooned with evergreens and decked with flags, command-
ing the highest admiration and reflecting great credit on the decorating
committee." Amid these surroundings they enjoyed a hearty early feast.
"The tables were elevated about three and a half or four feet above the
floor, were covered with white linen, and presented as neat and cleanly an
appearance as any private table in the city. They were covered with all the
substantials and many of the delicacies of the season." No one departed
hungry or unhappy.[10]

PASSENGER EQUIPMENT

Celebrants who took the cars to New Albany found rolling stock that had
changed dramatically from what had first appeared on the pioneering Baltimore & Ohio. By the mid-1850s the demonstration period for American
railroads had largely passed. Steam locomotives had become larger and
more powerful, prototypes of later ones, and coaches had quickly evolved
from stagecoach-like contraptions on four flanged wheels to eight-wheel
ones that resembled future passenger equipment. The track structure, too,
was different. Solid iron rails, rather than "strap" rails—iron-on-wood
stringers—made for a faster and safer ride.

The relentless tide of progress continued. Most importantly for passengers, coaches became more attractive and comfortable. About 1860
the introduction of a radical roof profile, known as the clerestory design,

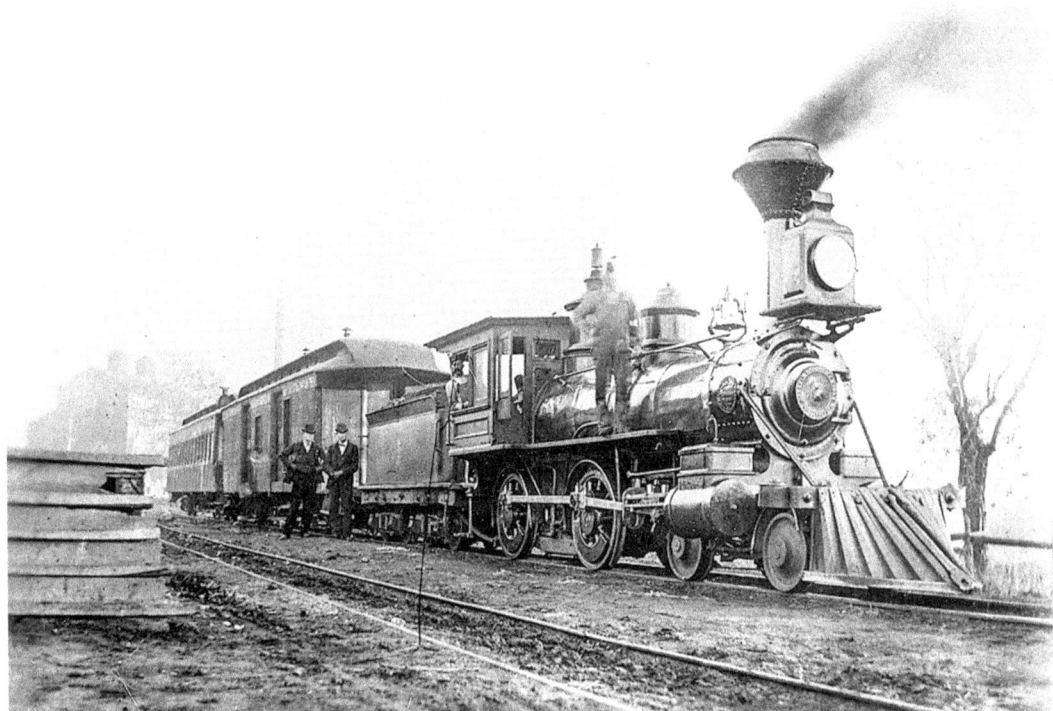

provided openings that enhanced interior daylight, created better ventilation, and added a touch of architectural grandeur. A similar style had already appeared on steamboats. Seating, lighting, heating, toilets, and other features also improved. By the 1890s the Pennsylvania Railroad, immodestly proclaiming itself as the "Standard Railway of the World," owned coaches that featured adjustable red plush seats, carpeted floors, gas or electric lights, and steam heat. An extra-wide clerestory roof gave interiors a feeling of added space. Throughout the passenger era, older rolling stock did not immediately go to the scrap heap or appear in work-train consists. Vintage coaches might be assigned to branchline, emigrant, or suburban service.[11]

Coinciding with improvements to day coaches was the introduction of sleeping and dining cars. The need to offer these accommodations did not exist on early railroads; trains customarily operated only during daylight hours and over short distances. As longer roads appeared by mid-century, the trackside hotel, either railroad or privately owned, allowed passengers to have a more pleasant overnight experience and access to hot meals. Yet the quality of food and service at such places was often poor before the 1870s, when entrepreneurial and hands-on restauranteur Fred Harvey began to set the standard for such trackside operations.[12]

While a few sleeping cars had appeared by the 1840s, none were especially comfortable. Still the need existed. Businessmen, most of all

Motive power and passenger equipment built during the post–Civil War era often remained in service for decades. The narrow-gauge craze of the 1870s and early 1880s, which led to construction of the sixty-one-mile Fulton County Narrow Gauge Railway (FCNG), resulted in the continuing use of its diminutive rolling stock. This 1900 photograph shows a classic American Standard locomotive with its aging passenger consist about to depart the FCNG station in Galesburg, Illinois, for its southern terminus in Havana, Illinois. The baggage car and coach feature that distinctive clerestory roof design.

Author's Collection

salesmen, or "drummers," wanted to arrive at their destinations as quickly
as possible, and they did not care to waste time staying overnight in hotels.
The old proverb of "Necessity is the mother of invention" prompted a
number of individuals to devise improved sleepers. The breakthrough
came with a car designed by George Mortimer Pullman, who created
what was dubbed a "hotel on wheels." He knew from his own travels that
attempting to sleep in a coach seat made for a grueling overnight experience. Although Pullman had tinkered with sleeping cars prior to the Civil
War, it was during that conflict that he created a popular prototype, the
Springfield. This long eight-wheel, double-truck car could accommodate
fifty-six passengers in multiple lower and upper convertible berths, and
it offered a feature that was lacking in existing sleeping cars: mattresses

made of the best materials and covered by snowy-white linens. Next Pullman designed and had constructed what was called car *A* but was soon renamed the *Pioneer*. This sleeper contained a dozen open sections with such luxurious appointments as rare hardwoods and plush upholstery. In April 1865 this lavish car may or may not have been attached to the much-viewed funeral train of President Abraham Lincoln between Chicago and Springfield, Illinois. Soon, though, the *Pioneer* attracted considerable press and public praise, setting the stage for the highly successful Pullman Palace Car Company, a firm that built, maintained, and operated fleets of sleeping cars. Although the Pullman firm had rivals, most notably the Woodruff Sleeping Car Company and the Wagner Palace Car Company, it dominated the business by the 1870s. By the start of the twentieth century, Pullman enjoyed a near monopoly; purchase of the Wagner firm, which served the New York Central System, made that possible.[13]

During their prolonged trips, travelers not only relished these posh, comfortable sleeping cars, with their convertible berths, dressing rooms, lavatories, and other amenities, but also showed great fondness for the Pullman porters. These employees of the Pullman Company, nearly all of whom were men of color, pampered patrons. And they would be carefully supervised by white Pullman conductors. George Pullman spoke for his company when he remarked: "[African Americans] by nature are adapted faithfully to perform their duties under circumstances which necessitate unfailing good nature, solicitude, and faithfulness." No wonder travelers for decades commonly referred to Pullman porters as "George," a direct reference to the company founder and later a most politically incorrect honor.[14]

George Pullman was not content with offering overnight travelers a superior sleeping car. He realized that a market existed for luxury onboard dining. In 1868 his firm introduced the palace dining car, the first one being the *Delmonico*, named after the famed New York City restaurant, Delmonico's, located in Lower Manhattan. Unlike sleeping cars, the appearance of dining cars came about more gradually. They were not profitable, and at times they were big money losers, in part because many less affluent passengers balked at what they considered to be overpriced meals. Yet onboard dining became attractive for well-heeled travelers and necessary for those in a hurry. Anyone who partook in a meal in a Pullman or non-Pullman diner was likely to be satisfied. Excellent food—frequently with an amazing choice of entrées—came out piping hot from tiny albeit efficient kitchens to be served by accommodating waiters at attractively set tables.

The Gilded Age also saw the Pullman Company, competing sleeping-car firms, and individual railroads providing deluxe library,

The attractiveness of a pre–World War II era parlor car is revealed in this 1930s photograph. Unlike in earlier years, there is no gender segregation; men and women move freely in this well-appointed piece of equipment.

Author's Collection

parlor, smoking, and observation cars. More affluent passengers willingly paid the extra charges for traveling in these pieces of specialized rolling stock. Women welcomed the privacy and "Victorian safety" of parlor cars, and men showed a fondness for smokers, where they relished opportunities for camaraderie and business interplay. These first-class trains were truly ones of delight. In the 1880s a railroad employee correctly observed that these consists were "equipped with all the luxuries and conveniences a millionaire could desire at home."[15]

The railroad enterprise continued to enhance travel experiences, aided by faster and safer trains. During the early years of the twentieth century, there occurred the second building of the nation's busiest lines. Major roads, including the North Western, New York Central, Pennsylvania, Southern, and Union Pacific, invested heavily in heavier rail, multiple tracks, grade reductions, improved signaling, more powerful locomotives, all-steel passenger cars, new stations and terminals, and other betterments.[16]

A good example of these train improvements took place on the New Haven, a company that operated a high-speed main line between New York City and Boston. In 1913 one of its premier trains, the *Merchants' Limited*, became reequipped, and the company claimed it to be "the most gorgeous train in America." The all-steel and "practically indestructible" consist featured a dining car, four parlor cars, and an observation-smoking car. "The interior finish [of the parlor cars] is Mexican mahogany, except the smokers, in which it is cocoa wood. Each of the parlor cars has 36 chairs, the usual drawing-room having been omitted." There was more to laud. "At night the cars have indirect lighting, each having ten 100-watt lamps distributed along the center. These lamps, with ornamented brass shields beneath them, throw their light up against a white ceiling. The cars are heated by steam. In the observation smoking car there is a buffet for making coffee."[17]

The leading passenger roads were never shy about promoting these classy trains. Early in the twentieth century, the Chicago, Rock Island & Pacific had this to say about its *Rocky Mountain Rocket*, its premier Chicago-to-Denver train: "It's a perfect train—perfectly equipped, perfectly conducted, and perfectly scheduled—a solid, substantial, well-balanced train, with a solidity of construction that spells the utmost safety—a richly finished and appointed train, but restfully and elegantly simple—electric lights for illumination, electric fans for ventilation, large, airy coaches, in whose building the sanitary engineer has had much to say." The company continued to sing the praises of this train. "And then there is that wonderful buffet-library-observation car, the 'clubhouse' of the train—complete and replete with everything that can lift the strain of the journey and edge its enjoyment."[18]

During this pre–World War I period, there were hints of what was to come during the 1930s when diesel-powered streamliners made their debut. Early in the new century, inventors, entrepreneurs, and railroaders saw the possibilities of a compact, internal-combustion-propelled passenger vehicle. It was Union Pacific employee William R. McKeen Jr. who in 1904 built the prototype of his famous knife-prowed gas-electric cars with their distinctive streamlined design. It did not take long before McKeen launched his own company, and for about a decade or so it produced scores of these futuristic units, which served more than four dozen railroads. McKeen cars and those of several competitors gave riders who patronized local, branchline, and shortline trains relief from the smoke, soot, and cinders emitted by steam locomotives. These metal McKeen cars featured air-tight porthole windows and a ventilating system that every few minutes screened and changed the air. Neatness and sanitary

The Union Pacific and Southern Pacific were two of the largest railroads that operated McKeen Cars. *Above*, A relatively new McKeen car awaits departure ca. 1915 in Omaha on Union Pacific rails. *Below*, In 1925 a somewhat battered McKeen car stands at the Beaverton, Oregon, station of the Southern Pacific. This car operated as train #149 between Portland and Timber, Oregon, on the Portland-Hillsboro-Tillamook branch.

Los Angeles Railroad Heritage Foundation Collection

conditions characterized the passenger section, and a roomy interior, comfortable seats, and improved heating added to a sense of travel cheerfulness. "Passengers on the R. O. & N. E. [Red Oak & North Eastern] railway will ride in the latest and most approved gasoline motor cars," a pleased Red Oak, Iowa, newspaper in 1909 editorialized on the likelihood of having a McKeen car serve this gestating, albeit never opened, hundred-mile Hawkeye State road. Unfortunately, though, early on these

Burlington

and Presents America's ====▶ *First Diesel Streamline Train*

Zephyr

THE WEST WIND

internal-combustion McKeen cars had the nasty habit of breaking down, often at some distance from a depot or terminal.[19]

While McKeen and other motor cars remained in operation, there were the well-equipped luxury passenger trains that were steam-powered and consisted of heavy-weight steel cars. By the 1920s various trunk roads claimed the most modern equipment. The *Pan-American*, pride of the Louisville & Nashville Railroad (L&N), is representative. This flagship train ran between Cincinnati and New Orleans via Louisville, Nashville, Birmingham, Montgomery, and Mobile. In May 1925 the *Pan-American* featured an all-Pullman consist, being described by the L&N as "the last word in De-Luxe Passenger Equipment." Amenities included a club car, observation car, "dining car service for which this line is famous," men's and women's showers, radio with earphones, and maid and valet service.[20]

Then in the 1930s a new era dawned with the advent of diesel-powered streamliners. The kickoff for this major upgrade in intercity travel came in 1934 with two Union Pacific (UP) trains called M-10000 and M-10001, built by the Pullman Car Company, and the *Zephyr*, constructed for the Burlington by the Edward G. Budd Company. Yet these articulated units were noticeably different. The UP trains were made of aluminum and featured a distillate-burning engine, and the Burlington one had stainless-steel construction with a diesel power plant. During 1934 the M-10000, dubbed "the Train of Tomorrow," made a twenty-two-state, 13,000-mile tour, while the *Zephyr* captured national attention by sprinting 1,015 miles nonstop from Denver to Chicago at an average speed of 77.6 miles per hour to take part in the festivities at the Century of Progress Exposition on the city's lakefront.

In 1934 the Chicago, Burlington & Quincy Railroad proudly introduced its *Zephyr* streamliner. A promotional folder distributed at its debut proclaimed: "Burlington Pioneers Again in Gleaming Stainless Steel."

Author's Collection

The Union Pacific and the Burlington quickly lost their monopoly on snappy streamliners. By the outbreak of World War II, various railroads operated this latest rolling stock, including such roads as the Boston & Maine, Great Northern, Illinois Central, New York Central, Pennsylvania, Rock Island, Santa Fe, Seaboard, and Southern Pacific. Unlike the pioneer trains, these were not articulated but rather diesel-powered locomotives containing individual lightweight stainless-steel coaches, dining, parlor, and sleeping cars. It did not take long before the UP and Burlington relegated their first streamliners to shorter routes and expanded their fleets of these modern passenger trains. Main lines saw fewer and fewer steam locomotives pulling fast trains with heavy-weight cars. Soon that would be true for diesel locomotives handling similar consists.

The Burlington remained innovative, hoping as did other major passenger carriers to attract those former passengers who had opted to drive their automobiles or to take airplanes for their long-distance journeys. In 1945 the company introduced the industry's initial Vista-Dome car. Two years later the road's *Twin Cities Zephyrs* became the first regular-service trains with Vista-Dome equipment, which proved so popular that the Burlington immediately ordered forty more of these luxury viewing cars. After March 19, 1949, dome cars became a favorite attraction of the newly introduced *California Zephyr*—commonly dubbed the "Silver Lady"—a deluxe Chicago to Oakland [San Francisco], California, train operated in conjunction with the Denver & Rio Grande Western and Western Pacific railroads. Additional carriers, mostly in the trans-Chicago West where lines lacked height restrictions, followed suit with their own dome cars.[21]

Railroads in the East did not fail to make attractive upgrades to their passenger train sets. Take the New York Central. When the postwar *Twentieth Century Limited* made its inaugural trip between New York City and Chicago on September 17, 1948, this diesel-powered all-Pullman streamliner contained such travel-friendly innovations as train-radio-telephones, fluorescent lighting, pneumatically operated doors, and enclosed toilets in all two-person rooms.[22]

Notwithstanding efforts to make train travel competitive with automobiles and airplanes, by mid-century passenger business continued to erode. Nevertheless, various attempts took place to create even better rolling stock, namely ultramodern jet age trains. Dome cars and train-radio-telephones were not enough. A good example of the desire to offer travelers cutting-edge technology came in 1949 when the American Car & Foundry Company (AC&F) constructed its *Talgo* diesel-powered trainsets. Designed in Spain but built by Saint Louis–based AC&F, these marvels of the rail employed a tilt mechanism with a low center of gravity, permitting faster track speeds. The low-slung articulated, lightweight aluminum *Talgos*, however, never caught on, largely because of their poor riding qualities and high interior noise level. Low ceilings, small seats, and tiny toilets hardly added to their popularity. Yet a much later direct descendant of these AC&F products appeared in the Pacific Northwest, trains of the National Railroad Passenger Corporation, better known as Amtrak, this quasi-public corporation that made its debut in 1971. Other mid-century experiments with jet age technology, including *Train X* and *TurboTrain*, failed to make an impact on travel.[23]

In the 1960s and 1970s, a more conventional form of passenger equipment emerged. During the latter part of the 1960s, the Budd Company built for the Pennsylvania Railroad an electrified fleet of lightweight tubular, stainless-steel *Metroliners*. These fast, comfortable trains sped between the company's New York City and Washington, DC, terminals and attracted considerable public support. About a decade later the Pullman-Standard Company constructed for Amtrak a large order of *Superliner* bi-level cars, influenced by similar cars developed in the mid-1950s by the Santa Fe. After Bombardier acquired Pullman-Standard, more of these bi-levels went into service. More recently, travelers along the electrified Northeast Corridor between Boston, New York City, Philadelphia, and Washington, DC, could take the *Acela Express*, trains built by Bombardier/GEC Alstom. This sleek rolling stock was fitted with a tilting capability and could reach 150 miles per hour, although there were few stretches of track that permitted such speeds.

TRAIN CREWS

Each form of intercity transportation had its iconic worker: stagecoach driver, riverboat pilot, packet boat captain, bus driver, and airplane pilot. For railroads a strong case can be made for the locomotive engineer, or "hogger." Passenger trains, of course, had other personnel, including a fireman, or "tallowpot"; conductor, who legally was in charge; multiple brakemen; and likely a flagman. Then there were crew members who were assigned to the sleeping, dining, parlor, or lounge cars. And for decades "news butchers," lads who worked for news companies or as private contractors, sold passengers newspapers, candy, and assorted oddments. The trainmen's smart uniforms, with their shiny brass or nickel cap badges and buttons, might impress youngsters. "The conductors were V.I.P.'s," remembered a Coloradan. "Proud, indeed, was the grimy-faced boy who could boast of having been patted on the tousled head and spoken to by one of those brass-buttoned, swallow-tail-coated members of an exclusive fraternity."[24]

Lads, however, probably wanted to sit in the engineer's seat on the right-hand side of the locomotive cab. The hogger was the one who controlled the whistle, throttle, and various other levers (later switches) and

Enginemen even on the smallest railroads commonly took pride in their work. This ca. 1910 photograph attests to that commitment. In Douglas, Georgia, a Georgia & Florida Railway fireman (with shovel) and engineer (with oil can) are joined by a lad and likely an official in front of locomotive No. 17, a 4-4-0. A decorative set of antlers and a circular painting of an American Indian with bow and arrow, likely the property of the engineer, rest on the front of the engine.

Author's Collection

had that bird's-eye view of the track ahead. Having that flair for making cinders fly, he was seen as the individual who could work under pressure and likely make up lost time if the train were seriously delayed. As with the captain of a ship, the engineer was that heroic figure who stuck to his post. He might command the fireman and head brakeman to jump off before a crash. The engineer surely resembled the real-life Casey Jones of the Illinois Central, who on that eventful day in April 1900 remained at the throttle, attempting to slow down before slamming into a stalled freight train and to signal warnings to its crew about the impending wreck. There is no question that Jones was a brave engineer who died an American

Although railroad engineers saw technological improvements, including the cab-to-train telephone, on their steam locomotives, the job continued to require skill and alertness. About 1950 a hogger on the Missouri Pacific watches the track ahead while he talks to a crew member.

Author's Collection

hero. His personal life, too, was that of a good role model; he was a tee-totaler and loyal family man. One late-nineteenth-century instructional publication, *The Science of Railways*, succinctly explained what makes a good engineer: "He, above all men, must be practical and conservative and possessed of a comprehensive mind. He must not only be alive to his own duty, but alert to that of others. There must be nothing of the brag-gadocio about him, nothing pyrotechnical nor spectacular. He must be a conscientious man, taking the safe course, not because the rules tell him so, but because it is his nature."[25]

So who became a locomotive engineer and how? From the dawn of railroading, companies sought out young men—women did not win rec-ognition until late in the twentieth century—who were deemed to be honest, dependable, and sober. Those who met these requirements and who had a knowledge and fondness for things mechanical were ideal can-didates. In that dominant nineteenth-century agricultural society, future engineers commonly came from farming backgrounds, where youngsters had a familiarity with tools and the art of machine repair. But these future hoggers might hail from urban areas, where they had had exposure to blacksmithing or a related trade. Frequently, these lads had only limited formal education, even well into the twentieth century.

Engineers seemingly liked their jobs. Not only was their pay generally good, but they gained positive recognition from colleagues, friends, and neighbors. Even on the lowliest pikes, including the narrow-gauge Mis-souri Southern, this apparently held true. The railroad's first locomotive, which burned pine knots, produced plenty of black, acrid smoke. "The engineer and fireman had little protection from the resinous black smoke that wafted back over them, but because of the prestige aspects of their job, they probably gave little thought to such slight discomforts," ruminated a lifelong resident who lived along this fifty-four-mile road. "Even with their sooty and begrimed faces, they were looked up with much of the same type of admiration and respect we accord our Astronauts today."[26]

The process of gaining access to the right-hand seat in the locomotive cab was relatively simple. Future engineers started out as firemen, a dirty and backbreaking job. Much of this crewman's time was consumed stoking and watching the firebox and regulating the supply of oxygen to the burning fuel. If the locomotive used wood, the fireman had to carry the logs from the attached tender to the deck. Coal, though, could be scooped directly into the firebox. In time mechanical stokers lessened the physical burden, as did introduction of oil-burning engines. Later the diesel revolution changed everything. A "boomer" fireman described the rigors of the job prior to the advent of the much-appreciated technology replacements:

> Now on most of those fast passenger trains in those days made that one hundred and forty-five mile run over the Hudson division [of the New York Central between New York City and Albany] in about two hours and forty-five minutes. And I have been told by some of the firemen on those fast runs, that they never left the deck to climb upon their seat boxes to sit down for a moment, for they were kept busy shoveling coal into the roaring hot fire box in order to keep the engine hot so that the engineer could make the time, and the best they got was to step to one side of the gangway and suck in a few breaths of cool air until they reached the end of their runs.[27]

Seniority affected everyone in the cab. It did not take long for railroads to establish a nearly universal system where the hiring date of an employee placed him on a list for job promotion and protection. A fireman gained experience by watching the actions of the engineer, and it was not unknown for the engineer to allow his fireman to take the throttle. Companies had extra boards, and so a qualified fireman, when needed, could work temporarily as an engineer. In time, if all went well, the fireman became the highly respected and better paid engineer.

The work of passenger conductors, or "captains"; brakeman; and other train crew members was in some ways more attractive. The conductor ruled the train, although he might spar with an independent-minded engineer. "The conductor was the one contact between the company and the passengers," opined one commentator, "to them he was the company." Usually this elite trainman began his career as a brakeman and then worked as a conductor on a freight train, and with good job performance and seniority, advancement took place. Toward the end of the nineteenth century, a conductor for the East Tennessee, Virginia & Georgia Railroad (Southern Railway component) made this observation: "The majority of conductors in this section of the county commenced braking on a

freight-train, or as flagman or baggage-master, and worked themselves up to freight conductor, and on up to passenger conductor." These captains required only a modest education, needing to be able to read and write and do simple arithmetic. Their duties were usually clean and relatively comfortable. Yet conductors had to manage their subordinates and passengers; the latter likely posed greater challenges. At times conductors had to be something of a politician to survive. "The railroad conductor is eminently a practical man," observed *Harpers Monthly* in 1874. "He is apt to be a self-made man."[28]

Brakemen, flagmen, and others usually had advanced through the seniority ranks from freight to passenger train service. Before air brakes, the brakeman (perhaps two) needed to handle the pesky brake wheels located on the car platforms. Still, this was highly preferable to turning braking devices located on the tops of freight cars, which necessitated walking along the moving train in all kinds of weather. Prior to the advent of knuckle, or "Janney," couplers in the post–Civil War years, brakemen also faced the dangerous task of managing link and pin couplers.[29]

As with all crewmen, hours on duty were long and daily. Eventually legal limits on the hours of service for train personnel went into effect. In 1907 the federal government limited continuous work to sixteen hours. Nine years later the Adamson Act strengthened this measure by mandating the eight-hour day. Not until after World War II did annual vacations

Early in the twentieth century, various employees, travelers, and visitors pose for a photographer at the Chicago & North Western depot in Oakland, Nebraska. The agent is probably the one standing in front of the bay-window office wearing a white shirt and cap. To his left are likely other railroad and express workers.

Author's Collection

In this unidentified photograph taken at the turn of the twentieth century in a combination-style depot, an agent is at work in his office. Located near him are the ticket case and dater that will be used prior to the train-time rush.

Author's Collection

become the norm, meaning that if an employee wished to take time off, he did so without pay.

On a typical railroad, hundreds of support personnel made passenger operations possible. Critical to this function were employees who served as train dispatchers and station agents. The former men, occasionally women, had the nerve-racking job of making certain that trains, both freight and passenger, ran safely over a division, usually one hundred miles or so in length or along even longer distances. They would telegraph or later telephone tower operators and depot agents to inform engineers and conductors of where to pass slower trains or where to take sidings for faster-moving ones. They would also receive telegraphic or telephone reports from these sources when trains passed designated locations. Agents, who included some women, not only assisted in train movements but also met the public when they planned travel itineraries; sold tickets; managed baggage, less-than-carload and carload freight; and performed other duties. As with the train crews, dispatchers and agents had similar backgrounds. The former were nearly always former agents, ones who had thoroughly mastered that cryptic Morse code and who accepted the pressures of the train dispatching. The latter were often youngsters from villages and towns who at an early age hung out at the depot, where they did chores for agents, including sweeping floors; cleaning windows; filling coal buckets, hand lanterns, and switch lamps; and running errands. In return for such tasks, agents taught them how to send and receive telegraphic messages and to do station bookkeeping and other tasks. This was classic on-the-job training, comparable to the unpaid internship of today.

From the time of the first scheduled railroad service, Americans overwhelmingly embraced this revolutionary form of travel. Yet as with every new technology, there were detractors. "This railroad is a pestilential, topsy-turvy, harum scarum, whirligig scheme," editorialized the *Vincennes* (Indiana) *Western Sun*. "Give me the old, solemn, straightforward, regular Dutch canal—three miles an hour for expresses and two for jog or trot journeys. I go for beasts of burden; it is more primitive and scriptural and suits a moral and religious people better. None of your hop, skip and jump whimsies for me."[30]

Notwithstanding individuals who preferred the tried and true, Americans mostly found railroads to be exciting, fast, safe, and dependable. A passenger who rode the New Castle & Frenchtown Rail Road (later part of the Pennsylvania) in late 1832 wrote, "Not an incident happened to break the spell of the enchantment which we all felt in cutting the air at this rate—the houses and trees all seemed to be rapidly passing us, and sometimes a bird would, when we were descending, look to the eye as if its wings were of no use to it." A few years later, renowned traveler and writer Freeman Hunt recounted his trip over the recently opened Rensselaer & Saratoga Railway (later the Delaware & Hudson). "The arrangement for carrying passengers are quite extensive. There are twenty-four cars belonging to the company—at once spacious, elegant, and convenient." He went on to comment, "The passage over the islands to Waterford, and indeed the whole route to Balston and Saratoga Springs is really delightful. The engineers are experienced, and, although 'flying as it were on the wings of the wind,' one feels perfectly safe from accident." In 1835, a director of the Boston & Wooster Rail Road (later New York Central System), upon entering a company meeting in Boston, said, "Well, here we are, friends—we came by rail almost fifty-two miles in less than three hours." Arguably Nathaniel Hawthorne captured the public's attitude toward the developing railway age when he wrote in *The House of Seven Gables*, "Railroads are positively the greatest blessing that the ages have wrought out for us. They give us wings; they annihilate the toil and dust of pilgrimage; they spiritualize travel!"[31]

Positive responses to rail travel have long persisted, and for many they continue to this day. Americans, most of all, love speed. Until the appearance of airplanes, trains were the fastest commercial vehicles on the planet. The iron horse could move faster than any flesh hay-burner and could sustain its speeds. In 1869 a rider on the recently opened Virginia & Truckee Railroad, headquartered in Carson City, Nevada, expressed this widely held feeling: "Nothing is more exhilarating than speed. It is physically and mentally exciting. You feel—well, just as happy as a big sunflower and you think quick, pleasantly and liberally. So we felt and thought a great deal as we sped across the plain." When compared to other land travel, even with the fully developed automobile age, the steam-powered train was viewed as being fast, and incredibly so with the much later *Acela*-type trains.[32]

Speed records or unusually fast runs captivated Americans. New Englanders and others elsewhere were abuzz when they learned of the first mile-a-minute run. In 1848 this historic accomplishment occurred on the Boston & Maine Railroad (B&M) between Boston and South Lawrence, Massachusetts. At the request of Charles Minot, B&M general superintendent and later the great innovator at the Erie Railroad, the appropriately named locomotive *Antelope* and a single coach filled with railroad officials and newspaper reporters made this trip in exactly twenty-six minutes. Part of the run, though, was over a poor stretch of track, and the primitive strap-iron rails "flew up behind in a shower of curling snakeheads." By the time the train reached its destination, the extremely hot boiler had blistered off most of the gilt and red lacquer paint on the locomotive. This lightning-fast experience rattled the fourth estate. "The reporters were in no shape to write their copy until they had been treated at the nearest sample room by the populace. [They] said they never purposed to duplicate the performance. It was plainly against the will of God."[33]

While a sixty-mile-per-hour trip over a considerable length of rail line was most impressive for a railroad at mid-century, a much better remembered speed record occurred forty-five years later. On May 10, 1893, New York Central No. 999, a husky, high-stepping American Standard (4-4-0)-type locomotive, pulled the first train in the world to attain a speed of over 100 miles per hour, running a mile in allegedly thirty-two seconds (112.5 miles per hour) near Batavia, New York. This racer pulled more than a single car, having a consist of a diner-coach, two coaches, and a parlor car. Although it was a well-planned event, the *Empire State Express* was on a regularly scheduled run, and fare-paying passengers were potentially being placed in harm's way for the sake of corporate publicity. But all went well. Soon the Central proudly put the engine on display at the World's Columbian Exposition, which was then being held in Chicago, and where it became a star attraction. In fact, so great was this accomplishment that in 1901 the US Post Office portrayed the famed No. 999 on the two-cent postage stamp.[34]

Other examples of contemporary ballast scorching took place. On November 16, 1886, a locomotive and two-car Michigan Central train raced on its Canada Southern Division from Saint Clair Junction to Windsor, Ontario, in ninety-seven minutes and included several stops. The average speed was about sixty-nine miles per hour, and in places the special reached seventy-five or more miles per hour. Then in July 1905 one of the more amazing speed records was established. Walter "Death Valley Scotty" Scott, a mine owner who adored speed, arranged for the Santa Fe to operate a special train that would dash along its main line between Los Angles and Chicago. Dubbed the *Coyote Special* and costing Scott a whopping $5,500 ($135,500 in current dollars), the train consisted of a locomotive, baggage car, diner, and Pullman observation car. The trip, which necessitated a series of locomotive and crew changes, took just forty-four hours and fifty-four minutes to cover the 2,265-mile route, averaging 50.4 miles per hour. At times the *Coyote Special* achieved great speeds, clocking 106 miles per hour between the Illinois communities of Cameron and Surry. It even made good time over some of the heaviest grades on this transcontinental line. Scott and the Santa Fe took pride in this exceptional run, which shattered the previous record by more than seven hours.[35]

Regularly scheduled passenger trains also scorched the rails. Although the vast majority of passenger train movements operated at slow or modest speeds on branch and secondary main lines, a number of deluxe named trains sped over "high iron" between major terminals. A red-letter day occurred on June 15, 1902. On that date the two greatest passenger roads in the nation, the Pennsylvania (PRR) and New York Central System, embarked upon what was called the "Great Speed War" between New York City and Chicago. PRR trains Nos. 28 and 29, known as the *Pennsylvania Special* but later rebranded as the *Broadway Limited*, raced between New York City (Jersey City) and Chicago, a distance of nearly a thousand miles in twenty hours, cutting eight hours off the fastest schedule. Three years later these PRR trains reduced the time to just eighteen hours. The Central would not be outdone. The same day that the PRR offered travelers a twenty-hour trip, its rival introduced the *Twentieth Century Limited*, and it, too, connected Gotham with the Windy City in twenty hours. When the PRR slashed the running time to eighteen hours, so did the Central. Ironically each railroad billed its marque varnish as the "Fastest Long Distance Train in the World." Competition continued to mean speed on the rails, and for the PRR and Central, this lasted into the diesel era.[36]

The Pennsylvania and New York Central were determined to maintain speed, and some would say at any cost. Engineers understood that if they fell behind their schedule, they must make up as much lost time as possible. On the inaugural trip of the faster *Pennsylvania Limited* in 1905, the westbound train developed a hotbox on the locomotive, which caused a twenty-six-minute delay, but replacement power was quickly found. The engineer opened the throttle of the 4-4-2 Atlantic and ran hot. The *Limited* claimed to cover the 131.4 miles between Crestline, Ohio, and Fort Wayne, Indiana, in just 115 minutes, and for the three miles near Elida, Ohio, it boasted a world speed record of 127.1 miles per hour. "It is almost as easy to mark the flight of an artillery shell as that of a train making from 85 to 100 miles an hour," observed an amazed correspondent for the *Chicago Tribune*.[37]

For much of the passenger-train era, speed reigned supreme. In 1900 the public cherished such speedsters as the B&O's *Royal Limited*, Central's *Empire State Express*, the PRR and Reading's Camden–Atlantic City expresses, and the Wabash's *Continental Limited*. It was hardly surprising that a writer for the mass-circulation *World's Work* magazine in 1907 described this passion for speed and explained a troubling consequence. "Our railroads kill their thousands every month in wreck or trespass. In more than half the cases, the real truth underlying the tragedy is the fact that the train was running at forty or fifty or sixty miles an hour over tracks that were built for trains that never ran but thirty miles an hour. The people demand it. The railroads must obey." He added, "Each year, the manufacturers of locomotives are called upon by the big lines to produce and deliver more and more engines that can haul a ten-car passenger train at sixty miles an hour. The cry is ever for more speed." And for decades that publication's assessment generally rang true. Yet railroads did improve their physical plants with heavier rail, better curve elevations, grade reductions, and line cutoffs for higher sustained speeds, along with better safety devices and employee training.[38]

It would be during the Great Depression that additional speed records were set. Carriers needed to respond to hard times and the growing popularity of private automobiles and commercial buses and airplanes. Steam locomotives continued to pound the rails with their named-train consists, and newly introduced diesel-electrics did the same. Just as the rivalry between the PRR and Central in 1902 produced that dramatic reduction in the time of travel between New York and Chicago, a similar competitiveness erupted between the three premier railroads that linked Chicago and the Twin Cities. It became a battle for speed between the Burlington, North Western, and Milwaukee Road on this highly competitive route. The North Western led the way on January 2, 1935, with introduction of its *400* crack standard-weight, steam-powered trains. These "new aristocrats of the rails" clipped hours from the previous fastest time between Chicago, Milwaukee, and the Twin Cities: four hundred miles in four hundred minutes. However, neither the Burlington nor Milwaukee Road was asleep at the switch. Soon the former introduced its diesel-powered *Twin Cities Zephyr* streamliners, and the latter its steam-powered *Hiawatha*,

In the mid-1930s the Milwaukee Road responded to the speed race between competitors Burlington and North Western for the Chicago–Twin Cities passenger trade with its streamlined rolling stock. A pair of powerful Hudson-type 4-6-4 steam locomotives grace the cover of this timetable folder.

Author's Collection

"the First of the Speedliners." By the end of the 1930s, both the North Western and Milwaukee Road operated diesel streamliners as well.[39]

The public approved, reading about or watching these positive happenings during a time of economic trauma—new sleek trains, fast speeds. The June 1935 issue of the *Milwaukee Magazine* shared with employees the excitement of the test run of the *Hiawatha*:

> At 91 m.p.h. everyone remarked that it didn't seem as though the *Hiawatha* was traveling much faster than about 45. At 100 m.p.h. a shout went up. One hundred and one, they calculated; 103.5, then 105, 105.5; faster and faster it went until 109 miles per hour the *Hiawatha* decided that that was a very comfortable pace and continued along at that speed for five or six miles without a change, but as interest began to wane in seeing 109 mile per hour marked up as mile after mile went by Ed Donahue, the man at the throttle, gave it another notch and in very short order there were figures of 110.5, 111.3 and the 112.5 m.p.h.

Engineer Donahue summarized the *Hiawatha's* performance: "Faster it ran, the better it rode."[40]

Following World War II, those longtime passenger rivals, PRR and Central, did not rest on their speed laurels. In September 1948 the Central inaugurated a state-of-the-art streamlined diesel-powered *Twentieth Century Limited*. Built by Electro-Motive and Pullman-Standard, the train operated between New York City and Chicago on a sixteen-hour schedule. And the *Broadway Limited* matched this impressive speed.[41]

While comfort never characterized travel on poky locals or combination freight-passenger accommodations—"mixed trains"—it unquestionably highlighted the better trains. Just as rolling stock evolved rapidly during the nineteenth century, so did creature comforts. By the post–Civil War period, the quality of train travel rivaled or surpassed the best that coastal, lake, or river vessels could offer. Yet in the demonstration period, especially during the 1830s, complaints about coaches were more common than not. "This morning at nine o'clock I took passage in a railroad car [on the Boston & Providence Rail Road] from Boston for Providence. Five or six other cars were attached to the locomotive, and uglier boxes I do not wish to travel in," wrote an annoyed Samuel Breck. "They were made to stow away some thirty human beings, who sit cheek by jowl as best they can."[42]

During Breck's lifetime those uncomfortable "boxes" could no longer be found on the busier rail routes and much less so on the minor lines. Most had been sent to junkyards, relegated to work trains, employed as wayside shelters or storage sheds, or used for some other adaptive purpose. In 1869 an accountant for R. G. Dun & Company said it well: "Cars are infinitely preferable to our old fashioned ones." In the early 1880s, a trade journal writer repeated much the same about travel during the early years. "Sleeping-cars were undreamed of; comfortable seats were

In the late 1930s a Kishacoquillas Valley mixed train works at the Pennsylvania Railroad interchange at Reedsville, Pennsylvania. A vintage baggage car and coach are attached in the customary fashion to the rear of the freight cars.

Robert G. Lewis photograph, Author's Collection

not devised. There have been no good old days in railroading." By the latter half of the nineteenth century, the commonly used two-by-two seats with reversible backs adequately served day-coach riders. In cold weather a pot-bellied stove supplied warmth. Admittedly there were complaints about too much or insufficient heat, but those early cars lacked any heat source, forcing passengers to bundle up and perhaps take along foot or lap warmers. And by that time kerosene lamps had largely replaced tin-plated candle sconces for illumination. Within two decades the popular Pintsch gas lamps also had appeared. Soon electric lights made their debut. Moreover, chair cars had become relatively spacious, although seating might remain somewhat cramped. Unlike in the pioneer equipment, toilet facilities were available, relieving one of the excruciating discomforts of any train trip. A satisfied traveler, who journeyed from his home in Detroit to Chicago on the Chicago & Grand Trunk Railway, in a November 18, 1888, letter to his sister in England, remarked on the features of a typical coach. "The cars have the entrances at each end opening from a railed platform reached by means of steps on either side. The seats are placed on either side of the car leaving an aisle or passage through the centre—and usually face the way the train is going. They seat 2 people each. The backs of the seats are reversible thus a party of four can sit two and two facing each other." There were these amenities: "Overhead are metal racks fitted to the sides of the car to hold parcels, etc. The windows are fitted with latticed wooden

Pennsylvania
Railroad
The Standard Railroad of the World

Dining Car
MENU

Pennsylvania Station, New York—one of the cross-roads of world travel

Christmas on the Railroad

Christmas holidays are fittingly a time of home-coming, family reunions, and visits to those held dear. There is unmistakably a " going home " expression on the traveler's face.

Happily the railroad may participate in this observ-ance of the spirit of Christmas by making the holiday journey a real part of it.

On the Pennsylvania Railroad more than 175,000 men are helping to give you a safe, comfortable, and pleasant trip.

In no better way could they tell you that they wish you a Merry Christmas.

Is There a Santa Claus?

Little Virginia O'Hanlon, perplexed by this question, wrote to the Editor of the *New York Sun*. The following editorial from the pen of Francis P. Church answered the question for all time:

"Yes, Virginia, there is a Santa Claus. He exists as certainly as love and generosity and devotion exist, and you know that they abound and give to your life its highest beauty and joy. Alas! how dreary would be the world if there were no Santa Claus! It would be as dreary as if there were no Virginias. There would be no childlike faith then, no poetry, no romance to make tolerable this existence. We should have no enjoyment, except in sense and sight. The eternal light with which childhood fills the world would be extinguished. Not believe in Santa Claus! You might as well not believe in fairies! You might get men to watch in all the chimneys on Christmas eve to catch Santa Claus, but even if they did not see Santa Claus coming down, what would that prove? Nobody sees Santa Claus, but that is no sign that there is no Santa Claus. The most real things in the world are those that neither children nor men can see. Did you ever see fairies dancing on the lawn? Of course not, but that's no proof that they are not there. Nobody can conceive or imagine all the wonders that are unseen and unseeable in the world.

You tear apart the baby's rattle to see what makes the noise inside, but there is a veil covering the unseen world which not the strongest man, nor even the united strength of all the strongest men that ever lived could tear apart. Only faith, fancy, poetry, love, romance, can push aside that curtain and view and picture the supernal beauty and glory beyond. Is it all real? Ah, Virginia, in all this world there is nothing else real and abiding.

No Santa Claus! Thank God! he lives, and he lives forever. A thousand years from now, Virginia, nay, ten times ten thousand years from now, he will continue to make glad the heart of childhood."

BEVERAGES

	Bottle
Pale Moon	30
Cereal Beverages	25
Ginger Ale (Imported)	40
Ginger Ale (Domestic)	30
Ginger Ale (Dry)	35
Sarsaparilla (Imported)	35
Sarsaparilla (Domestic)	25
Grape Juice (Individual)	20
Lemonade (Carbonated)	20-25
Lemonade (Plain) (Glass)	10
Orangeade (Glass)	25
Coca-Cola	Split 10

MINERAL WATERS

Carbonated	Split 20-25
Carbonated	Bottle 25-30-35
Natural	35-30
Purgative	20
Vichy	Split 30-40
Bromo-Seltzer	15

BRIAR PIPE 75

CIGARETTES

Assorted Brands 20-25
Cigarettes will not be sold within the state of Ohio.

CIGARS

Imported	25-35
Domestic	10; 2 for 25; 15-20

PLAYING CARDS

Straight or Pinochle Decks	60
Bridge Decks (2)	1.20

CANDIES

Pulled Cream Mints 25
Ultra Assorted 35
Chocolate Peppermints, half pound 60
Assorted Chocolates, half pound 65

Aspirin Tablets 25

FIELD-14-21-21-25

The name of your waiter is

DINNER

SOUPS—Puree of Yellow Split Peas 35; Cup 25
Clam Bouillon, Hot or Cold 30
Clear Green Turtle 80 — Consomme 35; Cup 25

RELISHES—Sliced Tomatoes 40 — Mixed Pickles 30 — Midget Gherkins 30
Sweet Pickled Onions 30 — Celery 35

OYSTERS AND FISH—Oysters, Fried, Chili Sauce 80
Stewed in Cream 75 — Stewed in Milk 60
Filets of Sole, Saute, Fine Herbs 80
Kippered Herring on Toast 45

SPECIAL DINNER $1.10

PLEASE WRITE ON MEAL CHECK "SPECIAL DINNER" AND EACH ITEM DESIRED

Filets of Sole, Tartar Sauce
Hashed Browned Potatoes — String Beans
or
Fricassee of Veal with Mushrooms
Mashed Potatoes — Green Peas
or
Individual Boneless Chicken Pie
New Beets in Butter
or
Roast Prime Ribs of Beef
Browned Potatoes — Creamed Carrots and Celery
or
Vegetarian Dinner with Poached Egg
Includes Bread, Rolls or Muffins and Tea, Coffee, Cocoa or Milk

Omelet with Stewed Fresh Cranberries, Glazed Sweet Potatoes 85
Minute Steak, French Fried or Hashed Browned Potatoes 1.00

ROAST—Leg of 1926 Prize Lamb with String Beans and Rissole Potatoes 1.20
GRILLED—Lamb Chop 55 — Young Chicken (Half) 1.25 — Sirloin Steak 1.50
Ham and (1) Egg 65; (2) Eggs 80
Bacon and (1) Egg 65; (2) Eggs 80
Ham 80; Half Portion 45
Bacon 80; Half Portion 45; per Slice 15
EGGS AND OMELETS—Poached on Toast (2) 50
Eggs—Boiled, Fried, Shirred or Scrambled (1) 30; (2) 40
Omelets, (2) Eggs, Plain 55; Ham, Parsley or Jelly 70
COLD MEATS, ETC.—Boiled Ham 80 — Ox Tongue 85
Sliced Chicken 1.00 — Roast Beef 85
Assorted Cold Meats 1.10 — Pickled Lamba Tongue Vinaigrette 65
Potato Salad Served with Cold Meats if Desired
Imported Sardines 60 — Baked Beans (Hot or Cold) 45
VEGETABLES—Carrots, Saute 30 — Lima Beans 30 — Peas 30
String Beans 30 — Creamed Carrots and Celery 30 — Beets in Butter 30
Stewed Tomatoes 30 — New Spinach with Egg 35
Potatoes:— Baked Idaho Russet 30 — Boiled 25 — Mashed 25
French Fried 30 — Glazed Sweet 30 — Hashed Browned 30
SALADS—Apple and Celery, Mayonnaise 65
Head Lettuce, French Dressing 40; with Tomato 60
Pineapple or Egg, French Dressing 55 — Chicken 90
Combination 60 — Asparagus, Vinaigrette 50 — Potato 40
Dressings:— Mayonnaise 20 — Russian 25 — Roquefort 25
BREAD, ETC.—Vienna, Raisin, Graham or Rye 15 — Rolls 15
Toast—Dry, Buttered or Raisin 20; Milk 30
Boston Brown 15 — Bran Muffins (2) 15
Doughnuts (2) 15 — Whole Wheat Wafers 15
Bran Cookies 15 — Crackers 10
DESSERTS—Fig or Plum Pudding, Fruit Sauce 35
Apple Pie 25; Deep Dish Blueberry Pie (Baked on Car To-day) 30
Baked Apple with Cream 25 — Raw Apple 15
Orange 20 — Grape Fruit 30
French Ice Cream 35; with Crushed Pineapple 45
Preserved Figs in Syrup 45 — Preserved Strawberries 30
Orange Marmalade 30 — Hawaiian Pineapple 30
Old Virginia Fruit Cake 25 — Bar le Duc 35
Guava Jelly 30 — Wafers 15
Stewed Fresh Cranberries 25
CHEESE AND CRACKERS—Imperial 30 — Swiss Gruyere 35
Cream 30 — Camembert 35 — Roquefort 40 — Yeast Cake 10
COFFEE, TEA, ETC.—
Coffee, Tea, Postum, Cocoa (Pot for One) 25 — (Demitasse) 15
Koffee Hag or Sanka Coffee (Pot for One) 25
Certified Milk (Individual Bottle) 20 — Malted Milk 25
Service charge of twenty-five cents will be made
for each person served outside of Dining Car.
Pay only upon presentation of check; see that extensions and totals are correct.
Passengers are requested to report any unusual service or attention on the part of the employees. This enables us to recognize the exceptional efficiency which we wish to encourage in our service.
D. N. Bell, Passenger Traffic Manager, Philadelphia, Pa.
F. W. Conner, Passenger Traffic Manager, Pittsburgh, Pa.
C. E. Milliron, Superintendent, Dining Car Service, New York.

................................., Steward in Charge

---

shutters or sun blinds—which slide up and down as do the windows. From the roof along the centre of the car, the ornamental lamps descend. On a bracket in the corner is a tank of ice cold drinking water and a cup. In a corner stands the small heater furnace, steam pipes from which pass all around the cars and under each seat. While in the opposite corner is a W.C. [water closet]." At the turn of the twentieth century, a coach on the Colorado Midland Railway, "which operated passenger equipment equal to that of any standard-gauge line in the country," impressed the commentator. "The coach in which I rode seated about fifty-five persons. It was elegantly finished and furnished with mahogany and oak panels, bronze trimmings, four massive gas lamps, highbacked mahogany seats upholstered in maroon and old-gold plush, lavishly decorated ceilings, and little embossed glass windows in the clerestory." The account concluded: "It had a smoking compartment, done in mahogany and at large plate-glass mirror, and two salons with marble washstands and tin basins."[43]

Sleeping cars likewise became more comfortable and pleased those who demanded luxury as a birthright. "I delayed a journey because I could not get a Pullman berth," admitted an individual who sought personal pampering. That Detroit-to-Chicago traveler had no complaints about the Pullman equipment, and he offered this description: "Entering from the rear platform, I find myself in the smoking room. In one corner by the door is the Gentleman's lavatory. Marble topped with two marble basins sunk in level with the top. Two silver plated taps to each basis for hot & cold water. Two ditto for ice cold drinking water, clean towels, ad. lib. Tumblers, brushes, combs clothes brushing, etc. all complete." He further elaborated:

> The lavatory is rendered private by rich curtains hung from silver plated rods completely shutting it in, in the opposite corners is a W.C. Passing through a passage at the side of the smoking room I come to the "buffet" or more properly speaking pantry which is supplied with a small oil stove arrangement for making tea, coffee, chocolate and boiling eggs, etc., next comes the main body of the car. This part of the car is divided into 8 sections, 4 on each side. These sections will each hold 4 people. That is a party of 4 can take a section sleeping 2 in the Lower berth and 2 small ones in the upper. Of course if a single passenger takes a berth in any section he has the berth to himself. The seats are upholstered in the blue plush gobelin blue, in the centre panel between the windows is a mirror plate & beveled edges.

The configuration of this sleeping car was one of various floor designs used by the Pullman Company.[44]

By the peak years of intercity passenger travel, which occurred in the 1920s following the end of federal wartime control, equipment on major lines had continually improved, and onboard amenities on premier trains rivaled what might be reserved for royalty. While trips might be recalled fondly, pleasant memories of first-class train travel lasted longer, perhaps indelibly emblazoned in individuals' minds. On a cold, snowy day in January 1918, members of a well-to-do Cedar Rapids, Iowa, family boarded the all-steel *Overland Limited*, which sped over the rails of the North Western and Union Pacific Railroads between Chicago and San Francisco, for their annual winter sojourn to California. The usual consist of this deluxe train included a club-buffet car, which contained a barber and bath; dining car; sleeping cars; drawing-room compartment cars; and an observation car with rear platform. "The first day on the train was just as exciting as getting on it," remembered author and philanthropist Ellen Douglas Williamson, and she found this long-distance train to her satisfaction. "After we had taken turns getting dressed in our narrow floor space, and getting washed up in our small washroom with the shiny nickel-plated washbowl and its toilet, a waiter arrived all the way from the dining car, bringing us breakfast on a huge silver tray. He and George, our porter, set up a table in the adjacent compartment." She elaborated, "The waiter spread a white tablecloth, unloaded his tray, and soon we were peeking into one covered silver dish after another and filling our plates with hot corn muffins, bacon and jam. Besides that we poured hot cocoa from thermos jugs into our cups, and topped them off with whipped cream. Through the windows we could see flat snow-covered Nebraska. We were on our way!"[45]

Middle- and upper-class travelers flocked to Pullmans. By the end of the Roaring Twenties, the company operated nearly ten thousand cars, which were staffed by an army of conductors, porters, and attendants. During these halcyon years, Pullman cars carried as many as thirty-nine million passengers annually, nearly one-third of the nation's population. Pullman had become essentially a giant hotel operation.[46]

What continued to please passengers were multiple features, and the coming of the streamliner era provided additional improvements. Air-conditioning made summertime travel a pleasure. Not only did first-generation streamliners offer this amenity, but many older cars were refitted to supply the much-appreciated "refrigerated air." If the train had a coal-burning locomotive, the annoyances of smoke and the like no longer were part of the trip; open windows were a thing of the past. Moreover, noise levels were reduced, contributing to a more restful journey. Other, often less remarked upon upgrades occurred, ranging from better car suspension systems to non-glare window glass. There also existed the visual benefits of that streamliner look. "The whole point of streamlining is not to lower air resistence," admitted a railroad official, "but to lower passenger resistence [to rail travel]." In the 1930s premier trains developed a modern, sexy appearance, and the traveling public loved them.

Then there was the dining-car experience. Railroad officials came to realize that they were more than people movers; they needed to become food providers. Meal stops continued to disappear as the railway age matured, being replaced by onboard dining. Passengers did not complain. As the senior John D. Rockefeller once described the earlier wayside stops: "You stuff your cheeks like a squirrel and jump back on the train." Time might be limited to only twenty minutes. Many, if not most, of these earliest trackside eateries lacked positive customer qualities, although some were noted for their good food and service. An outstanding illustration was the Logan House, a station restaurant at Altoona, Pennsylvania, opened in the 1850s on the Pennsylvania main line. Patrons loved its bread and pastries and especially its ice cream—"excellent texture and flavor." An English traveler considered the Logan House "better than any in Europe and equal to any in America." Somewhat later Lady Duffus Hardy recalled pleasant meals along the New York to Chicago corridor. "No hotel or dining-cars accompany the morning train from New York, but eating-stations are erected at certain portions of the road, where you may get rid of the most wolfish appetite at an admirably spread table, and plenty of time allowed for the knife and fork engagement." By early in the twentieth century, those famed Harvey Houses, scattered over half the continent, had made their appearance, and patrons raved about their

The Baltimore & Ohio Railroad offered an elegant ambience for its dining-car patrons who traveled on its best trains. This car was one of the "Colonial Class" of diners, and the photograph dates from the 1920s.

William Howes Collection

food, their service, and the attractiveness of the waitresses, the renowned "Harvey Girls."[47]

By the zenith of intercity passenger train travel, the dining-car experience had reached maturity. In 1924 the Bureau of Railway Economics reported that the several scores of railroads that provided this service annually served as many as fifty million meals. For decades patrons had a wide range of breakfast, luncheon, and dinner food choices, finding offerings that surely pleased every palate. One who had ridden the *New England States,* a crack train on the New York Century System, recalled, "Breakfast in the diner—what an unforgettable experience: linen tablecloths, complete silver service, a full menu, large windows affording a panoramic view of the passing landscape. Also at one end of the car is the full though snug kitchen where the staff labors over charcoal stoves to prepare our food. Everything is very fresh and very tasty." A Minnesotan commented about onboard meals: "I would go to the diner, have a seven-course dinner for a dollar and get off at Minneapolis an hour later full of good vittles." The renowned chief chemist of the Department of Agriculture, Dr. Harvey Wiley, best remembered for spearheading the Food

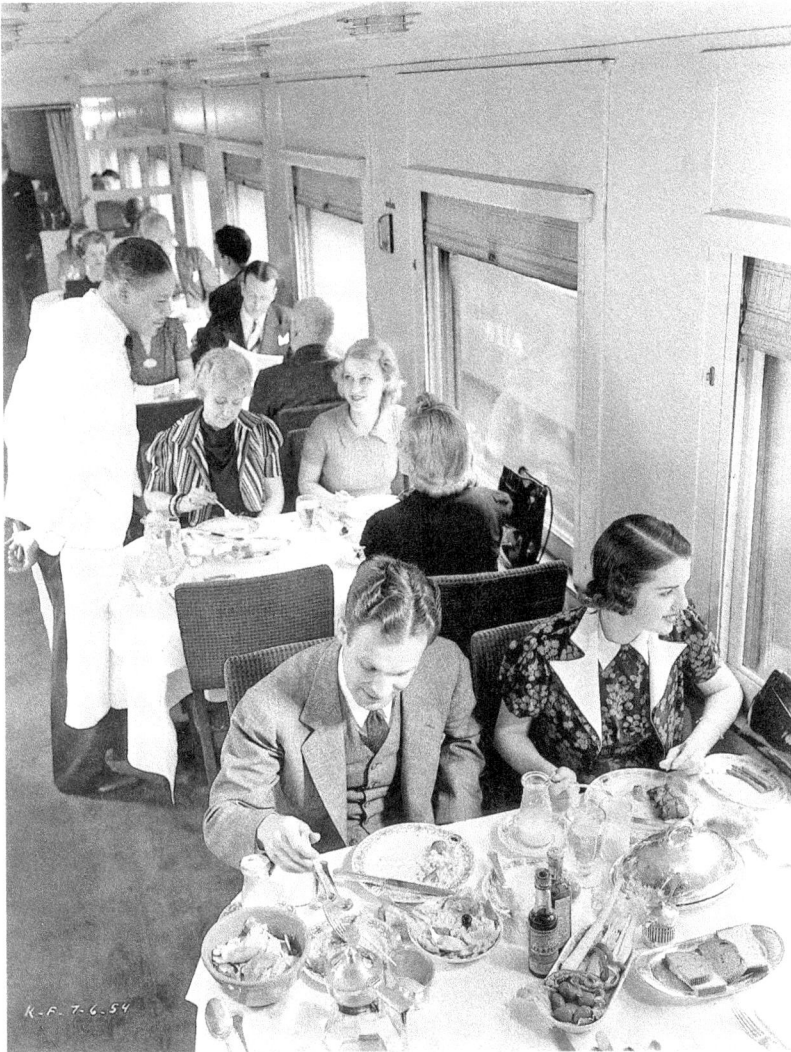

In the 1930s the Chicago & North Western staged this publicity photograph of "Dinner in the Diner" onboard the *Overland Limited*, a crack Chicago to San Francisco train that ran over its rails and those of the Union Pacific and Southern Pacific. Food and service were always memorable.

Author's Collection

and Drug Act of 1906, had this to say about the food quality provided by the Northern Pacific Railway: "Pure food must be the foundation upon which the health of the nation is built, and you have one of the best illustrations of what can be done in feeding the people along the right lines with the right kind of food here in the Northwest in the dining service of the Northern Pacific Railway." He told a Seattle newspaper, "Most of the food which they serve comes from their own model farms, and the way in which it is prepared should be copied by others who wish to serve the public food that is healthful." While dining-car food quality was generally good or improved over time, carriers commonly responded to regional tastes. "Northerners like their marmalade rather tart, while southerners prefer it sweet," recalled a veteran dining-car superintendent. "Southerners also like heavy, syrupy coffee, which Northerners won't stand for." Railroads, too, became known for their signature dishes. There was the

A group of business-men, who are riding in a Baltimore & Ohio club car, are intensely focused on the words of a fellow passenger. A bar attendant dutifully provides liquid refreshments.

William Howes Collection

french toast on the Missouri Pacific; creole entries on the Illinois Central; the salad bowl on the Southern Pacific; the Cuban sandwich, Ybor City–style, on the Atlantic Coast Line; and the Chesapeake Bay fish dinner on the Chesapeake & Ohio. One memorable offering was the "Great Big Baked Potato" served for decades on the Great Northern Railway. It was a monster, measuring on average slightly more than nine inches in length. Ever proud and always promoting, the company went so far as to distrib-ute sheet music about its famed spud, with lyrics written by a Mrs. A. F. Wolfschlager and set to the tune of "You're a Great Big Blue-Eyed Baby." Some railroads pampered children. The Northern Pacific, the principal competitor of the Great Northern, early in the twentieth century created a special "Tiny Tots' Menu." One cover featured this clever verse:

> Little Miss Muffet
> Sat in a buf-et
> Weary of curds and whey;
> Along came a waiter
> Who brought a Big "Tater"—
> Miss Muffet decided to stay![48]

Whether in dining cars, in coaches, in parlor cars, or somewhere else on board, rail passengers resembled all travelers by perhaps relishing conversations with others. There might be much to discuss and learn, especially when businessmen and salesmen gathered in smoking or parlor cars. While traveling from western Pennsylvania to New York City late in the nineteenth century, poet and prose writer Harry Kemp found such exposures fascinating. "In the smoker I listened till late to the talk of the drummers who clenched big black cigars with their teeth, or slender Pittsburgh stogies, expertly flicking off the grey ash with their little fingers, as they yawned."[49]

As with all forms of land and water travel, those who took trains frequently commented positively about the passing landscapes. Typical of the multitude of scenery descriptions is this one made in 1882 by a passenger who rode on the recently opened narrow-gauge South Pacific Coast Railroad between Alameda (San Francisco Bay area) and Santa Cruz, California, a distance of seventy-one miles: "A noticeable feature is the glistening white cones which look like the tents of an army, but are heaps of salt gathered from the marshes where the sun has evaporated the sea water. Flocks of water fowl, including ducks of almost every known variety, suggest abundant pleasure for the sportsman, and numerous gardens, in whose rich black soil vegetables and small fruits are growing luxuriantly, indicate that nature yields liberal returns of the necessaries of life for the minimum of labor," which he observed during the initial part of his trip. As the train continued southward, "We enter the famous Santa Clara valley, which many have pronounced the garden spot of the continent. Here grapes, oranges, lemons, figs, melons, nuts of many kinds and vegetables innumerable flourish abundantly, and the fruits, foliage and climate remind the traveled visitor of southern France and Italy, except that there is a more bracing quality to the air, disposing one to cheerful exercise rather than to indolent dreaming." There was more to savor. "At Los Gatos, we commence the ascent of the Santa Cruz mountains, and from this point on to the end of the road at Santa Cruz bay, every inch of the way abounds in scenery beautiful and grand." Just like stagecoach passengers, railroad travelers found that even the great expanse of mid-America offered opportunities for pleasant viewing. Writing in the later part of the nineteenth century, English novelist Robert Louis Stevenson noted, "But Ohio was not at all as I had pictured it. The country was flat like Holland, but far from being dull. All through Ohio, Indiana, Illinois, and Iowa, or for as much as I saw of them from the train and in my waking moments, it was rich and various, and breathed an elegance peculiar to itself." He added, "The tall corn pleased the eye; the trees were graceful in themselves, and framed the plain into long, aerial vistas; and the clean, bright, gardened townships spoke of country fare and pleasant summer evenings on the stoop. It was a sort of flat paradise." Railroads, especially those that served the West, like the little South Pacific Coast, helped to expose the grandeur of the nation. James J. Hill's Great Northern promoted the concepts of "See America First" and "See More of America." Early in the twentieth century, one response involved attaching open-top cars to the rear of the crack *Oriental Limited* through the Rocky Mountains of Montana.[50]

What did it cost to travel the vastness of America? Fares levied by the pioneer carriers might be considered pricey, approaching ten cents or more per mile, but by the mid-nineteenth century charges had dropped sharply. Competition had slashed them to two and a half or three and a half cents per mile in New England and the Mid-Atlantic states, and up to five cents in the remainder of the country. Then during the reform bursts of the post–Civil War era and into the early years of the next century, railroads voluntarily, or were forced by law to, set prices at the two-to-three-cent level. At times rate wars broke out, providing travelers with incredibly low prices. Examples abound, especially during the 1880s. In 1881 a ticket between New York City and Chicago once dropped to only five dollars. About the same time, the Chicago & Alton and Wabash entered a cutthroat marketing contest, slashing a one-way ticket to just fifty cents for the 280 miles between Chicago and Saint Louis. Companies commonly offered bargain-basement fares for land-seeking, shopping outings, fairs, fraternal and political conventions, or something else. For these special occasions they might average a penny or so per mile. Some went so far as to provide partially free rides. In the 1850s Indiana railroads offered delegates to a temperance convention free passage home "on any railroad upon presentation of a certificate verifying their attendance." Then there were times when passengers jumped on trains at the last minute and negotiated with conductors for reduced fares, expecting trainmen to pocket these cash transactions. Since railroads did not charge for children under age six, required half fare for those after the age of six, and charged full fare when they reached twelve, some parents insisted that their offspring were only five when they were actually seven or eight, or only eleven when they were somewhat older. "Parents often pushed their darlings into a corner between them and the window sill so they could not be observed too closely by the conductor."[51]

Some travelers found a way to ride the rails, to enjoy the scenery, and to do so at costs that were more attractive, namely free. For decades there were individuals, including clergy, journalists, politicians, railroaders, and others, who received complimentary annual or trip passes. Then early in the twentieth century the federal government outlawed free franks to most everyone, except railroad employees and their families. Many more, though, stole rides. "It is no exaggeration to say that every night in the year ten thousand free passengers of tramp genus travel on the different railroads, and that ten thousands more are waiting at watering-tanks and in railroad yards for opportunities to get on the trains," surmised a tramp expert in the late 1890s. "I estimate the professional tramp population at about sixty thousands, a third of whom are generally on the move." While such theft was illegal and frequently dangerous, there was that thrill in seeing new vistas and experiencing different places. "When I was pulled through the door of the boxcar, I was pulled into another world, a world of adventure and hardship," explained a young man who took free passage on both freight and passenger trains. "I felt that my past life had been shut out. I was no longer a plodding farmhand. The idea filled me with an elation hard to describe." Said another, "I stood for long moments at the box-car door and gazed at the passing landscape. Over in the next valley were life and dreams and hopes. Monotony and the wretched routine of a drab Ohio town would be unknown."[52]

There were many free-riding individuals who could not be classified as "professional tramps." Hoboes, or "'bos," usually sought employment, either permanent or temporary, rather than an alternative lifestyle or travel excitement. Beckoning attractions were wide-ranging seasonal jobs, whether harvesting wheat on the Great Plains, picking fruit in the Pacific Northwest, or cutting sugarcane in Louisiana. At times many of these men (and occasionally women and older children) sought jobs that simply did not exist; this was painfully true during the horrific depressions of the 1890s and 1930s. Shortly after the Panic of May 1893 struck Wall Street, a Denver & Rio Grande trainman observed: "The result was that all along the main line were crackling bonfires shooting red tongues into the cold night and casting flickering shadows along the cliffs and fills. From half to a dozen disgruntled men lay around these fires, or huddled over them for warmth." These likely desperate souls were awaiting a passing train for a ride to some anticipated or unknown destination.[53]

How did these determined travelers without tickets make their way? Usually their travel involved hopping trains by riding the rods (using a board—the "universal ticket"—placed on metal support braces) beneath freight cars; taking "side-door Pullmans" (boxcars); standing in the blinds of passenger cars, usually between head-end mail and express cars; or "decking" on top of freight or passenger cars and preferably on a speeding limited or mail train. These places, hopefully concealed from unfriendly train crews and potentially vicious railroad police ("dicks" or "bulls"), could be more than uncomfortable, especially during inclement weather; they were dangerous. The out-of-pocket costs for any trip might be very little. "I dined fairly well on two dollars a week," said a 'bo at the turn of the twentieth century. Of course, there were no train fares to pay. Crew members, however, might shake down unauthorized riders, charging a dollar or so to ride over a division or demanding watches, clothing, or anything of value. Or they might be heartless. In 1882 this "Tramps" account appeared in the *Raleigh News and Observer*: "One of the conductors on the Raleigh & Augusta road [later Seaboard Air Line] found that in an empty box car were no less than fifteen tramps, all asleep and snoring loudly. He locked the door of the car and when he reached Hamlet [North Carolina] they begged to be allowed to get out, saying they wished to go to Charlotte, that some were sick and one had a fit." Added the newspaper, "But their racket didn't work, their car was attached to the Wilmington train, and they were shipped as livestock, east instead of west." This era of tramp and hobo travel generally lasted from after the Civil War until the outbreak of World War II, peaking during hard times. After 1945 hitchhiking grew in popularity until the advent of the Interstate Highway System, which made it more difficult and often illegal to thumb a ride in a passing car or truck.[54]

Just as some 'bos and others sought thrilling experiences; varying degrees of excitement might be part of only a modest rail journey. In January 1908 Mary Baker Eddy, Discoverer and Founder of Christian Science, planned to move permanently from her residence at Pleasant View in Concord, New Hampshire, to Chestnut Hill in Boston, Massachusetts. Being one of the most famous women in America because of her rapidly growing metaphysical faith, she did not wish to be bothered by a bevy of pushy reporters who frequently penned sensationalized accounts of her and her church. The train trip, which Mrs. Eddy organized between the two cities, was superbly executed. Her assistant John Lathrop recalled: "Mrs. Eddy went for her usual [carriage] drive in Concord. In the meantime her household boarded the [Boston & Maine] train of two cars. Instead of returning to Pleasant View, she drove to the station and boarded her special car." Yet her departure became known. "The news spread like wildfire. People scurried. Reporters tried to board the train, but were gently brushed off. Where was Mrs. Eddy going? Was she leaving Concord? were the questions asked. The reporters hastened to telephone to Boston, but just such an emergency had been foreseen by Mrs. Eddy." Her rail travel plan then emerged. "Arrangements had been made to detour [the special train] on the Boston & Albany tracks just before reaching Boston. So Mrs. Eddy arrived at the Chestnut Hill Station, instead of at the Boston North Station, thus avoiding many who had congregated at the North Station to see her arrive [following the expected 75 mile trip]. At the Chestnut Hill Station, carriages awaited her and her party, and within a few minutes she was in her new quarters in her commodious and beautiful new home."[55]

TRAVEL ADVERSITIES

No one who hopped a train failed to encounter some sort of travel adversity. The list is lengthy, ranging from exposure to inclement weather to shakedowns and physical abuse by trainmen and railroad police. Yet for many this was the only practical way to reach employment destinations, to enjoy a rite of male passage, or to escape personal or family problems.

Those individuals who paid for their fares might face hardships or at least petty annoyances, albeit usually never as great as those faced by people who jumped trains. Before the common availability of dining cars and quality trackside eating facilities, passengers habitually complained about not having a decent meal. "Fruit we could buy upon the cars; and now and then we had a few minutes at some station with a meager show of rolls and sandwiches for sale; but we were so many and ravenous that, though I tried at every opportunity, the coffee was always exhausted before I could elbow my way to the counter," observed Robert Louis Stevenson about his 1879 cross-country trip.[56]

Where companies employed mixed trains, passengers often did not relish being in a coach, usually an old one, at the end of a freight train. Schedules were uncertain, being largely dependent on the amount of switching that the crew needed to conduct along the way. "It isn't in the order of things that such trains should travel very rapidly, and sometimes there is considerable growling among the 'traffic,'" commented the *Railroad Gazette* in the late 1880s. These passengers, of course, should have expected departures from the published timetables.[57]

While being unable to acquire a satisfying meal or even a liquid refreshment or enduring a poky "mixed" were hardly the most disappointing aspects of train travel, there were greater concerns. However, it is difficult to say what the worst were. It probably being in a train wreck or getting stranded, especially during a howling blizzard. Children's author Laura Ingalls Wilder expressed a common feeling when in *By the Shores of Silver Lake* she suggested the ever-present dangers of a train journey. "You can not tell what may happen when you go traveling on a train. It is not like starting out all together in a wagon." Yet during the formative decades of railroading, serious accidents were uncommon. Slow speeds, limited train movements, absence of nighttime operations, and a small mileage network explain the mode's relative safety. But somewhat prior to the Civil War, more wrecks and deaths occurred. Increasing speeds, defective tracks, poorly constructed bridges, limited maintenance, or careless crews were the principal culprits. The public became alarmed with several extensively reported disasters. These included the 1853 wreck at South Norwalk, Connecticut, when a New York & New Haven passenger train ran through an open drawbridge and killed forty-eight; the 1867 "Angola Horror," when the trailing cars of the Lake Shore & Michigan Southern's *New York Express* derailed outside Angola, New York, and plunged into Big Sister's Creek, resulting in the death of forty-two passengers; and the time in 1876 when a Lake Shore train broke through a faulty bridge at

Although details of
this wreck on the
Chicago & North West-
ern are not known,
a westbound local,
including a coach,
baggage car, and
Railway Post Office
car, had jumped the
rails on August 1, 1899,
near the Des Moines
River Bridge outside
the Moingona sta-
tion in central Iowa.
The locomotive and
tender are not visible
in this professionally
made photograph.
The mishap drew a
sizable crowd, includ-
ing youngsters who
ventured down the
steep embankment
for a closer look.

Author's Collection

Ashtabula, Ohio, killing eighty-one.[58] For countless railroad passengers there was that persistent fear that something bad would happen. The president of the Connecticut River Railroad, who traveled in August 1869 on the Michigan Central Railroad, commented in his notebook: "The speed of the train is fearful. Nobody seems to desire it. Everybody doubts its expediency."[59]

Although the industry responded to wrecks large and small with improved technologies, maintenance, and employee training, accidents haunted the nation. In 1902 a trade publication commented about "The Week's Accidents": "In the seven days from July 21 to 27, inclusive, 28 serious railway accidents—an average of four every day—were reported, not including numerous derailments and minor wrecks. In these 28 occurrences, 23 lives were lost and more than 60 persons were injured. In 20 of the accidents there was loss of life or personal injury, and 18 of them involved passenger trains." These early years of the new century marked a particularly high amount of carnage. In 1905 the number peaked at 537 passengers killed. The worst single wreck, though, occurred on July 9, 1918, when 101 passengers and crew members, most of whom were African American factory workers, died after two Nashville, Chattanooga & St. Louis passenger trains collided near Nashville, Tennessee. Many more were seriously injured. Human error was to blame.

As with all active transportation forms, passenger deaths have continued. Take what happened on May 12, 2015, when an Amtrak Northeast Regional train headed to New York City from Washington, DC, left the rails at high speed outside Philadelphia. This mishap killed eight passengers and injured more than two hundred. Once again human error explained the tragedy.[60]

Far less deadly than wrecks were trains that had become stranded, usually because of adverse weather. It might be a flood, heavy snow, extreme cold, or some other natural occurrence. A mechanical breakdown might also cause a lengthy delay. In January 1879 a not-so-rare happening took place on the main line of the New York Central & Hudson River Railroad in upstate New York when a blinding blizzard stalled a six-car westbound passenger train east of Batavia. "That day before Batavia lies in memory like a month," wrote Linda Thayer Guilford, a schoolteacher from Cleveland, Ohio. "All morning we were without fire or water. How we crowded around the battered stove in the corner when it was filled once more: How delicious the drink from the tin watering can and its grimy cup after our long waiting: On the cramped seats packed hard by years of use we twisted into every lawful position and found each intolerable after the first moment." In time a brakeman brought this weary passenger "two slices of hot saleratus bread with a lump of stale butter melting between." Finally that night a rescue party arrived. A snowplow, coupled to multiple locomotives, allowed the trapped train to be brought into the welcoming surroundings of the Buffalo station.[61]

As with other modes of transportation, rail travelers might fret about the likelihood of contracting some communicable disease. It could be the common cold or something far worse. Just as canal-boat passengers and canal-town residents feared cholera outbreaks, a variety of deadly or serious illnesses, including cholera, yellow and typhoid fever, measles, tuberculosis, and influenza, disquieted railroad travelers and public health officials. In 1879 the Kentucky Board of Health responded to a yellow fever outbreak by issuing this order: "Whenever a railroad train departs from an infected station no person with fever shall be allowed to take passage on such trains. At a point not less than 50 nor more than 75 miles from the point of departure from an infected place there shall be an entire transfer of passengers and baggage to another train of cars, which train shall never enter an infected district. This transfer shall be made under the supervision of a medical officer." Then in 1893 the federal government enacted this measure that may have lessened traveler anxieties: "No common carrier shall accept for transportation any person suffering with a quarantinable disease, nor any interested article of clothing, bedding or personal property." Yet an even greater concern took place in 1918–1919 when the Spanish influenza pandemic ravaged the country.[62]

When Americans realized that a fatal or life-threatening disease was spreading, they might respond in a proactive fashion. As in past decades some decided to limit their travels or avoid railroad stations and trains altogether. If they did board a coach or Pullman during the time of the Spanish influenza outbreak, vigilant passengers might wear protective masks or take other precautions.

Railroads and public health officials shared a mixed record on combating disease. For decades they posted signs that warned about the dangers of spitting on the floors of trains and depots, along with other unsanitary acts. "All the diseases of the lungs and air passages, also certain other diseases, are spread by dried spit," noted the *Railway Surgical Journal* in 1907. Extensive spitting, in fact, had been ongoing since the dawn of the railway age. In the 1830s a traveler from Worcester to Boston remarked, "Our journey would have been agreeable, except for the annoyance of constant showers of tobacco saliva squirted on the floor at our feet." At times employees either did not understand or did not care about other health hazards. Generally cars, particularly on local or branchline trains, were not fumigated or sterilized, and at best seats and headrests received only cursory cleaning. Railroads that operated crack main line trains and the Pullman Company maintained higher standards of cleanliness and hygiene. Then there was the matter of onboard toilets. Until more recent times, cars lacked chemical retention commodes, and human waste went directly onto the tracks. This increased the possibilities for the spread of cholera, typhoid, and similar feces-borne illnesses, most of all among railroad maintenance workers who walked or worked along the rights-of-way.[63]

While fears of an impending accident, threats of disrupting weather, or the prospect of contracting a sickness lingered in the minds of many travelers, reoccurring complaints centered on fellow passengers, resembling patron comments about those who used *all* forms of public transportation. "Everybody talks to you, or to anybody else who hits his fancy," observed Charles Dickens, who in 1842 rode on the Boston & Lowell Railroad. And he was annoyed:

> If you are an Englishman, he expects that that railroad is pretty much like an English railroad. If you say "No," he says "Yes?" (interrogatively), and asks in what respect they differ. You enumerate the heads of difference, one by one, and he says "Yes?" (still interrogatively), to each. Then he guesses that you don't travel faster in England; and on your replying that you do, says "Yes?" again (still interrogatively), and it is quite evident, doesn't believe it. After a long pause he remarks, partly to you, and partly to the knob on the top of his stick, that "Yankees are reckoned to be considerable of a go-ahead people too;" upon which *you* say "Yes," and then *he* says "Yes" again (affirmatively this time); and upon your looking out of the window, tells you that behind that hill, some three miles from the next station, there is a clever town in a smart lo-ca-tion [*sic*], where he expects you have con-cluded [*sic*] to stop.

There was more to this bothersome exchange. "Your answer in the negative naturally leads to more questions in reference to your intended route (always pronounced rout); and wherever you are going, you invariably learn that you can't get there without immense difficulty and danger, and that all the great sights are somewhere else."[64]

Charles Dickens, this most distinguished antebellum traveler, also found it irritating that railroad passengers were thrown together, a situation that dominated coaches until the advent of sleepers and other extra-fare accommodations. He preferred to be with the "civilized" or "gentleman" class of passengers. Another Englishman, Thomas Cather, agreed. While riding in the South somewhat earlier, he discovered a "troubling" societal mix. There was "the slaveholder from the South, the abolitionist from the North, the merchant, the Congress man, the lawyer, the artizan [sic] and labourer, all huddled together in glorious equality, smelling of antifogmatics, and in the most independent manner, spitting and smoking almost in each other's faces." A displeased Cather went on to say, "One man thinks himself as much entitled as another to dub himself gentleman. If they could assume the character along with the name, it would add immeasurably to the comfort of those who travel among them." Still another English resident, Isabella Bird Bishop, was not so pleased with her fellow passengers when in 1856 she traveled by train across Illinois. "What strange people crammed the cars! Traders, merchants, hunters, diggers, trappers, and adventurers from every land, most of them armed to the teeth."[65]

Long before the advent of extra-fare accommodations that produced a class-like system, passenger cars frequently segregated women and children from "coarse and vile" males. As early as the 1840s, Dickens, for one, noted that on the Boston & Lowell there was "a gentlemen's car and a ladies' car." Although there were no first- and second-class coaches in the consist, he explained that "the main distinction between which is, that in the first everybody smokes; and in the second, nobody does." Added Dickens, "If a lady take a fancy to any male passenger's seat, the gentleman, who accompanies her gives him notice of the fact, and he immediately vacates it with great politeness." Railroad managements refined the segregation of sexes in these semipublic spaces. In the 1880s, the Burlington was one company that placed "palace smoking cars" for "the comfort of male passengers" on its best trains.[66]

For decades there existed that not-so-attractive mixing of men and women in open section sleeping cars. Theresa Yelverton (Viscountess Avonmore) did not care for such arrangements when she traveled on the Overland Route to San Francisco not long after the opening of what she called "the biggest railroad in creation!" Her thoughts: "There are no special cars for ladies, and if your opposite neighbour is a gentleman in the day, in all probability you will have him on your shelf at night, and it will be well for you if he does not either snore or have nightmare." There was more. "Although you have blankets, sheets, and pillows, you have to go to bed in your boots—at least, ladies have, and indeed they cannot undress at all, because they cannot shroud themselves behind the curtains without placing themselves in recumbent positions. Besides, what could be done with their clothing?"[67]

Then there was racial segregation. Even in the North, prior to the Civil War African Americans often felt the sting of the forced separation from whites. When traveling from Baltimore to York, Pennsylvania, in the late 1830s, a traveler observed this racial arrangement: "What surprised me was the baggage wagon, in which three divisions were found, the first for baggage, the second for Negroes, and the third for specific destinations." The advent of state-enacted Jim Crow laws during the post–Civil War years became part of *all* public travel in the Southlands. In the landmark case of *Plessy v. Ferguson*, the US Supreme Court ruled in 1896 that racial segregation did not violate the due process and equal protection clauses of the Fourteenth Amendment to the Constitution. Hence it would be "separate but equal" until the civil rights movement of the 1950s and 1960s. Yet during the Jim Crow era train accommodations were usually anything but equal, blacks being relegated to the older, less well-maintained "Negro coach" or to the combination multiracial Jim Crow car.[68]

Just as African Americans commonly encountered dirty and dingy passenger cars, all passengers, irrespective of time period, probably endured less than satisfactory equipment. Negative descriptions appeared widely. Travelers fussed (and rightly so) about broken seats and doors, unswept floors, dirty windows, smelly "dump" toilets, cigar smoke, expectorated tobacco juice, and much more. Even the quality of the ride itself might be unpleasant. In 1847 a traveler commented about his upstate New York trip: "Of the railroad from Albany to Buffalo I can say but little and that little by no means to its praise. Never was I more disappointed. Dragging along all day over a crazy track of flat [strap] rail with a black, dirty looking engine of about the power of a cast iron teakettle, the cars shaking and rocking like a steamboat in a rough sea. I arrived at Auburn late in the evening and found myself tired out and not half way to my journey's end."[69]

The quality of the passenger experience improved after the Civil War, but much later it often deteriorated, especially after World War II. Companies frequently under-maintained track and downgraded service on branch and secondary lines. A good description of this decline came from a Huron College English professor who blasted the North Western for what she recently had experienced on its daily train from Sioux City, Iowa, to Huron, South Dakota. "It is the kind of thing one sees in nightmares from which ones awakens, thankful that such a monster as one has

dreamed about simply cannot exist. It contains windows through which the light of day cannot penetrate because of decades of accumulated dirt. No one dares to touch the back of the seat, and the hand returns to its owner unrecognizable because of its sudden coating of black soot." Her biting closing thoughts: "Let me suggest that on the coaches of this monstrous imposition be painted in yellow lettering: 'Abandon hope all ye who enter here.' The Hades of the ancients must have been a Paradise in comparison."[70]

That disgusted passenger who encountered the tired, grimy North Western coach had opportunities to protest. In this case it was a letter to the editor of her hometown newspaper. Before the advent of meaningful state railroad commissions, which appeared beginning in the 1870s, travelers expressed their unhappiness on a plethora of matters, ranging from inadequate accommodations to poor service, the latter being a recurring concern. These complainants wrote to railroad officials, newspaper editors, or politicians, but more likely they vented their frustrations to the local depot agent. As regulations tightened, there might be a flood of complaints about slow and dirty trains, missed stops, or surly employees. Depot services, which were provided or not, likewise made

In the decade before the advent of Amtrak in 1971, intercity passenger service declined rapidly. Yet in 1966 the Erie Lackawanna Railroad still sought to provide the best possible service, refusing to allow its several long-distance trains to sink to disgraceful levels. Nevertheless, business was hardly brisk. A lone passenger is about to board the westbound *Phoebe Snow* in Owego, New York.

Author's Collection

the list of patron charges. Fortunately, regulators, through either moral suasion or statutory authority, had clout to rectify most of these alleged deficiencies.

Two contemporary examples from Iowa, the quintessential railroad state, reveal the common unhappiness about service and depots. Residents of the farming community of Cromwell, located in Union County six miles west of the county-seat town of Creston and connected by the Burlington main line, had long grumbled about train service between the two places. Although Cromwellians could take an eastbound train that reached Creston about noon, there was no train returning on the same day, notwithstanding that a westbound train passed through Cromwell at 7:35 p.m. without stopping. Once it had been convenient to go to and from Creston during the same day. In a hearing held in Des Moines in December 1912, a lawyer, who represented the village, told the Board of Railroad Commissioners that "said railroad company is thereby failing to promote the security, convenience and accommodation of the public." Even though the distance between Cromwell and Creston was relatively short, the connecting public road was at times virtually impassable because of weather conditions—mud, snow, ice. And, of course, Cromwellians wanted to go to Creston to shop or transact business and to return home the same day. Otherwise they would have to pay for an evening meal, a hotel room, and breakfast or stay with friends or relatives. The railroad, on the other hand, argued that it was unreasonable to force that early evening train to stop at Cromwell. "No. 9 was an interstate, through train, running on fast schedule, and that the passenger business to be accommodated by the running of an additional train would not be sufficient to pay actual expenses of operating the train." The matter was not resolved until 1917. Ultimately Iowa regulators sided with the Burlington, and so the citizens of Cromwell had to wait until a better road to Creston allowed them to travel freely by wagon, carriage, or more likely automobile.[71]

While residents of a southwestern Iowa village sparred with the Burlington, a community in the northwestern section of the Hawkeye State complained about the lack of a depot or shelter provided for them by the Chicago, St. Paul, Minneapolis & Omaha Railroad (Omaha Road), an affiliate of the Chicago & North Western System. The citizens of Ritter, located in O'Brien County, and the surrounding countryside demanded some sort of structure. As their legal representative told state railroad commissioners: "For passengers, it is a flag station. There is no accommodation for passengers. In the winter, when it is cold, passengers go into the office of the elevator company, which is close to the point at which passenger trains stop." He elaborated, "Of course, this office was not erected as a depot, nor was it built at a proper point to serve the ordinary purposes of a depot." The railroad, however, was not interested in satisfying the villagers' request. And its position was hardly unreasonable. The commission commented, "The company states that the revenue from passengers at Ritter does not average over $600 a year. The maintenance of an agent at this point would be largely for the accommodation of passengers. If it be true that the total passenger revenue is not greater than $600 yearly, it would about pay the salary of the agent, aside from such other expenses as light and heat." Still commissioners announced a compromise in their formal decision released on May 14, 1913. "We will make no order requiring the furnishing of an agent, as we do not believe the revenues justify the same. We fully realize the hardship that will be worked upon the residents of Ritter and vicinity during cold weather. It will simply require these parties to go on further to a neighboring town where proper accommodations exist, or else accept the courtesy of the elevator company." The specific order: "The defendant herein will be expected to take immediate steps towards the purchase of the necessary land and the erection of the necessary shelter at the town of Ritter to accommodate passengers." The Omaha Road complied.[72]

Whether in Iowa or elsewhere, the public often complained bitterly about passenger train discontinuances, which accelerated after World War I and continued during the following decades until the Amtrak era. For some patrons this meant a severe inconvenience, but others, especially by the mid-century years, wanted only backup transportation when weather turned nasty, producing impassible or dangerous snow-packed or ice-slick highways and grounding commercial aircraft. Until passage of the Transportation Act of 1958, railroads repeatedly faced difficulties achieving these takeoffs. Nevertheless, they did occur. Sometimes a carrier employed the tactic of offering substitute bus service, either its own or one provided by a contractor, and state and federal regulators might readily approve such a proposal. In the 1950s two railroads, Bangor & Aroostook and Northern Pacific, crowed about how they benefited from using small buses to eliminate money-draining passenger trains. In a most unusual occurrence, which took place in the mid-1950s, *Railway Age* reported this tale of "Substitute Service": "The principal opponents of the abandonment of a particular train [on the Reading Railroad] were a couple of schoolmarms who used the train regularly. So the railroad bought the teachers a second-hand Ford and off came the train." This was a smart investment by the Reading for solving this red-ink case. "What's wrong with providing substitute service by private automobile at far less cost?" asked this trade journal.[73]

Although passengers might be satisfied with rolling stock, trackside accommodations, and service, there were those who complained about the boredom of train riding, particularly on long trips. While arguably minor, the complaint was not unusual. When Amos Jay Cummins, a journalist with the *New York Sun*, traveled in 1873 from Kansas to California not long after the Union Pacific-Central Pacific transcontinental route opened, he had these thoughts about crossing the vastness of the Great Plains: "The trip by railroad over the plains is monotonous. It is generally understood that passengers have not a thing to do during the journey but to gaze at immense buffalo herds and shoot antelopes." But Cummins failed to have even these visual pleasures while riding on the Kansas Pacific Railroad. "Although it was in the buffalo season, I saw none of the animals. I counted twenty-one antelopes, but they were at a great distance. We passed about fifty prairie dogs, one prairie hen, and quantity of snipe and turtle dove, four black ducks, and a weasel—and that was all. Not an Indian." As for the landscape: "The plains spread north and south as far as the eye could reach, but a tree was a rarity. At one time we ran 150 miles without seeing a leaf or a tree. There was neither wood nor water—not a stick as big as a man's thumb." Taking a train through the pine forests of Maine, the wiregrass region of Georgia, or some other locale might elicit similar responses.[74]

Even in the nineteenth century (and later, too), travelers, both native residents and foreign visitors, complained occasionally about visual pollution along railroad corridors. About 1880, English tourist Walter Gore Marshall grumbled about the abundance of trackside advertisements. "On both sides of the railway along the shore of the Hudson River, for 150 miles to Albany, the following information and advice 'USE CARBOLINE FOR THE HAIR;' 'TARRANT'S SELTZER APERIENT CURES DIARRHEA;' 'GARGLING OIL;' 'TWIN BROTHERS YEAST;' 'SAPOLIO;' 'DIXON'S ICE CREAM,' etc. You cannot look on the beauties of this river from the train without being reminded that there are hair dyes, pills, and horse-powers—claiming your immediate attention etc." He went on to complain: "No one who has not travelled in the United States, has the least idea how sadly the country is disfigured by the daubing I have referred to."[75]

INTERURBAN INTERLUDE

What became a pleasurable experience for countless rail travelers after the mid-1890s, but often troubled steam railroads, involved electric intercity railways. Seemingly overnight, "interurban mania" swept America. "[The interurban] performs a service for mankind as notable and perhaps ultimately as great as that rendered by its steam-operated precursor," proclaimed one enthusiast. By the turn of the twentieth century, 3,132 miles of "juice" lines were in operation, being largely concentrated in southern New England, the Middle Atlantic region, states of the Old Northwest, and California. Trackage peaked in 1916 at an impressive 15,580 miles, and it knew no geographical bounds, although the South, excluding Texas, had a much lighter density of this competing transportation form.[76]

Although the majority of interurban roads operated less than seventy-five miles, they repeatedly drew short-haul travelers away from steam railroads. The public liked their new travel option for multiple reasons. Most significantly, electric cars were quiet and clean—"Dustless—Cinderless—Smokeless"—were relatively fast, and stopped at convenient locations, including in the heart of a village, town, or city and at crossroads and elsewhere along their routes. Moreover, they provided hourly or more frequent service throughout much of the day, unlike steam roads, which for many communities offered at best only double-daily service. Interurban fares were consistently less per mile than what their rivals charged. "Juice" roads frequently offered coupon ticket books at discounted prices, making trips even cheaper. In some cases electric lines served places that had been missed by steam roads, allowing the railway age finally to arrive. "Better late than never at all," said a Lee Center, Illinois, resident in 1910, adding that "this new electric line is a true blessing." Interurbans were almost always the last, best hope for obtaining a railroad.

Although individuals with access to interurbans embraced them, their interest eventually flagged. It would be automobiles, buses, and all-weather roads that would explain the spectacular decline of intercity traction by the eve of World War II. In 1941 only 3,197 miles remained in service. A significant amount of this trackage centered in greater Chicago, where the Chicago, Aurora & Elgin; Chicago, North Shore & Milwaukee; and Chicago, South Shore & South Bend continued in operation, but after 1963 only that latter road remained. The argument can be made that for many Americans the interurban served as the transition between the steam train and the family car.[77]

RAILROAD ENTHUSIASTS

Flanged-wheeled transport, whether railroads or interurbans, has long been the darling of enthusiasts. This has not been a recent phenomenon. As early as the 1840s, there were individuals who could be described as "train spotters," reminiscent of the well-known and somewhat maligned British fans. They noted locomotive types, engine numbers, and locations. By the era of World War I, there were enthusiasts, including some railroad employees, who mainly photographed rolling stock, usually locomotives, or perhaps became fanciers of railroad fiction, both in book and magazine form. Countless others had long taken pleasure from watching a passing train, especially a fast-moving express. Then in 1921 a group of enthusiasts, mostly New Englanders, launched the Railway & Locomotive Historical Society (R&LHS). "Some were interested in photographs of the old-time

locomotives; others preferred only the modern and, armed with cameras, took these photographs, but a few others set to work to acquire timetables, tickets, posters, hat checks, etc." Importantly, the R&LHS launched a semiannual publication, *The Bulletin of the Railway & Locomotive Histori-cal Society*, and occasionally it produced topical supplements. Much later, in 1972, the *Bulletin* became *Railroad History*, a more scholarly publication and a tradition that remains. No longer does the journal publish antiquar-ian pieces and the once-ubiquitous steam locomotive rosters. The R&LHS also sponsored member meetings.[78]

Most of those men—there were no women—who joined the Railway & Locomotive Historical Society showed little or no interest in the rapidly disappearing electric interurbans. Some, in fact, had disdain for "streetcars." Die-hard traction fanciers understandably sought to have their own organizations. Two pioneer juice clubs, Lancaster (Pennsyl-vania) Railroad & Locomotive Historical Society and Interstate Trolley Club (New York–Philadelphia), which date from the early 1930s, morphed into what became America's largest railfan organization, National Rail-way Historical Society (NRHS). This group attracted both steam and electric fans, and over several decades it grew into scores of local chapters nationwide. Some of its members showed an almost fanatic obsession for trains. Although the NRHS published a quarterly magazine, its activi-ties centered on chapter meetings, annual national conventions, and rail excursions.

And there were membership overlaps with railroad enthusiast organi-zations. Since the R&LHS leadership early on showed an iciness toward fan trips, some members flocked to the National Association of Railroad Enthusiasts (NARE), later Railroad Enthusiasts. They sought to have excursions "sponsored by the railfans, for the railfans." On August 26, 1934, NARE claimed to have operated the first fan excursion in America. This involved a trip over the Boston & Maine and Hoosac Tunnel & Wilmington Railroads. More followed, usually in rail-line-and member-rich New England. Participants always relished old equipment and preferred steam to diesel locomotives.[79]

In more recent decades enthusiasts have developed a fondness for "fallen flag" companies, a process accelerated by the widespread corporate mergers of the 1960s. These organizations focus on a single railroad or closely related ones, and they include the Anthracite Railroads Historical Society, Baltimore & Ohio Railroad Historical Society, Erie Lackawanna Historical Society, Southern Pacific Historical & Technical Society, Southern Railway Historical Association, and Wabash Railroad Historical Society. Some fans have found the Dining Car Preservation Society, Railroad Station Historical Society, and other specialized organizations to their liking. Traction enthusiasts formed the Chicago-based Central Electric Railfans' Association (CERA). This group resembled more the R&LHS than the NRHS, focusing on publications, which in time often became sophistical works on specific interurbans, those in a region or state, or some related topic like trolley freight. Recently, an increasingly popular organization, the Center for Railroad Photography and Art, has emerged. A high percentage of the members of this vibrant group also belong to other railroad organizations.

The intense interest in rail transport encompasses much more. There are tens of thousands of model railroaders. They have their own organizations and clubs, publications, and other activities, including conventions, shows, and museums. Then there are national enthusiast-specific magazines. The widely circulated *Trains*, a product of Kalmbach Publishing Company, has been a longtime favorite. Even before the debut of *Trains* in 1941, Kalmbach produced *The Model Railroader*, and more recently it introduced *Classic Trains*. And books, including biographies, company histories, and pictorials, have become ubiquitous, especially since the 1960s. Many are buff works, published by fan-oriented presses or privately printed. Commercial and university presses, too, have entered the field. Donald Duke, whose Golden Western Books sold both steam and electric titles, said, "I can't image a railroad book not selling. Even the crappiest book probably makes money or at least it breaks even." And for decades there have been preservation efforts, saving rolling stock, depots, hardware, paper ephemera, and the like. Private collections and railroad-oriented museums have appeared from coast to coast. Some of the leading public ones are the Baltimore & Ohio Museum in Baltimore,

Maryland; California State Railroad Museum in Sacramento; Illinois Railroad Museum in Union; Lake Superior Railroad Museum in Duluth, Minnesota; and the Railroad Museum of Pennsylvania in Strasburg.

Americans, whether railfans or not, have had a variety of railroad-related experiences in addition to train travel, more so than any other commercial transport. A plethora of songs, works of art, photography, poetry, novels, and motion pictures have railroad themes. There are also those railroad-created names of towns, counties, streets, and other places, as well as common railroad-inspired phrases: "off the rails," "asleep at the switch," "sidetracked," and many more. Railroad monuments and memorials also dot the landscape. The Golden Spike Monument, part of the Golden Spike National Historic Site in Utah, is a leading example. Railroads surely will remain a source of interest and pleasure for generations to come and probably will retain their supremacy among transportation enthusiasts.[80]

ELECTRIC INTERURBANS AND MOTOR BUSES

When one examines American intercity transportation, the motor bus shares strong similarities with the electric interurban railway. They might be considered cousins. Early in the twentieth century, interurbans burst on the American scene, and not long thereafter buses made their debut. Both grew rapidly, and the traveling public embraced them, often preferring these modes of travel to steam railroads. Resembling interurbans, buses operated on frequent, convenient schedules. In 1923, for example, Range Rapid Transit Company dispatched its equipment between Virginia and Duluth, Minnesota, on an hourly basis throughout a fifteen-hour operating day, except on Sundays. Both transport forms brought passengers into the heart of commercial centers and commonly used as their depots existing businesses, perhaps a drugstore, hotel, or café. When railroad owned, a bus likely stopped at a railway station. Moreover, interurbans and buses usually boarded and discharged passengers at the lesser villages and crossroads. The bus division of the Sioux Falls Traction System, which connected Sioux Falls, South Dakota, with Sioux City, Iowa, proclaimed: "We Pick Up Passengers Any Place along the Highway." Each form also vigorously promoted charter trips. "Special coaches are available at all times for business or social functions," announced one bus carrier. "They may be chartered for any length of time—for any distance." By the 1920s the typical interurban car had a single employee, the motorman, while the bus had only the driver. Both transport forms likewise offered patrons clean accommodations and not the soot and grime that had been the curse of railroad travelers. And fares for interurbans and buses were nearly always less than what competing steam roads charged. In 1926 a bus patron, who used an All-States Motor Coach between Chicago and Saint Louis, noted, "The fare of $7 for the 300-mile run is one of the lowest I found. Being somewhat less than the railway fare, the buses are largely patronized by those desiring to save the difference." Interurban and bus

Right and facing, An example of the similarity between interurbans and buses can be found in their practice of using joint timetables. In June 1919 the Illinois Electric Railway Association distributed a comprehensive schedule (with map) of the more than a dozen interurbans that served the Prairie State. In August 1933 more than two dozen Midwestern and Southern bus companies advertised in the *Official Bus Schedule,* a monthly publication of the Benas Advertising Service of Louisville.

Author's Collection

JUNE, 1919

ILLINOIS ELECTRIC RAILWAYS

ILLINOIS ELECTRIC RAILWAYS ASSOCIATION

OFFICIAL TIME TABLES IN

ILLINOIS

with

CONNECTIONS

PUBLISHED BY AUTHORITY OF
ILLINOIS ELECTRIC
RAILWAYS ASSOCIATION

OFFICIAL
BUS
SCHEDULE

HOTEL GUIDE
LOWER FARE EVERYWHERE

Volume 6   Number 4
EFFECTIVE AUGUST 20, 1933
TO SEPTEMBER 20, 1933

Following steam railroads, a few long-distance electric interurbans operated sleeping cars. In the mid-1920s the American Car & Foundry Company built this petite steel sleeper for the Interstate Public Service Company, and it saw service on this 117-mile road between Indianapolis and Louisville.

ACF Photo, Krambles-Peterson Archive

firms frequently issued mileage books, designed to further reduce the cost for daily or frequent riders and also to retain their patronage. The Cleveland-Ashtabula-Conneaut Bus Company announced: "We have thousands of mileage book customers. There's a reason!" Similarly, in the 1920s and 1930s interurban and bus companies regularly published joint public timetable guides, in part because they both consisted of a plethora of small companies. Even when Greyhound Lines emerged as the monster carrier in the late 1920s, officials wished to recognize smaller connecting lines, allowing for more seamless and less stressful travel experiences. Both interurban and bus companies also sought to be good corporate citizens. It was hardly surprising that the Cleveland, Southwestern & Columbus Railway adopted the straightforward motto "The public be pleased," and the Vermont Transit Bus Company proclaimed, "The people will be served." Such heartfelt slogans were a far cry from what William H.

For several decades the Illinois Terminal Railroad and predecessor Illinois Traction Company dispatched sleeping cars between Saint Louis and several destinations in Illinois, including Springfield and Peoria. In 1940 Illinois Terminal withdrew its last sleeper, one that served the Peoria line.

IT Photo by Venard Film Corp., Krambles-Peterson Archive

Vanderbilt of the New York Central Lines allegedly had said in the 1880s: "The public be damned!"[1]

Interurbans and buses emerged as advanced forms of transportation, and each demonstrated creative features. Admittedly, a similar case can be made for early steamboats, streamliners, and airplanes. In 1926 the New Hampshire Public Service Commission pointedly said: "Buses are this modern mode of travel." Such a statement about modernity seemed particularly appropriate during the first several decades of their existence; equipment got larger, more powerful, and more luxurious. Both interurbans and buses had companies that operated "parlor cars," interurbans with specially designed ones with deluxe features, including some with rear observation platforms, and buses introduced vehicles that resembled them. Bus companies, though, provided this service for a much shorter duration, mostly in the late 1920s and early 1930s. Each form went so far as to dabble with overnight sleepers: interurbans with modified Pullman-type cars and buses with cleverly designed, self-contained sleeper vehicles. The former appeared prior to World War I, and the latter made their debut about 1930. Yet this specialty equipment usually lasted only for a short time, being killed off by low customer demand. Generally interurban and bus operators concluded that they would not have any class-based service, unlike steam railroads and later airlines. A few interurbans and bus companies went so far as to coordinate air service. The Cleveland, Southwestern Railway & Light Company allowed its passengers the convenience of joint rail-air ticketing and a direct connection with Stout Airlines in Cleveland. Pickwick Stages transported patrons overnight between San Diego and Seattle by "Nitecoach" and during daytime by air on its own Pickwick Airways. This arrangement created a travel time of one day and two nights between these far-flung

In the early 1930s a short-lived long-distance bus was the "Nite Coach." Several companies offered this equipment, including Columbia Nite Coach Lines (*facing*) and Pickwick-Greyhound Lines (*above*). The latter described its luxury sleeper service this way: "[The Nite Coach] is a beautiful stream-lined vehicle, with 26 air-cushioned chairs by day—26 comfortable berths by night. Hot meals are prepared and served on board. Two lavatories. Crew of 3—pilot, steward, porter."

Author's Collections

West Coast destinations. Neither electric interurbans nor intercity buses provided the same flexibility of personal movement as private automobiles; cars could more or less go where and when people wanted. Still, interurban and bus availability was usually greater than service on contemporary steam roads, except perhaps on commuter lines. Then as the interurban industry faded, some surviving juice roads added connecting or supplementary bus service. A few, like the Cincinnati & Lake Erie Railway, junked their rolling stock for buses, embracing the philosophy of "if you can't beat'em, join'em."[2]

Nevertheless, significant differences exist. For embryonic bus companies, the cost of entry was surprisingly low. Usually it involved minimal equipment, initially a roomy motorcar and somewhat later a specially designed bus. Indeed, prototype buses, the "jitneys," used mass-produced automobiles, including Overlands and Ford Model Ts. A garage or some type of maintenance facility was also required. On the other hand, an electric interurban needed right-of-way, track, carbarn, electric power supply, poles and overhead wire, and often pricey rolling stock. This costly fixed physical plant meant no flexibility; buses, on the other hand, could be sent over any drivable route. Electric roads also faced sizable property taxes on their facilities and equipment; bus companies paid only modest taxes, largely on fuel and any real estate. After all, buses traveled on public roads. While it is possible to identify the initial interurbans, the early growth of intercity bus travel has neither a distinctive nor a unique origin. Interurbans were regional in appearance, being most heavily concentrated in the Northeast, Midwest, Texas, and California; buses were ubiquitous, even in the Southlands, where electric roads were scattered. Moreover, buses focused on passengers, although they might carry "Uncle Sam's mail bags" and express packages. Only a few bus companies, especially during the 1930s, operated motor freight subsidiaries for less-than-truckload (LTL) shipments. Interurbans handled more than US mail and express; they hauled less-than-carload (LCL) freight and some carload freight. Before the triumph of the "good roads" movement, a bus jaunt was hardly as smooth as an interurban ride. Holes, rocks, ruts, and sharp curves made taking a nap or getting longer periods of restful sleep difficult. "It is not possible to sleep in a bus," complained a rider in 1934. "Everything the huge wheels meet upon the road is transferred to the sitting body, and one vibrates and shakes."[3]

Unlike other forms of American transport—even more so than railroads—the bus industry experienced impressive and rapid consolidation, much of which occurred during the 1920s and 1930s. Hundreds of small firms entered the fold of larger companies. By 1929 Greyhound Lines offered coast-to-coast service, and within a few years it had amassed more than forty thousand miles of routes; owned nearly 1,500 buses; generated about twenty million coach miles; and employed thousands. Such growth allowed the industry to claim that it reached more places than any other form of public transportation. Interurbans, on the other hand, remained largely localized, averaging less than seventy-five route miles, although there was modest system building and some forged interline service agreements.[4]

Initially, buses, unlike interurbans, faced no or limited public regulation, although in 1916 Pennsylvania blazed the way. Still, years later only thirty-eight states wielded oversight, much of it directed at the licensing of drivers, vehicle safety, and mandatory accident and liability insurance coverage. If buses were regulated, some states did so lackadaisically. When public controls existed, carriers often expressed their support. Minnesota bus operators pronounced (even gloated) in 1925: "While laws passed at the last session of the legislature laid down certain rules which must be followed by vehicles which carry passengers for hire, those regulations were not necessary as far as the member companies of the Minnesota Motor Bus Association were concerned." By the mid-1930s states had instituted a degree of regulation over intrastate bus carriers, yet it varied widely. Generally regulations included operator's licenses, assignment of routes, establishment of tariffs, filing of annual reports, and requirements for insurance and other financial responsibilities. It would not be until the federal government passed the Motor Carrier Act of 1935 that *interstate* bus lines (and also trucking firms) experienced the same controls that railroads and interurbans had long encountered. "A thick fog of comprehensive regulation now settled over all [transportation] industries," concluded one scholar. Strikingly different from interurbans, buses were not a flash-in-the-pan phenomenon. By the time of World War II, most interurbans had folded, yet buses flourished, reaching their peak popularity during those hectic war years and immediately thereafter. Then the shine was off the apple. Ridership declined as long-distance automobile travel became more convenient, economical, and pleasant, and attractive airline options beckoned. By the 1960s surviving bus firms, including the dominant Greyhound Lines and Trailways System, focused on their profitable charter and tour operations, reducing or ending their scheduled intercity runs. This trend continued into the twenty-first century.[5]

TAKING THE BUS

By the 1930s intercity buses offered practical alternatives to traditional steam railroads and thus attracted a range of travelers. Moreover, the bus network had the geographical coverage that was necessary to bind the nation. Yet passenger composition changed. Early on, riders might have been ones who lacked other transportation options. "It was not a great many years ago that the motor bus was regarded as a necessary evil—to be used as a means of travel only when one wanted to go to some out-of-the-way, off-the-beaten-path town or rural community without any of the more comfortable passenger carriers," remarked the *Greyhound Traveler* in 1929. "It was in these days that motor buses might justly be referred to as 'Rough Riders.' To stand the wear and tear of such a trip in a bus of doubtful dependability over highways (if so we may favor them) that jolted and bounced a person who had to be equipped with about as rugged a constitution as the men in [Theodore] Roosevelt's famous [Spanish-American War] regiment." These hardy souls might have been traveling to a remote sawmill in Washington State, oil patch in Texas, or turpentine camp in Florida.[6]

By the mid and late 1920s, bus owners and managers had done much to convince Americans, who have always sought increased mobility, that their equipment was dependable, safe, and comfortable. Publicity took the form of splashy demonstrations, radio spots, and newspaper and magazine advertisements. On June 21, 1929, the Wisconsin Motor Bus Line dispatched three new buses, painted an eye-catching bright orange, from

Just as stagecoaches commonly made railroad connections, at times so did buses. In 1927 travelers to the Black Hills of South Dakota could step from a Chicago & North Western train at the Rapid City station onto a Black Hills Transportation Company White-built auto bus. These intermodal riders could expect safe travel experiences on both the train and the compact highway vehicle.

Author's Collection

its headquarters in Madison for an inaugural convoy tour along Highway 19 to Dubuque, Iowa. Throughout the well-publicized trip, company representatives showed off their state-of-the-art equipment and distributed fresh oranges and orange-colored timetables and promotional materials. Its popular slogan, "Have an Orange on the Orange Line," evolved from this much-watched public relations stunt. Two months later a Yelloway and Greyhound Lines advertisement in the *American Magazine*, with the headline "Master Seven-Years-Old Travels 2600 Miles Alone," told of the journey of a youngster from the West Coast to the Midwest. The copy read in part: "With a ten-dollar bill, a suitcase too big for him to carry, and a bulletin from the District Traffic Manager to all drivers and agents en route, Master Seven-Years-Old boarded an East-bound bus. Drivers and agents watched over him, supervised his meals and menu, turned him over to other drivers at transfer points." There was a happy ending: "On time, fresh and hale, he danced from his bus at Chicago into the arms of his brother."[7]

By the 1930s the clientele who regularly rode intercity buses largely reflected a cross section of the American population, particularly the middle and lower-middle classes. Some contemporaries went so far as

to suggest that ridership represented virtually all segments of society. Travelers selected this transport option because of cost, convenience, and perhaps comfort. "Bus-minded travelers are finding motorized transportation increasingly convenient and comfortable," proclaimed railroad-owned Interstate Transit Lines in 1931. "Schedules provide frequent service; routes lie through interesting scenic and historic sections—altogether, buses fill a definite travel need." Riders included workers (and those looking for work), commercial travelers, shoppers, students, children, senior citizens, nondrivers, people seeking medical attention, and pleasure seekers. In a self-serving fashion, Atlantic Greyhound Lines identified a range of individuals who liked bus travel. In a 1934 timetable insert, "We Changed Our Minds about Bus Trips," a housewife said: "I didn't think it could be so comfortable and you see much more!" A businessman announced, "From now on my salesmen go by Greyhound. We'll cut travel expenses in half." An older woman commented, "I've never seen such careful drivers and they are so considerate!" Except for the World War II era when military personnel packed buses, this passenger mix continued into the postwar period. During these years the complexion of riders who frequented a south Texas bus station was remembered this way: "Through the portals came service men and women of all ranks; drunks, bums, mean truck drivers,

In the 1930s riders often took a White-built bus. The railroad-owned Interstate Transit Lines, composed of Chicago & North Western Stages and Union Pacific Stages, operated a fleet of these heavy-duty, over-the-road vehicles.

Author's Collection

salesmen, teachers, farmers, farm hands, blind people with dogs, sick people who threw up in handkerchiefs, elderly people who were not sure where they were going, illegal aliens trying to avoid the immigration police, students of all descriptions, telephone operators and beautiful women of all ages." About the same time, writer Thomas Wolf, who described his cross-country bus trip for *Collier's*, provided this description of his fellow riders: "The people I rode with were more of America: harvest hands and C.I.O. [labor] organizers; butchers and ministers; stenographers and farmers; house wives and house painters; students and mill hands; waitresses and missionaries; drifters and loafers; veterans and stay-at-homes; teenagers and grandparents." He added, "They were white and black; Methodist and Baptist; Amish, Jewish, Catholic, Protestant, Church of Jesus Christ [of Latter-day Saints], and African-Methodist." Intercity buses often became a refuge for those travelers who were unable or unwilling to pay for usually faster and more comfortable train trips.[8]

Specialized markets emerged. Take what began in the 1920s and continued for decades. Bus companies, large and small, annually transported tens of thousands of northern factory workers to and from their traditional homes in the South. As regional agricultural and mining conditions changed, the lure of steady, high-paying jobs in such manufacturing centers as Akron, Chicago, Cleveland, Detroit, Pittsburgh, Toledo, and other places north of the Mason-Dixon Line prompted these trips. One carrier that thrived on this clientele was Brooks Bus Line, based in Paducah, Kentucky. Starting in 1929 with a Plymouth sedan, founder J. Polk Brooks established regular service between Paducah and Detroit. Bigger and better equipment followed, and patronage increased and then stabilized, augmented by charter operations. "By 1938 Brooks had built up a following of passengers who preferred his 'Detroit Express,'" observed company chronicler Ora Bailey Brooks. "Even though the economy had improved and many of his passengers could now afford their own automobiles, they preferred to leave the problems of the road to professional and experienced drivers." She added, "Frequently parents sent their children south to visit grandparents and other relatives, trusting them to the care of the bus driver." This family firm charged less than competing railroads and provided continual passage that did not necessitate changing trains in Cincinnati or elsewhere.[9]

But as the immediate post–World War II era passed, the composition of bus ridership changed. Because of increased automobile ownership; better roads, highlighted by a rapidly expanding interstate network after 1956; and enhanced domestic airline service, more Americans shied away from intercity buses. This occurred in part because of the clientele, which was dominated by the poor, college students, elderly, and

substance abusers and other "unde-
sirables." Core patrons tended to be
those individuals who had limited
alternatives or who wished to pay less
for their travels. There also might be
"incurably romantic riders," vacationers, and charter and tour groups. In
the 1970s a federal agency determined
that nearly two-thirds of bus passengers were younger than twenty-five or
older than sixty-four, and 60 percent
had family incomes under $15,000,
compared with 40 percent of all commercial travelers.[10]

Pennsylvanians, espe-
cially those who lived
in greater Pittsburgh
and Harrisburg, could
for a brief time ride
the *Steel City Flyer*.
On November 24,
2009, its initial day of
operations, the three
initial passengers
stand at Crowne
Plaza in Harrisburg
for the westbound
trip to the Steel City.

*Courtesy of Henry
Posner III*

By the twenty-first century another sea change was occurring,
sparked by the 1982 passage of the Bus Regulatory Reform Act, which
relaxed entry controls and liberalized rate making. With the introduction
of the New York City–based Chinatown bus lines, along with Boltbus,
Megabus, and other start-ups, the public, including business executives,
professionals, and other nontraditional riders, found that these carriers had become an attractive way to travel for short and intermediate
distances. Not only were they inexpensive, but tickets and reservations
could be easily made on the internet for popular routes at convenient
departure and arrival times. Some buses featured such amenities as seats
with extra leg room, Wi-Fi connections, and power outlets. "The coach
was in excellent condition with no obvious dents or damage," reported a
Megabus rider. "The interior was clean and neat with no obvious problems or smells." And there were special come-ons. Boltbus created this
policy: customers for every four round trips earned a free fifth trip. The
intended purpose of these discount bus operations was (and remains) to
get people between point A and point B as cheaply as possible. Yet this
budget-carrier philosophy has downsides, namely the usual absence of
ticket offices and waiting rooms along with poorly marked curbside load-
ings and perhaps no scheduled on-route rest stops. Passengers usually find
curbside boarding acceptable during pleasant weather, but it becomes an
annoyance in the rain, snow, heat, or cold. In a sense bus history repeated
itself. Throughout most of the 1920s Chicago, for one, lacked any kind of
bus terminal; coaches used curbside stops at hotels, including the cen-
trally located Congress Hotel on Michigan Avenue.[11]

In recent years this phenomenon of inexpensive yet upscale bus service, however, has led to ill-fated attempts to make such operations permanent. Take the *Steel City Flyer*, introduced in 2008 between Pittsburgh and
Harrisburg by the Pittsburgh-based Railroad Development Corporation

COMFORT—that reaches a new height of luxury —makes every minute you travel in an An-X Motor Coach thoroughly enjoyable Although built to accommodate 16 passengers, the capacity is limited to 10 people, assuring greater roominess and extra width window seats for every passenger. Latest type individual reclining swivel chairs with footstools.

VALET SERVICE—A courteous attendant caters to your wants. His duty is to make your journey as pleasant as possible.

REFRESHMENTS—served in the coach from a refrigerator. Confections are also obtainable.

LIBRARY—consisting of popular books and magazines, are at your disposal.

RADIO—installed to give you entertainment at the turn of a switch.

SMOKING—permitted at all times.

BAGGAGE—checked and carried in forward power car. Coats and wraps cared for by valet in lockers.

REST STOPS—made every 100 miles. Emergency stops made upon request.

LOUD SPEAKER and Telephonic communication between driver and passengers.

The An-X Motor Coach is provided with every device for the comfort and protection of its passengers. Equipped with vacuum brakes on both the Coach and Power Car. Driven by trained, experienced chauffeurs at safe speeds along scenic, express highways.

TIME TABLE
NORTH
Lv. New York   9:00 A. M.

Daily   Except   Sundays

From Hotel Cadillac Bus Depot
43rd Street and Broadway

Ar. Buffalo 10:30 P. M.

Time 13½ Hours

SOUTH
Lv. Buffalo   9:00 A. M.

Daily   Except   Sundays

From Hotel Statler, Hotel Lafayette, Hotel Buffalo or Ford Hotel

Ar. New York 10:30 P. M.

Time 13½ Hours

NEW YORK   ·   ·   ·   ·   ·   -   -   -   -   - BUFFALO

EXTRA FARE SERVICE AT NO ADDITIONAL COST

All forms of public transportation have experimented with equipment; buses were not an exception. In the early 1930s travelers between Buffalo and New York City could ride in a hybrid automobile/bus, the "AN-X DeLuxe Motor Coach." The services of a "courteous attendant" and access to refreshments, radio, and a small library were included in this odd car-trailer combination.

Author's Collection

(RDC). This intrastate bus line catered to Pittsburgh hospital employees, business travelers, politicians, and lobbyists who no longer had access to direct airline connections between the two cities and who did not wish to take a Greyhound bus or the once-daily Amtrak train. And it offered attractive fares and customer-friendly schedules. RDC dispatched a bus with first-class amenities, featuring an attendant, movies, reading lights, reclining seats, pillows, and a restroom. Since business travelers were targeted, Wi-Fi and laptop desks were available. The initial response was positive. "There are a lot of days I drive to Harrisburg and back in the same day, and it makes for a long day when you do that," explained the head of the Greater Pittsburgh Chamber of Commerce. "And I could get some work done when I'm riding the bus." But alas, patronage did not reach the break-even revenue point, largely because hospital workers wanted to keep their mileage reimbursements. The *Steel City Flyer* also failed to gain convenient access to Amtrak's intermodal facility in Harrisburg, preventing a truly seamless connection to high-speed trains to and from

Philadelphia and its connecting rail service. The last run took place on July 9, 2009.[12]

Almost from the dawn of intercity bus transportation, companies of all sizes exploited the opportunity to cater to pleasure seekers, individuals who came largely from the middle class. They could "ride the rubber" and not be annoyed by dirty steam locomotives or the unsightliness of rail yards, factories, or other unpleasing sites along the railroad corridor. In the 1920s Motor Transit Company, which operated between Los Angeles and San Diego, sought sightseers and advertised: "A ride of unmatched scenic beauty awaits the traveler by Motor Stage between Los Angeles and San Diego. Thru miles of orange groves, beautiful farms and along picturesque stretches of California seacoast, the road leads to the state's most southern metropolis." Another Golden State carrier, Crown Stage Lines, proclaimed on the front page of its May 1, 1922, timetable: "See the Orange Groves at Santa Ana!" Later in the 1920s Northland Transportation Company offered this commentary: "This growing form of transportation has demonstrated its wonderful utility. To the summer traveler the motor bus makes available the pleasures of Minnesota's wonderful highway development. Motor buses provide a safe, comfortable, and economical access to the lakes, the woods, the places of beauty and pleasure for which Minnesota is so famed. Minnesota by Northland bus will be a revelation of beauty and pleasure." In 1929 Pickwick Stages glamorized its service when it told prospective patrons: "The last barrier to full keen enjoyment of America's highways has been conquered. Pickwick motor coaches make possible a journey of travel thrills never before fully enjoyed. For they offer all the pleasure of private car tours at much less cost, and without the fatigue. Days are saved, too." In the 1930s Oregon Motor Stages branded itself as "The Beach Route Serving Oregon's Playground" and boasted: "Here is the West that still is Paradise for Vacationists and Sportsmen." In 1933 Greyhound operated a fleet of buses on the grounds of the Century of Progress Exposition in Chicago and set up tours to this popular fair from every state. "This sparked the birth of Greyhound Highway Tours," recalled a company executive. "To sell these tours, Greyhound established travel agencies in many key cities and towns, not only in the United States, but also in Europe and South America." The industry consistently made much of citizens having new, exciting experiences. "By taking a bus Americans could become fashionable and relax in some exotic location at any time of the year," observed bus historian Margaret Walsh. "Indeed, this romantic or perhaps even therapeutic appeal of seeing new places came to dominate bus advertising." No wonder the Trailways System in 1954 launched a nationwide advertising campaign that announced: "See America at Scenery Level."[13]

The best-known pleasure ride in a touring car or bus prior to World War II involved the joint Indian-detour operation offered by the Atchison,

Topeka & Santa Fe Railway (Santa Fe) and the Fred Harvey Company. When the service began in 1926, the railroad explained: "The *Indian-detour* [italics in original] service is daily the year round. This unusual educational tour comprises visits to the old city of Santa Fe, also the inhabited Indian pueblos of Tesuque, Santa Clara, San Juan, Santo Domingo and other places in the picturesque valley of the Upper Rio Grande. Three days and three hundred miles of sunshine and relaxation and mountain air in a land of unique human contrasts and natural grandeur." This coordinated bus and rail trip allowed westbound Santa Fe passengers to detrain at Las Vegas, New Mexico, and reboard at Albuquerque and eastbound passengers to take a reverse course. The two sponsoring firms formed the Santa Fe Transportation Company and acquired a fleet of Yellow and White-built buses, called "Harveycoaches." This equipment provided wide windows and ample baggage space for passengers, or "dudes" as employees called them. Riders received the benefits of expert guides and the caring staffs of Harvey Houses in Las Vegas, Santa Fe, and Albuquerque who facilitated these "bother-eliminated" travel experiences.[14]

The Great Depression hurt the Indian-detour business, and World War II ended these once-popular tours. With the return of peacetime, numerous companies nationally either launched or expanded their pleasure operations, offering a variety of regularly scheduled runs or more likely special trips. Some travel agents promoted "bus vacations," where they created individualized package tours that included hotel reservations and sightseeing excursions. Peter Pan Bus Lines, headquartered in Springfield, Massachusetts, was one such firm. In the early 1930s, founder Peter Picknelly realized the potential of charter and tour operations, and his company advertised extensively about group transportation. Although war suspended charter runs, except for military personnel, peacetime saw their resumption. "Picknelly went after the business 'in spades,' as he liked to say, courting companies, clubs, organizations, and the public," explained the Peter Pan historian. "In addition, he built an extensive schedule of daily service to seasonal events and locations in New England, from ball games to flower shows to ski resorts."[15]

Nonscheduled firms also specialized in bus vacations. The Tauck Company has been enduring. In summer 1925 Arthur C. Tauck Sr., a traveling salesman and first-generation German American, launched his initial motor tours in a Studebaker touring car through rural New England. It did not take long before Tauck expanded operations with a small fleet of buses providing what he considered to be "life-enriching motorcoach experiences for discerning travelers." Typical of its pre–World War II promotions of a growing number of trips through the East, South, and Atlantic Canada was a seven-day, 1,200-mile "Easter and Spring" bus journey through the "Heart of Virginia," in "Luxurious Parlor Motor Coaches."

The cost for this experience in 1930: "All Expenses $98." The tour would be conducted by a "competent courier in addition to an efficient chauffeur." Tauck made it clear that "ladies need not feel the least bit timid about traveling alone, because they are bound to make acquaintances immediately from the start of the tour with others in the same position." The company also contended that "there is no commercial atmosphere about this tour. It is conducted purely as an 'Ideal Vacation'—long to be remembered," and that became the hallmark of its quality travel brand.[16]

There were bus companies that originally concentrated on common carrier service but by the latter part of the twentieth century had morphed into the motor coach charter business. Arrow Stage Lines, based in Norfolk, Nebraska, is one example. In the late 1920s the firm began with a seven-passenger Buick sedan on a Norfolk to Sioux City, Iowa, route, and later it added larger, specialized equipment and launched additional regional operations. Following World War II, Arrow Stages began its focus on the charter and tour business. Ultimately it launched Black Hill Stage Lines for its remaining scheduled bus operations, thus permitting its core unit to handle charters for school, church, military, and other groups and for extended over-the-road vacations. By the twenty-first century, Arrow exploited the high-end touring niche market by offering luxury coaches with premium features, which include padded seats, flat-screen monitors, Wi-Fi, and outlets for consumer electronics.[17]

When Greyhound used that "Rough Rider" analogy to describe pioneer bus travel, it was not far off the mark. These buses offered minimal comfort. Seats were often covered with woven cane or held up by spiral springs, and leg room was minimal. Even the specially designed Fageol Safety Coach, when introduced in 1921 as the "PALACE CAR of the Highway," squeezed four or perhaps five passengers in their several single-row bench seats, which had sedan-type doors. Heating systems were primitive, usually a metal exhaust pipe that extended along one side of the coach and that could become dangerously hot, burning anybody and anything that came in contact with it. Buses, admitted one carrier, were "crude and undeveloped." They were often locally fabricated bodies that were attached to stock truck chassis. Then there were the roads. By the early 1920s only a small percentage of intercity roads could be classified as "all weather"; most were "unpaved and wrinkled." Dirt roads with ruts, whether of mud, ice, or snow, made for an uncomfortable ride. Mud, especially, disrupted schedules. During wet periods buses frequently became trapped in messy quagmires, prompting a wag to describe springtime roads in New England as "16 feet wide and 2 feet deep." In what was surely an extreme case, a bus operated by Red Ball Transportation Company of Iowa in the 1920s became stuck for two weeks in "mud up to the axles" midway between Charles City and Nashua. Hopefully, passengers were able to flee the stranded bus within a reasonable length of time. Winter storms might delay a bus for hours, occasionally days. If a snowbound vehicle were in a fortunate location, passengers and driver might find shelter, food, and drink, but otherwise conditions might become dire, even life threatening. Inclement weather and road conditions also contributed to annoying equipment breakdowns. Likewise dangerous was the initial use of vacuum brakes. If the motor died, so did the braking system. Air brakes subsequently solved that safety problem. There were, of course, roadway collisions. But differing from steamboat, rail, interurban, and air transport, the industry met with no horrendous disasters, largely because bus speeds during the formative years were relatively low and because during World War II the federal government mandated a thirty-five-mile-per-hour limit. It would not be until the turnpike and interstate highway era that the number of fatal injuries increased. Yet they commonly were the fault of neither the equipment nor the driver.[18]

The "Rough Rider" conditions that intercity bus travelers faced did not spark repeated complaints to regulatory authorities. After all, what could a state railroad or commerce commission do about muddy roads or bad weather? There were concerns early on about illegitimate ticket brokers and fly-by-night operators who sold travel on an unscrupulous or poorly equipped bus line or who made it difficult or impossible for riders to make reasonable connections to their destinations. R. L. Lannon, who in 1927 chaired the Colorado Public Utilities Commission, remarked, "This commission has on file dozens of complaints against brokers handling tickets for various touring cars and buses. In fact the office of this Commission is completely littered with numerous complaints from practically all of the companies operating in interstate traffic in Colorado. It is indeed deplorable to this Commission that such brokers and irresponsible operators are allowed to continue such practices."[19]

A long, perhaps cross-country bus trip prior to World War II usually involved some passenger inconveniences, discomforts, or unanticipated adventures. Such experiences were most common as bus travel developed. In the late 1920s Yelloway Lines, which operated between Denver and Los Angeles, ran over hundreds of miles of primitive roads with steep grades that on occasion forced passengers to temporarily leave their bus before they could continue their journey. A novice driver related his experience with taking his vehicle over Oatman Pass in the Black Mountains of Arizona. "The motor began to moan from its labors until I could count the last weak efforts of the cylinder explosions as the coach coughed to a standstill." He recalled telling his passengers, "'Well, folks, I guess you'll just have to walk over the hill. The old hack won't make it with a load.'" No one objected. "'I'm used to walking over the hill. I travel this route quite often,' remarked one of the men sitting near the front of the bus." The driver continued: "Without the weight of my passengers, I was able to climb in low gear to the crest of the grade, although I had to back down the hill for a start." Even a contemporary long-distance traveler, who expressed positive comments about his trip over multiple bus lines between Chicago and Los Angeles, admitted that there were delays and inconveniences, including a time-consuming broken axle and miles of poor roads. As for the latter, he remarked about crossing the Arizona desert: "There was some sand, and in one patch of this we stalled, so that all of the men had to get out and push." Yet he opined, "Over most of even the worst of this section better time could be made than on some of the run-down gravel roads of Arkansas, Louisiana and Texas."[20]

As with all intercity transport, there were complaints, and over time they revealed some consistency. Even though the industry evolved rapidly from its gestation stage, gaining maturity by the end of the 1930s, passengers, representing all backgrounds, fussed about meal stops where food might be tasteless and even stomach-turning, menu choices limited, and poor service endemic. Whether bad food, rotten service, or not, prices might also be out of line. One rider in the 1930s said, "[Food] prices were high, especially in the lonely places where there was no competition." In 1947 another traveler commented, "When I went into [the] restaurant as a bus passenger Cokes were ten cents. But when I returned for a second one, after the bus had pulled out, the price had dropped to a nickel." Some bus companies apparently paid attention to food matters. The short-lived Golden Eagle Transcontinental Lines, headquartered in Tulsa, Oklahoma, made it a point to reassure prospective riders, "Meals are served at the best places en route, at reduced prices to all passengers."[21]

A frequent complaint involved toilet facilities, commonly lacking on board the gasoline- and early diesel-powered buses. Bathrooms at rest stops were often inconveniently located. In 1929 investigators, affiliated with the Trans-Continental Passenger Association, rode across the country and offered these observations: "Many restroom stops are made, but in the majority of cases the transportation company does not operate the restrooms and passengers are forced to use the facilities of hotels, garages, barber shops, etc. In some cases even railroad stations are used." More troubling were the conditions of bus-owned or related restrooms. Passengers fussed about these facilities being dirty and smelly and lacking toilet paper, towels, soap, and hot or even cold running water. There were exceptions. A newspaper feature writer from Seattle, who in the mid-1930s journeyed cross country by bus, explained, "Only *one* stop, exclusive of hotels and terminals, offered the complete service. Rock Springs, Wyo., wins the blue ribbon and the Union Pacific Stages can take the honor." This observant reporter concluded, "As a general rule the stops west of

Minneapolis are superior to those in the east. They are much cleaner and even where there is no sanitary plumbing a real effort seems to have been made to make them acceptable."[22]

Roadside and terminal amenities did improve, especially along routes served by Greyhound after it began to open, in 1939, its chain of Post House restaurants: "quality food and sanitary and adequately equipped restrooms." Unfortunately the company's plan to establish nearly six hundred of these rest and lunch stops along its far-flung system fell short of the projected number. Yet many appeared, although progress did not always create perfection. Over time some urban bus terminals, whether served by Greyhound or not and mostly in the largest cities, became potentially dangerous. The chief of police in Columbus, Ohio, characterized the local bus station as a hot spot, saying, "Pickpockets, con-men, perverts—they all come there to prey on the travelers. We give the terminal quite a bit of attention." Even if a facility were relatively new, food and janitorial services might deteriorate.[23]

The public may have been more concerned about how the outbreak of World War II affected Greyhound and other bus operators. During the four-year conflict, Americans realized that they must make sacrifices, including their travels. The US Office of Defense Transportation ordered the bus industry: "1. To save rubber, 2. To save gasoline, and 3. To conserve equipment to make it last for the duration." Companies repeatedly warned the public about traveling. In 1944 the Minneapolis-based Jefferson Transportation Company offered these pointers on how to cope with wartime conditions: "1. Don't take unnecessary trips. 2. Travel on Tuesdays, Wednesdays, Thursdays—instead of on crowded week-ends. 3. Avoid traveling on holidays, during rush seasons and at rush hours. 4. If you are sometimes inconvenienced, smile it off as a contribution to winning the war. 5. Take as little baggage as possible on any trip. 6. Buy bus tickets in advance to avoid delay at crowded terminals." Greyhound announced: "Don't travel unless your trip is essential. Serve America now so you can see America later." Not only did motorists discover that gasoline, tires, and automobiles and their replacement parts were rationed or difficult, if not impossible, to acquire, but Congress mandated restrictive highway speeds. Public transport—trains, surviving interurbans, airplanes, and buses—operated at capacity, becoming regularly jammed with members of the armed services and their family members, war workers, and those unable to drive themselves. These conditions required some bus riders to stand for part or all of their trips. Bus companies encountered the same limitations that affected car owners, ranging from lack of spare parts to reduced speed limits. Terminals and other facilities became crowded and delays frequent. One driver told of pulling into the San Antonio, Texas, bus station in 1943 only to watch the press of exiting humanity tear off the entrance door, delaying his departure for two hours. But bus and other transportation firms continually told citizens that putting up with wartime inconveniences was a patriotic duty. They surely agreed, helping to explain why ridership peaked in 1945 with more than twenty-seven billion passenger miles, still far less than the record-setting ninety-eight billion passenger miles that railroads carried the previous year.[24]

Capturing the spirit of wartime travel, a traffic manager for Santa Fe Trailways penned a creative piece that he called the "Diary of Bus No. 326":

> August 1, 1943 . . . Oh boy, what a wonderful day! I had my bath down at the shop. Surely miss Jack, the car-cleaner. Understand he's in Guadalcanal. It still embarrasses me to have girls working on me. I knew this was my lucky day when I saw Charley climb into the driver's seat.
>
> He's so careful and cheerful. He brought me up to the depot and boy oh boy, what a crowd. I couldn't take all of them although I stretched my sides as much as I could. I'm glad they got that soldier's wife aboard, she wanted so much to get to California to see her hubby before he went overseas.
>
> I've got a terrific pain in my baggage-rack where that fellow's extra luggage is. I wish folks would travel light like Santa Fe Trailways asks them to. It would make things better for all of us.
>
> Oh well, I'm not complaining. I'm doing a swell job for my Country . . . in fact, I'm doing a bigger job than has ever been done before. And I'm going to do a whole lot more.[25]

Although companies did their best to serve the traveling public and carriers like Mid-Continent Coaches proclaimed "Courtesy is not rationed," some wartime riders believed that with the return to peacetime buses should be avoided. Memories of bad travel experiences have a long shelf life; automobiles and airplanes became preferred options.[26]

Notwithstanding the crush of wartime business and discomforts and challenges posed by equipment and unsatisfactory amenities, many bus patrons for decades found this mode of intercity travel attractive. "Motor Bus Transportation gives the advantages and pleasures of the highways to those who would otherwise get no benefit of them," argued Motor Transit Lines in the early 1930s, more than a decade or so before automobility exploded. As the industry matured, a traveler caught the essence of such an experience. "A trip on the bus is as scenic as a trip in your own automobile and you have none of the responsibility. The driver never fails to point out places of interest and importance." There was more: "The freedom and the gaiety that always prevail in a bus crowd are fun. If a crank gets on, someone laughs him out of it. No one seems in any particular hurry to get to their destination and they all enter into the holiday spirit of the trip. There is usually someone on a bus who is more or less an entertainer and the time goes by pleasantly." A decade later another rider said much the same. "We all quickly became friends. The little girl who with her mother was going back to Texas acquired many almost-fathers and

many packages of chewing gum and peanuts. [A man] had a mouth organ, and that night he played for us, and we sang, and visited, and a couple of budding romances were started." In the 1970s a veteran traveler made this observation: "As a traveler who is familiar with most of the western world's transport, I say going across the country by Greyhound is really the best way to see America. It not only gets you to almost all the cities, but also to the wonderful parks and wildernesses."[27]

The interest in, and even the glamour of, bus travel, especially for longer trips, was heightened by a popular Hollywood movie. In 1934 Columbia Pictures released *It Happened One Night*, based on a short story, "Night Bus," by Samuel Hopkins Adams and starring Claudette Colbert and Clark Gable. This Frank Capra–directed romantic comedy, which won an astonishing five Oscars, showed the comfort of bus travel, depicted the professionalism of the well-groomed driver, and revealed how such a journey assimilated all socioeconomic classes. Characters included a wealthy socialite played by Colbert and a tough, recently fired newspaper reporter played by Gable. In what was a classic movie of escapism during the depths of the Great Depression, one message said that excitement, perhaps even love, could be found on an intercity bus.[28]

Also in 1934, a less famous but still positive Hollywood endorsement of bus travel appeared, *Cross Country Cruise*, featuring June Knight, Alice White, and Lew Ayres. This Greyhound run from New York City to San

Francisco captured the maturing nature of an extended journey. Not only were there optional layovers, including a jaunt on the *Maid of the Mist* at Niagara Falls, but there was the comradery that quickly developed among the passengers, including a solo sung by a female passenger that sparked a group sing. As expected, "You meet a lot of strange people on a bus," and these travelers included a talkative commercial salesman, a bewildered immigrant, husband and wife con artists, a drunk, and a crying baby. And there is engine trouble, "washday" to accommodate the needs of through passengers, and a grand finale in this Universal Pictures melodrama.

Not only do *It Happened One Night* and *Cross County Cruise* depict the fashions of the 1930s, but they correctly indicate that bus patrons dressed up for their trips. Rail and air passengers would do much the same, a tradition that continued through the 1950s. But by the 1960s bus riders became known for their "sloppy" attire, and in time this free-and-easy dress spread to air and the remaining rail service. Still, bus companies before World War II did not expect their passengers to don their Sunday best, and in their publications they took pains to suggest what to wear. "No special type clothing is necessary for a Greyhound bus trip," explained Pacific Greyhound Lines. "A woman will usually choose a street dress or some comfortable sports wear. The latter especially for a trip of several hundred miles or across the continent. A sweater or light weight coat is usually welcome on long trips."[29]

Equipment steadily evolved. By the eve of World War II, bus builders were providing riders with greater comfort, including air-conditioning. In 1941 the bus affiliates of the Santa Fe Railway, Santa Fe Transportation Company, and Santa Fe Trail Transportation Company bragged that "Santa Fe's new fleet of cream and crimson motor stages are completely air-conditioned. Amazingly smooth riding, these new buses are cool, quiet, absolutely dustproof. Deeply cushioned reclining chairs, adjustable to four positions, provide greater comfort." There was this attraction: "Extra wide safety-glass windows offer full view along scenic highways." By the time of the Pearl Harbor attack, Greyhound Lines operated nearly six hundred of its famed fleet of "Silverside" buses, which were introduced in 1938 and compared favorably to the Santa Fe coaches. Progress continued after the government lifted wartime restrictions on bus manufacturing. Equipment became more powerful and luxurious and offered glare- and heat-resistant window glass, wider seats, and controlled temperatures. In 1953 General Motors built for Greyhound its popular forty-three-passenger Scenicruiser bus, a vehicle that featured two diesel engines, power steering and brakes, air suspension, and, of course, air-conditioning. Greyhound proclaimed: "New Era in travel history! This luxury bus offers 4-way sightseeing, raised observation decks, huge picture windows, washroom facilities." Three years later Short Way Lines

NEW *Air-Conditioned* LUXURY DIESELINERS

AIR-CONDITIONED TRAVEL COMFORT AT NO INCREASE IN FARES

of Michigan announced that its new buses offered "adjustable foot rests for added comfort on long trips, reading light for each seat, spot-focused, and a $6,800 General Motors diesel engine that has proven dependable by millions of miles of operation that means on-time schedules for you." In subsequent decades ever more comfortable buses entered service. By the 1980s the South Dakota–based Jack Rabbit Bus Line, for example, promoted its "Executive Hares," coaches that provided the latest in seating comfort, a public address system, and easy-to-see television monitors that offered recent Hollywood releases.[30]

BUS DRIVERS

Then there was the bus driver, the man who was in charge. (Occasionally there were women—"jitneyettes" during World War I, temporary ones during World War II, and permanent hires in more recent years.) Until the early 1950s he was *always* white. Unlike with the steamboat captain, locomotive engineer, airplane pilot, and perhaps the interurban motorman, there was an interaction between driver and passengers that resembled that earlier relationship between the stagecoach driver and his passengers. In fact, scores of early bus companies called themselves "Auto Stages" or "Motor Stages."[31]

The bus driver welcomed passengers, collected tickets, pointed out scenic attractions and places of interest, and announced stops. Early on a few companies dispatched multiple drivers. "Two courteous uniformed drivers alternate in driving on every stage," bragged Interstate Stages in 1927. "One operator is always available to care for comforts of the passengers and to dispense information regarding interesting points along the route." Passengers surely felt pampered. Even without an extra driver or attendant, the man behind the wheel usually had the same effect.

"A personal atmosphere pervades the coach," observed a writer for *National Geographic Magazine* in 1950. "Unlike the plane pilot or railway engineer, the operator stays in touch with riders, who often ask him questions or converse." At the height of the great Florida land boom of the 1920s, the Auto Bus Line, which operated between Bonaventure, Rockledge, and Cocoa, encouraged passengers to discuss real-estate purchases. "DO YOU WANT TO BUY A HOME? Consult the driver. He will meet every requirement." And company after company stressed its courteous operators. The Cleveland-Pittsburgh Motor Stage announced in 1927: "The unfailing courtesy of our experienced Pilots makes you feel as though you are traveling in your own 'private car.'" A year later a small carrier that linked the Northern Great Plains cities of Bismarck and Aberdeen announced: "COURTESY IS KINDNESS—It is an asset that costs nothing and upon which we can draw without reserve. It is an OPEN ACCOUNT and should never be in the RED and therefore the Interstate Transportation Company requests its patrons to report any employee whose actions jeopardize a strict compliance with our Slogan—SAFETY, COURTESY, SERVICE." Understandably safety was always the recurring theme. "If every private car owner had the same performance record as the average Greyhound operator, the highways would be many times as safe," proclaimed the company in 1946. "Greyhound's safety record is outstanding in transportation! The reason: rigid training, strict observance of safety rules, and a literal application of 'courtesy of the road.'" Then in the latter part of the twentieth century, while courtesy and safety remained industry priorities, the personal connections between operator and passenger became more restricted. On some buses, partitions appeared between the driver's seat and the passenger section, and later they became nearly universal.[32]

Who were these bus drivers? Resembling their passengers, these individuals hailed from varied backgrounds. As the industry emerged during the era of World War I, drivers often had had some mechanical experience, perhaps associated with a farm, garage, or machine shop. Then as the nation slipped into recession in 1921, producing that "forgotten depression," the unemployed, whether truck drivers, miners, railroad shop workers, store clerks, or even college students, might turn to the burgeoning bus industry for jobs, including driver positions. When the economy rebounded after 1923, bus firms continued to tap a similar employment pool. From sketchy evidence, the turnover rate was relatively small, even though in the 1920s pay was hardly that of unionized railroad workers, and hours in service might be much longer than those of their train counterparts. Companies, especially giants Greyhound and Trailways, would later report having drivers who remained in their employ for twenty-five, thirty, or more years. Take the career of Russell A. Byrd, a veteran driver and author of several bus-related books. He began his bus career in 1918 at age fourteen driving and shuttling jitneys in Fort Travis, Texas, and later he joined Yelloway Lines and then Greyhound in Los Angeles, retiring in 1980 at age seventy-six. Wages and eventually fringe benefits were frequently comparable with other blue-collar jobs, and working conditions were mostly pleasant and stimulating, although they could become stressful. Early on there was the opportunity for the driver to wear a snappy uniform with military-style across-the-chest belt, puttees (leather leggings), necktie, and cap. Such a neat attire conveyed a sense of skilled professionalism. Styles changed, but drivers continued to dress up for their runs.[33]

During the formative years a bus driver likely had little or no formal training, although in most states he needed a chauffeur's license. Still, some early carriers (and later ones, too) bragged that they carefully screened and trained their drivers. "No driver is permitted to take out a bus until he has completed an intensive course of training and satisfied the management that he is reliable, dependable and naturally courteous toward the patrons of the line," announced the Cleveland-Akron Bus Company in 1926. A few years later Great Lakes Stages said much the same. "Great Lakes drivers are all graduated from Great Lakes training school before they are permitted to take a bus on the road. Applicants are selected according to their physical fitness, their ability to think quick, and are required to give references showing their complete history for five years prior to the application." This company went on to note: "He is taught the rudiments of mechanics as pertaining to motor coaches and is skilled in the manner of how to handle our patrons, and is tested for courtesy under all conditions." Maine Stages said: "Our drivers are selected with utmost care. They are required to stop at all railroad crossings; to drive well on their side of the road, to dim lights in passing cars at night. They are prohibited, under penalty of dismissal, to speed or pass cars on curves or hills, or to cut in and out of traffic." It was common for smaller companies, old and not so old, to have their owners personally screen applicants. The founder and longtime head of Peter Pan Bus Lines "carefully considered every man who applied to sit behind the wheel of a Peter Pan bus. With all employees, and most particularly with drivers, he stressed courtesy, helpfulness, and, most importantly, safety. Driver performance was closely documented, and a program was instituted to recognize and reward its best drivers." Carriers liked to boast that they stressed driver safety. In 1938 United Motor Coach Company of Des Plaines, Illinois, announced that since 1931 it had paid drivers $4,556 in "Safety Bonuses," and that June it had awarded "Nineteen Ace Driver Awards [for safety]." All managers surely would concur that one of the ingredients that made a good driver was a sense of humor, but character and responsibility were basic.[34]

With training or not, having a mechanical aptitude and physical strength early on allowed a driver to master his job, perhaps with confidence and ease. Not only were buses underpowered, especially in the 1920s, but they often fell victim to mechanical breakdowns. No wonder the driver carried a well-equipped toolkit. This large box would store not only needed tools, particularly wrenches or spanners of varying sizes, but also cables, nuts and bolts, fan belts, inner tubes, light bulbs, and other essential replacement parts, including spark plugs. The latter engine component frequently failed or pre-ignited, forcing the driver to stop when he heard the telltale popping sound. When he replaced the fouled plugs, which were quickly identified since they turned a light blue, he had to be careful because "those bad plugs were extremely hot." And it was not unusual for the driver to tinker with a cranky transmission or clutch plate.[35]

More so than mechanical breakdowns, flat tires were endemic. Neither did tire quality, being described as iffy in the 1920s and seldom lasting for more than two thousand miles, nor dirt and rock roads help. Drivers became intimately acquainted with the spare tire, screw jack, and lug wrench, things they customarily checked before departing a bus garage or terminal. Being muscular helped any driver who faced a tire problem. Even in the 1920s tires were heavy, being at least forty by eight inches in size and weighing one hundred pounds or more. A veteran driver recalled that it might be difficult to find a level place along the road. "I had to use one of those old-fashioned jacks, and it could slip if I didn't have a relatively flat stopping space." It commonly took about forty-five minutes to change out a bad tire. In addition to building up his physique handling tires, the driver also did so at the steering wheel. Even on improved roads, "driving demanded two strong arms." Power steering came later.[36]

A pioneer driver usually had access to additional travel aids. He frequently carried a water can for the radiator, especially along roadways with limited service facilities. Early equipment commonly overheated. During hot weather Packard vehicles were notorious for requiring frequent radiator refills. And removing a hot radiator cap could be potentially dangerous. Motor oil was also stored. Some vehicles were heavy oil burners, requiring several quarts every few hundred miles.[37]

Notwithstanding the challenges presented by early buses, whether mechanical, tire, or something else, including roads, weather, and accidents, there could be problems with passengers. Nearly all riders behaved, but occasionally troublemakers appeared. The most common were intoxicated passengers who became noisy, used profane language, and occasionally turned belligerent. Before establishment of large interstate carriers and their accompanying book of rules, drivers used their best judgment when dealing with any unruly rider. "I looked tough," recalled a driver on how he handled drunks. By the mid-1930s Greyhound had established a clear policy. "The most important thing is for the bus driver to protect respectable passengers rather than show undue courtesy to an objectionable drunk. When a drunk is removed from the bus, the removal should take place at a station where there are facilities for shelter. Drivers should not involve other passengers by asking them to assist, but should call upon the ticket agent, rest or lunch stop owner, or some one closely connected with Greyhound for assistance." There was more. "It is not advisable for the bus driver to swear out a warrant of arrest for intoxicated passengers. Passengers removed should be left with endorsed transportation [ticket] so they may continue their trip when they sober up, or be able to secure a refund on the unused portion of their ticket." About the same time, Crescent Stages of Anniston, Alabama, made known its policy: "Right is reserved by the Company to refuse conveyance to any passenger who is intoxicated, or obnoxious through use of profane language, as in the judgment of our employees. We also reserve the right to eject from the Buses any passenger who may be judged guilty of the same, or any other misconduct while en route."[38]

Although alcohol issues never vanished, the advent of a widespread drug culture in the 1960s forced drivers to cope with a new challenge. "I have always enjoyed people and I have never been at a loss for words when talking to them," commented a Greyhound driver. "However, I was constantly having problems with the younger generation wanting to smoke pot on the bus. Smoking was confined to the last two rows of seats and to cigarettes only." This driver kept a watchful eye out for rule violators. "When I left the Stockton [California] depot each trip I would make an announcement pertaining to smoking. I would hear some giggling in the rear of the bus and I knew I had some pot smokers aboard. I always wore sunglasses and adjusted the big rear view mirror in the bus, so I could see to the back of the bus without raising my head. I always kept the little six-inch window open by my side so I would create a draft and bring any smoke from the rear of the bus." His strategy worked. "I usually got about five miles out of Stockton before I would smell marijuana. I immediately started looking to the rear and watching the kids (usually 16 to 20 years old) passing the marijuana around." He then took action:

> It was twenty miles to Tracy, my first stop, and by the time I arrived, I would
> have everyone that was involved with smoking, identified by clothing or
> looks. I would nonchalantly step off the bus and walk into the baggage room. I
> immediately picked up the phone and called the Tracy PD [Police Department]
> and in less than two minutes there would be two police cars and usually three,

screeching to a halt surrounding the bus. I would then come out of the baggage room and greet the officers. I would go on the bus ahead of the officers and point out the ones I wanted removed.[39]

A much more serious passenger matter involved treatment of African Americans in the Jim Crow South. Ten states legally controlled the mingling of the races in public places, whether on trains and buses or in air, bus, and rail terminals. Like steam railroads and electric interurbans, bus companies honored state laws about the separation of blacks and whites, meaning that people of color needed to take rear seats. Unlike on many southern transit buses, intercity buses, whether interstate or intrastate, had no clear line dividing the space between races. Yet Colored or Colored Only and White or White Only signs were posted in bus stations and terminals, and companies implied in their schedules that Jim Crow reigned. An Albany, Georgia-based affiliate of the Trailways System announced in the Rules and Regulations section of its public timetables: "Modern Coaches reserve to themselves full control and discretion as to seating of passengers and reserve the right to change such seating at any time during the trip." In the South, riders, black and white, knew what this meant.[40]

For passengers of color, racial segregation was a humiliating experience. Pauli Murray, North Carolina native, lawyer, and civil rights activist, recalled that of all the segregated institutions in the Jim Crow era, she hated the bus the most. The intimacy of the seating, Murray wrote, "permitted the public humiliation of black people to be carried out in the presence of privileged white spectators, who witnessed our shame in silence or indifference."[41]

Drivers in Dixie nearly always enforced code and custom. They allowed white passengers to be seated first and then blacks. During World War II, white soldiers boarded first, then white civilians, black soldiers, and finally black civilians. These drivers made certain that blacks took their proper place. There were instances when a driver and a person of color got into verbal clashes and occasionally physical altercations. In December 1946 a dramatic event occurred in Houston, Texas, when a white bus driver killed a sixty-five-year-old black barber who intervened in a dispute between the driver and a black teenager. Six years later a driver of a Southeastern Greyhound bus in Georgia and his white passengers ignored pleas for help from an elderly black minister who was being beaten by two white men because he refused to move to a rear seat. The injured man then left the bus.[42]

Changes occurred. The NAACP and the larger civil rights movement, which spearheaded antidiscrimination US Supreme Court decisions, including *Browder v. Gayle* in 1956, and later an Interstate Commerce Commission desegregation edict led to the demise of Jim Crow in the late 1950s and early 1960s. Interstate and then intrastate runs became desegregated, although not immediately. Some companies were slower than others in ending the practice, mostly on intrastate runs. As for the latter, bus officials authorized drivers to ask, not force, black passengers to occupy rear seats. "Some of the drivers, knowing they could not enforce a segregation request, made no effort to jim crow intrastate riders," observed historian Catherine Barnes. "Others did, and on all lines, some drivers segregated even interstate patrons in defiance of company policy and federal law." The US Department of Justice, however, reported that by June 1963 it knew of no segregation by any air, rail, or bus facility, not even in the Deep South, and freedom to travel for the bus rider of color took on a new meaning.[43]

Native Americans might likewise feel the sting of racial discrimination. In certain areas with large American Indian populations—for example, Arizona and South Dakota—drivers might insist that members of this minority, especially adult males, sit in the back of the bus. Their principal objection: passengers who were already inebriated or who started to imbibe. Troublemakers usually would be ejected while en route.

Except in the racially segregated South or in Native American areas, drivers usually did not encounter passenger problems. Rather there were happier happenings. In the late 1920s and early 1930s, drivers at the end of a long-distance trip might receive a handsome tip from their passengers, not unlike what became customary for drivers who later handled charter and tour runs. A Yelloway driver described a popular practice. "Old timers explained to me that no driver ever drove day and night just for the sake of being on time. It was the custom to drive through the last night at the suggestion of the passengers, who, in turn, gave the driver what they would have paid for the night's lodging." The sum was not insignificant. "This netted the driver about seventy-five dollars bonus for the trip, and put the passengers in a day early. As the drivers were paid only one hundred twenty-five to one hundred fifty dollars a month, this bonus comprised the bulk of their earnings." And this example: regular riders during the holiday season might present a favored driver with food, drink, or other small gifts.[44]

Bus drivers continually sought the best runs and came to prefer charter and tour assignments. Even a rookie driver, who could not hold a good-paying regular route because of limited seniority, might be assigned to an attractive run. "By working the extra board you would get the overloads [of assigned runs] and it paid the same as being on the regular run," explained a Greyhound driver. "We also had lots of charters that were worked from the extra board and they were always interesting. We went on lots of trips to baseball and football games and the drivers always go to the game free." Advancing on the seniority roster, drivers could expect good assignments and better income. "My life as a Greyhound Driver was a happy one and an educational one, geographically," recalled a veteran employee. "I have seen many things that I would never have had the opportunity to see if I had not been behind the steering wheel of a Greyhound bus."[45]

The longevity of bus drivers attests to an occupation that so many enjoyed. Yet at times hard feelings flared between workers and managers. As with all transportation forms during the twentieth century, labor unrest occurred, although it was not common among bus employees until the more recent past. Smaller carriers, especially mom-and-pop operations, usually hired nonunion workers, and these individuals generally avoided confrontations with their owners, benefiting often from friendly paternalism. Yet larger carriers, especially Greyhound, faced repeated strikes in the 1970s and later, mostly involving their drivers and ticket agents who belonged to the Amalgamated Transit Union (ATU) rather than from unionized maintenance workers.

By the latter part of the twentieth century, Greyhound had become the eight-hundred-pound bus gorilla, operating a fleet of nearly four thousand buses and carrying about 60 percent of intercity bus riders. In October 1983 thousands of drivers hit the bricks, protesting a 9.5 percent salary cut, a required contribution to their pension plan, and other concessions that amounted to wage and benefit reductions that totaled 20 to 40 percent. Immediately ATU members put up informational and protest signs, including this one in Mobile, Alabama: "Caution, scabbing can be hazardous to your health." Some wore T-shirts saying "Go Trailways." Violence erupted. In Zanesville, Ohio, a "scab" driver ran over and killed a union driver who was on picket-line duty, and vandalism of buses— broken windshields and mirrors and slashed tires—became widespread. It took more than two months to hammer out and ratify a new contract before peace returned, and most drivers were reinstated. Some employees, though, received pink slips for their strike activities.[46]

Yet for Greyhound, which experienced its own internal problems due to corporate mismanagement and competition from discount airlines and Amtrak, that 1987 contract led to greater unrest when it expired three years later. History repeated itself. In March 1990 drivers struck, and violence returned. A replacement driver struck down a striker in San Francisco, killing him, and additional havoc, including gunfire, took place. This dispute lasted thirty-eight months, during which time the company slipped into bankruptcy. Although the National Labor Relations Board awarded the ATU damages for unfair labor practices, the bankruptcy reorganization discharged these corporate liabilities. Retrenchment was another result of the strike; Greyhound ended service to hundreds of smaller communities, mostly in rural areas of the Midwest and Great Plains, causing the permanent loss of jobs.[47]

Union power, however, waned, and drivers found that in an era of transportation deregulation, wages and benefits declined. Firms like Bolt and other low-cost newcomers hardly paid top dollar. Still, the charter and tour business remained attractive for those behind the wheel, and the remaining scheduled runs continued to provide employment. Significantly, buses during the post–World War II era have experienced neither the secular decline of passenger rail nor the rapid growth of commercial air travel.

No different from other forms of transportation, the bus industry has attracted enthusiasts, but it pales in comparison to the long-standing (and continuing) popularity of railroads. After all, individuals and groups of railfans can often be seen at trackside taking photographs and making videos of passing trains, but few if any bus devotees appear along highways and interstate interchanges capturing images of buses. Following World War II, the National Motor Bus Association, later renamed the Motor Bus Society, came into being with this announced purpose: "The collection and publication of information about the history and development of the bus industry in North America." By the second decade of the twenty-first century, the organization claimed about seven hundred members domestically and from abroad; kept its small group of supporters informed through a quarterly publication, *Motor Coach Age*; and created a modest archive and reference library, one of only a limited number that have been established. Bus aficionados also have opened several small museums, including the Museum of Bus Transportation in Hershey, Pennsylvania, and the Pacific Bus Museum in Fremont, California. The latter was founded in 1989 by "a group of bus enthusiasts who enjoyed getting together and talking about buses." Fans have wholeheartedly supported preservationists in their efforts to save several classic bus stations. When it comes to bus nostalgia, the autobiographical writings and collecting of Jim Lehrer, an avowed "bus nut," are best known. This retired journalist and former anchor of the *PBS Newshour* has amassed probably the largest collection of bus memorabilia in the country, featuring cap badges, timetables, signs, and a restored 1946 Flexible bus. Yet Lehrer's accomplishments represent the unusual, whereas over the decades there have been scores of railroad and traction fans who have accumulated as many and possibly more collectable artifacts.[48]

While bus enthusiasts are scant in comparison to those of steam and electric railroads, bus-related place names are virtually nonexistent. Hundreds of "depot" and "railroad" streets dot the urban landscape, as do a smaller number of "interurban" and "traction" ones. Yet barely a handful of such names testify to or honor the intercity bus. There is a notable exception. In July 1984 Hibbing, Minnesota, named a section of Third

This beautifully preserved Greyhound Bus Lines station, which dates from 1937, stands on its original site adjoining US Highway 61 in Blytheville, Arkansas. Designed by Memphis architect William Norland Van Powell, this functional facility represents the Streamline Moderne style, created to suggest the speed lines of Greyhound buses and the firm's dynamic nature.

Courtesy of Mindi Rice, Main Street Blytheville

Avenue "Greyhound Boulevard." The town and Greyhound claim that this Iron Range community is where the company traces its corporate roots. "Hibbing is our birthplace," said a Greyhound official. "It's like Plymouth Rock."[49]

Strikingly different from those of railroads, few bus facilities have been listed on the National Register of Historic Places. A prominent one, however, is the former Greyhound bus station in Blytheville, Arkansas. This structure, constructed in the late 1930s and designed by Memphis architect William Noland Powell, is one of a limited number of surviving Art Deco bus stations. Although closed about 2001 and falling into disrepair, a community preservation effort led to municipal ownership. The building was refurbished, and in 2010 it reopened as a visitor center and transportation museum.[50]

Even though scheduled bus service has declined in recent decades, with thousands of communities no longer having access to this form of intercity transportation, Americans continue to board intercity coaches. Expansion of low-fare, regular-route carriers will enable a cross section of travelers to have bus experiences, both good and bad. Riders are often individuals who take advantage of this transport alternative for relatively short trips or who for longer ones perhaps have a minimal value of their time. An industry bright spot: an aging population undoubtedly will increase the need for more drivers and support personnel. Also younger travelers—"millennials"—might not agree that the automobile symbolizes freedom and independence and might find owning a car too expensive and burdensome. And charter and tour segments will likely remain strong. As in the past there will be those accommodating and professional drivers behind the wheel. Nevertheless, that once-prevailing sense of optimism among bus advocates will probably never return.

Airplanes and the American People

TAKING OFF

In the 1920s American advocates of commercial aviation considered the airplane to be the "most modern way" for intercity travel. Yet a decade or so earlier, they would not have expressed such an opinion. In fact, there were those who had long believed that "a flying machine is impossible, in spite of the testimony of the birds." When the generally accepted first heavier-than-air flight took place at windswept Kill Devil Hills near Kitty Hawk, North Carolina, on December 17, 1903, the Wright brothers, Orville and Wilbur, had constructed an airplane that resembled a toy more than a useful machine. But it did not take long before their Wright Flyer could claim to be the world's first practical airplane. In 1905 at Huffman Prairie, a cow pasture near the brothers' home in Dayton, Ohio, test flights demonstrated that a flying machine was sophisticated enough to bank, to turn, to circle, and to be fully controlled. The Wrights concluded that their invention had passed from the initial experimental stage. It did not take long for self-styled futurists to fantasize about air travel. In 1910 an editorial writer for the *Minneapolis Journal* predicted that aircraft would someday take people "through the clean, fresh, dustless roads of the air" with the ground below "like a green alluring map, with no mountains or valleys or rivers or ravines to conquer."[1]

Other aviation pioneers joined the famous Ohioans. In 1908 Glenn Curtiss, who became the first major American airplane manufacturer, flew his *June Bug* a distance of one mile, and *Scientific American* awarded him a trophy for this memorable achievement. More aviation triumphs followed. Two years later, for example, Thomas Baldwin in his home-built *Red Devil* became the first person to fly across the Mississippi River at Saint Louis. Then in 1911 a Wright airplane, piloted by Calbraith Perry Rodgers, crossed America, although his well-publicized exploit took eighty-four days and involved numerous forced landings. Not to be overlooked were aeronautical advances made by Europeans, especially aviation pioneers in France, Germany, and Great Britain.[2]

This gestation period for aviation produced more excitement and entertainment than any meaningful commercial possibilities. Americans considered "aeroplanes" to be mechanical curiosities and aviators to be daredevils or madmen. Those who had the opportunity to watch these fragile craft—described as "flimsy kites"—at air shows and stunting exhibitions, where brave pilots "thrilled the throngs," numbered often in the thousands. It did not take long before public interest increased, becoming ever more lucrative for air-show promoters and aviators.[3]

Notwithstanding aircraft limitations, companies made brief attempts prior to the early 1920s to create commercial passenger service. The first notable (and successful) experiment took place in Florida when civic boosters launched the Saint Petersburg–Tampa Airboat Line. This operation involved using a two-passenger wood-and-muslin Benoist Type XIV flying boat to cross Tampa Bay, and it allowed wealthy vacationers and others the opportunity to take a thirty-minute flight rather than an extended rail journey, a three-hour boat trip, or a nearly fifty-mile road detour. Apparently most passengers saw this more as a novelty rather than a way to negotiate the bay barrier. The twice-daily (except Sunday) service, which began on New Year's Day, 1914, cost $5 ($115 in current dollars) for a one-way ticket, and passengers were limited to a gross weight of two hundred pounds, including personal luggage. Lasting for the three months of the subsidized contract, the flying boat safely made about one hundred trips and carried nearly two hundred passengers. Plans to continue flights during the following tourist season and to expand the frequency of service fizzled; the venture ended largely because of the financial uncertainties caused by the outbreak of the European war.[4]

By the time of World War I, however, airplanes had become faster, more dependable, and capable of flying relatively long distances. Better aerodynamic designs, more powerful engines, and stronger structural components made these impressive advancements possible. Optimism was in the air.

With the signing of the Armistice in November 1918 and the return to "normalcy," domestic aviation enthusiasts renewed their efforts to establish commercial flights. Not only were they encouraged by technological advancements, but the availability of inexpensive surplus military aircraft became an additional incentive. Yet most of these immediate postwar ventures either never became more than unrealized plans or quickly failed. The Curtiss-Iowa Corporation, based in Monmouth, Illinois, was one example. In April 1922 the firm inaugurated a passenger and freight service between Chicago and Kansas City, yet it operated for only a month. Still there were ventures that lasted much longer. More durable were the Seattle-Victoria Air Mail Line, commencing in March 1919 and later becoming part of Northwest Air Service, and the Aeromarine company. Inglis Uppercu, a college-trained engineer turned aviation promoter, headed the better-known latter venture. Using modified F-5L ex–US Navy seaplanes that could accommodate eleven passengers, Uppercu launched the Aeromarine Sightseeing and Navigation Company in 1920, and he set out to demonstrate the reliability, safety, and speed of air travel.[5]

The savvy Uppercu varied where his Aeromarine seaplanes flew. Initially his infant firm served summer passengers who went from New York City to nearby resorts in Atlantic City, New Jersey; Newport, Rhode Island; and Southampton, Long Island, what became its Eastern Division. After carrying more than a thousand fare-paying riders, Uppercu and his associates decided to expand; the firm of Aeromarine-West Indies Airways made its corporate debut in October 1920, operating two daily flights between Key West, Florida, and Havana, Cuba. Although the cost for a one-way ticket was pricy—$75 ($375 in current dollars)—time savings were impressive: one hour and fifteen minutes by air rather than eight hours by steamship. Potentially there were other attractions. Water travelers who suffered from seasickness would be spared that discomfort. And there was the airborne experience itself. *Scientific American* explained, "The enchantment the aerial traveler experiences aloft will offer a further inducement to go via the air route." Still, in order to combat public concerns about flying, Aeromarine publicized that it was committed to "Safety First, Last, and All the Time." Unfortunately for this upstart carrier, many potential riders found the $16 to $20 charged by water carriers more attractive. The airline also encountered multiple operational problems, yet it did not abandon its Cuban flights. During the winter of 1921–1922, the company slashed fares, and passenger loads tripled. The following year a US Post Office contract for Cuban mail and added flights between Miami and Nassau generated precious revenues. Thirsty Americans, hindered by national prohibition, found easy access to wet Cuba and the Bahamas to their liking.[6]

The concept of a varied service area resulted in what proved to be more encouraging ventures. In calendar year 1922 Aeromarine operated the Eastern Division in New York City, where it offered charter and sightseeing trips and benefited from a new dock facility at Eighty-Second Street on the North (Hudson) River. It also launched a Great Lakes Division, where on July 17, 1920, it inaugurated daily flights between Cleveland and Detroit, and this soon became double-daily service because of an aggressive advertising campaign. In order to promote this business, the company opened the first branch office for regularly scheduled flights in the lobby of the upscale Hollenden Hotel in downtown Cleveland.

During the two months that these trips operated, nearly 4,500 passengers took to the air.[7]

The popularity of the flights on the Great Lakes Division stemmed from speed ("The Ninety Minute Line") and the thrill of flying over the waters of Lake Erie between the Cleveland public docks and the Detroit River near Detroit's commercial center. There was more. Harry Bruno, Aeromarine's traffic and sales head, showed creativity when he confronted the public's fear of flight and his desire to make everyone "air minded." He launched what he called "a new bag of promotion tricks." The company flew various opinion makers—mayors, bankers, journalists—over the Great Lakes Division, with the expectation that their safe and enjoyable trips would convince others that no one needed to worry about these seaplanes. More imaginative was an arrangement with the *Detroit Times* in which the airline sponsored a weekly limerick contest. A free round trip went to the person who wrote the best last lines. A typical limerick challenge:

> A pretty young woman named Jean
> Flew to Cleveland by Aeromarine.
> Said she: "It's just fine;
> In Detroit I can dine;
> . . . .

After the winner was selected, newspaper coverage followed. "Pictures of the winner in the plane and an interview on how he enjoyed the flight appeared next," related Bruno. "Thousands competed for these free rides." The service also received free advertising and goodwill when it arranged with used-car dealers in Cleveland and Detroit for anyone who bought a vehicle that cost $300 or more to receive a complimentary round trip. "Aeromarine and flying made more valuable friends."[8]

Although the northern units of Aeromarine, most of all its Great Lakes Division, showed promise, the company failed to become profitable. Rising maintenance costs and the seasonal need to relocate equipment and personnel had become financial drains. Furthermore, absence of a federal subsidy or a domestic mail contract hardly helped. Then disaster struck. A fatal accident and loss of an aircraft in the Havana harbor nearly shut down operations. But the New York and Great Lakes Divisions continued the following year, although New York service ended in July 1923. The Cleveland and Detroit flights proved to be more popular (and remunerative), and they remained operational throughout the 1923 summer season, hauling more than five thousand passengers and without any serious difficulties. Yet the writing was on the wall. Uppercu, who had sought and failed to gain an aircraft-manufacturing contract from the US

Navy, quit the aviation business. Having invested heavily in his money-losing Aeromarine, he was unwilling to endure further losses."[9]

Commercial aviation did not die with Aeromarine. The federal government came to the rescue and involves the story of domestic airmail. In spring 1918 when airmail service began between New York and Washington, DC, it was the US Army, not private carriers, who was involved. The US Post Office soon expanded the army's role by establishing a transcontinental air route. Although this expansion took shape in several stages, veteran pilots from the Great War on September 8, 1920, flew "aero mail" between New York City and San Francisco via Cleveland, Chicago, Omaha, Cheyenne, Salt Lake City, and Reno. More feeder routes followed, including runs between Chicago and Minneapolis/Saint Paul, Chicago and Saint Louis, and Cleveland and Cincinnati.[10]

Then in February 1925 a sea change occurred. Congress passed and President Calvin Coolidge signed the Contract Air Mail Act, popularly known as the Kelly Act after its sponsor, Representative Clyde Kelly of Pennsylvania. This law accelerated commercial air transport by authorizing the postmaster general to determine air routes and to pay private carriers to fly mail over them. A mail contract, coupled with revenue passengers, promised the potential for profits. No other non-technological event so directly encouraged commercial aviation; it was not long before passengers shared space with sacks of mail. Also of significance was enactment the following year of the Air Commerce bill that created the Aeronautics Branch within the US Department of Commerce. This measure was designed to promote aviation through navigational support equipment and other improvements.[11]

Two years after the Kelly Act, what many considered to be the foremost single event of the Roaring Twenties occurred—the Charles Lindbergh trans-Atlantic flight. On May 20, 1927, this twenty-five-year-old accomplished airmail pilot—the "Flying Fool"—took off in his single-engine Ryan airplane, the *Spirit of St. Louis*, from New York's Roosevelt Field; thirty-three and a half hours later, he landed at Le Bourget Field outside Paris. This epic solo flight, so perfectly executed, captured the imagination of the American public. According to the *New York World*, the Minnesota native had performed "the greatest feat of a solitary man in the records of the human race." His daring and success triggered an aviation frenzy, providing the impulse for air transport expansion in those go-go years of the late 1920s. After all, Lindbergh redefined the possibilities of human flight. If the *Spirit of St. Louis* could fly 3,610 miles, thought many, why couldn't a larger commercial aircraft bind the nation, even the world? This air-mindedness was also stimulated by the Richard Byrd and Floyd Bennett flight over the North Pole in 1926 and two years later by Byrd's flight across the South Pole. By the close of 1928, there were forty-eight commercial airlines in the United States, serving 355 cities and claiming a combined total of approximately twenty thousand route miles. The aviation age was at hand.[12]

The Kelly Act and the Lindbergh flight were pivotal events in the development of commercial aviation. By the late 1920s an employee of Lincoln Financial Service in New York City penned these thoughts about the emerging airline industry. "Today we cannot judge by yesterday. Air progress is much too fast. Estimates do not avail, for who can estimate Americans' reactions to this new, time-saving, money-saving means of communication and transportation." He continued, "Airplanes are built in every growing numbers. Loads increase amazingly. Miles flown begin to assume railroad proportions. Air service is actually an industry."[13]

A milestone in commercial aviation came in 1928 with the creation of a daring business venture, Transcontinental Air Transport, or simply TAT. Soon this fledgling carrier promoted itself as "The Lindbergh Line," to honor "Lucky Lindy." Lindbergh chaired the TAT technical committee, and the company sought to capitalize on his fame as the "Hero of the Century." This New York to Los Angeles service, which began in summer 1929, brought to public attention the practicality of long-distance air travel.[14]

The concept of TAT came from the creative mind of Clement Melville "C. M." Keys, founder of the financial firm of C. M. Keys & Company and an investor in the developing aviation industry. Keys, his backers, and others realized that there were those businessmen who wanted to connect quickly with distant associates and customers rather than to rely on established methods of contact, whether long-distance telephone calls, airmail letters, or the fastest rail passenger service. If someone wished to travel physically between Gotham and the City of Angels with speed, it necessitated taking a limited train, perhaps going to Chicago via either the New York Central or Pennsylvania, and from there on the Atchison, Topeka & Santa Fe (Santa Fe); Chicago, Rock Island & Pacific-Southern Pacific; or Chicago & North Western-Union Pacific. The length of time for these cross-country journeys was seventy-five hours or longer, and they involved a change of trains and perhaps stations in the Windy City.[15]

TAT made a difference "for those whose time is too important to waste." It offered New York to Los Angeles in only forty-eight hours. Furthermore, it was a first-class experience where travelers did not need to be brave and hardy. "It is Modern Transportation's answer to the demands for faster travel without sacrifice of safety or comfort," exhorted the company. Since night flying remained problematic, especially over mountainous terrain, this service involved coast-to-coast transit by tri-motored plane and deluxe train.[16]

The Airway Limited

Between

New York and Port Columbus, Ohio

Columbus, O., and Indianapolis, Ind.

Rail-Air Service

COAST TO COAST IN 48 HOURS

Beginning July 7, 1929

RAIL-AIR Passenger Service will be inaugurated by the Pennsylvania Railroad Transcontinental Air Transport, Inc., and the Atchison, Topeka and Santa Fe Railway between New York and Los Angeles and San Francisco in both directions.

Pennsylvania Railroad

On the eve of the Transcontinental Air Transport and joint rail service via the Pennsylvania and Santa Fe railroads, the former road issued a small brochure on its soon-to-be-introduced *Airways Limited*. The cover image reveals (correctly) a mighty passenger train and two less physically impressive airplanes.

Author's Collection

In its introductory timetable, Transcontinental Air Transport proclaimed that "air-rail passenger service brings Atlantic and Pacific coast cities two days near to each other, and speeds up travel between local points in TAT territory." That publicity statement assumed neither mechanical nor weather delays.

Author's Collection

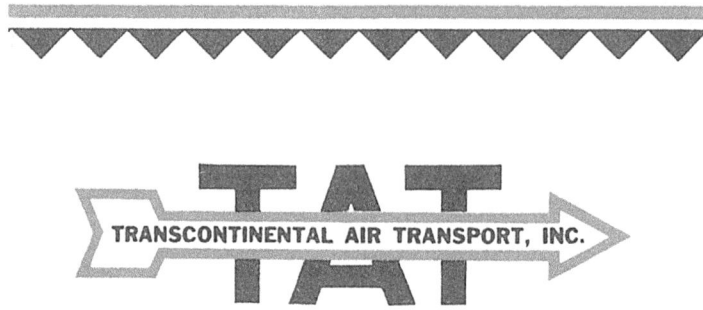

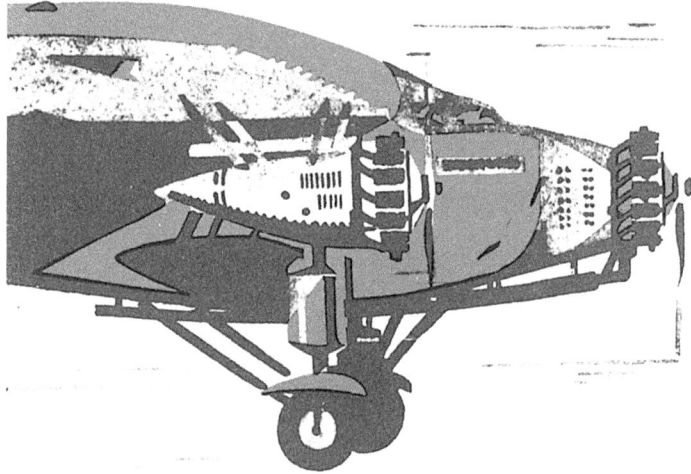

TAT
TRANSCONTINENTAL AIR TRANSPORT, INC.

Coast to Coast by Plane and Train

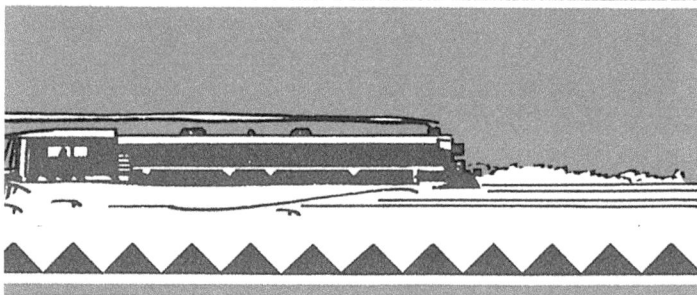

Passengers who partook of the TAT experience, which began officially on July 7, 1929 (there had been rehearsal flights), boarded the *Airway Limited*, a classy Pennsylvania Railroad train that offered an array of amenities: "Barber, bath, valet, ladies' maid, train secretary, writing desk, stock quotations, magazines, newspapers, baseball and football scores (in season)." At 6:05 p.m. this all-Pullman consist steamed out of Pennsylvania Station in New York City for a newly established station at Port Columbus, Ohio, a specially designed one-of-a-kind air-rail facility seven miles east of Columbus (the train, though, continued on through Columbus to Dayton and Indianapolis). There would be dinner in the diner and Pullman berths where TAT patrons enjoyed "sleep, deep and peaceful, as the train glides smoothly over well-laid rails." Upon the 7:55 a.m. arrival at Port Columbus following breakfast, passengers walked under an orange and black canopy to an awaiting all-metal Ford-Tri-Motor airplane—the *Tin Goose*—and soon an attendant proudly announced: "All aboard by air for Indianapolis, St. Louis, Kansas City, and points west."[17]

Passengers boarded quickly; after all, saving time was the advertised raison d'être for this cross-country journey. "Enter the cabin with nine fellow passengers, relax in the comfortable chairs with their reclining backs and prepare to enjoy your flight," announced a TAT publication. Ann Morrow Lindbergh, Charles Lindbergh's wife, commented in a letter to her sister about the plane and service. "It is beautifully comfortable and businesslike; I feel as though I were in a private [railroad] car." She added, "I am crazy to have you take this trip. You simply must. Even Mother would enjoy it." A male cabin attendant—called a courier by TAT—greeted passengers; reviewed safety features; indicated that portable tables were available for food service, card playing, and letter writing; pointed out the lavatory at the rear of the cabin; and passed out balls of cotton to soften the deafening engine noise and chewing gum to help clear ears in the non-pressurized craft. Fortunately, when the plane reached its cruising altitude of about 2,500 feet, the decibel level dropped. The attendant also provided maps that showed the flight route. Then there was the food, initially coffee, small bottles of milk, and rolls. Later a noon meal would be served, prepared by the Fred Harvey Company, TAT's famed caterer, and in midafternoon the attendant offered hot or iced tea. Passengers were encouraged to enjoy the scenery from their personal window as the plane cruised at the steady rate of 110 miles an hour.[18]

During the day there would be several stops. After being airborne for two hours, the plane first landed in Indianapolis. This new terminal offered passengers several amenities, including a dining room and telegraph office. Following stops at Saint Louis, Kansas City, and Wichita, Kansas, the TAT craft touched down at approximately 6:30 p.m. several miles outside Waynoka, Oklahoma. Passengers deplaned and boarded a "luxuriously upholstered trailer bus," which TAT called an "Aero Car," to the Santa Fe Railway station. Before they boarded a nearby set-out Pullman car, they had dinner in an adjoining Harvey House restaurant. At 10:00 p.m. a train crew attached the sleeper to the *Missionary*, which then speed through the night to Clovis, New Mexico. Once at the station, passengers boarded another Aero Car and rode five miles to the Portair landing strip for the second day's plane trip.[19]

The routine of the final leg resembled that of the first day. There were stops at Albuquerque, New Mexico, and the Arizona communities of Winslow and Kingman, and late in the afternoon the trimotor touched down at the Grand Central Air Terminal in Glendale, California, a route that largely followed the Santa Fe main line. During this portion of the journey, a luncheon and midmorning and midafternoon refreshments were served aloft. In Glendale an Aero Car whisked passengers to downtown Los Angeles "in ample time for dinner and the evening's business or social engagements."[20]

The inaugural trips (eastbound and westbound) received extensive newspaper and radio coverage, and thousands of spectators jammed the airports and landing strips along the route. Velva Darling, a passenger on board the first scheduled westbound flight, reflected about her TAT experience in a *World's Work* magazine article: "It proved two facts to me: First, that the luxury, comfort, and speed of this method of transportation have never been equaled, much less surpassed; second, that the popularity of air travel, as demonstrated by the passengers themselves and by the obviously interested and enthusiastic crowds that greet the plane at every airport, is only the first stirrings of a much greater popularity shortly to come." She would be correct. Darling also mentioned this widely held point of view: "Heretofore I have ranked flying along with outdoor sports like horseback riding and tennis. A lot of fun, you know, but not to be taken too frightfully seriously."[21]

The TAT offered a nonpareil operation. It involved about nine hundred miles by rail and two thousand miles by air and came with a hefty one-way price, roughly 16 cents per mile, although the fare varied from a minimum of $337 ($4,690 in current dollars) to a maximum of $403 ($5,600 in current dollars), depending on the choice of Pullman accommodations. Los Angeles passengers could continue their flight (with an additional charge) by connecting directly with Maddux Air Lines, which operated a fleet of Ford trimotors between Los Angeles (Glendale) and San Francisco. Then in late 1929 TAT acquired Maddux, and this corporate relationship led to a rebranding, TAT-Maddux Air-Lines.[22]

Throughout its existence TAT repeatedly printed in its publications, including its illustrated *Plane Talk* magazine, positive passenger commentaries. Typical of these songs of praise for "Flying De-Luxe" came these words from W. U. Moyer, a Pennroad Corporation vice president in New York City: "Clean, quick, dependable, are the three words I would use to describe my trip which I enjoyed to the full and which I hope to be able to take again soon." John B. Windsor, an executive with the Monogah Glass Company in Fairmount, West Virginia, said much the same: "My trip from Los Angeles to Port Columbus far exceeded my expectations in the way of comfort, convenience and real pleasure. I have never seen such consideration and courtesy as was shown by every one of your men."[23]

Notwithstanding glowing testimonials, not every passenger found a TAT (or any other contemporary) flight delightful. Considering the state of air technology, TAT passengers understandably had their share of unpleasant experiences. Although the length of time between New York and Los Angeles would be further reduced, owing to installation of government navigation beacons between Waynoka and Clovis that eliminated the *Missionary* segment, passengers complained not only about deafening noise but about the more serious problem of ear discomfort when the non-pressurized trimotor soared above seven or eight thousand feet over mountainous terrains. Ears popped, and in some cases hearing damage resulted. When air turbulence struck, the attendant offered slices of lemon or encouraged everyone to open the windows. Still, motion sickness occurred, necessitating queasy passengers to use what the airline called "waxed bags." The cabin might not smell as good as when passengers first boarded. No wonder the uncarpeted floor was designed for an easy wash-down and cleanup following a rough trip. Since these planes could not fly over thunderstorms, flight cancellations and other weather-related delays caused by fog, ice, and snow became more than occasional occurrences. Some wags said that TAT really stood for "Take a Train!" Although a day or so slower than TAT, trains were nearly always more dependable.[24]

TAT certainly did not want to print any negative comments about its coast-to-coast service. The following one from a not-so-pleased passenger is perhaps more revealing about a rail-air journey. "I saved thirty-six hours, and I was glad that I'd done it once, but *never again* [italics in original]." The reason was this: "It took me a week to recover. Besides being quite deaf from the roar of the motors, and dizzy from the constant rolling and yawing, as well as a little queasy from the more gentle motion of the trains at night, I ended up just plain tired from all the hectic rushing from one moving object to another."[25]

Even though TAT-Maddux morphed into Transcontinental & Western Air Lines following a merger in October 1930 with Western Air Express and later was rebaptized as Trans-World Airlines, the coast-to-coast service failed to turn a profit, losing nearly $3 million during its brief life span. Although the company added four eighteen-passenger Curtiss Condor biplanes to its fleet and slashed fares to a basic cross-country inclusive price of $159.93 ($2,380 in current dollars), the financial bleeding never stopped. The lack of a US mail contract, dependability problems, and the coming of the Great Depression destroyed the bottom line. A crash at Mount Taylor, New Mexico, on September 4, 1929, which killed all eight persons on board, also had an adverse effect.[26]

Americans who desired to take advantage of coordinated air-rail service in areas beyond the path of TAT-Maddux had other options during this period of transition between air-rail and all-air travel. A number of recently launched airlines offered such arrangements, and several of these carriers involved railroads that were not giants like either the Pennsylvania or the Santa Fe. The 1,500-mile Chicago Great Western Railroad (CGW) was one such road. Coinciding with the advent of TAT, this innovative Midwestern carrier for about a year offered overnight service from points in Minnesota, Iowa, and Illinois to a connection in Chicago with Universal Air Lines System for Cleveland, Ohio, and Saint Louis, Missouri. By way of example, an individual could board a CGW train with Pullman accommodations in Waterloo, Iowa, at 11:50 p.m., arrive in the Windy City at 7:35 a.m., leave on a 4:00 p.m. Fokker tri-motored plane for Cleveland, and land there at 7:45 p.m. Eastern time. If Saint Louis were the destination, the flight left at 9:45 a.m. and reached Saint Louis at 1:00 p.m. As with TAT and other air-rail linkages, the value for the businessperson was described as follows: "Calculate the value of your time, Mr. Business Man, and see what waste can be avoided by flying!" And for the pleasure traveler there was this message: "This journey provides the sightseer with the best possible means for viewing the endless panorama of lakes, rivers, forests, the symmetrical pattern of fertile fields and the compact and towering cities."[27]

Universal and other airlines expected that these coordinated arrangements with railroads that "sprouted wings" would bolster patronage, which was critical since their low-capacity planes needed revenue riders to fill virtually every seat. Mail and express contracts were essential, but profit or loss depended on passenger volume. No wonder Universal hyped this air-rail service as "the New Era of Modern Transportation." A combination of plane and train "turns days into hours and makes neighbors of distant places." The promotional copy continued:

> By night, comfortable Pullmans on America's finest trains are used. During the day the perpetual landing fields of the nation's great level stretches are covered by air in comfortable planes—cool and dustless in summer, warm and cozy through perfected heating systems in winter. Air-Rail journeys may begin by train at night with transfer to plane in the morning or the start may be by plane during the day for transfer to train at night. The former gives a comfortable night's rest before the air journey, the latter provides a relaxing, restful flight in preparation for the night's sleep.[28]

Universal argued that daytime flying was safe, suggesting perhaps unintentionally that a nighttime flight was risky. Throughout the late 1920s and later, airlines told potential customers that they had no need to fret about taking to the skies. They also downplayed anyone's fear of heights. "Though ordinarily you may suffer from fear of heights," Stout Air Services told the public in 1929, "this fear when in the air does not touch you now, for there are no lines of perspective drawing you earthward."[29]

Passengers on these early commercial craft might actually become bored, making long flights especially tedious. Speeds, while faster than land transport, were hardly supersonic, likely only one hundred or so miles per hour. American Airlines provided on its Fokker aircraft an elementary precursor to later inflight movies and other onboard forms of personal entertainment. These were the long popular stereoscopes. With these handheld devices, passengers could view three-dimensional pictures of scenery, movie stars, and others of general interest. Theoretically, time passed more quickly, but passengers may have found reading a book, magazine, or newspaper more absorbing.[30]

While airlines stressed safety and speed, they avoided comments about their ground facilities. The earliest airports left much to be desired. "Most of them were perfectly terrible," remembered an early air traveler. "Some were just a grass runway with a hangar and a wind sock, some had rickety wooden sheds filled with flies, furnished with a kitchen chair or two and a bench." But improvements came. "The sheds gradually grew larger and became buildings. Some had lunch counters and waiting rooms that looked like [railroad] station waiting rooms with a ticket-office-check-in counter." Take Washington Hoover Airport. By 1932 this expanding facility had an information desk, telegraph and telephone access, a restaurant, and news and cigar stands, and it claimed a "magnificent new swimming pool for Mr. and Mrs. John J. Public." With improved facilities or not, a passenger still needed to walk (or run in a rainstorm) to the awaiting plane.[31] The efforts of TAT, Universal, and other carriers with their air-rail service, along with other firms that took to the skyways, contributed to a growing number of Americans who included airplanes in their travel plans. In 1926 the number stood at a mere 5,782; three years later it increased to 161,933, and in 1931 it soared to 472,438. Even with the Great Depression, these figures remained on an upward trend throughout the 1930s and beyond. Helping to increase an awareness of the advantages of air travel was the Pittsburgh-based Air Travel League of America, a nonprofit organization that consisted of representatives from aviation, professional, and business circles. Its purpose was to remove the fear of flying and to foster interest in commercial aviation, in part by sponsoring educational programs designed for schoolchildren.[32]

During the 1930s commercial aviation made impressive gains, paralleling the rapid changes that occurred in other modes of transportation, most notably intercity buses and railroad streamliners. Air service advanced, increasing its value to the person in a hurry. In the process, there were corporate births and deaths and important mergers. Early in the decade, United Air Lines was just that—united—a unification of multiple carriers, consisting of Boeing, National, Pacific, Stout, and Varney.[33]

Yet more important than evolving corporate genealogies were the larger, faster, and safer commercial airplanes. In 1935 *Popular Science Monthly* made these observations about a decade of technological advances: "[The latest aircraft] is far ahead of the 1925 plane as the Twentieth Century Limited is ahead of the Lincoln funeral train; as far ahead of Louis Bleriot's cross-channel plane as the latest streamline train is ahead of the Pony Express."[34]

It would be in the 1930s that modern airliners (or "ships" as some carriers called them) moved skyward. One impetus came from Washington. In spring 1930 Congress passed and President Herbert Hoover signed what became known as the McNary-Watres Act. This measure made the earlier airmail legislation more attractive, permitting airlines that held mail contracts to be paid on the basis of the *space* they provided rather than the *weight* of the mail they actually handled. Managements wanted bigger planes to exploit this enhanced compensation opportunity.[35]

Similarly, airlines wished to expand air express and air freight. Since the late 1920s, this had been a growing business. Service became more attractive, and customers willingly paid a premium to have this fast, convenient option for their high-priority items. In October 1933 United Air Lines advertised its service in conjunction with the Air Express Division of the Railway Express Agency. "Pick-Up and Special Delivery at No Extra Cost. Rapid, Dependable, Nationwide. Practically all types of merchandise accepted up to $5,000 in value, 200 lbs. in weight and 106 inches in length and girth. Larger and heavier shipments can be forwarded by arrangement."[36]

Manufacturers responded to carrier equipment needs. Shortly they would please contract airmail carriers and those who wished to increase ridership. In 1933 the Boeing Aircraft Company introduced its 247 model, the world's first civil airplane that offered real economic advantages to its owners. This twin-engine monoplane featured all-metal construction, retractable undercarriages, more space for mail, and a passenger cabin that comfortably accommodated ten. To the delight of the traveling public, United Airlines by the end of June 1933 had placed in service thirty of these state-of-art planes. Earlier that month it had established a

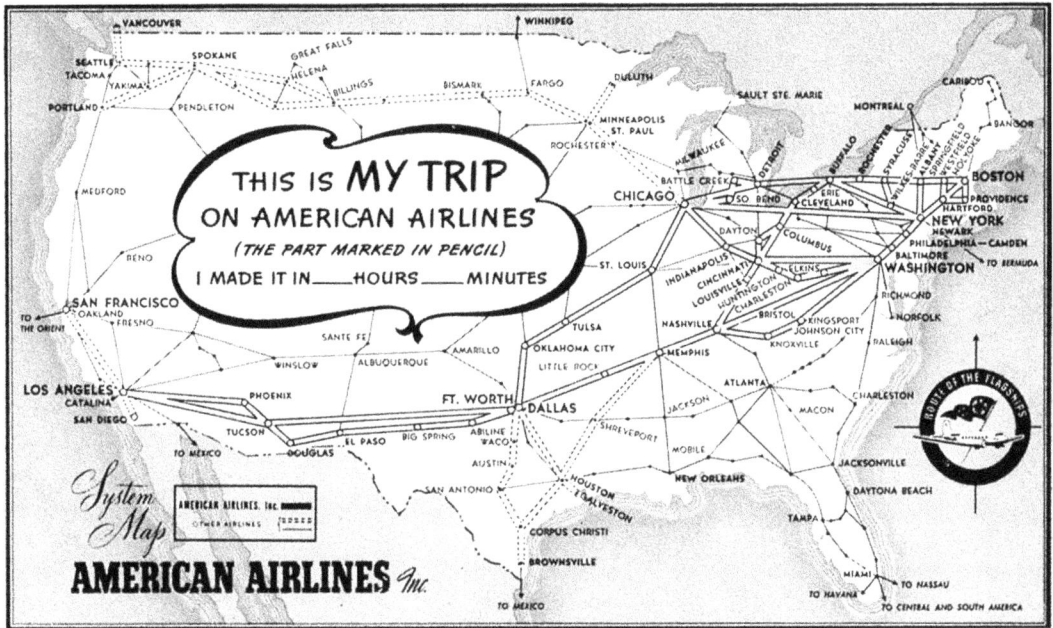

THIS IS MY TRIP
ON AMERICAN AIRLINES
(THE PART MARKED IN PENCIL)
I MADE IT IN___HOURS___MINUTES

System Map

AMERICAN AIRLINES Inc.

coast-to-coast record schedule of slightly under twenty hours, being much faster than the aircraft used by rival TWA.[37]

Transcontinental & Western Air was not about to let United outpace it in a growing passenger market. But because of United orders and an unwillingness to expand production, for two years Boeing could not deliver any of its 247s to additional customers, including TWA. This situation led the carrier to convince the Douglas Aircraft Company to design a 247-like model, but one that was better. And it did. Initially there was the two-engine prototype DC-1 (*DC* standing for Douglas Commercial), which reached TWA in December 1933. Shortly a modified DC-2 entered full-scale production; now the company would have an aircraft that could seat fourteen passengers rather than the twelve accommodated in the prototype. TWA pleased travelers when on August 1, 1934, it introduced the DC-2 on its New York–Los Angeles route with an eighteen-hour schedule westbound and sixteen hours eastbound (because of prevailing westerly winds), making intermediate stops in Chicago, Kansas City, and Albuquerque. Soon TWA advertised "4 Famous Fastest Coast to Coast flights, *The Sky Chief, The Comet, The Sun Racer* and *The Sky Queen*." Other domestic airlines started to fly this aircraft, although TWA bragged of having "Douglas Air Liners on all schedules."[38]

Positive testimonials about modern aircraft dwarfed negative commentary. "Fourteen passengers are seated in comfortable reclining chairs," wrote a passenger on the inaugural TWA New York to Los Angeles flight. "The cabins are quiet and air-conditioned, and most passengers prefer to sleep at night. The height [cruising at eight thousand feet] and

As the decade of the 1930s waned, American Airlines operated an impressive route structure with its fleet of dependable DC-3 aircraft. On the reverse side of this promotional postcard, the company commented: "With freedom from tipping, complimentary meals, and no 'extras,' it's not hard to figure a saving of money as well as time." A growing number of passengers agreed.

Author's Collection

few stops give an entirely new panorama from above; human beings are indistinguishable, automobiles are seen only with careful watching, fields are mere patches, and only the main highways, like white ribbons, stand out on the globe." Enhancing the flying experience on a DC-2 was a cabin system of individual ventilation and frequent air changes and also automatic aircraft stabilizers. Individuals who embraced air travel and who could afford it flocked to these planes. No wonder TWA announced that its "passenger list resembles a page from Who's Who."[39]

While competitors improved their aircraft, attempting to meet the challenges posed by the DC-2, Douglas Aircraft did not rest on its laurels. The company showed real imagination. Its next version, the DC-3, turned out to be 85 percent new and just 15 percent DC-2. On December 17, 1935, the first test flight of a DC-3 took place. The initial aircraft, built for American Airlines, was the Douglas Sleeper Transport (DST), which contained fourteen berths. On September 18, 1936, "American Sky Sleeper" service began between New York and Los Angeles, although two years earlier the company started flying Curtiss-Condor biplanes between Dallas-Fort Worth and Los Angeles, with "twelve comfortable berths, comparable in every respect with [Pullman] Sleeping Car service," and it claimed the "World's First Air Sleeper." With the new Douglas craft, American announced: "QUIET PLEASE at 10,000 feet!" The advertising copy added, "Between dusk and dawn you may eat a delightful dinner, play bridge, smoke, chat and yawn. When you yawn, you will undress and retire to your comfortable bed to read until deep, sweet sleep puts an end to such time-wasting." Passengers, though, discovered to their dismay that with intermediate stops, there was little quiet time for that promised restful sleep. Just as joint air-rail service disappeared, faster planes later led to the demise of domestic sleeper operations. In the 1990s, however, bed-like sleeping reappeared in international travel when British Airways began this service, and other overseas carriers followed.[40]

The Douglas firm also produced a daytime version of the DST, the DC-3, with a twenty-one-seat capacity, and American would be a customer. No wonder it boasted in its November 1936 public timetable: "American Airlines is able to offer you the finest air services in history with the new Flagship Fleet by Douglas, the largest, most luxurious land transport planes in America with their record non-stop cruising range of 2,000 miles." The range of the DC-3 was attractive, but its cruising speed of about 180 miles an hour was not that impressive.[41]

The DST/DC-3, known affectionately as "Gooney Bird" and later as the "Grand Old Lady of Aviation," became "the most popular and reliable propeller-driven airline in aviation history." For the first time an airline could make money by carrying *only* passengers, no longer needing to rely on a mail contract, no matter how lucrative. The DC-3 therefore single-handedly turned commercial aviation into a profitable business. It would be the DC-3 that became the "plane that changed the world" and "taught the public to fly." By the time production ended in 1946, Douglas had constructed about eleven thousand DC-3s and its cargo version, the C-47, "the World War II military workhorse." As years passed some airplane aficionados considered the DC-3 to be "the most remarkable piece of machinery ever built," and a government report went so far as to call it "the best single airplane ever built."[42]

Testimonials abound about the DC-3 during its early years in service. "By 1936 the memory of the noisy and fatiguing airplane, and I changed my mind about flying," remembered an air traveler. "As more and more friends flew in commercial planes there began to be something very alluring (as well as practical) about walking onto a plane at 4 P.M. in New York and walking off in Chicago at 8:33 P.M. and being able to sleep in one's own bed; so in 1936 found me returning to Chicago by American Airlines in the very latest of planes, the DC-3."[43]

Yet whether one was boarding a DC-3 or a comparable craft, flying always held a degree of uncertain dependability. Usually it was weather related and not mechanical. After a March 1939 journey from Seattle to Dayton, Ohio, Edward Gates, an aeronautical engineer for Boeing, provided his family with this description of his badly disrupted business trip on United Airlines.

> The weather was good from Portland to Pendleton [Oregon], but there was a delay at Pendleton to decide whether to take off for Salt Lake to beat the weather, or to take off for Boise to wait for an improvement at Salt Lake. We then took off for Boise and there we took a taxi downtown for a wait of about an hour while the fog lifted at Salt Lake. We arrived at Salt Lake without incident except that there weren't very many holes in the low ceiling, and waited there for about an hour while conditions improved. Upon arriving at Cheyenne, we were rolled into a hangar to keep the ship warm, while we slept the rest of the night. About nine o'clock in the morning we were rolled out again and took off for Omaha, landing there in a snow storm. Weather was getting worse at Chicago, so after waiting in Omaha all day we finally took the train overnight to Chicago, and I took the day train to Dayton, arriving one day late.

Still, Gates made this positive comment about his not-so-timely journey: "It was quite a trip, but encouraging in one way, in that the airlines appear to be much more cautious and sensible about the weather they fly in now than they were formerly." And he added, "Their attitude will be reflected in their safety record."[44]

In a competitive airplane market, Douglas did not stop with its remarkable DC-3; a more powerful four-engine model, the DC-4 (the C-54 military transport) emerged at the start of World War II. Its passenger-carrying capacity was nearly twice that of a DC-3, at forty passengers instead of twenty-one, and it could cruise at two hundred miles per hour. By this time passengers enjoyed being in a pressurized cabin that permitted flights to soar above much of the air turbulence that had caused airsickness and ear discomfort. In 1938 rival Boeing had introduced this technological betterment with its four-engine 307 Stratoliner. "Mark it down in your notebook that the Stratoliner has achieved one of the greatest boons air travel has yet had," opined an aviation specialist. "At no time either westbound or eastbound, despite altitudes of 18,000 and 19,000 feet and despite a rate of climb of 800 to 1,000 feet a minute, was there the slightest discomfort to the ears."[45]

By 1940 industry experts believed that commercial air travel had largely matured. "Facilities for passengers traveling by air have now reached a level of comfort which can be compared with 1st class accommodations by trains," went the argument. "While there is not as much room for walking about, other items of comfort are comparable. Excellent meals are served aloft, hostesses or stewards are present to care for the wants of passengers, seats are comfortable, and noise has been reduced to about 70 decibels or approximately the same as that in Pullman cars. Some passengers still suffer from air sickness, but the number is quite small and appears to be decreasing." And this overall assessment of what had happened in the industry rang true: "Transport aviation may be said to have had its infancy to 1911, its romantic childhood to 1926, its painful adolescence to 1931, its satisfactory progressing young manhood to the present time [1940], and gives great promise for greater maturity for the future."[46]

Throughout the 1930s and later, airlines repeatedly sought to increase ridership; fully occupied aircraft meant revenues that satisfied executives and investors. By the late 1930s United Air Lines, for instance, had created a women's traffic division. In 1937 Helen Stansbury, who headed that department, told members of the Advertising Women of New York City that the way to attract female riders was not to point out technological improvements to aircraft and commercial aviation but rather to take the "feminine" approach. "Tell them how comfortable they'll be, how delicious their meals are, how capable the stewardesses are, how luxurious their surroundings will be, and you can 'sell' women on air travel." United did just that in its advertising.[47]

For the flying public, World War II was no time for leisure travel. Those who wanted to go near or far would need to either take a train or bus or drive an automobile. This disruption in air service came about when federal authorities commandeered scores of commercial aircraft for military purposes and instigated a rigid priority system for using the remaining planes in service. "Nowhere does priority carry more weight, more downright authority, than on commercial air lines," commented journalist Don Eddy. These four priority categories made civilian air travel difficult if not impossible: (1) those who worked for the White House or were connected directly with it; (2) pilots who needed to ferry aircraft; (3) military, government personnel, and civilians who were on urgent missions; and (4) civilians on war assignments of a less urgent nature, or for military personnel on leave just before or just after overseas duty.[48]

Some intrepid travelers took their chances. The likelihood of being stranded because of someone with a priority classification was great. One person, who sought to fly from New York to San Francisco, experienced repeated "bump offs," in a trip that took days rather than hours. When this stranded passenger was forced off in Albuquerque, the airline ticket agent told him that "he had 52 people waiting for seats and could give me no hope whatever. 'Why don't you take a train?'" He refused. Eventually this individual completed his transcontinental air journey. Ticket agents often had to call these non-protected customers to inform them that the government had requisitioned their seats. According to Delta historians David Lewis and Wesley Newton, "Responses to this sort of news ranged from patriotic understanding to a petulant 'Why didn't you call sooner?' or a threatening 'Wait until after the war!'"[49]

Although it is impossible to say precisely when an air-minded America came about, perhaps it was during or immediately after World War II. "You used to hear people say, 'I'm afraid to fly,'" remarked a traveler in 1945. "You don't hear that any more. Nowadays it appears that everybody wants to fly. It isn't a new air-minded generation; all at once, since the war, the *entire* population yearns to soar the airways." Whether this was true or not, air travel during the postwar years would become a greater part of national life.[50]

Between 1945 and 1960, volume soared. Airlines annually boarded millions of passengers, compared to only thousands in the 1930s. No longer did a cabin contain mostly businessmen, celebrities, and others with high incomes or generous expense accounts; an expanding and more affluent middle class found flights affordable and ideally suited for long-distance journeys. Intercity train travel, especially via Pullman cars, steadily declined, while personal automobile usage increased dramatically.[51]

Airlines took advantage of the growing number of Americans who wanted to fly, and they continually upgraded their equipment, making use of innovations created by airplane manufacturers. The results were aircraft designed for greater speeds, high-altitude and over-the-weather flying, and more travel comfort. Passengers were likely to board a four-engine Boeing Stratocrusier, Douglas DC-6, or a Lockheed Constellation, or "Connie," for their long-distance trips. These airplanes were more commodious, more reliable, and much cheaper to operate per seat mile than their prewar counterparts. On shorter runs, carriers, particularly "feeders" like Allegheny, Inland, North Central, Ozark, and Piedmont, continued to fly the always-reliable DC-3, but they also acquired from such manufacturers as Convair and Martin twin-engine crafts that not only were faster and pressurized but also contained more seats.[52]

Like other forms of public transportation, airlines, large and small, promoted during the post–World War II era a variety of "package" vacations. In the late 1940s Allegheny Airlines touted a relatively inexpensive "All-Expense Golfer's Holiday" in the resort community of Bedford Springs, Pennsylvania. The special featured "Golf on one of America's championship courses, including greens fees and 2 lessons by the Hotel's Professional, 3 days and 2 nights at the historic Bedford Spring Hotel and 7 delicious meals." Flights from New York, Philadelphia, and Washington to airports in either Johnstown or Altoona, Pennsylvania, were offered, and the hotel met deplaning passengers with its limousine.[53]

Taking a flight in the postwar era was mostly a pleasant experience, even on airplanes that offered only coach service. Passengers were especially taken by the Boeing 377 Stratocruiser, which offered roomy seats in its luxury class and sported a spiral staircase leading to a lower deck lounge, being "a sensation for early postwar airline travelers." Author Bernard DeVoto, who in 1952 took a transcontinental flight, raved about his first-class experience. "Once in the air, you are surrounded with luxury above your station and treated with a deference elsewhere reserved for movie stars." He continued, "My trade supplies an apt test: I can correct galleys and I can read the notes I write, neither of which is possible on a train. And it is quieter; the muffled sound of the engines is far less wearing than the badly orchestrated tone poem of groans, creaks, squeals, and kettledrum pounding of any train." And for DeVoto there was that lingering sense of adventure.[54]

While Bernard DeVoto traveled in style, the frill of first-class service would not be part of the airborne experiences for a growing number of travelers. When carriers offered discounted family-fare plans in the late 1940s for newly inaugurated "air coach" service, price-sensitive travelers were pleased, and more Americans, especially children, became first-time air goers. In 1949, the first full year of air coach offerings, domestic scheduled airlines, which gave this alternative to first class, saw about 4 percent of their revenue miles consisting of these budget-minded passengers. Yet that figure rose rapidly. Then in 1960 coach-class air travel exceeded first-class traffic for the first time on the country's domestic trunk carriers. More passengers felt that with the faster times made by newly introduced jets, the differences in luxury between coach and first-class tickets were not worth the substantial added expense.[55]

Passengers did have complaints about their in-air experiences. They were mostly minor and predictable—crying babies, occasional turbulence, delayed departures and arrivals. One, however, stands out: food.

Bernard DeVoto, for one, was not pleased with his meals. He recalled the fine box lunches that airlines had once served. "They ran an excellent lunch counter in those days; they run a poor restaurant now. I have seldom had even a mediocre meal at it; most are definitely bad." Yet food quality improved, attributable to specialized contract meal preparers, led by Dobbs and Marriott, who blazed the way with frozen, reheatable meals. Passengers still were not convinced that they were about to eat a tasty meal, and snide remarks about inflight food became common. But as air speeds increased and multiple stops decreased, a sky meal became less of a necessity and a possible annoyance.[56]

What bothered the increasing number of airline patrons during the postwar years were growing problems in airports. Check-ins became time consuming, as counters were clogged with customers buying and altering tickets, changing reservations, checking luggage, and asking questions. Fortunately carriers, spearheaded by the trunk lines, began to install computers as that technological revolution took hold by the 1960s. Complaints, too, mounted about the slowness of having baggage delivered to claim areas. Some airports, especially in major metropolitan centers like Detroit and New York City, could not cope with the flood of passengers. Food and bar services were limited, restrooms overtaxed, and seating hard to find. The Federal Airport Act of 1950 offered some relief, providing much-needed government funding for airport construction and expansion. Some patrons, however, did not approve of where new airports were located, grumbling about how they further diffused the city. Airports frequently appeared on the far outskirts of a city or perhaps between cities. The latter practice would occur in such places as Dallas and Fort Worth and Akron and Canton, Ohio.[57]

No matter the constant reassurances by airlines about safety, some passengers remained tense about air travel. They simply could not relax. Comments made in the late 1960s by David Morgan, editor of *Trains Magazine*, are revealing. "[In the air] I'm much too busy back-seat flying. Modesty forbids that I enumerate for you the planes (not to mention the passengers) I've saved from looming disaster by pulling up on my seat armrests at the critical moment or communicating our plight to the captain through mental telepathy." He had these thoughts about landing: "*Get her down* [italics in original]. Ah, wonderful—the wheels have touched. The engines almost expire, cough, explode back to life in reverse pitch, and wonderfully, surely, we're slowing. Time now to give the controls back to the crew and compose oneself for the casual descent of the stairway that marked the seasoned passenger." Added Morgan, "Never, never kiss the ground upon leaving the aircraft; it's bad form."[58]

When David Morgan admitted to being a "white-knuckle flyer," the era of jet airplanes had been ongoing for more than a decade. There was a transition of sorts between piston-engine and "pure" jet aircraft, namely the turbo-prop airliner. It would be the Lockheed Electra II that claimed this honor, entering regular service on American Airlines in December 1957. Although turbo-props or prop-jets were to be the equipment bridge between the piston and jet, the latter quickly appeared. On October 28, 1958, a Boeing 707-121 ushered in the jet age with its inaugural flight on Pan American World Airlines from Idlewild, the New York International Airport, and Le Bourget Airport in Paris. It would be National Airlines that became the first domestic carrier to provide 707 service, starting in December 1958 with flights between New York City and Miami. Soon more 707s and the Douglas DC-8 jets went airborne.[59]

The Boeing and Douglas jets offered much to the traveler. They were large and fast. Both the 707 and DC-8 accommodated more than 120 passengers in their first-class and coach sections. Their four powerful jet engines allowed the 707 to cruise at six hundred miles per hour and the DC-8 at a slightly slower speed. Each jetliner could fly more than 2,500 miles nonstop and at altitudes above thirty thousand feet. "The introduction of the Boeing 707 and the competing Douglas DC-8 jetliners revolutionized air travel in America," observed aviation historian Daniel Rust, and others have agreed. These airplanes attracted millions more annually to the skyways, and for good reason. "First-jet-flight anxiety drifted away. Passengers relaxed as if to say, 'Why didn't someone tell us it was like this!' Jets cut more than three hours and many decibels off the bone-rattling ordeal presented by cross-country propeller-plane flights." It did not take long before the 707 and DC-8 became the DC-3 workhorse of the jet age.[60]

By the early 1960s more and more air passengers saw America from thirty thousand feet. A tongue-in-cheek statement went like this: "The United States is an east-coast and west-coast connected by United Air Lines." For many, much of the nation became flyover country. Still, a jet that flew at such altitudes did offer those who had window seats and who did not want to read or to converse with fellow passengers opportunities to see something that could be quite memorable. Conservationist Harry James, who took his first trip on a United jet in 1960, disagreed with the widely held view that "flying by jet is awfully boring—you can't see a thing at 30,000 feet." On a trip from Los Angeles to New York City, he marveled at being able to view such natural features as the Grand Canyon, Monument Valley, and Shiprock, New Mexico, concluding that "only at great altitudes does our Southwest fall into perspective." James answered the rhetorical question, "Flying by jet boring? Nothing to see at 30,000 feet? Ridiculous!"[61]

With the impressive success of commercial jet aircraft, piston and prop-jets began to disappear from the fleets of trunk carriers. In spring 1967 Trans-World Airways claimed to be the first domestic company to fly only pure jets. And in the late 1960s Boeing introduced the 747 Jumbo Jet, an airplane that for the next three decades would set the standard for the largest passenger craft, including the wide-bodied Lockheed L-1011 and the McDonnell Douglas DC-10. The massive 747 could accommodate 350 to 500 passengers and provided ten-abreast seating, double aisles, and eight lavatories in the coach section. By 1970 the jet era had been firmly established, but other airplane types, including a few venerable DC-3s, continued to serve patrons of smaller carriers.

The decade that followed the widespread employment of jet-powered aircraft remained rather predictable for the average flier. Flights tended to operate on schedule, cabin service was usually acceptable, and airports, both new and old, became more traveler friendly. The industry remained largely stable, although there were some highly publicized accidents and labor disputes. Then on October 24, 1978, a sea change took place in commercial aviation. On that date President Jimmy Carter signed the Airline Deregulation Act, a bipartisan measure that within a few years inspired deregulation statutes for other forms of domestic transportation. Since the New Deal, the Civil Aeronautics Board (CAB) had regulated commercial carriers as a public utility, having the authority to establish routes, fares, and schedules. And the CAB had promoted creation of feeder airlines, in part because in some areas topographical features made surface connections between cities inconvenient. The 1978 law allowed the CAB to oversee the process of deregulation before its official closure on January 1, 1985. By the early 1980s airlines, established or upstarts, could enter the market without the need to await blessings from Washington bureaucrats, and fares were left unregulated.[62]

Not everyone applauded airline deregulation. An open-market environment, with its largely unfettered competition, worried established trunk and some smaller carrier executives; troubled labor union members, who anticipated nonunion hires; and caused concerns for safety advocates. Their collective feelings about deregulation were hardly unfounded; a new and often tumultuous era for domestic aviation resulted. It did not take long for the typical flier to grasp that the former days of aviation were largely gone.[63]

Air travelers sensed certain positives that came from deregulation. Fares were one. In 1996 the US Government Accounting Office reported that the average fare per passenger mile was about 9 percent lower in 1994 than it had been in 1979. While that feature of the law was consumer friendly, rate cuts more likely appeared on the most competitive routes, notably between major cities. Fare fluctuations might also become an annoyance. Those who lived on less trafficked and shorter routes often found that ticket prices actually increased. Individuals who had access to a new breed of low-fare, no-frill airlines, best represented by People's

Express and Southwest Airlines, liked their ticket prices, although many thought their operations resembled "buses that had taken to the air." Passengers on People's Express, which started in 1981, may have been surprised (or shocked) that fares were paid in cash or by credit card aboard the aircraft and that they were permitted only one carry-on bag for free and paid for all others. People's became the first domestic airline to charge for checked luggage. Onboard food and beverages also came with a price.[64]

With entry into markets no longer rigidly controlled by the CAB, existing, or "heritage," carriers frequently expanded their scope of operations. And in the process they often reduced or ended service to lesser destinations. Northwest Airlines, based in Minneapolis, for one, added new flights to several cities in the Southwest but ended them to such smaller markets as Jamestown, North Dakota, and Miles City, Montana. Such adjustments made passengers and community boosters happy in places that gained service but angry in those places that lost service.

Nevertheless, communities that felt the sting of the exodus of heritage carriers welcomed an expanding or new carrier, perhaps a low-cost but more likely a so-called commuter one. Dozens of these companies filled vacuums or provided competitive service to usually larger regional carriers. Significantly, the government guaranteed continued air flights for all places on a certified list of cities that existed at the time of deregulation. Thus for a time "essential air service" would be a godsend for travelers and for commuter operators. Yet these markets might not warrant such operations. When subsidies ended, airline after airline vanished by the late 1980s, especially those that served sparsely populated states like Montana, Nebraska, and the Dakotas. Sadly for travelers to and from three state capitals—Dover, Delaware; Salem, Oregon; and Olympia, Washington—direct air service was no longer available. Unfavorable load factors meant bankruptcy and then either a reorganization or merger but more likely liquidation.[65]

Commuter airlines, which maintained service to smaller communities, might incense patrons. Perhaps only one or a limited number of flights were provided, and they might be canceled because of bad weather, equipment problems, or too few passengers to justify a trip. Aircraft might be old or uncomfortably small and lack any sort of onboard amenities, including a flight attendant.

Affecting all passengers, whether they used a commuter line or not, was the rapid expansion of the "hub-and-spoke" or the "fortress hub" concept. This routing arrangement differed from what had prevailed prior to deregulation, when the CAB had commonly required airlines to fly directly between stops. Thus a plane scheduled to connect major terminals served smaller places along the established route. But with "hub-and-choke," as some critics called it, planes fed passengers into a hub airport,

TO FULLY ENJOY YOUR FLIGHT...

Sink back into your comfortable seat and relax! Read these tips and take advantage of the many conveniences designed to make your flight more pleasant. Eastern Flight Attendants are experts in the art of making you feel at ease. If there is anything at all that will contribute to your further comfort, feel free to ask your Flight Attendant. To call, simply push the button that is located directly above your seat.

FOR YOUR ADDED COMFORT

It's a medical fact that "motion sickness" hits only a small fraction of one percent of people who fly. The Flight Attendant will be glad to help you —and for your convenience there is a handy receptacle in the seat pocket just in front of you.

LIGHT UP

You may smoke cigarettes at any time, except when the airplane is on the ground or the "No Smoking" sign is on. You are requested to smoke only at your seat. Since the heavier smoke of cigars and pipes is objectionable to some passengers, we ask that you restrict your smoking to cigarettes only. (Exception: you can smoke pipes and cigars in the lounge of *standard fare* Golden Falcon flights.) You'll find a convenient ash tray in the arm of your seat.

ENJOY GROUND-LEVEL COMFORT AT ANY ALTITUDE

Your airplane is air-conditioned and air-controlled so that you may enjoy ground-level comfort at high altitudes. You may regulate the fresh air vent over your seat to control the flow of air in your immediate area.

In 1956 Eastern Air Lines provided passengers with "Your Souvenir Flight Pack," which contained a variety of trip commentaries and tips, including "Light Up." Smoking was generally permitted, being a far cry from later restrictions for those with a tobacco habit.

Author's Collection

perhaps dominated by one or two heritage carriers, where they boarded their second or even third flight of the day. Complaints multiplied. Hub airports frequently became crowded at peak arrival and departure times, waiting for connecting flights might consume hours and involve changing terminals or walking long distances to the departure gates, and air traffic congestion and weather problems might delay or cancel connections. The hub-and-spoke concept did not sit well with one Boonton Township, New Jersey, traveler. "People who fly are no longer travelers; they are now 'same-day delivery' parcels. The Hub and Spoke System of Levitating Everything (acronym HASSLE?) was first designed to move parcels from city A to city B. So the good old Salt Lakes, Raleighs, Minneapolises and Newarks of 'Airport America' are now part of a warehouse-sorting-shipping operation for 'people parcels,' whose identities are canceled the movement they turn themselves over to the airlines for shipment." This disgruntled New Jerseyan had more to say. "Instead of suffering from HASSLE, one might simply write the destination on his forehead and check in at the nearest air-freight warehouse for sorting and shipping."[66]

Then there was this complaint about air deregulation: travelers served by commuter lines often faced time-consuming circuitous routes. The governor of Nebraska, for one, observed that with deregulation, direct service ended between communities in the eastern and western sections of his state and that caused problems. "I love to have people from all parts of the state appointed to boards and commissions, but when people from the western part of the state ask me how often they would have to meet and I tell them once a month, they say they can't do it."[67]

Although the public may not always have welcomed the presence of smaller airlines, the major ones usually did. Resembling a railroad that spun off an unproductive or underproductive branchline to a shortline operator and still retained most or all of the freight generated on that discarded trackage, heritage carriers not only saved money by not operating in and out of smaller markets but likely got that connecting business at a designated hub. For example, TWA liked that Resort Air had become a partner, and Delta welcomed Comair for the same reason.

Toward the close of the twentieth century, domestic passengers experienced new rules and procedures. One involved onboard smoking. The earliest commercial carriers did not permit smoking; the presence of combustible materials made it dangerous to allow lighted pipes, cigars, or cigarettes. By the early 1930s, however, as all-metal planes became universal, some companies allowed cigarette smoking, but only when the craft was airborne. Once off the ground, smokers were segregated from nonsmokers, being seated in the forward section. Still, if passengers complained, smoking might be banished. "You may enjoy a cigarette if your fellow passengers do not object," was the United Air Lines pronouncement. Smoking continued, as it seemingly became more fashionable and also allegedly calmed a flier's nerves. But in the 1950s medical experts began to warn that smoking had negative health effects, even on airliners. "Obviously the average airline passenger might find his flight more comfortable if he avoids excessive smoking," concluded a physician in 1954. It would not be for another three decades that stiff antismoking actions occurred, a delayed response to the US surgeon general's 1964 report on smoking and health. In 1988 the federal government banned smoking on all domestic flights of two hours or less, and two years later smoking was eliminated entirely on all flights lasting fewer than six hours. A deprived, even desperate smoker could take some solace; lung associations and other health groups might supply them with emergency kits, containing mints, sugarless gum, and toothpicks. By this time smokers were in a minority; most Americans believed that the tobacco habit was unhealthy, and they did not want to be in an environment where they encountered secondary smoke. Finally, in 2000 the government made all flights smoke-free, and by this time airport terminals had created designated interior smoking areas that later would be eliminated.[68]

The matter of smoking restrictions caused some passenger complaints, but airplane safety became a more important issue. In the 1960s skyjacking grabbed media headlines. Between 1968 and 1972, hijackers on average took over commercial planes every week or so. Most hijackings involved forced trips to communist Cuba and caused no physical harm to passengers and crew members. Lax airport security was largely to blame. A good illustration involved a 707 airliner operated by Continental Airlines. In August 1961 this plane was hijacked by two men in Los Angeles but was prevented from taking off to Cuba. Next came this striking twist. Less than a year later, the same craft exploded en route from Chicago to Kansas City, as the result of a bomb carried on in an individual's briefcase. The crash near Centerville, Iowa, killed the perpetrator and forty-four other passengers and crew members. The reason for this suicide bombing involved attempted insurance fraud. Such happenings could occur because travelers did not need to show any personal identification to security agents, who worked for private contractors, and less than 1 percent of all passengers were screened. The federal government, though, began to place armed guards—"sky marshals"—on scheduled flights, and the Federal Aviation Administration (FAA) launched a program to screen passengers and their luggage with metal detectors and x-ray machines. Then in the 1980s and 1990s, the FAA implemented additional security measures.[69]

Expanding security made an airplane journey dramatically different from earlier years. "It was once possible to pass through an entire airport, from curbside to gate, without encountering a single inconvenience—no X-ray machines, no metal detectors, no uniformed security personnel and grabby hands and bitter dispositions," observed a student of aircraft hijacking. "Anyone could stroll onto a tarmac and queue for boarding without holding a ticket or presenting identification."[70]

Airplane security took a quantum leap after terrorists on September 11, 2001, hijacked multiple airplanes, which they rammed into the North and South Towers of the World Trade Center in New York City and the Pentagon in Washington, DC, and crashed in Somerset County, Pennsylvania. It did not take long for the federalization of airport security personnel and more careful screening procedures to take place. The newly created Transportation Security Administration (TSA) announced that a lengthy list of items, including box cutters and pocket knives and later various liquids, could not be carried onto an airliner. And TSA permitted only ticketed passengers who had been screened to proceed to airline gates. Passengers accepted enhanced security, although complaints multiplied. Some called TSA employees "security goons" and fussed about long delays at entry points.

If heightened security procedures were not enough for domestic air travelers to worry or to be annoyed about, the industry itself experienced turmoil. In recent decades mergers, acquisitions, and liquidations have occurred with astounding frequency. The corporate graveyards are crowded with well-known carriers, including Braniff, Eastern, National, Ozark, and TWA. Scores of upstart commuter carriers also have had their corporate funerals, whether Air Nebraska, Independence, or Liberty airlines. Deregulation, mismanagement, labor disputes, high fuel prices, and economic downswings have left their marks. In order to respond to these forces and to satisfy consumer demands for cheap fares, existing domestic carriers have altered onboard amenities, either reducing or eliminating meal service, crowding coach sections with additional seating, and adding extra charges, most notably for baggage and in a few cases for carry-on items. Recent ultra-discounters, most famously Spirit Airlines, which first flew in 1993, have slashed services to the bone and tacked on a host of user fees. Sprint management explained its pricing policies this way: "We believe in only paying for what you use, not what you don't need." Under its Bare Fare Plan, one personal item is included with a standard ticket, but the first checked bag costs forty-seven dollars and the second one adds another ten dollars. Spirit and other carriers, including the majors, though, have embraced or expanded frequent-flier rewards programs, attempting to establish brand loyalty in the midst of their own economy moves.

The sorting out of carriers, which has produced new policies, has not gone unnoticed. Customer complaints have mounted, and tempers have flared. "As airlines have forced passengers into smaller spaces and turned flying into a physical test of endurance," commented a New York City traveler in 2015, "more passengers have gotten thrown off planes or otherwise become confrontational and angry." He asked, "If I put you in a box and poke you with a stick enough times, what do you expect? What's changed in the last five years, airlines or humans?" Another remarked, "I don't fly coach; I don't like to fly in a cage." A University of Illinois design professor said, "The seating is an absolute scandal. More seats with shrinking space between and this at the same time that passengers are getting larger. We should all be protesting this kind of inhumane treatment." In spring 2017 Americans expressed shock when they watched video accounts of the forced removal of a passenger from a United flight, allegedly because of an overbooking problem. A howl went up for corrective responses. A Pound Ridge, New York, resident, who spoke for many passengers, commented: "Collectively airlines have degraded the flying experience by forcing inadequate leg-room and seating conditions on their customers. If the government is going to get involved, it should admonish the industry to increase efforts to minimize delays, police the misuse of overhead compartments, runaway additional fees and the over-all cattle-drive experience that flying has become." Coach passengers, however, have been forced to cope. A decade ago an Atlanta resident explained one set of strategies: "Having flown in commercial airlines quite a bit, I have learned the following: 1. Compliment the flight attendants. You'll get extra cookies or drinks. 2. Behave, be polite and keep your mouth shut. 3. Help women, older passengers and those with physical limitations with their luggage and other needs if it's convenient. 4. Be patient. You'll get there at the same time. All this works!"[71]

Adjustments at major airports have caused more unhappiness. Dominant trunk carriers have relocated hubs, and those cities that have lost such facilities, most notably Cincinnati, Memphis, and Saint Louis, have suffered, causing special difficulties for the frequent business flier. Cincinnati is representative. As recently as 2004 the Cincinnati-North Kentucky Airport served as a major Delta Airlines hub that provided direct service to 129 major cities, including four in Europe. Because of a corporate policy decision, Delta closed the Cincinnati hub, resulting in the number of flights dropping by two-thirds and in an entire concourse shutting down. One result of this cutback led Procter & Gamble, a major area employer, to move a travel-dependent division to Charlotte, North Carolina, a busy locus for American Airlines (née US Airways). Before deregulation the federal government viewed airline service as "a public convenience and necessity," but that no longer holds true.[72]

ICONIC EMPLOYEES

With every form of commercial transport, a variety of workers have historically facilitated the flow of people. Airlines are no exception. Although employing far fewer employees than steam railroads during the golden decades of the railway age, the air industry has hired thousands, including mechanics, counter personnel, dispatchers, and office workers, but two occupations stand out, at least from the passenger's perspective: pilots and flight attendants.

The story of the airline pilot is an evolutionary one. The earliest aviators were mostly airplane developers and "barnstorming" performers, but soon came better aircraft and the Great War. With America's entry into that conflict, experienced fliers and individuals who were keen on having their own aerial experiences rallied to the colors by joining the ranks of the US Army Air Corps. Not all of these men saw action in Europe; most remained stateside to train others and also to handle newly instituted airmail runs. Yet by the 1920s a pilot mystique had evolved. "Aerial record setters dominated the front pages of American newspapers, making the pilots seem larger-than life," concluded Daniel Rust. And he offered this astute observation: "Pilots were the fastest men on earth—participating in the cutting edge of technological advancement." Another scholar said: "The pilots who began flying regularly scheduled passenger trips after 1926 fell heir to this mystique and, in addition, to the tradition of technical expertise which the public had previously associated with locomotive engineers, steamboat captains, and the master of ocean vessels." The public saw these aeronauts as "men's men" who skillfully and calmly managed a multitude of airborne challenges, a perception that did not fade. "Our boss pilot is a straight, clean, well-built, military-looking man about thirty-five years old," observed an air traveler in the mid-1930s. "He is typical of the boss pilots you find on these air lines; he learned to fly in the Army, a hard school; he got his postgraduate course in the mail service. Flying is the only profession he knows. The copilot is a younger edition of the boss pilot." By this time most airlines had their cockpit crew members wearing smart-looking caps and uniforms, appearing not that different from contemporary bus drivers and passenger train crewmen. Such apparel was designed to instill passenger confidence; a professional was in charge.[73]

Over time a new generation of pilots emerged. Rather than having "circus" or "flying postmen" backgrounds, they might have more formal educations, perhaps taking courses or earning degrees from aviation-training programs and colleges. Then came World War II. Commercial pilots commonly saw wartime service in various capacities, and the military itself trained thousands of additional pilots.

With the return to peacetime and rapidly expanding commercial flights, military air veterans entered service as flight engineers, copilots, and pilots. The joys of flying and good pay were strong incentives to seek such occupations. Of course, there was that well-established mystique. If

LARRY HARRIS, *pilot for Interstate Airlines, Inc., on the day shuttle route between Nashville, Tenn., and Atlanta, Ga., and Chief Flight Instructor in the Sky Harbor Flying School near Nashville and Murfreesboro, has been flying since 1915, and to May 11, 1930, had a total of 3,426 hours flying to his credit. His home is in Washington, D. C. During his career as a flyer, Larry has flown for various motion picture companies, and before joining Interstate, conducted a flying school in Nashville. Pilot Harris has never had an accident of any kind during his flying career.*

In the early 1930s commercial airlines continued to emphasize the safety of their service and the skills of their pilots. Interstate Airlines, launched in 1928 and linking Chicago and Atlanta, distributed a printed card that glorified pilot Larry Harris. Interstate ultimately became a unit of American Airlines.

Author's Collection

the rank of pilot were achieved, one enjoyed total authority in the cockpit and airplane, a power that continued for decades. And air carriers continually needed more (and ideally already experienced) personnel in the cockpit. Understandably, major firms also established their own flight academies that provided specialized training.[74]

Yet it took decades before women entered the commercial pilot profession. There had been pioneer women aviators (also called "aviatrixes") in the 1910s and 1920s, and during World War II, hundreds of females, members of the Women Airforce Service Pilots (WASP), had ferried military aircraft to various domestic locations "to relieve fighting men for combat duty." Not until the 1970s and 1980s did major carriers place women in the cockpit. It would be in 1973 that American Airlines became the first commercial carrier to employ a female pilot, and thirteen years later it had its first female captain. Yet by the twenty-first century, the percentage of female pilots remained low. In 2008 American, for example, had approximately 11,000 pilots, but only 478 were women, and by 2017 only 3 percent of pilots worldwide were female.[75]

Although the personal stories of pilots are individualistic, whether male or female, the career of a Houston, Texas, pilot reveals a work history that is representative.

I learned to fly at 16 years old in 1970. Continuing flight training, I was a commercial multi-engine, instrument pilot by 18. On my 20th birthday, I was hired as a full-time professional pilot, flying on a corporate turboprop. Over the next few years, I advanced to large turboprops and jets. Piedmont Airlines hired me soon after my 26th birthday. Thanks to Piedmont's rapid growth, I was upgraded to captain when I was 29. When Piedmont bought Fokker F-28's, I was part of the introduction team. By 1986, I upgraded to the Boeing 737 and flew it until 1999 when I switched to the Airbus 319/320/321. I retired in 2004 with more than 12,000 hours.

During my time at Piedmont/USAir/US Airways, I was a safety representative for the Air Line Pilots Association and became an aircraft accident investigator and safety advocate. After retiring from US Airways I founded an aviation safety consulting firm where I work today [2015] with airlines, regulators, manufacturers and the media.[76]

This autobiographical reference to the Air Line Pilots Association (ALPA) is not surprising. Early in the history of the industry, commercial pilots unionized. Launched in 1931, their national organization, which grew out of meetings of pilots from Transcontinental & Western and United airlines, resembled other trade unions, designed to improve working conditions and bolster wages and benefits. "Pilots presented an ideal situation [for unionization], for they were an exceptionally cohesive and stable group," concludes labor historian George Hopkins. By the late 1940s the ALPA had produced impressive benefits for members, most of all making them the highest-paid unionized workers in the nation. There would be labor disputes and strikes, but the ALPA flourished.[77]

Although it took generations before women became eligible for ALPA membership, they did fly, not in cockpits but rather in cabins. As commercial aviation began, carriers usually had copilots serve passenger needs, whether filling their coffee cups from thermos bottles or answering their questions about the aircraft, the trip, and the like. Yet these men had their flying duties. Stout and some other airlines, though, employed male stewards to take care of its passengers. It would be Boeing Air Transport, soon a component of United Air Lines, that hired the first female stewardesses, called at times "flying hostesses" or "air hostesses." In May 1930 seven young women assumed their roles on flights between San Francisco and Chicago. "Boeing's patrons liked the new touch to air travel luxury." Boeing pilots and copilots, according to a United company historian, were "glad to be relieved of chores for passengers in flight [and] swung around from critics to boosters."[78]

The Boeing innovation caught on throughout the industry, although it was not immediate. Northwest Airlines, for example, did not place a stewardess in service until 1939, and Delta Air Lines would not follow suit until a year later. Carriers generally adopted standards set by Boeing-United. Before World War II stewardesses were required to be between the ages of twenty-one and thirty, single, a registered nurse in excellent health, and of a certain weight and height. They also needed to have a pleasant disposition, to stay calm during any adversity, to be physically attractive, and to be "morally irreproachable." As cabin attendant, "the girl" would serve food and drink; attend to other passenger needs, including airsickness; serve as an onboard guide; and instill confidence in air travel, being always mindful of matters of safety. Since businessmen usually occupied most of the seats, their wives supposedly felt better that if their husbands

When Pennsylvania-Central Airlines in 1941 issued its onboard booklet, "Service at Your Fingertips," the company pictured an "Air Hostess," who represented the quintessential female flight attendant of the period.

(Author's Collection)

Ring the Chimes

By simply pressing the button above the window, you will summon the Air Hostess, who is trained to make your trip on Pennsylvania-Central Airlines a pleasant, interesting and invigorating experience. This booklet has been prepared to familiarize you with the many little "extras" on THE CAPITAL FLEET that give you

PERFECT

COMFORT

ALOFT

had a medical emergency, perhaps a heart attack or stroke, a nurse would be close by. The stewardess could diagnose a problem, give what aid she could, and tell the pilot to radio the nearest airport for an unscheduled landing and the required medical assistance. The nurse requirement had its justifications in addition to medical expertise. "Nurses were hired because of their intelligence, poise, friendliness and ability to deal tactfully and graciously with people."[79]

Male passengers seemed pleased with having the special attention of a pleasant, attractive, and experienced stewardess. Women might have these special feelings: "The presence of another woman, who also happened to be a trained nurse, eased the minds of apprehensive female passengers," observed Daniel Rust. "After the arrival of the stewardess, more women took to the skies in the less socially threatening environment [of male dominance]." Yet wives or girlfriends might worry that the man in their lives might become romantically attracted to a young, petite, and perky stewardess.[80]

There would be major modifications in cabin crew hiring standards. During World War II the nurse requirement ended; hundreds of nurse-stewardesses had joined the armed forces, causing a shortage of qualified personnel. Some carriers, however, demanded that prospective stewardesses have at least two years of college education. This requirement would be dropped, as would that of maximum age and gender limitations. In the late 1960s the US Equal Employment Opportunity Commission decided that age restrictions were an illegal sex discrimination, and a court decision in the early 1970s ruled that a person's sex was not a bona fide occupational requirement. By the 1980s the no-marriage rule had been eliminated. Earlier the color barrier had slowly begun to disappear. In 1958 the first African American stewardess assumed her duties, and regional Mohawk Airlines took that honor.

More changes occurred. With larger aircraft in the post–World War II era, it became necessary to have additional cabin attendants. More passengers were carried on individual flights, and drink and food service had become more elaborate. During this period major airlines also either launched or expanded their training programs, with some establishing their own "colleges." As in the past, appearance remained important. In the early 1950s United, for one, expected their stewardesses to follow this checklist before going on duty: "Stewardesses: Is your hat straight, Make up neat, Hair length correct, Blouse clean, Insignia on costume jewelry off, Slip showing, Hose seams straight, Shoes shined?"[81]

By the 1960s duties of stewardesses remained largely the same as in the past, but a few carriers, notably PSA and Southwest, decided to abandon the professional image for the sexy look. This resulted in stewardesses dressing in miniskirts or hot pants and wearing go-go boots. Supposedly this made for happy, repeat adult male passengers and a radical departure from more than 30 years before, when United Airlines female attendants wore green berets, green capes, and nurse's shoes. Later sex would be downplayed, and Southwest flight attendants, for one, shed their body-revealing attire.

Replicating cockpit crews, cabin attendants also unionized, albeit a decade or so after the ALPA. The Association of Flight Attendants (AFA), which grew out of the Airline Stewardess Association, founded in 1946, has become a strong force in company-employee negotiations. After the attacks of September 11, 2001, which resulted in less passenger demand and hence flight attendant layoffs, the AFA merged with the powerful Communications Workers of America. Significantly, the AFA has played a key role in ending age and sex discrimination. With such victories, thousands of males have entered the profession, making flight attendants more reflective of the general public. Earlier some men, though, had continued to serve as stewards, and in 1949 their small union, the Air Line Stewards Association, joined with their female counterpart.

AIRLINE ENTHUSIASTS

There are those individuals who fancy aviation history, but the majority are interested in the airplanes themselves, most likely military aircraft. Perhaps they belong to the Academy of Model Aeronautics, the Air Racing Historians Society, or the Antique Airplane Association. Then there is the Douglas DC-3/Dakota Historical Society, which reflects the excitement of some for the commercial and military versions of this iconic flying machine. The fascination with commercial aviation per se is more limited. Those who experience it may focus on collecting airline china, baggage labels, timetables, and other memorabilia. And thousands of Americans, mostly the youthful set, have long been making or assembling models of military and commercial airplanes.

There is agreement that one of America's finest museums, whether commercially oriented or not, is the Smithsonian Institution's National Air and Space Museum. Although established in 1946, the popular Washington, DC, mall facility did not open until 1976. Then on the centennial of the Wright brothers' historic 1903 flight, the Smithsonian launched companion Steven F. Udvar-Hazy Center on the grounds of the Washington Dulles International Airport in northern Virginia. In addition to its display of an extensive variety of air and space artifacts, it also houses a restoration facility and archive, and it has become one of the jewels in the Smithsonian's crown.

Airline enthusiasts have joined the general public in their interest in Hollywood productions. The majority of airplane-related movies have been war oriented, especially ones that deal with World War II. The industry, however, did not overlook the dog fighting of World War I. An early film, *Wings*, released in 1927 and starring Clara Bow, Cary Cooper, and Charles "Buddy" Rogers, focused on the Battle of Saint-Mihiel, which took place in September 1918. This silent film claimed the honor of winning the first Academy Award for Best Picture. While scores of films depict commercial flights, a memorable one is *The High and the Mighty*, a 1954 Warner Brothers release based on Ernest Gann's 1953 novel by the same name and with Laraine Day, Robert Stack, and John Wayne leading the cast. This action-packed movie features an onboard confrontation with a troubled passenger, a propeller loss, an engine fire, and a damaged wing tank. Miraculously, this DC-4 airliner, flying from Honolulu to San Francisco, reaches its destination, being mechanically crippled and virtually out of fuel. Reviews of this template for later disaster-themed pictures were positive, and the theme song won an Academy Award for Best Original Music Score.

Arguably, enthusiast interest in American aviation is second only to the fascination of railroads. And in Alaska and Hawaii it might be much greater. After all, it would be commercial and private aircraft that for decades knitted together each state and linked it to the remainder of the nation.

The nearly a century of commercial aviation does not close the social history of public transportation on an elegiac note. Airplanes are not likely to make their passage into the mists of history. That has not been the case for stagecoaches, steamboats, canal packets, and nearly all electric interurbans. Yet trains and buses remain, although their former passenger volumes have greatly diminished from their highs during and immediately after World War II. For Americans today, transportation is mostly automobiles and airplanes.

NOTES

1. STEADY BUT UNCOMFORTABLE

1. George Rogers Taylor, *The Transportation Revolution, 1815–1860* (New York: Holt, Rinehart and Winston, 1951), 142.

2. John H. White Jr., *Wet Britches and Muddy Boots: A History of Travel in Victorian America* (Bloomington: Indiana University Press, 2013), 22; Frederick J. Wood, *The Turnpikes of New England and Evolution of the Same through England, Virginia, and Maryland* (Boston: Marshall Jones, 1909), 51; Oliver W. Holmes, "The Stage-Coach Business in the Hudson Valley," *Quarterly Journal of the New-York State Historical Association* 12 (July 1931): 233.

3. Wood, *Turnpikes of New England*, 51; *American Traveler* (Boston), October 12, 1827.

4. William I. Hair, "Stagecoaches and Public Accommodations in Antebellum Georgia," *Georgia Historical Quarterly* 68 (Fall 1984): 324; Ulrich Bonnell Phillips, *A History of Transportation in the Eastern Cotton Belt to 1860* (New York: Columbia University Press, 1908), 122–123.

5. White, *Wet Britches and Muddy Boots*, 26; H. Roger Grant, *Ohio on the Move: Transportation in the Buckeye State* (Athens: Ohio University Press, 2000), 5–7.

6. Roger Matile, "John Frink and Martin Walker: Stagecoach Kings of the Old Northwest," *Journal of the Illinois State Historical Society* 95 (Summer 2002): 119–120.

7. Oscar Osburn Winther, *The Transportation Revolution: Trans-Mississippi West, 1865–1890* (New York: Holt, Rinehart and Winston, 1964), 50–52.

8. William Harland Boyd, "The Stagecoach in the Southern San Joaquin Valley, 1854–1876," *Pacific Historical Review* 26 (November 1957): 365–371.

9. Fred A. Rozum, "Buckboards and Stagecoaches: Establishing Public Transportation on the Black Canyon Route," *Journal of Arizona History* 30 (Summer 1989): 165–180.

10. Jameson's Stage Line public timetable broadside, June 27, 1892.

11. Trenton W. Batson, "The Troy Car Works: A History of Eaton and Gilbert," *Railroad History* 123 (October 1970): 5–22.

12. Edwin G. Burgum, "The Concord Coach," *Colorado Magazine* 16 (September 1939): 175; Ruth S. Beitz, "Iowa's Stagecoach Era," *Iowan* 9 (April–May 1961), 25.

13. Captain Basil Hall, *Travels in North America in the Years 1827 and 1828* (Edinburgh: Robert Cadell, 1830), 94; Thomas B. Searight, *The Old Pike: A History of the National Road* (Uniontown, PA: Privately published, 1894), 148.

14. One California stagecoach driver, Charlie Parkhurst, known affectionately as "Old Charlie," had a long and respected career. Charlie chewed tobacco, smoked cigars, and drank moderately. "No more than five feet seven inches tall, Charlie was broad-shouldered, smooth-faced, and sun-browned, and had gray-blue eyes and a rather sharp, high-pitched voice." That latter characteristic may have been a gender tip-off. When Charlie's body was being prepared for burial in 1880, it was discovered that Charlie was a woman, "and upon examination by a doctor it was definitely established that she had been a mother." See Ralph Moody, *Stagecoach West* (New York: Thomas Y. Crowell, 1967), 320–322.

15. *The Oregonian* (Portland), January 3, 1925; White, *Wet Britches and Muddy Boots*, 60–61; Alice Morse Earle, *Stage-Coach and Tavern Days* (New York: Macmillan, 1900), 325; *The Works of Mark Twain: Roughing It* (Berkeley: University of California Press, 1993), 20.

16. Moody, *Stagecoach West*, 20; Carlos Arnaldo Schwantes, *Long Day's Journey: The Steamboat & Stagecoach Era in the Northern West* (Seattle: University of Washington Press, 1999), 199; Earle, *Stage-Coach and Tavern Days*, 332.

17. George Estes, *The Stagecoach* (Troutdale, OR: George Estes' Publishers, 1925), 36; Searight, *Old Pike*, 156–157; Schwantes, *Long Day's Journey*, 200.

18. Earle, *Stage-Coach and Tavern Days*, 323; Charles Dickens, *American Notes* (Gloucester, MA: Peter Smith, 1968, rept.), 216.

19. Earle, *Stage-Coach and Tavern Days*, 323–324; Everett Dick, *Vanguards of the Frontier: A Social History of the Northern Plains and Rocky Mountains from the Fur Traders to the Sod Busters* (New York: D. Appleton-Century, 1941), 326.

20. Moody, *Stagecoach West*, 34.

21. Holmes, "Stage-Coach Business in the Hudson Valley," 254.

22. Emily C. Blackman, *History of Susquehanna County, Pennsylvania* (Philadelphia: Claxton, Remsen & Haffelfinger, 1873), 325, 511.

23. Earle, *Stage-Coach and Tavern Days*, 346; Clara von Gerstner, "Description of a Journey through the United States of North America (1838–1840)," unpublished English manuscript translated by Steven Rowan; Demas Barnes, *From the Atlantic to the Pacific Overland: A Series of Letters* (New York: D. Van Nostrand, 1866), 22; Philip D. Jordan, *The National Road* (Indianapolis, IN: Bobbs-Merrill, 1948), 207.

24. Charles P. Brown, *Brownie the Boomer: The Life of Charles P. Brown, an American Railroader*, edited by H. Roger Grant (DeKalb: Northern Illinois University Press, 1991), 47.

25. Fred Erving Dayton, *Steamboat Days* (New York: Tudor, 1939), 178; *Works of Mark Twain: Roughing It*, 84.

26. Thomas Yoseloff, ed., *Voyage to America: The Journals of Thomas Cather* (New York: A. S. Barnes, 1961), 45; *Works of Mark Twain: Roughing It*, 4.

27. Hall, *Travels in North America*, 104; Lester B. Shippee, ed., *Bishop Whipple's Southern Diary, 1843–1844* (Minneapolis: University of Minnesota Press, 1937), 69; Allen W. Trelease, *The North Carolina Railroad, 1849–1871, and the Modernization of North Carolina* (Chapel Hill: University of North Carolina Press, 1991), 10.

28. Jordan, *National Road*, 198.

29. Yoseloff, ed., *Voyage to America*, 128–129; *Paoli* (IN) *American Eagle*, September 24, 1930; Dickens, *American Notes*, 222.

30. Charles Augustus Murray, *Travels in North America, Including a Summer Residence with the Pawnee Tribe of Indians in the Remote Prairies of the Missouri, and a Visit to Cuba and the Azore Islands* (London, 1854, 3rd rev. ed., 2 vols.), I, 127–128; George F. Pierce, *Incidents of Western Travel: In a Series of Letters* (Nashville, TN: E. Stevenson & F. A. Owen, 1857), 14; Herman A. Mueller, ed., *History of Madison County [Iowa] and Its People* (Chicago: S. J. Clarke, 1915, 2 vols.), I, 402–403; Harry Kemp, *Tramping on Life: An Autobiographical Narrative* (Garden City, NY: Garden City Publishing, 1922), 242; Horace Greeley, *An Overland Journey from New York to San Francisco in the Summer of 1859* (New York: Alfred A. Knopf, 1964 ed.), 37–38.

31. *Davenport (IA) Gazette*, January 17, 1855.

32. John Lewis Peyton, *Over the Alleghanies and across the Prairies. Personal Recollections of the Far West One and Twenty Years Ago* (London: Simpkin, Marshall & Company, 1869), 139–140.

33. C. Robert Haywood, *Trails South: The Wagon-Road Economy in the Dodge City-Panhandle Region* (Norman: University of Oklahoma Press, 1986), 42–43; Hair, "Stagecoaches and Public Accommodations in Antebellum Georgia," 328; Jordan, *National Road*, 205.

34. Barnes, *From the Atlantic to the Pacific Overland*, 8.

35. Barnes, *From the Atlantic to the Pacific Overland*, 8; Moody, *Stagecoach West*, 244; Schwantes, *Long Day's Journey*, 207.

36. Shippee, ed., *Bishop Whipple's Southern Diary*, 70.

37. Hair, "Stagecoaches and Public Accommodations in Antebellum Georgia," 331.

38. Moody, *Stagecoach West*, 305–306.

39. Moody, *Stagecoach West*, 109; Barnes, *From the Atlantic to the Pacific Overland*, 21.

40. In 1995 the Library of Congress deemed *Stagecoach* to be "culturally, historically, or aesthetically significant" and selected it for preservation in the National Film Registry.

2. WATERWAYS AND THE AMERICAN PEOPLE

1. Guillaume Tell Poussin, *Travaux d' ameliorations interieures, projetes ou executes par le gouvernement general des Etats-Unis d'Amerique, de 1824 a 1831* (Paris: Anselin, 1834).

2. Mark Twain, *Life on the Mississippi* (New York: Modern Library, 2007 ed.). For a detailed listing of navigable rivers for the Mississippi River watershed, see Adam I. Kane, *The Western River Steamboat* (College Station: Texas A&M University Press, 2004), 26.

3. H. Roger Grant, *The Louisville, Cincinnati & Charleston Rail Road: Dreams of Linking North and South* (Bloomington: Indiana University Press, 2014), 16.

4. William L. Heckman, *Steamboating Sixty-Five Years on Missouri's Rivers: The Historical Story* (Kansas City, MO: Burton, 1950), 19; George F. Pierce, *Incidents of Western Travel: In a Series of Letters* (Nashville, TN: E. Stevenson and F. A. Owen, 1857), 24; Jerry MacMullen, *Paddle-Wheel Days in California* (Stanford, CA: Stanford University Press, 1944), 18; Charles S. Potts, *Railroad Transportation in Texas* (Austin: Bulletin of the University of Texas, 1909), 10; Florence L. Dorsey, *Master of the Mississippi: Henry Shreve and the Conquest of*

the *Mississippi* (Boston: Houghton Mifflin, 1941), 58; Balthasar Henry Meyer, *History of Transportation in the United States before 1860* (Boston: Peter Smith rept., 1948), 94–95.

5. Charles Henry Ambler, *A History of Transportation in the Ohio Valley* (Glendale, CA: Arthur H. Clark, 1932), 25–26; John A. Jakle, *Images of the Ohio Valley: A Historical Geography of Travel, 1740 to 1860* (New York: Oxford University Press, 1977), 27.

6. See Leland D. Baldwin, *The Keelboat Age on Western Waters* (Pittsburgh, PA: University of Pittsburgh Press, 1941); Michael Allen, *Western Rivermen, 1763–1861: Ohio and Mississippi Boatmen and the Myth of the Alligator Horse* (Baton Rouge: Louisiana State University Press, 1990), 145.

7. Erik Haits, James Mak, and Garry Walton, *Western River Transportation: The Era of Early Internal Development, 1810–1860* (Baltimore, MD: Johns Hopkins University Press, 1975), 17–18; Kane, *The Western River Steamboat*, 8–9.

8. Herbert Quick and Edward Quick, *Mississippi Steamboatin': A History of Steamboating on the Mississippi and Its Tributaries* (New York: Henry Holt and Company, 1926), 47–53.

9. George Rogers Taylor, *The Transportation Revolution, 1815–1860* (New York: Holt, Rinehart and Winston, 1951), 57, 63.

10. *Knoxville* (TN) *Register*, March 5, March 12, 1828.

11. Randall V. Mills, *Stern-Wheelers up Columbia: A Century of Steamboating in the Oregon Country* (Palo Alto, CA: Pacific Books, 1947), 21–22.

12. Basil Hall, *Travels in North America in the Years 1827 and 1828* (Edinburgh: Robert Cadell, 1830), 46.

13. Louis C. Hunter, *Steamboats on the Western Rivers: An Economic and Technological History* (Cambridge, MA: Harvard University Press, 1949), 75–76; Garnett Laidlaw Eskew, *The Pageant of the Packets: A Book of American Steamboating* (New York: Henry Holt and Company, 1929), 56; John L. Ringwalt, *Development of Transportation Systems in the United States* (Philadelphia: J. B. Lippincott, 1888), 114.

14. Heckman, *Steamboating Sixty-Five Years on Missouri's Rivers*, 28; Ambler, *History of Transportation in the Ohio Valley*, 127; John H. Morrison, *History of American Steam Navigation* (New York: Argosy-Antiquarian Ltd., 1967 rept.), 220; Oscar Osburn Winther, *The Transportation Frontier: Trans-Missouri West, 1865–1890* (New York: Holt, Rinehart and Winston, 1964), 86; John H. White Jr., *Wet Britches and Muddy Boots: A History of Travel in Victorian America* (Bloomington: Indiana University Press, 2013), 184.

15. Ambler, *History of Transportation in the Ohio Valley*, 395–396; Clara von Gerstner, "Description of a Journey through the United States of North America (1838–1840)," unpublished English manuscript translated by Steven Rowan; Mills, *Stern-Wheelers up Columbia*, 49.

16. Fred A. Bill, "Early Steamboating on the Red River," *North Dakota Historical Quarterly* 9 (1942): 79.

17. Frederick C. Gamst, ed., *Early American Railroads: Franz Anton Ritter von Gerstner's "Die innern Communicationen" (1842–1843)* (Stanford, CA: Stanford University Press, 1997), 775–776.

18. Hunter, *Steamboats on the Western Rivers*, 442–451; Michael Allen, ed., "Reminiscences of a Common Boatman," *Gateway Heritage* 5 (Fall, 1984): 44.

19. Quick and Quick, *Mississippi Steamboatin'*, 190.

20. Bonnie Stepenoff, *Working on the Mississippi: Two Centuries of Life on the River* (Columbia: University of Missouri Press, 2015), 51–61, 37–43; Allen, ed., "Reminiscences of a Common Boatman," 40, 46.

21. Hunter, *Steamboats on the Western Rivers*, 473–478; Eskew, *Pageant of the Packets*, 81.

22. Hunter, *Steamboats on the Western Rivers*, 22, 24; "Fast Steamboat Time," *Railroad Gazette* 14 (January 6, 1882): 5.

23. William J. Petersen, *Steamboating on the Upper Mississippi* (Iowa City: State Historical Society of Iowa, 1968), 261.

24. Stephen H. Hayes, "Letters from the West in 1845," *Iowa Journal of History and Politics* 20 (January 1922): 49.

25. Marquis W. Childs, *Mighty Mississippi: Biography of a River* (New York: Ticknor and Fields, 1982), 60.

26. Hunter, *Steamboats on the Western Rivers*, 381, 420; Gamst, ed., *Early American Railroads*, 775; Childs, *Mighty Mississippi*, 54; Fred Erving Dayton, *Steamboat Days* (New York: Tudor, 1939), 337–338.

27. Hall, *Travels in North America*, 80; Allen, ed., "Reminiscences of a Common Boatman," 38; Eskew, *Pageant of the Packets*, 95.

28. Margaret L. Coit, *John C. Calhoun: American Portrait* (New York: Houghton Mifflin, 1950), 415; Hunter, *Steamboats on the Western Rivers*, 412–415; Petersen, *Steamboating on the Upper Mississippi*, 358, 360; Jakle, *Images of the Ohio Valley*, 32; Pierce, *Incidents of Western Travel*, 20, 225–226; Alfred Falk, *Trans-Pacific Sketches: A Tour through the United States and Canada* (Melbourne: 1877), 258; Gerstner, "Description of a Journey through the United States of North America"; Frederick Trautmann, ed., "Alabama through a German's Eyes: The Travels of Clara von Gerstner, 1839," *Alabama Review* 36 (April 1983): 136; Mills, *Stern-Wheelers up Columbia*, 43; Jay Mack Gamble, *Steamboats on the Muskingum* (Staten Island, NY: Steamship Historical Society of America, 1971), 38–39.

29. Thomas Yoseloff, ed., *Voyage to America: The Journals of Thomas Cather* (New York: A. S. Barnes, 1961), 80.

30. Hunter, *Steamboats on the Western Rivers*, 413.

31. Thomas Low Nichols, *Forty Years of American Life, 1821–1861* (New York: Stackpole Sons, 1937), 121.

32. John L. Scripps, *Rock Island and Its Surroundings in 1853* (Chicago: Democratic Press Steam Print, 1854), 4.

33. Eskew, *Pageant of the Packets*, 74; Theresa Yelverton, *Teresina in America*, vol. 1 (London: Richard Bentley and Son, 1875), 98–99.

34. *Chicago Daily Tribune*, September 23, 1910; H. Roger Grant, *Electric Interurbans and the American People* (Bloomington: Indiana University Press, 2016), 119.

In his book *Sultana: Surviving Civil War, Prison, and the Worst Maritime Disaster in American History* (New York: HarperCollins, 2009), Alan Huffman explains the loss of life. "Many people boarded without being counted, and the counting itself was questionable. By the most reliable accounts, more than twenty-four hundred people were aboard—about six times the boat's legal carrying capacity. Of the more than seven hundred who initially survived the disaster, between two hundred and three hundred died in Memphis hospitals in the days after. Even allowing for a fairly wide margin of error, the accepted toll of about seventeen hundred made it the worst known maritime disaster in American history" (p. 232).

35. White, *Wet Britches and Muddy Boots*, 203; Mills, *Stern-Wheelers Up Columbia*, 114.

36. White, *Wet Britches and Muddy Boots*, 203.

37. *New-York Daily Tribune*, January 9, 1846.

38. *New-York Daily Tribune*, January 9, 1846; *Hartford* (CT) *Courant*, January 13, 1846.

39. S. A. Howland, *Steamboat Disasters and Railroad Accidents in the United States* (Worcester, MA: Warren Lazell, 1846), 135–149.

40. White, *Wet Britches and Muddy Boots*, 207.

41. Daniel J. Boorstin, *The Americans: The National Experience* (New York: Random House, 1965), 101.

42. Hunter, *Steamboats on the Western Rivers*, 532–546; John H. Morrison, *History of American Steam Navigation* (New York: W. F. Sametz and Company, 1903), 591.

43. Brian McGinty, *Lincoln's Great Case: The River, the Bridge, and the Making of America* (New York: W. W. Norton, 2015), 121.

44. Howland, *Steamboat Disasters and Railroad Accidents in the United States*, 97–98.

45. Petersen, *Steamboating on the Upper Mississippi*, 354–355.

46. Heckman, *Steamboating Sixty-Five Years on Missouri's Rivers*, 153.

47. Gamst, ed., *Early American Railroads*, 416; Walter Havinghurst, *The Long Ships Passing: The Story of the Great Lakes* (New York: Macmillan, 1942), 121; *Cleaveland* (OH) *Gazette*, September 8, 1818; Grace Hunter, "Life on Lake Erie a Century Ago," *Inland Seas* 22 (Fall 1966): part 1, 21.

48. Havinghurst, *Long Ships Passing*, 141.

49. Havinghurst, *Long Ships Passing*, 124.

50. James P. Berry, *Ships of the Great Lakes: 300 Years of Navigation* (Berkeley, CA: Howell-North Books, 1973), 79; White, *Wet Britches and Muddy Boots*, 229.

51. *Buffalo* (NY) *Commercial Advertiser*, April 18, 1854; Havinghurst, *Long Ships Passing*, 139–140.

52. Gamst, ed., *Early American Railroads*, 417–418.

53. James L. Elliott, *Red Stacks over the Horizon: The Story of the Goodrich Steamboat Line* (Grand Rapids, MI: William B. Eerdmans, 1967), 97–98; George W. Hilton, *Eastland Legacy of the Titanic* (Stanford, CA; Stanford University Press, 1995); Carl Sandburg, "Looking 'Em Over," *International Socialist Review* 16 (September 1915): 132.

54. Taylor, *Transportation Revolution*, 72.

55. James P. Barry, *Ships of the Great Lakes: 300 Years of Navigation* (Berkeley, CA: Howell-North, 1973), 164–165; Ralph W. Hidy, Muriel E. Hidy, and Roy V. Scott with Don L. Hofsommer, *The Great Northern Railway: A History* (Boston, MA: Harvard Business School Press, 1998), 122.

56. The Detroit & Cleveland Steam Navigation Company public timetable, April 1891; David D. Van Tassel and John J. Grabowski, eds., *The Encyclopedia of Cleveland History* (Bloomington: Indiana University Press, 1987), 609; James A. Toman and Blaine S. Hays, *Horse Trails to Regional Rails: The Story of Public Transit in Greater Cleveland* (Kent, OH: Kent State University Press, 1966), 98.

57. Cleveland & Buffalo Transit Company public timetable, May 1, 1927; A. T. Zillmer, "The Erie Excursion Company," *Inland Seas* (Winter 1960): 275–282; *Muskegon* (MI) *Chronicle*, April 11, 2011; Van Tassel and Grabowski, eds., *Encyclopedia of Cleveland History*, 38.

58. White, *Wet Britches and Muddy Boots*, 251.

59. T. J. Stiles, *The First Tycoon: The Epic Life of Cornelius Vanderbilt* (New York: Alfred A. Knopf, 2009), 107.

60. John H. Morrison, *History of American Steam Navigation* (New York: W. F. Sametz and Company, 1903).

61. Howland, *Steamboat Disasters and Railroad Accidents in the United States*; Dayton, *Steamboat Days*, 190–191; White, *Wet Britches and Muddy Boots*, 253–254.

62. Roger Williams McAdam, *The Old Fall River Line* (New York: Stephen Daye, 1955), 85–88; Edward L. Dunbaugh, *The New England Steamship Company: Long Island Sound Night Boats in the Twentieth Century* (Gainesville: University Press of Florida, 2005), 33–65.

63. Dayton, *Steamboat Days*, 202.

64. *The Pilot* 18 (February 1909): 8–9, 12, 17.

65. Lester B. Shippee, ed., *Bishop Whipple's Southern Diary, 1843–1844* (Minneapolis: University of Minnesota Press, 1937), 7; Charles P. Brown, *Brownie the Boomer: The Life of Charles P. Brown, an American Railroader*, edited by H. Roger Grant (DeKalb: Northern Illinois University Press, 1991), 139–140, 244.

66. *Seattle* (WA) *Daily Times*, January 4, 1902.

67. David I. Folman Jr., *The Nicaragua Route* (Salt Lake City: University of Utah Press, 1972); Hubert Howe Bancroft, *The Works of William Howe Bancroft, 1848–1859* (San Francisco: History Company, n.d.) 6: 137.

68. Giles T. Brown, *Ships That Sail No More: Marine Transportation from San Diego to Puget Sound, 1910–1940* (Lexington: University of Kentucky Press, 1966), 9; Don L. Hofsommer, *The Southern Pacific, 1901–1985* (College Station: Texas A&M Press, 1986), 152; Gregory Lee Thompson, *The Passenger Train in the Motor Age: California's Rail and Bus Industries, 1910–1941* (Columbus: Ohio State University Press, 1993), 31; Gordon R. Newell and Joe Williamson, *Pacific Coastal Liners* (Seattle, WA: Superior, 1959), 33.

69. Hidy, et al., *Great Northern Railway*, 122; Brown, *Ships That Sail No More*, 13; *Palaces of the Pacific* (Portland, OR: Great Northern Pacific Steamship Company, 1915), 4–5.

70. Roy Minter, *The White Pass Gateway to the Klondike* (Fairbanks: University of Alaska Press, 1987), 17; Gordon R. Newell, *The H. W. McCurdy Marine History of the Northwest* (Seattle, WA: Superior, 1966), 12–26; David Henderickson, "Knots, Liberties & Lollipop Ships: Postwar Cargo Ships of the Alaska Steamship Company," *PowerShips* 299 (Fall 2016): 25.

71. Tappen Adney, *The Klondike Stampede* (New York: Harper and Brothers, 1900), 31.

Pierre Berton, in his book *The Klondike Fever: The Life and Death of the Last Great Gold Rush* (New York: Alfred A. Knopf, 1958), makes clear that the initial wave of gold seekers to the Klondike region nearly universally encountered horrible conditions. One passenger aboard the *Amur* described it as "a floating bedlam, pandemonium let loose, the Black Hole of Calcutta in an Arctic setting" (p. 138). Vessels were badly overcrowded, some filthy and smelly, and food awful or limited.

72. *Wall Street Journal*, November 5, 2016.

1. Robert Payne, *The Canal Builders: The Story of Canal Engineers through the Ages* (New York: Macmillan, 1959), 10, 35–62; Benjamin Franklin to Samuel Rhoads, August 22, 1772, William Willcox, ed., *The Papers of Benjamin Franklin*, vol. 19 (New Haven, CT: Yale University Press, 1975), 279; Harry Sinclair Drago, *Canal Days in America: The History and Romance of Old Towpaths and Waterways* (New York: Clarkson N. Potter, 1972), 7–9; Ronald E. Shaw, *Canals for a Nation: The Canal Era in the United States, 1790–1860* (Lexington: University Press of Kentucky, 1990), 11–15; Frederick C. Gamst, ed., *Early American Railroads: Franz Anton Ritter von Gerstner's "Die innern Communicationen," 1842–1843* (Stanford, CA: Stanford University Press, 1997), 293–295; Ronald E. Shaw, *Erie Water West: A History of the Erie Canal, 1792–1854* (Lexington: University of Kentucky Press, 1966).

A remarkable and highly attractive feature of the Erie Canal involved the swiftness of its completion, and the final price tag of $7.1 million did not result in a cost overrun.

2. See Robert H. Wiebe, *Opening of American Society: From the Adoption of the Constitution to the Eve of Disunion* (New York: Alfred A. Knopf, 1984), chapter 10.

3. George Perkins, "The Ohio Canal: An Account of Its Completion to Chillicothe," *Ohio Archaeological and Historical Quarterly* 34 (October 1925): 597; Charles R. Poinsatte, *Fort Wayne during the Canal Era, 1828–1855* (Indianapolis: Indiana Historical Bureau, 1969), 256.

4. George Rogers Taylor, *The Transportation Revolution, 1815–1860* (New York: Holt, Rinehart and Winston, 1951), 152; Andrew R. L. Cayton and Peter S. Onuf, *The Midwest and the Nation: Rethinking the History of an American Region* (Bloomington: Indiana University Press, 1990), 36; Harvey H. Segal, "Cycles of Canal Construction," in Carter Goodrich, ed., *Canals and American Economic Development* (New York: Columbia University Press, 1961), 172.

By way of comparison, Great Britain in 1840 claimed 4,003 miles of canal and improved or canalized rivers. See Charles Hadfield, *The Canal Age* (Newton Abbot, UK: David and Charles, 1968), 208.

5. Carter Goodrich, "The Gallatin Plan after One Hundred and Fifty Years," *American Philosophical Society Proceedings* 102 (October 1958): 437; John Lauritz Larson, "'Bind the Republic Together': The National Union and the Struggle of Internal Improvements," *Journal of American History* 74 (September 1987): 372–374.

6. Shaw, *Canals for a Nation*, 33, 66, 98, 110; George W. Knepper, *Ohio and Its People* (Kent, OH: Kent State University Press, 1989), 150.

7. Carol Sheriff, *The Artificial River: The Erie Canal and the Paradox of Progress, 1817–1862* (New York: Hill and Wang, 1996), 36; Catherine Tobin, "The Lowly Muscular Digger: Irish Canal Workers in Nineteenth Century America" (PhD diss., University of Notre Dame, 1987), 38.

8. Robert J. Kapsch, *Historic Canals & Waterways of South Carolina* (Columbia: University of South Carolina Press, 2010), 41–42; Ernest Teagarden, "Builders of the Ohio Canal, 1815–1832," *Inland Seas* 19 (1963): 95.

9. Sheriff, *Artificial River*, 40; Harvey Chalmers II, *How the Irish Built the Erie* (New York: Bookman Associates, 1964), 16, 132; *Cleveland* (OH) *Herald*, July 22, 1825; Harry N. Scheiber, *Ohio Canal Era: A Case Study of Government*

and the Economy, 1820–1861 (Athens: Ohio University Press, 1969), 45; David D. Van Tassel and John J. Grabowski, eds., *The Encyclopedia of Cleveland History* (Bloomington: Indiana University Press, 1987), xxiii; Tobin, "Lowly Muscular Digger," 41.

10. Sheriff, *Artificial River*, 191; Teagarden, "Builders of the Ohio Canal," 96–97; Charles Nordhoff, *The Communistic Societies of the United States* (New York: Hillary House, 1961 rept.), 103; Kathleen Fernandez, "The Hands of the Diligent," in Lynn Metzger and Peg Bobel, eds., *Canal Fever: The Ohio & Erie Canal, from Waterway to Canalway* (Kent, OH: Kent State University Press, 2009), 109–110.

11. Ralph D. Gray, *The National Waterway: A History of the Chesapeake and Delaware Canal, 1769–1985*, 2nd ed. (Urbana: University of Illinois Press, 1989), 52–53; Tobin, "Lowly Muscular Digger," 122; Terry K. Woods, *Twenty Five Miles to Nowhere: The Story of the Walhonding Canal with Canal Guide* (Coshocton, OH: Roscoe Village Foundation, 1978), 23–25; Peter Way, *Common Labour: Workers and the Digging of North American Canals, 1780–1860* (Cambridge, UK: Cambridge University Press, 1993), 146–148; Michael P. Conzen and Kay J. Carr, eds., *The Illinois & Michigan Canal National Heritage Corridor: A Guide to Its History and Sources* (DeKalb: Northern Illinois University Press, 1988), 8.

12. Taylor, *Transportation Revolution*, 1951; John J. George Jr., "The Miami Canal," *Ohio Archaeological and Historical Publications* (1927): 96; Alan Conway, ed., *The Welsh in America: Letter from the Immigrants* (Minneapolis: University of Minnesota Press, 1961), 60–61; Tobin, "Lowly Muscular Digger," 46.

13. Sheriff, *Artificial River*, 43; Shaw, *Canals for a Nation*, 167; W. J. Rorabaugh, *The Alcoholic Republic: An American Tradition* (New York: Oxford University Press, 1979), 140, 143–149.

14. Teagarden, "Builders of the Ohio Canal," 101–102.

15. *Fort Wayne* (IN) *Sentinel*, August 27, 1842.

16. Perkins, "Ohio Canal," 599; Teagarden, "Builders of the Ohio Canal," 102; Charles E. Rosenberg, *The Cholera Years: The United States in 1832, 1849, and 1866*, part 1 (Chicago: University of Chicago Press, 1962); Tobin, "Lowly Muscular Digger," 129–130; Woods, *Twenty Five Miles to Nowhere*, 55.

An additional indication of the challenges facing diggers is this ditty sung by those who built the Erie Canal:

> We are digging the ditch through the mire;
> Through the mud and the slime and the mire, by heck!
> And the mud is our principal hire;
> Up our pants, in our shirts, down our neck, by heck!

17. Shaw, *Canals for a Nation*, 171–172; Rorabaugh, *Alcoholic Republic*, 143–144; James E. Davis, *Frontier Illinois* (Bloomington: Indiana University Press, 1998), 302.

18. *Lancaster* (OH) *Gazette*, July 20, 1825; "Commencement on the Ohio Canal at Licking Summit," *Ohio Archaeological and Historical Quarterly* 34 (January 1925): 66–99.

19. Drago, *Canal Days in America*, 198–199; Alvin F. Harlow, *Old Towpaths: The Story of the American Canal Era* (New York: D. Appleton and Company, 1926), 61–62; Benjamin F. Taylor, *The World on Wheels and Other Sketches* (Chicago: S. C. Griggs and Company, 1874), 26; Shaw, *Canals for a Nation*, 42–44.

20. Cadwallader D. Colden, *Memoir, Prepared at the Celebration of the Completion of the New York Canals* (New York: W. A. Davis, 1825), 122.

21. Lionel D. Wyld, *Low Bridge! Folklore and the Erie Canal* (Syracuse, NY: Syracuse University Press, 1962), 16; Madeline Sadler Waggoner, *The Long Haul West: The Great Canal Era, 1817–1850* (New York: G. P. Putnam's Sons, 1958), 151.

22. John H. White Jr., *Wet Britches and Muddy Boots: A History of Travel in Victorian America* (Bloomington: Indiana University Press, 2013), 171; Sheriff, *Artificial River*, 138, 144; Lloyd Corkan, "The Beaver and Lake Erie Canal," *Western Pennsylvania Historical Magazine* 17 (September 1934): 185; Wyld, *Low Bridge!*, 20, 70.

23. Waggoner, *Long Haul West*, 138–139; Sheriff, *Artificial River*, 141; Taylor, *World on Wheels*, 27; Eugene F. Moran Sr., "The Erie Canal as I Have Known It," *Bottoming Out* 3 (1959): 2–3; Harlow, *Old Towpaths*, 333.

24. Marvin A. Rapp, *Canal Water and Whiskey: Tall Tales from the Erie Canal Country* (New York: Twayne, 1965), 20.

25. Horatio Alger Jr., *From Canal Boy to President, or the Boyhood and Manhood of James A. Garfield* (New York: John R. Anderson and Company, 1881), 44–60; Allan Peskin, *Garfield: A Biography* (Kent, OH: Kent State University Press, 1978), 12–13.

26. Walter D. Edmonds, *Rome Haul* (Boston: Little, Brown and Company, 1929), 50; Sheriff, *Artificial River*, 141, 144; Maurice Thompson, *Stories of Indiana* (Cincinnati, OH: American Book Company, 1898), 218.

27. Paul Fatout, *Indiana Canals* (West Lafayette, IN: Purdue University Studies, 1972), 131; Harlow, *Old Towpaths*, 329–330.

28. Wyld, *Low Bridge!*, 19; Rapp, *Canal Water and Whiskey*, 161; Fatout, *Indiana Canals*, 130.

29. Thompson, *Stories of Indiana*, 217; White, *Wet Britches and Muddy Boots*, 166.

30. Theodore Dwight, *The Northern Traveller* (New York: G. & C. Carvill, 1828), 38.

31. White, *Wet Britches and Muddy Boots*, 168; Harlow, *Old Towpaths*, 342.

32. Shirley S. McCord, compiler, *Travel Accounts of Indiana, 1679–1961* (Indianapolis: Indiana Historical Bureau, 1970), 198.

33. Drago, *Canal Days in America*, 276.

34. Shaw, *Canals for a Nation*, 186; Warren S. Tryon, ed., *A Mirror for Americans: Life and Manners in the United States 1790–1870 as Recorded by American Travelers*, vol. 1: *Life in the East* (Chicago: University of Chicago Press, 1952), 113.

35. Captain Basil Hall, *Travels in North America in the Years 1827 and 1828*, vol. 1 (Edinburgh: Robert Cadell, 1830), 119; Clara von Gerstner, "Description of a Journey through the United States of North America (1838–1840)," unpublished manuscript translated by Steven Rowan; George W. Bagby, *Canal Reminiscences: Recollections of Travel in the Old Days on the James River and Kanawha Canal* (Richmond, VA: West, Johnson, 1879); Moran, "The Erie Canal as I Have Known It," 11; Charles Dickens, *American Notes for General Circulation*, vol. 2 (London: Chapman & Hall, n.d.), 49; Harlow, *Old Towpaths*, 359.

36. White, *Wet Britches and Muddy Boots*, 169; Dickens, *American Notes*, 48; Philip D. Mason, ed., "Diary of a Trip Rochester to Mackinac Island, 1830," *Michigan History* 37 (1953): 27; Sheriff, *Artificial River*, 70; Harlow, *Old Towpaths*, 360.

37. White, *Wet Britches and Muddy Boots*, 172–173; *History of Scott County, Iowa* (Chicago: Inter-State, 1882), 545; Thompson, *Stories of Indiana*, 218; Corkan, "The Beaver and Lake Erie Canal," 187; Tryon, ed., *A Mirror for Americans*, 107; Waggoner, *Long Haul West*, 77; Russell P. Bellico, *Life on a Canal Boat: The Journals of Theodore D. Bartley, 1861–1889* (Fleischmanns, NY: Purple Mountain, 2004), 37.

38. Wyld, *Low Bridge!*, 69.

39. White, *Wet Britches and Muddy Boots*, 169.

40. Bagby, *Canal Reminiscences*; Fatout, *Indiana Canals*, 136–137.

41. Thompson, *Stories of Indiana*, 221–222.

42. McCord, compiler, *Travel Accounts of Indiana*, 199.

43. "Notes on a Tour through the Western Part of the State of New York," *Ariel* (1829–1830).

44. Jacob Abbott, *Marco Paul's Voyages & Travel* (New York: Harper and Brothers, 1852), 79.

45. George W. Knepper, *Akron: City at the Summit* (Akron, OH: Summit County Historical Society, 1994), 26; Wyld, *Low Bridge!*, 31; Tryon, ed., *A Mirror for Americans*, 113; Thomas Yoseloff, ed., *Voyage to America: The Journals of Thomas Cather* (New York: A. S. Barnes, 1961), 163; Sir Arthur Cunynghame, *A Glimpse of the Great Western Republic* (London: Richard Bentley, 1851); Dickens, *American Notes*, 52; Doris M. Reed, ed., "Journal of James Darwin Maxwell," *Indiana Magazine of History* 46 (March 1950): 77.

46. Thompson, *Stories of Indiana*, 219.

47. Harlow, *Old Towpaths*, 353.

48. White, *Wet Britches and Muddy Boots*, 170; Waggoner, *Long Haul West*, 154.

49. Harlow, *Old Towpaths*, 352.

50. "Notes on a Tour through the Western Part of the State of New York."

51. Taylor, *World on Wheels*, 26–27; Harlow, *Old Towpaths*, 351.

52. Fatout, *Indiana Canals*, 118; Mason, ed., "Diary of a Trip Rochester to Mackinac Island," 30.

53. Shaw, *Erie Water West*, 214.

54. Hall, *Travels in North America*, 159; Ernst A. Stadler, ed., translator, *Journey through a Part of the United States of North America in the Years 1844 to 1846* (Carbondale: Southern Illinois University Press, 1972), 33.

55. Stadler, ed., translator, *Journal through a Part of the United States*, 36–37.

56. Harlow, *Old Towpaths*, 334; Drago, *Canal Days in America*, 280; Kenneth L. Nichols, "In Order of Appearance: Akron's Theaters, 1840–1940," (MA thesis, University of Akron, 1968), 17–22.

57. Whitney R. Cross, *The Burned-Over District* (Ithaca, NY: Cornell University Press, 1950); H. Roger Grant, *Spirit Fruit: A Gentle Utopia* (DeKalb: Northern Illinois University Press, 1988).

58. Samuel Rezneck, "A Traveling School of Science on the Erie Canal in 1826," *New York History* 40 (July 1959): 255–269.

59. Shaw, *Canals for a Nation*, 236; Poinsatte, *Fort Wayne during the Canal Era*, 73.

60. George, "Miami Canal," 96; Way, *Common Labour*, 176; Woods, *Twenty Five Miles to Nowhere*, 59.

61. Burton P. Porter, *Old Canal Days* (Columbus, OH: Heer, 1942), 63–65.

62. Way, *Common Labour*, 157; R. Max Gard and William H. Vodrey Jr., *The Sandy and Beaver Canal* (East Liverpool, OH: East Liverpool Historical Society, 1952), 170–171; Ray Allen Billington, *The Protestant Crusade, 1800–1860: A Study of the Origins of American Nativism* (New York: Macmillan, 1938), 42.

63. H. Roger Grant, *Getting Around: Exploring Transportation History* (Malabar, FL: Krieger, 2003), 61.

64. Shaw, *Canals for a Nation*, 236.

1. John F. Stover, *American Railroads*, 2nd ed. (Chicago: University of Chicago Press, 1997), 205; "1900–1950," *Railway Age* 129 (October 28, 1950): 106; "Era of Railroad Building," *Air Line News* 1 (February 1907): 6; *Harper's Monthly*, June 1907; *Historical Statistics of the United States, Colonial Times to 1957* (Washington, DC: US Bureau of the Census, 1960), 429; Jim McClellan, *My Life with Trains: Memoir of a Railroader* (Bloomington: Indiana University Press, 2017), 256.

2. Robert G. Athearn, *Union Pacific Country* (New York: Rand McNally and Company, 1971), 89–112.

3. H. Roger Grant, *Twilight Rails: The Final Era of Railroad Building in the Midwest* (Minneapolis: University of Minnesota Press, 2010), 129–147.

4. Don L. Hofsommer, *The Quanah Route: A History of the Quanah, Acme & Pacific Railway* (College Station: Texas A&M University Press, 1991), 12.

5. Ben Hur Wilson, "Abandoned Railroads of Iowa," *Iowa Journal of History and Politics* 26 (January 1928): 46–47; *Omaha World-Herald*, March 10, 1956.

6. Edward Hungerford, *The Story of the Baltimore & Ohio Railroad, 1827–1927*, vol. 1 (New York: G. P. Putnam's Sons, 1928), 37–47; James D. Dilts, *The Great Road: The Building of the Baltimore & Ohio, the Nation's First Railroad, 1828–1853* (Stanford, CA: Stanford University Press, 1993), 7–12; William Prescott Smith, *The Book of the Great Railway Celebrations of 1857* (New York: D. Appleton and Company, 1858), 13.

7. George W. Hilton, *American Narrow Gauge Railroads* (Stanford, CA: Stanford University Press, 1990), 537–538; Victor Moore, *36 Miles of Trouble: The Story of the West River R.R.* (Brattleboro, VT: Stephen Green Press, 1959), 7.

8. George W. Hilton, *Monon Route* (San Diego, CA: Howell-North Books, 1978), 27; *New Albany* (IN) *Ledger*, July 5, 1854.

9. *Louisville* (KY) *Weekly Courier*, July 8, 1854.

10. *Louisville* (KY) *Weekly Courier*, July 8, 1854.

11. John H. White Jr., *The American Railroad Passenger Car*, part I (Baltimore, MD: Johns Hopkins University Press, 1978), 105.

12. H. Roger Grant, "Frederick H. Harvey and the Revolution in Nineteenth-Century Food Service," in Virgil W. Dean, ed., *John Brown to Bob Dole: Movers and Shakers in Kansas History* (Lawrence: University Press of Kansas, 2006), 91–111.

13. V. R. Willoughby, "A Century of Car Design and Examples of Present Construction," *Bulletin of the Railway & Locomotive Historical Society* 46 (April 1938): 7–13; Liston Edgington Leyendecker, *Palace Car Prince: A Biography of George Mortimer Pullman* (Niwot: University Press of Colorado, 1992): 71–95.

14. Alan Grubb and H. Roger Grant, eds., *Epic Peters: Pullman Porter* (Clemson, SC: Clemson University Digital Press, 2012), ix.

15. Amy G. Richter, *Home on the Rails: Women, the Railroad, and the Rise of Public Domesticity* (Chapel Hill: University of North Carolina Press, 2005), 68.

16. Albro Martin, *Enterprise Denied: Origins of the Decline of American Railroads, 1897–1917* (New York: Columbia University Press, 1971), 51–95.

17. *Railway Age* (February 28, 1913).

18. *The Rocky Mountain Limited* (Chicago: Rock Island Lines, n.d.), 5–6.

19. "The McKeen Motor Cars," *Railway Age Gazette* 46 (December 17, 1909): 111; Mark Reutter, "The Life of Edward Budd, Part I: Pulleys, McKeen Cars, and the Origins of the *Zephyr*," *Railroad History* 172 (Spring 1995): 17; H. Roger Grant,

"The Des Moines & Red Oak Railway, A Stillborn Interurban," *Railroad History* 206 (Spring–Summer 2012): 70.

20. Arthur D. Dubin, *More Classic Trains* (Glendale, CA: Interurban Press, 1974), 224; *Official Guide of the Railways* (New York: National Railway Publication Company, February 1928), 517.

21. Richard C. Overton, *Burlington Route: A History of the Burlington Lines* (New York: Alfred A. Knopf, 1965), 496; Bruce A. MacGregor and Frederick W. Benson, *Portrait of a Silver Lady: The Trains They Called the California Zephyr* (Boulder, CO: Pruett, 1977), 111–115.

22. Arthur D. Dubin, "The 20th Century Limited: A Chronicle of the Land's Most Famous Train," *Trains* 22 (August 1962): 32.

23. White, *American Railroad Passenger Car*, II, 627–628; Michael P. Chaney, "United Aircraft's Turbo Train: The Transfer of Aerospace Technology to Rail Transportation," *Railroad History* 154 (Spring 1986): 115–124.

24. Gilbert A. Lathrop, *Little Engines and Big Men* (Caldwell, ID: Caxton Printers, 1954), 17.

25. Marshall M. Kirkman, *The Science of Railways*, vol. 4 (New York: World Railway Publishing Company, 1902), 34.

26. James H. Ducker, *Men of the Steel Rails* (Lincoln: University of Nebraska Press, 1983), 10, 79; Kathern I. Sutterfield, "The Missouri Southern Railroad (As I Remember It)," unidentified newspaper story, ca. 1965, in possession of author.

27. Charles P. Brown, *Brownie the Boomer: The Life of Charles P. Brown, an American Railroader*, edited by H. Roger Grant (DeKalb: Northern Illinois University Press, 1991), 144.

28. Cary Clive Burford, "The Twilight of the Local Passenger Train in Illinois," *Journal of the Illinois State Historical Society* 51 (Summer 1958): 170; James A. Ward, ed., *Southern Railroad Man: Conductor N. J. Bell's Recollections of the Civil War Era* (DeKalb: Northern Illinois University Press, 1994), 143; *Harpers Monthly*, August 1874.

29. Ward, ed., *Southern Railroad Man*, 143.

30. *Vincennes* (IN) *Western Sun*, July 24, 1830.

31. H. Roger Grant, *Railroads and the American People* (Bloomington: Indiana University Press, 2012), 11; Willoughby, "A Century of Car Design and Examples of Present Construction," 10; Charles E. Fisher, ed., "Some Notes on Our Early Railroads," *Bulletin of the Railway & Locomotive Historical Society* 81 (1950): 61–63; Agnes C. Laut, *The Romance of the Rails* (New York: Tudor, 1936), 66.

32. Gilbert H. Kneiss, "The Virginia and Truckee Railway," *Bulletin of the Railway & Locomotive Historical Society* 45 (January 1938): 12.

33. Lucius Beebe, *Boston and the Boston Legend* (New York: D. Appleton-Century, 1935), 133–135.

34. There is a question about whether No. 999 set that world speed record. Clocking devices were not sophisticated, and the locomotive may not have been mechanically able to reach and sustain such a high speed.

35. Thomas Curtis Clarke, et al., *The American Railway: Its Construction, Development, Management and Appliances* (Secaucus, NJ: Castle, 1988), 404; Keith L. Bryant Jr., *History of the Atchison, Topeka and Santa Fe Railway* (New York: Macmillan, 1974), 213–216.

36. Arthur D. Dubin, *Some Classic Trains* (Milwaukee, WI: Kalmbach, 1964), 60, 64, 82–83; Dubin, "20th Century Limited," 16–35.

37. Dubin, *Some Classic Trains*, 83.

38. "The Pace that Kills," *World's Work* 13 (March 1907): 8,595–8,596.

39. H. Roger Grant, *The North Western: A History of the Chicago & North Western Railway System* (DeKalb: Northern Illinois University Press, 1996), 157–159; Dubin, *More Classic Trains*, 304–319; Overton, *Burlington Route*, 398.

40. August Derleth, *The Milwaukee Road: Its First Hundred Years* (Iowa City: University of Iowa Press, 2002 rept.), 238–239.

41. Dubin, "20th Century Limited," 32.

42. Samuel Breck, "A Ride from Boston to Providence in 1835," in Richard Pike, ed., *Railway Adventures and Anecdotes: Extending over More Than Fifty Years* (London: Hamilton, Adams and Company, 1887), 80–84.

43. "Stewart's Journal–Railway Travel in 1869–1871," *Railroad History* 127 (October 1972): 56; "Old Buffalo Railroads," *Railroad Gazette* 14 (August 28, 1882): 253; H. Roger Grant, ed., "Detroit to Chicago in 1888," *Railroad History* 165 (Autumn 1991): 102; Lathrop, *Little Engines and Big Men*, 175.

44. Jim Tully, *Beggars of Life: A Hobo Autobiography* (Edinburgh: AK Press/ Nabat, 2004), 140; Grant, "Detroit to Chicago in 1888," 103–105.

45. H. Roger Grant, ed., *We Took the Train* (DeKalb: Northern Illinois University Press, 1990), 112–114.

46. Joe Walsh and Bill Howes, *Travel by Pullman: A Century of Service* (Saint Paul, MN: MBI, 2004), 8.

47. James D. Porterfield, *Dining by Rail: The History and Recipes of America's Golden Age of Railroad Cuisine* (New York: St. Martin's Griffin, 1998), 13–15; Lady Duffus Hardy, *Through Cities and Prairie Lands* (New York: R. Rorthington, 1881), 75.

48. Ray Neil Jr., *The American Railroad: Life after Death (Memories and Milestones)* (London: Minerva, 2000), 13; Porterfield, *Dining by Rail*, 100, 147, 189; *Post-Intelligence* (Seattle, WA), March 14, 1913; William A. McKenzie, *Dining Car Line to the Pacific: An Illustrated History of the NP Railway's "Famously Good" Food, with 150 Authentic Recipes* (Saint Paul: Minnesota Historical Society, 1990), 18.

49. Harry Kemp, *Tramping on Life: An Autobiographical Narrative* (Garden City, NY: Garden City Publishing Company, 1922), 31.

50. *Railway Age* 5 (July 20, 1882): 395–396; Robert Louis Stevenson, *The Amateur Emigrant* (London: Hogarth, 1984 rept.), 101; Ralph W. Hidy, et al., *The Great Northern Railway: A History* (Boston, MA: Harvard Business School Press, 1988), 179–180.

51. Stover, *American Railroads*, 31, 108, 160; "Rate Wars," *Railroad Gazette* 14 (June 23, 1882): 370; Gayle Thornbrough, et al., eds., *The Diary of Calvin Fletcher, 1853–1856*, vol. 5 (Indianapolis: Indiana Historical Society, 1977), 159; Burford, "Twilight of the Local Passenger Train in Illinois," 170–171.

52. Tully, *Beggars of Life*, 5.

53. Josiah Flynt, "The Tramp and the Railroads," *Century Illustrated Magazine* 58 (June 1899): 258; Grant, *Railroads and the American People*, 54.

54. "Tramps," *Railroad History* 128 (Spring 1973):34; "Tramps," *Railroad Gazette* 14 ((December 1, 1882):745; Lathrop, *Little Engines and Big Men*, 214; Erling E. Kildahl, "Riding Freight to Jamestown in 1936: A Brief Memoir," *North Dakota History* 55 (1988):14–24.

55. *We Knew Mary Baker Eddy* (Boston: Christian Science Publishing Society, 1943), 20–21.

56. Stevenson, *Amateur Emigrant*, 98.

57. "A Mixed Train," *Railroad Gazette* 14 (September 8, 1882): 555.

58. Charity Vogel, *The Angola Horror: The 1867 Train Wreck That Shocked the Nation and Transformed American Railroads* (Ithaca, NY: Cornell University Press, 2013).

59. "Memoranda Concerning the Union Pacific R.R.," *Bulletin of the Railway & Locomotive Historical Society* 32 (October 1933): 29.

60. "The Week's Accidents," *Railway Age* (August 1, 1902); *Historical Statistics of the United States*, 437; *Washington Post*, July 4, 2015; *New York Times*, July 10, 1918.

61. Linda Thayer Guilford, "A Winter Railroad Ride," n.d., Linda Thayer Guilford papers, Western Reserve Historical Society, Cleveland, Ohio.

62. *New York Times*, July 20, 1879.

63. *Railway Surgical Journal* 13 (July 1907): 424.

64. Charles Dickens, *American Notes* (Gloucester, MA: Peter Smith, 1968 rept.), 80.

65. Eugene Alvarez, *Travel on Southern Antebellum Railroads, 1838–1860* (Tuscaloosa: University of Alabama Press, 1974), 127; Thomas Yoseloff, ed., *Voyage to America: The Journals of Thomas Cather* (New York: A. S. Barnes, 1961), 136; Cicely Palser Havely, ed., *This Great Beyond: The Travels of Isabella Bird Bishop* (London: Century Publishing, 1984), 32.

66. Dickens, *American Notes*, 79–80; *Railway Age* 29 (July 1880): 402.

67. Theresa Yelverton, *Teresina in America*, vol. 2 (London: Richard Bentley and Son, 1875), 3, 5.

68. Theodore Kornweibel Jr., *Railroads in the African American Experience* (Baltimore, MD: Johns Hopkins University Press, 2010).

69. *Derby* (CT) *Journal*, October 1, 1847.

70. *Daily Plainsman* (Huron, SD), January 8, 1950.

71. *Fortieth Annual Report of the Board of Railroad Commissioners for the Year Ending December 3, 1917* (Des Moines: State of Iowa, 1917), 124–126.

72. *Thirty-Sixth Annual Report of the Board of Railroad Commissioners for the Year Ending December 1913* (Des Moines: State of Iowa, 1914), 17–18.

73. "Bus Produces Profits on 'Loser' Rail Lines," *Railway Age* 141 (August 20, 1956): 10; James G. Lyne, "After Hours," *Railway Age* 141 (August 13, 1956): 44.

74. Jerald T. Milanich, ed., *Dispatches from a New York City Journalist's 1873 Railroad Trip across the American West* (Boulder: University Press of Colorado, 2008), 70–71.

75. Walter Gore Marshall, *Through America* (London: S. Low, Marston, Searle, and Rivington, 1881), 112–113.

76. H. Roger Grant, *Electric Interurbans and the American People* (Bloomington: Indiana University Press, 2016), 11–23; George W. Hilton and John F. Due, *The Electric Interurban Railways in America* (Stanford, CA: Stanford University Press, 1960), 186.

77. Hilton and Due, *Electric Interurban Railways in America*, 187.

78. Grant, *Railroads and the American People*, 255–270.

79. Frank Kyper, *The Railroad That Came Out at Night: A Book of Railroading in and around Boston* (Brattleboro, VT: Stephen Greene, 1977), 135–155.

80. Grant, *Railroads and the American People*, 248–289.

1. Elizabeth Ann Pinkston, "The Intercity Bus Transportation Industry: An Industrial Organization Study" (PhD diss., Yale University, 1975), 4–6; Sioux Falls Traction System public timetable, July 4, 1924; Lewis R. Freeman, "From Chicago to Los Angeles on Common Carrier Lines," *Bus Transportation* 5 (June 1926): 295; Cleveland, Ashtabula, Conneaut Bus Company public timetable, June 19, 1926; H. Roger Grant, *Ohio on the Move: Transportation in the Buckeye State* (Athens: Ohio University Press, 2000), 129.

2. Larry Plachno, "Pickwick Stages System," *National Bus Trader* 25 (May 2002): 26.

3. Nathan Asch, "Cross-County Bus," *New Republic* 78 (April 25, 1934): 301; *Bus Transportation* 8 (June 1929): 566.

4. Pinkston, "Intercity Bus Transportation Industry," 119–120.

5. *Travel by Bus* (Minneapolis: Minnesota Motor Association, 1925); Federal Coordinator of Transportation, *Regulation of Transportation Agencies* (Washington, DC: Government Printing Office, 1934), 24–27; Warren J. Wagner, *A Legislative History of the Motor Carrier Act, 1935* (Denton, MD: Rue Publishing Company, 1935); Margaret Walsh, "The Motor Carrier Act of 1935," *Journal of Transport History* 8 (March 1987): 66–80; Elizabeth A. Pinkston, "The Rise and Fall of Bus Regulation," *Regulation: AEI Journal on Government and Society* (September–December 1984): 46; *National Bus Trader* 23 (May 2000): 8; Larry Plachno, "Greyhound and Laidlaw Update," *National Bus Trader* 23 (August 2000): 33.

A range of bus firms provided motor freight service, including the Short Line between New York City, Boston, and intermediate cities; Southern Michigan Transportation Company in Michigan and several adjoining states; and Southern Kansas Stage Lines between Wichita and various destinations in Kansas and Oklahoma.

As the bus industry developed, two long-distance companies came to dominate. Designed to facilitate long-distance transportation, Greyhound Bus Corporation emerged in the late 1920s, and in 1936 the National Trailways Bus System began as an alliance of independent firms, some of which were railroad owned.

6. *The Greyhound Traveler* 1 (March 1929).

7. John Gunnell, "The Orange Line of Wisconsin," *National Bus Trader* 25 (June 2002): 28–32; Robert Gabrick, *Traveling with Greyhound: On the Road for 100 Years* (Hudson, WI: Enthusiasts Books, 2014), 17.

8. Interstate Transit Lines public timetable, February 1, 1931; Atlantic Greyhound Lines public timetable, March 1, 1934; Jim Lehrer, *A Bus of My Own* (New York: G. P. Putnam's Sons, 1992), 27; Thomas H. Wolf, "Here Is America," *Collier's* (October 11, 1947): 11; Margaret Walsh, *Making Connections: The Long-Distance Bus Industry in the USA* (Aldershot, UK: Ashgate, 2000), 1–2.

9. Ora Bailey Brooks, *Brooks Bus Line: No "Common Carrier": The Story of J. Polk Brooks and His Enterprise* (Frankfort, KY: Heritage Printing, 1985), 6–7, 11–14.

10. Walsh, *Making Connections*, 2; *New York Times*, July 26, 2015; Pinkston, "Intercity Bus Transportation Industry," 132–134.

11. Larry Plachno, "Chinatown Buses," *National Bus Trader* 29 (September 2006): 14, 16, 22, 24–25; Larry Plachno, "Measuring Megabus," *National Bus Trader* 32 (September 2009): 24.

12. H. Roger Grant, *Railroaders without Borders: A History of the Railroad Development Corporation* (Bloomington: Indiana University Press, 2015), 203–208.

13. Motor Transit Company, "San Diego by Motor Stage," n.d.; Crown Stage Lines public timetable, May 1, 1922; "Thru Minnesota's Famous Playgrounds on Northland Buses," n.d.; Pickwick Stages public timetable, April 1, 1929; Oregon Motor Stages public timetable, April 1, 1935; Arthur S. Genet, *"Profile of Greyhound!" The Greyhound Corporation* (New York: Newcomen Society in North America, 1958), 18; Margaret Walsh, "'See This Amazing America': The Long-Distance Bus Industry's Use of Advertising in its First Quarter Century," *Journal of Transport History* 11 (March 1990): 64; Sandra J. Burgess, "Trailways," *National Bus Trader* 24 (October 2001): 20.

14. Atchison, Topeka & Santa Fe Railway public timetable, September 1, 1926; Jack Rhodes, *Intercity Bus Lines of the Southwest: A Photographic History* (College Station: Texas A&M University Press, 1988), 118–126.

15. Walsh, "'See This Amazing America,'" 75, 79; Deena Maniscalchi, *Driving Vision: The Story of Peter Pan Bus Lines* (privately printed, 2000), 37.

16. "Vacation Tours Easter and Spring by Tauck" (New York: Tauck Motor Tours, 1930).

17. Ann M. Kammerer, "Arrow Stage Lines Celebrates 85 Years," *National Bus Trader* 36 (May 2013): 24, 26–29.

18. Crown State Lines System public timetable, May 1, 1922; Interview with Arthur Lennartson, December 16, 1974, oral history recording in Minnesota Discovery Center, Chisholm, MN, hereafter cited as Lennartson interview; Genet, *"Profile of Greyhound!,"* 8; Northland Greyhound Lines public timetable, May 1930; *New York Times*, November 22, 1936; Margaret Walsh, "Iowa's Bus Queen: Helen M. Schultz and the Red Ball Transportation Company," *Annals of Iowa* 53 (Fall 1994): 334; Sylvia Nichols Allen, *The People Will Be Served: A History of the Vermont Transit Bus Company* (CreateSpace, 2011), 34.

19. "The Paradox Lines Have Always Fulfilled Contracts," *Paragrams* 2 (April 1927): 1.

20. Russell A. Byrd, *Russ's Bus: Adventures of an American Bus Driver* (Los Angeles: Wetzel, 1945), 24–25; Freeman, "From Chicago to Los Angeles," 297.

21. Wolf, "Here Is America," 13; Asch, "Cross-Country Bus," 301; Golden Eagle Transcontinental Lines public timetable, ca. 1934.

22. John A. Jakie and Keith A. Schulle, *Supplanting America's Railroads: The Early Auto Age, 1900–1940* (Knoxville: University of Tennessee Press, 2017): 184–185; Hazel Crosby Cizek, "What No Towels? The Theme Song of the Bus Traveler," *Bus Transportation* (January 1935): 4.

23. Gabrick, *Traveling with Greyhound*, 29; *New York Times*, April 3, 1969.

24. Genet, *"Profile of Greyhound!,"* 19, 20–21; Jefferson Transportation Company public timetable, October 1, 1944; Vermont Transit Company public timetable, December 4, 1942; Rhodes, *Intercity Bus Lines of the Southwest*, 70.

25. Santa Fe Trailways public timetable, August 15, 1943.

26. Mid-Continent Coaches public timetable, July 1944.

27. Motor Transit Stages public timetable, August 1931; Cizek, "What No Towels?," 6; Asch, "Cross-Country Bus," 301; *New York Times*, November 10, 1974.

28. William Kittredge and Steven M. Krauzer, *Stories into Film* (New York: Harper Colophon Books, 1979), 32–34.

29.	Pacific Greyhound Lines public timetable, July 20, 1937.

30.	Santa Fe Coordinated Rail-Bus timetable for California, June 8, 1941; *National Bus Trader* 19 (September 1996): 14; Gabrick, *Traveling with Greyhound*, 84–85; "Greyhound Scenicruiser: Introducing a Great New Era in Highway Travel," Greyhound pamphlet, ca. 1953; Short Way Lines public timetable, June 27, 1956.

31.	Gabrick, *Traveling with Greyhound*, 55.

32.	V. Scharff, *Taking the Wheel: Women and the Coming of the Motor Age* (New York: Free Press, 1991); Oriole Lines public timetable, July 6, 1927; Howell Walker, "You Can't Miss America by Bus," *National Geographic Magazine* 98 (July 1950): 3; Auto Bus Line public timetable, ca. 1925; Cleveland-Pittsburgh Motor Stage public timetable, June 20, 1927; Interstate Transportation Company public timetable, September 1, 1928; "Map of the United States—and Some Timely Tips on How to See It Best by Greyhound" (Greyhound Lines, 1946).

It was the Peter Pan Bus Company that likely hired the first black intercity/interstate bus driver. In 1953 Willie Taylor, an African American, joined the carrier. Maniscalchi, *Driving Vision*, 47.

33.	Kenneth R. Hixon, *Pick of the Litter: Greyhound's Once Finest Bus Line* (Lexington, KY: Centerville Books, 2001), 100; *National Bus Trader* 19 (March 1996): 38.

34.	The Cleveland-Akron Bus Company public timetable, ca. 1925; Great Lakes Stages public timetable, May 1, 1929; Maine Stages public timetable, June 21, 1930; Maniscalchi, *Driving Vision*, 42; United Motor Coach Company public timetable, October 1938.

35.	Lennartson interview.

36.	Genet, *"Profile of Greyhound!,"* 11; Interview with Merle Hemphill, 1976, oral history recording in Minnesota Discovery Center, Chisholm, MN, hereafter cited as Hemphill interview; Lennartson interview.

37.	Hemphill interview.

38.	Hemphill interview; Hixon, *Pick of the Litter*, 103–104; Crescent Stages public timetable, December 15, 1935.

39.	Grady H. Morgan, *Memoirs of a Greyhound Bus Driver* (West Conschohocken, PA: Infinity Publishing, 2005), 51–52.

40.	Modern Trailways bus timetables, August 1948.

41.	Kathryn Schulz, "Saint Pauli," *New Yorker* (April 17, 2017): 70.

42.	Catherine A. Barnes, *Journey from Jim Crow: The Desegregation of Southern Transit* (New York: Columbia University Press, 1983), 39, 62; *New York Times*, June 4, 1946; December 11, 1952.

43.	Barnes, *Journey from Jim Crow*, 130.

44.	Byrd, *Russ's Bus*, 41–42.

45.	Morgan, *Memoirs of a Greyhound Bus Driver*, 33, 54.

46.	Morgan, *Memoirs of a Greyhound Bus Driver*, 151–154; *New York Times*, November 3, 1983; November 18, 1983; November 26, 1983; December 4, 1983.

47.	*New York Times*, March, 4, 1990; April 2, 1990; July 11, 1991.

48.	*National Bus Trader* 20 (December 1996): 16; Tom Jones, "The Special Library of the Motor Bus Society," *National Bus Trader* 26 (August 2001): 26, 28–29.

49.	*Hibbing* (MN) *Daily Tribune*, July 29, 1984; August 1, 1984; Larry Plachno, "Hibbing, the Greyhound Museum, the Great Abyss and Bus Bash," *National Bus Trader* 25 (August 2002), 28–32.

50.	Mindi Rice, director, Main Street Blytheville, to author, May 30, 2017.

6. AIRPLANES AND THE AMERICAN PEOPLE

1. Craig S. Harwood and Gary B. Fogel, *Quest for Flight: John J. Montgomery and the Dawn of Aviation in the West* (Norman: University of Oklahoma Press, 2012), 28; Tom D. Crouch, *A Dream of Wings: Americans and the Airplane, 1875–1905* (New York: W. W. Norton, 1981), 13–15; David McCullough, *The Wright Brothers* (New York: Simon & Schuster, 2015), 105–106, 111–115; *Minneapolis* (MN) *Journal*, June 14, 1910.

2. Daniel L. Rust, *Flying across America: The Airline Passenger Experience* (Norman: University of Oklahoma Press, 2009), 3; William M. Leary Jr., ed., *Pilots' Directions: The Transcontinental Airway and Its History* (Iowa City: University of Iowa Press, 1990), 1–3; Jeremy R. Kinney, *Airplanes: The Life Story of a Technology* (Baltimore, MD: Johns Hopkins University Press, 2008), 19.

3. Harry Bruno, *Wings over America: The Inside Story of American Aviation* (New York: Robert M. McBridge and Company, 1942), 312; *Cincinnati* (OH) *Enquirer*, July 14, 1911.

4. Roger E. Bilstein, *Flight in America: From the Wrights to the Astronauts*, rev. ed. (Baltimore, MD: Johns Hopkins University Press, 1994), 27–28; *Wall Street Journal*, December 31, 2012.

5. Howard L. Scamehorn, *Balloons to Jets: A Century of Aeronautics in Illinois, 1855–1955* (Chicago: Henry Regnery, 1957), 141; R. E. G. Davis, *Airlines of the United States since 1914* (London: Putnam, 1972), 532; William M. Leary Jr., "At the Dawn of Commercial Aviation: Inglis M. Uppercu and Aeromarine Airways," *Business History Review* 53 (1979): 180–182.

6. Leary, "At the Dawn of Commercial Aviation," 186–187; Bilstein, *Flight in America*, 57.

7. Leary, "At the Dawn of Commercial Aviation," 189; Bruno, *Wings over America*, photo section.

8. Davis, *Airlines of the United States since 1914*, 8; Bruno, *Wings over America*, 119–120.

9. Leary, "At the Dawn of Commercial Aviation," 190–192.

10. Bilstein, *Flight in America*, 50–51; David B. Holmes, *Air Mail* (New York: Clarkson N. Potter, 1981).

11. Henry Ladd Smith, *Airways: The History of Commercial Aviation in the United States* (New York: Alfred A. Knopf, 1942), 374–376.

12. A. Scott Berg, *Lindbergh* (New York: G. P. Putnam's Sons, 1998), 112–131; Rust, *Flying across America*, 7.

13. *Air Transport Schedules for Spring and Summer 1929* (New York: Lincoln Financial Service, 1929), 1.

14. George E. Hopkins, "'TAT' Transcontinental Air Transport, Inc.," *American Heritage* 27 (December 1975): 25.

15. Hopkins, "'TAT' Transcontinental Air Transport," 23; "The TAT Air Rail Service," *Railway Age* 87 (July 6, 1929): 14–15.

16. *Coast to Coast in 48 Hours by Rail and Air* (Transcontinental Air Transport, 1929); Hopkins, "TAT Transcontinental Air Transport," 25; Transcontinental Air Transport public timetable, October 15, 1929.

17. *The Airway Limited* (Philadelphia: Pennsylvania Railroad, 1929); Hopkins, "'TAT' Transcontinental Air Transport," 25.

18. *Coast to Coast in 48 Hours by Rail and Air*; Rust, *Flying across America*, 48, 51; Hopkins, "'TAT' Transcontinental Air Transport," 26.

19. *Coast to Coast in 48 Hours by Rail and Air.*

20. Transcontinental Air Transport public timetable, October 15, 1929; Davis, *Airlines of the United States since 1914*, 85.

21. Velva G. Darling, "Across the Continent in Forty-Eight Hours," *World's Work* 58 (September 1929): 52.

22. Hopkins, "'TAT' Transcontinental Air Transport," 28; Davis, *Airlines of the United States since 1914*, 85, 87.

23. *Plane Talk* 2 (April 1930): 4.

24. Hopkins, "'TAT' Transcontinental Air Transport," 27; Rust, *Flying across America*, 55.

25. Ellen Williamson, *When We Went First Class* (Garden City, NY: Doubleday, 1977), 169.

26. Hopkins, "TAT' Transcontinental Air Transport," 28; *Plane Talk*, 1; *The Pennsylvania Railroad* (New York: Calvin Bullock, 1930), 76.

27. H. Roger Grant, *The Corn Belt Route: A History of the Chicago Great Western Railroad Company* (DeKalb: Northern Illinois University Press, 1984), 101; Universal Air Lines System public timetable, June 15, 1929.

28. Universal Air Lines System public timetable, November 1, 1929.

29. Stout Airlines public timetable, April 1, 1929.

30. Don Bedwell, *Silverbird: The American Airlines Story* (Sandpoint, ID: Airways International, 1999), 47.

31. Williamson, *When We Went First Class*, 173; *Tailwinds* (Washington, DC), December 31, 1931, 3.

32. US Bureau of the Census, *Historical Statistics of the United States, Colonial Times to 1957* (Washington, DC: US Government Printing Office, 1960), 467; *New York Times*, January 31, 1932.

33. Davis, *Airlines of the United States since 1914*, 195.

34. George R. Reiss, "From Coast to Coast in a Modern Airliner," *Popular Science Monthly* 127 (October 1935): 27.

35. Davis, *Airlines of the United States since 1914*, 114–116.

36. *The Official Aviation Guide of the Airways* (Chicago: Official Aviation Guide Company, October 1933), 10.

37. Davis, *Airlines of the United States since 1914*, 180–181; Rust, *Flying across America*, 96–97.

38. Davis, *Airlines of the United States since 1914*, 185–188; Transcontinental & Western Air public timetable, April 28, 1935.

39. Wayne W. Parrish, "Spanning the Continent from Dusk-to-Dawn," 27, copy in possession of the author; Transcontinental & Western Air public timetable, June 1, 1935.

40. Barbara Ganson, *Texas Takes Wings: A Century of Flight in the Lone Star State* (Austin: University of Texas Press, 2014), 81; American Airlines Air Sleeper Service timetable, May 5, 1934; American Airlines public timetable, November 15, 1936; Rust, *Flying across America*, 111.

41. Davis, *Airlines of the United States since 1914*, 190–191; American Airlines public timetable, November 15, 1936; January 10, 1937.

42. Kinney, *Airplanes*, 53–54; Rust, *Flying across America*, 95, 122; W. David Lewis and Wesley Phillips Newton, *Delta: The History of an Airline* (Athens: University of Georgia Press, 1979), 76; *New York Times*, June 25, 1961.

43. Williamson, *When We Went First Class*, 171–172.

44. Mary Wells Geer, *Boeing's Ed Wells* (Seattle: University of Washington Press, 1992), 73–74.

45. Wayne W. Parrish, "TWA Stratoliner Tops in Passenger Comfort; Cuts Flying Time to Coast," *American Aviation* 4 (July 15, 1940): 28.

46. T. P. Wright, "Trends in Air Transportation," *Aviation* 39 (March 1940): 115, 117.

47. *New York Times*, September 29, 1937.

48. Don Eddy, "Bumped Off," *American Magazine* 39 (February 1945): 32.

49. Eddy, "Bumped Off," 132; Lewis and Newton, *Delta*, 92.

50. Eddy, "Bumped Off," 32–33.

51. Bilstein, *Flight in America*, 176.

52. Bilstein, *Flight in America*, 171, 175.

53. Allegheny Airlines public timetable, August Schedules, n.d.

54. Bilstein, *Flight in America*, 172; Bernard DeVoto, "The Easy Chair: Transcontinental Flight," *Harper's Magazine* 205 (July 1952): 47–48; Rust, *Flying across America*, 153.

55. *New York Times*, July 8, 1956; August 22, 1960.

56. Rust, *Flying across America*, 164–165.

57. Bilstein, *Flight in America*, 176, 178.

58. David P. Morgan, *Fasten Seat Belts: The Confessions of a Reluctant Airline Passenger* (New York: ARCO, 1969), 6–7.

59. Kinney, *Airplanes*, 112; Davis, *Airlines of the United States since 1914*, 511–513; Rene J. Francillon, *Boeing 707: Pioneer Jetliner* (Osceola, WI: MBI, 1999), 79.

60. Rust, *Flying across America*, 190; Lou Davis, "The Inquiring Reporter on Flight 45," *Flying* 66 (March 1960): 29, 72.

61. Harry C. James, "40 Years Ago from 30,000 Feet Up," *Desert Magazine* 22 (June 1960): 15, 18.

62. *Survival in the Air Age* (Washington, DC: US Government Printing Office, 1948), 115; Martha Derthick and Paul J. Quirk, *The Politics of Deregulation* (Washington, DC: Brookings Institution, 1985), 1–8.

63. Rust, *Flying across America*, 213.

64. *Christian Science Monitor*, December 19, 1983.

65. I. E. Quastler, *Air Midwest: The First Twenty Years* (San Diego: Airline Press of California, 1985), 113–114.

66. *New York Times*, December 9, 1990.

67. *New York Times*, February 11, 2001.

68. Rust, *Flying across America*, 70–71, 204–205; Bilstein, *Flight in America*, 341.

69. Brendan I. Koerner, *The Skies Belong to Us* (New York: Crown, 2013); *Chicago Daily Tribune*, May 24, 1962; *New York Times*, May 25, 1962.

70. Koerner, *The Skies Belong to Us*, 7–8.

71. *New York Times*, November 22, 2015; *San Diego Union-Tribune*, July 16, 2017; *Wall Street Journal*, May 10, 2017.

72. Phillip Longman and Lina Khan, "Terminal Sickness," *Washington Monthly* (March–April 2012): 21–22.

73. Rust, *Flying across America*, 30–31; George E. Hopkins, *The Airline Pilots: A Study in Elite Unionization* (Cambridge, MA: Harvard University Press, 1971), 11; Reiss, "From Coast to Coast in a Modern Airliner," 26.

74. Jack El-Hai, *Non-Stop: A Turbulent History of Northwest Airlines* (Minneapolis: University of Minnesota Press, 2013), 43–45.

75. Ganson, *Texas Takes Wings*, 86; "Born to Fly," *American Way* (June 2007): 64.

76. *Greenville* (SC) *News*, November 30, 2015.

77. Hopkins, *Airline Pilots*, 52–77.

78. Frank J. Taylor, *High Horizons: Daredevil Flying Postmen to Modern Magic Carpet—The United Air Lines Story* (New York: McGraw Hill, 1962), 71, 245; *New York Times*, April 12, 1936.

79. Lewis and Newton, *Delta*, 71–72; El-Hai, *Non-Stop*, 71–80.

80. Rust, *Flying across America*, 77.

81. Bilstein, *Flight in America*, 236.

INDEX

Index pages in *italics* indicate illustrations

Abbot, Downing & Company, 6
Aberdeen, South Dakota, 173
Academy of Model Aeronautics, 217
Acela Express (passenger train), 111, 118
Acme, Red River & Northern Railway, 98
Adams, Charles Francis, 38
Adams, Samuel Hopkins, 170
Adamson Act (1916), 115
Aeromarine Airlines, 185–187
Airbus 319/320/321 (airplanes), 213
Airline Deregulation Act (1988), 205
Air Line Pilots Association, 214
Air Line Stewardess Association, 217
Air Line Stewards Association, 217
Air Nebraska, 210
Airplanes
    Aircraft, 184–185, 191, 193–199, 201–205
    Air express and air freight, 196
    Airports, 195, 203, 211
    Air-rail service, 188–194
    Beginnings, 183–186, 188
    Coach class, 202
    Corporate changes, 210
    Enthusiasts, 217–218
    Fares, 205–206
    Films, 217–218
    Flight attendants, 214, *215*, 217
    "Hub-and-spoke" routing, 206, 208
    Mail contracts, 187, 196
    Maturity, *197*, 200–201
    Package tours, 202
    Passenger volume, 195, 201
    Pilots, 212, *213*, 214

Regulation, 205–206
Security, 209–210
Skyjacking, 209
Smoking onboard, *207*, 208–209
Transcontinental Air Transport, 188, *189–190*, 191–193
Travel displeasures, 193, 195, 198–199, 202–203, 206, 208
Travel pleasures, 185, 188, 191–195, 197–200, 202, 204, 210–211
World War II travel, 200
Air Racing Historians Society, 217
Air Travel League of America, 195
Airways Limited (passenger train), *189*, 191
Akron, Ohio, 69, 76, 160, 203
Alameda, California, 131
Alaska, 59, 225n
Alaska Steamship Company, 60
Albany (steamboat), 34
Albany, Georgia, 177
Albany, New York, 3, 29, 34, 63, 80–81, 114, 140, 144
Albuquerque, New Mexico, 164, 192, 197, 201
Alcan Highway, 60
Alger, Horatio, Jr., 74
Alhambra (steamboat), 38
Allegheny Airlines, 201–202
All-States Motor Coach Company, 149
Alton (steamboat), 43
Altoona, Pennsylvania, 127, 202
Amalgamated Transit Union, 179
American Airlines, 195, *197*, 198–199, 204, 211, 213
American Canal Society, 92–93
American Car & Foundry Company, 110, *152*

Amtrak. *See* National Railroad Passenger Corporation
Amur (steamship), 225n
Angola, New York, 135
Antelope (locomotive), 118
Anthracite Railroads Historical Society, 147
Anti-Masonic Party, 89
Antique Airplane Association, 217
AN-X Deluxe Motor Coach, *162*
Aquarama (lake boat), 52
Ariel (steamboat), 29
Arrow Stage Lines, 165
Association of Flight Attendants, 216–217
Astoria, Oregon, 59
Atchison, Kansas, 21
Atchison, Topeka & Santa Fe Railway, 96, 98, 110–111, 119, 163–164, 188, 191
Atlanta, Georgia, 213
Atlantic City, New Jersey, 120, 185
Atlantic Coast Line Railroad, 130
Atlantic Greyhound Lines, 159
Atlas (steamboat), 28
Auburn, New York, 140
Audubon, John James, 38
Augusta, Georgia, 3, 40
Auto Bus Line, 173
Ayres, Lew, 170

Baldwin, Thomas, 183
Balston, New York, 117
Baltimore, Maryland, 100, 140, 147
Baltimore & Ohio Museum, 147
Baltimore & Ohio Railroad, 96, 100, 102, 120, *128*, 130
Baltimore & Ohio Railroad Historical Society, 147
Banger & Aroostook Railroad, 143

Batavia, New York, 118, 137
Beaver & Lake Erie Canal, 73, 81
Beaverton, Oregon, 108
Bedford Springs, Pennsylvania, 202
Belle Zane (steamboat), 42
Benas Advertising Service, *150*
Bennett, Floyd, 187
Ben Sherrod (steamboat), 42–43
Bingham, George Caleb, 61–62
Birmingham, Alabama, 109
Bishop, Isabella Bird, 139
Bismarck, North Dakota, 173
Black Hills, South Dakota, 20
Black Hills Stage Line, 165
Black Hills Transportation
    Company, *158*
Blair, Wisconsin, 98
Blue, Gilbert, 38–39
Blytheville, Arkansas, *181*
Boeing 247 (airplane), 196–197
Boeing 707 (airplane), 204–205
Boeing 737 (airplane), 213
Boeing Aircraft Company, 196–197,
    200, 204
Boeing Air Transport Company,
    196, 214
Boise, Idaho, 199
Bolivar, Ohio, 79
Bolt Bus, 161, 179
Bombardier Company, 111
Bonaventure, Florida, 173
Boston, Massachusetts, 2–3, 54–55,
    63, 77, 107, 111, 117–118, 122, 134,
    138
Boston & Albany Railroad, 134
Boston & Lowell Railroad, 5, 138–139
Boston & Maine Railroad, 110, 118,
    134, 147
Boston & Providence Railroad, 54,
    122
Boston & Wooster Rail Road, 117
Bow, Clara, 217
Braniff Airways, 210
Brattleboro & Whitehall Rail Road,
    100–101
Breck, Samuel, 122
Bridgewater and Wilkes-Barre
    Turnpike, 11
Bristol (steamboat), 55
British Airways, 198
Broadway Limited (passenger train),
    119, 122
Brooks, J. Polk, 160
Brooks Bus Line, 160
Browder v. Gayle (1956), 177

Brown, Ethan Allen, 71
Bruno, Harry, 186
Buffalo, New York, 47, 50–52, 74, 81,
    88, 137, 140, 162
*Bulletin of the Railway & Locomotive
    Historical Society* (journal), 146
Burlington, New Jersey, 2
Burlington Railroad. *See* Chicago,
    Burlington & Quincy Railroad
Burlington Trailways, *172*
"Burned-Over District," 89
Bus Regulatory Reform Act (1982),
    161
Buses
    Air service coordination, 153
    African-Americans, 177–178
    Beginnings, 155–156, 234n5
    Complaints and displeasures, 156,
        165–168
    Drivers, 172–179; background of,
        173–175; gifts to, 178; strikes, 179
    Enthusiasts, 180
    Equipment, 153, *154, 155, 158, 159,
        161–162,* 165–166, *170, 171, 172,
        175–178*
    Films, 170–171
    Future prospects, 182
    Motor freight, 234n
    Native Americans, 178
    Popularity and comforts, 149–150,
        151, 163–164, 170
    Preservation efforts, *181*
    Regulation, 156–157, 161, 166
    Ridership profiles and attires,
        157–163, 171
    Tours, 163–165
    World War II travel, 168–169
Butterfield, John, 4
Byrd, Richard, 187–188
Byrd, Russell A., 173–174
By the Shores of Silver Lake (book),
    135

C-47 (airplane), 199
C-54 (airplane), 199
Calhoun, John C., 37, 66
California State Railroad Museum,
    148
California Zephyr (passenger train),
    110
Camden, New Jersey, 120
Cameron, Illinois, 119
Canal Fulton, Ohio, 90–91
Canals
    Beginnings, 63–64

Canal fever, 64–65
    Celebrations, 71–72
    Civil engineers, 65–66
    Construction workers, 66–71;
        convict labor, 68; fighting,
        religious, and ethnic tensions,
        71
    Diseases, 70–71
    Legacies, 92–93
    Speeds, 81–82, 87
    Travel experiences, 76–92;
        boat decks, 78–80; costs,
        87–88; dangers, 80–81, 87, 91;
        line boats, 77–78, 79; meals,
        82–83; noise and annoyances,
        85–86; packet boats, 76–77,
        78, 80; passenger comradery,
        86; public contacts, 88–92;
        sleeping accommodations, 82,
        83–85; unpleasant passengers,
        86–87
    Workers, 72–76; boat captains,
        73–74; drivers, 73–55;
        helmsmen, 73; Irish, 67–69;
        maintenance and support, 76
*Canals for a Nation: The Canal Era
    in the United States, 1790–1860*
    (book), 92
Canal Society of Ohio, 92
Canton, Ohio, 203
Cape River Heritage Museum, 61
Carnes, Texas, 98
Carroll, Charles, 100
Carson City, Nevada, 118
Carter, Jimmy, 205
Cather, Thomas, 139
Center for Railroad Photography
    and Art, 147
Centerville, Iowa, 209
Central Electric Railfans'
    Association, 147
Central Pacific Railroad, 5, 96, 144
Centre Harbor, New Hampshire, 5
Century of Progress Exposition,
    109, 163
Champlain Canal, 82, 84
Charles City, Iowa, 165
Charleston, South Carolina, 3, 55
Charlotte, North Carolina, 14, 134,
    211
Chesapeake & Delaware Canal, 93
Chesapeake & Ohio Canal, 66,
    68–69, 71
Chesapeake & Ohio Railroad, 130
Chester (steamboat), 46

Cheyenne, Wyoming, 187, 199
Chicago, Aurora & Elgin Railway, 145
Chicago, Burlington & Quincy Railroad, 52, 96, *109*, 110, 120, 139, 142
Chicago, Illinois, 4, 48, 50, 52, 69, 84, 96, 102, 105, 107, 109–110, 119, 122–123, 126, 132, 145, 149, 160–161, 163, 167, 184, 187–188, 194, 197, 199, 209, 213–214
Chicago, Milwaukee, St. Paul & Pacific Railroad, 96–97, 120, *121*, 122
Chicago, North Shore & Milwaukee Railway, 145
Chicago, Rock Island & Pacific Railroad, 96, 107, 110, 188
Chicago, South Shore & South Bend Railroad, 145
Chicago, St. Paul, Minneapolis & Omaha Railroad, 142–143
Chicago & Alton Railroad, 132
Chicago & Grand Trunk Railway, 123
Chicago & North Western Railway, 96–98, *102*, 106, *115*, 120, 122, 126, *129*, *136*, 140, *146*, *158*, 188. *See also* Chicago, St. Paul, Minneapolis & Omaha Railroad
Chicago Great Western Railroad, 96–97, 194
Chicago Railroad Fair, 102
Chicago River, 48
Chinatown Bus Line, 161
Cholera, 44, 46, 147
Church of Jesus Christ of Latter-Day Saints, 96
Cincinnati, Ohio, 26–27, 34, 43, 86–87, 109, 160, 187, 211
Cincinnati & Lake Erie Railway, 155
Cincinnati & Whitewater Canal, 86
City of Cleveland (lake boat), *50*
Civil Aeronautics Board, 205–206
Classic Trains (magazine), 147
Cleveland, Ohio, 47, 50, 52, 71, 74, 88, 153, 160, 185–187, 194
Cleveland, Southwestern & Columbus Railway, 152
Cleveland, Southwestern Railway & Light Company, 153
Cleveland-Akron Bus Company, 174
Cleveland & Buffalo Transit Company, 52

Cleveland-Ashtabula-Conneaut Bus Company, 152
Cleveland-Pittsburgh Motor Stage, 173
Clinton, DeWitt, 63, 71–72
Clinton Line (packet boat company), 86
Clovis, New Mexico, 192–193
Cocoa, Florida, 173
Colbert, Claudette, 170
Colden, Cadwallader, 72
Colon, Panama, 58
Colorado Midland Railway, 125
Colorado Public Utilities Commission, 166
Columbia Nite Coach Lines, 154
Columbus (steamboat), 43
Columbus, Ohio, 3–4, 68, 168, 191
Columbus Lateral Canal, 68
Comair, 208
Communications Workers of America, 217
Concord, New Hampshire, 6, 134
Concord & Montreal Railroad, 5
Concord stagecoach, 6–7
Conemaugh River, 78
Constellation (steamboat), 35
Continental Airlines, 209
Continental Limited (passenger train), 120
Contract Air Mail Act (1925), 187–188
Coolidge, Calvin, 187
Cooper, Gary, 217
Coos Bay, Oregon, 59
Council Bluffs, Iowa, 100
Coyote Special (passenger train), 119
Crescent Stages, 176
Crestline, Ohio, 120
Creston, Iowa, 142
Cromwell, Iowa, 142
Crosbyton, Texas, 98
Cross Country Cruise (film), 170–171
Crown Stage Lines, 163
Cumberland, Maryland, 4
Cumberland River, 38
Cumberland Road. *See* National Road
Cummins, Amos Jay, 143–144
Currier, Nathaniel, 54
Curtis, Glenn, 183
Curtis Condor Biplane (airplane), 193, 198
Curtis-Iowa Corporation, 184

Dallas, Texas, 198, 203
Darling, Velva, 192
Darwin, Indiana, 88
Davenport, Iowa, 16
Day, Laraine, 218
Dayton, Ohio, 183, 191, 199
DC-1 (airplane), 197
DC-2 (airplane), 197–198
DC-3 (airplane), 198–199, 202
DC-4 (airplane), 199–200, 218
DC-6 (airplane), 201
DC-8 (airplane), 204
Delaware & Hudson Canal, 67
Delmonico (dining car), 105
Delta Airlines, 201, 108, 211, 214
Denver (steamship), 56
Denver, Colorado, 5, 107, 109, 166
Denver & Rio Grande Western Railroad, 110, 133
Des Plaines, Illinois, 174
Detroit, Michigan, 47, 50–52, 123, 126, 160, 185–186, 203
Detroit & Buffalo Steamboat Company, 53
Detroit & Cleveland Steam Navigation Company, 50, 51–52
DeVoto, Bernard, 202–203
Diana (steamboat), 32
Dickens, Charles, 9, 15, 80, 82, 84–85, 138–139
Dining Car Preservation Society, 147
Dossin Great Lakes Museum, 61
Double Wells, Georgia, 15
Douglas, Georgia, *112*
Douglas Aircraft Company, 197–199, 204
Douglas DC-3/Dakota Historical Society, 217
Douglas Sleeper Transport (airplane), 198
Dover, Delaware, 206
Dubuque, Iowa, 158
Duke, Donald, 147
Duluth, Minnesota, 51, 148–149
Dundaff, Pennsylvania, 11

Eastern Air Lines, 207, 210
Eastern Star (canal boat), 74
Eastern States (lake boat), 53
Eastland (lake boat), 41, 48–49
East Tennessee, Virginia & Georgia Railroad, 114
Eaton, Amos, 89–90
Eaton & Gilbert Company, 6

Eddy, Don, 200
Eddy, Mary Baker, 134
Edmonds, Walter, 92
Edward G. Budd Company, 109, 111
Electric interurbans, 144–146, 149, 150, 152–153, 155–156
Electro-Motive Division, General Motors, 122
Elida, Ohio, 120
El Paso, Texas, 4
Empire State Express (passenger train), 118, 120
Enterprise (steamboat), 28
Erie Canal, 63–67, 69, 72–73, 75, 77, 78, 80–87, 89, 93, 100, 226n, 227n
Erie Lackawanna Historical Society, 147
Erie Lackawanna Railroad, *141*
Erie Water (book), 92
Ettrick, Wisconsin, 98
Ettrick & Northern Railroad, 98
Evansville, Indiana, 65
Ewing, Thomas, 71–72
Excelsior (steamboat), 44, 46

Fageol Safety Coach, 165
Fairmount, North Dakota, 99
Fairmount & Veblen Railway, 99
Fall River, Massachusetts, 55
Fall River Line, 55
Farmer (steamboat), 38
Federal Airport Act (1950), 203
Federal Aviation Administration, 209
Fine Arts Museum of San Francisco, 61
Finney, Charles, 89
Fitch, John, 27
Floydada, Texas, 98
Fokker Tri-Motor (airplane), 194–195
Fontenac (steamboat), 46
Ford, John, 22
Ford Model T (automobile), 155
Ford Tri-Motor (airplane), 191
Fort Adams, Mississippi, 43
Fort Smith, Arkansas, 4
Fort Travis, Texas, 174
Fort Wayne (steamboat), 40
Fort Wayne, Indiana, 69, 90, 120
Fort Worth, Texas, 203
400s (passenger trains), 120
Fox sisters, 89
Frankfort, Kentucky, 12

Franklin, Benjamin, 63
Fred Harvey Company, 164, 191–192
Fremont, California, 180
Frink & Walker Company, 4
Frisco Railway. *See* St. Louis-San Francisco Railway
From Canal Boy to President (book), 74
Fulton, Robert, 28
Fulton County Narrow Gauge Railway, *103*

Gable, Clark, 170
Galena (steamboat), 46
Galena & Chicago Union Railroad, 4, 102
Galesburg, Illinois, 103
Gallatin, Albert, 65–66
Galveston, Texas, 55–56
Gann, Ernest, 218
Garfield, James A., 74
Gates, Edward, 199
Geddes, James, 66
General Motors Corporation, 171–172
General Survey Act (1824), 66
Georgia & Florida Railroad, *112*
Georgia Railroad, 15
Glendale, California, 192
Glen Ellyn, Illinois, 22
Golden Eagle Transcontinental Lines, 167
Golden Spike National Historic Site, 148
Golden West Books, 147
Goldsboro, North Carolina, 14
Goodrich Line, *49*
"Gooney Bird." *See* DC-3
Great Lake Stages, 174
Great Northern (steamship), 59
Great Northern Pacific Steamship Company, 59
Great Northern Railway, 50, 59, 110, 130, 132
Great Western Railroad. *See* Chicago Great Western Railroad
Greeley, Horace, 16
Green Bay & Western Railroad, 98
Greencastle, Indiana, 101
Grenville, South Dakota, 99
Greyhound Lines, 152, *155*, 156–158, 162–163, 168, 170–171, 173–174, 176–179, *181*. *See also* Atlantic Greyhound Lines

Guilford, Linda Thayer, 137

Hamlet, North Carolina, 134
Hardy, Lady Duffus, 127
Harris, Larry, 213
Harrisburg, Pennsylvania, 161–162
Harvard (steamship), 59
Harvey, Fred, 103
Harvey Houses, 127–128
Havana, Cuba, 185–186
Havana, Illinois, 103
Hawthorne, Nathaniel, 117
Henry, William, 27
Herman T. Pott National Inland Waterways Library, 61
Hershey, Pennsylvania, 180
Hiawatha (passenger train), 120, *121*, 122
Hibbing, Minnesota, 180–181
High and the Mighty, The (film), 217–218
Hill, James J., 50–52
Historical Collections of the Great Lakes, 61
Hone, Philip, 86
Honolulu, Hawaii, 218
Hoosac Tunnel & Wilmington Railroad, 147
Hoover, Herbert, 196
House of Seven Gables (book), 117
Houston, Texas, 177
Howland, S. A., 54
Hudson River, 27, 29, 37
Hudson River Day Line, 45
Hudsonville, Indiana, 88
Hunt, Freeman, 117
Huron, South Dakota, 140
Hydesville, New York, 89

Idlewild (lake boat), 51
Illinois & Michigan Canal, 4, 68–69, 71, 84, 92
Illinois & Michigan Canal Heritage Corridor, 92
Illinois Central Railroad, 96, 110, 112, 130
Illinois Electric Railway Association, 150
Illinois Electric Railways, *150*
Illinois Railroad Museum, 148
Illinois Terminal Railroad, *153*
Independence Air, 210
Indiana House of Representatives, 64
Indianapolis, Indiana, 4, 152, 191

Indian-Detour Tours, 163–164
Inland Air Lines, 201
Interstate Airlines, *213*
Interstate Commerce Commission, 95–96
Interstate Public Service Company, *152*
Interstate Stages, 172
Interstate Transit Lines, *159*
Interstate Transportation Company, 173
Interstate Trolley Club, 146
Interurbans. *See* Electric interurbans
Iowa & Omaha Short Line Railway, 99–100
Iowa Board of Railroad Commissioners, 142–143
It Happened One Night (film), 170

Jack Rabbit Bus Line, 172
Jacksonville, Florida, 56
James, Harry, 204
Jameson's Stage Line, 5
James River & Kanawha Canal, 66, 79, *80*, 83
Jamestown, North Dakota, 206
Jefferson, Thomas, 63, 65
Jefferson Transportation Company, 168
Jervis, John, 66
Jim Crow laws, 140
Johnstown, Pennsylvania, 202
Joliet, Illinois, 69
Jones, Casey, 112–113
June Bug (airplane), 183

Kalmbach Publishing Company, 147
Kanawha & James River Canal, 66, 79, *80*, 83
Kansas City, Missouri, 46, 184, 191, 197, 209
Kansas Pacific Railroad, 97, 144
Kelly, Clyde, 187
Kelly Act. *See* Contract Air Mail Act (1925)
Kemp, Harry, 131
Kentucky Board of Health, 137
Keokuk, Iowa, 15, 40
Keys, C. M., 188
Key West, Florida, 56, 185
Kill Devil Hills, North Carolina, 183
Kingman, Arizona, 192
Kingsland, Indiana, 41
Kishacoquillas Valley Railroad, *123*
Klondike gold rush, 59–60, 225n

Knight, June, 170
Know-Nothing movement, 89
Knoxville, Tennessee, 28

Lady of the Lake (steamboat), 5
Lafayette, Indiana, 70, 76
Lake Champlain, 84
Lake Erie, 46–48, 52
Lake Michigan, 48
Lake Ontario, 46
Lake Shore & Michigan Southern Railroad, 135–136
Lake Superior Railroad Museum, 148
Lancaster, Pennsylvania, 2, 146
Lancaster Railroad & Locomotive Historical Society, 146
Lancaster Turnpike, 2
Lannon, R. L., 166
La Salle, Illinois, 84
Las Vegas, New Mexico, 164
Leavenworth & Pikes Peak Express Company, 5
Leavenworth, Pawnee & Western Railroad, 97
Lee Center, Illinois, 145
Lehrer, Jim, 180
Lewis, Dixon Hall, 17
Lexington (steamboat), 53–55
Liberty Air Lines, 210
Life on the Mississippi (book), 61
Lighter Relieving a Steamboat Aground (painting), 62
Lincoln, Abraham, 105
Lincoln Financial Service, 188
Lindbergh, Ann Morrow, 191
Lindbergh, Charles, 187–188
Lisbon, Ohio, 92
Lockheed Constellation (airplane), 201
Lockheed Electra II (airplane), 204
Lockheed L-1011 (airplane), 205
Lockport, New York, 84
Logan House (station restaurant), 127
Lohrville, Iowa, 97
Long Island Sound, 53–54
Lord, Eleazar, 71
Lorena (steamboat), 24
Los Angeles, California, 4, 58–59, 96, 119, 163, 166–167, 188, 192–193, 197–198, 204, 209, 214
Los Gatos, California, 131
Lot Whitcomb (steamboat), 28

Louisville, Kentucky, 12, 15, 26, 28, 34, 36, 38, 109, 152
Louisville & Nashville Railroad, 109
Louisville & Portland Canal, 26
Low Bridge, Everybody Down! (song), 92
Lowell, Massachusetts, 63, 77

M-1000 and *M-1001* (passenger trains), 109
Maddux Airlines, 192
Madison, James, 65–66
Madison, Wisconsin, 158
Maid of the Midst (boat), 171
Maine Stages, 174
Mallory Steamship Lines, 57
Malta, Ohio, 24
Manitoba (steamboat), 31
Marshall, Walter Gore, 144
Maumee, Ohio, 91
May Flower (lake boat), 47
McClellan, James (Jim), 95
McDonnell Douglas DC-10 (airplane), 205
McKeen, William R., 107
McKeen Motor Car, 107, *108*, 109
McKinley, William, 51
McNary-Waters Act (1930), 196
Meek, Donald, 22
Mega Bus, 161
Memories of Mr. Judson (book), 87
Memphis, Tennessee, 4, 21, 41, 211
Merchants' Limited (passenger train), 107
Metroliners (passenger trains), 111
Metropolitan Museum of Art, 61
Miami, Florida, 185, 204
Miami & Erie Canal, 69, 88, *91*
Michigan Central Railroad, 48, 118, 119, 136
Michigan City, Indiana, 101
Mid-Continent Coaches, 169
Middlesex Canal, 63, 77
Miles City, Manitoba, 206
Milford and Owego Turnpike, 11
Milton, Indiana, 86
Milwaukee, Wisconsin, 47, 120
Milwaukee Road. *See* Chicago, Milwaukee, St. Paul & Pacific Railroad
Minneapolis, Minnesota, 96, 120, 128, 168, 187
Minneapolis, St. Paul & Sault Ste. Marie Railroad, 96–97, 99
Minneapolis & St. Louis Railway, 96

Minnesota Motor Bus Association, 156

Minnesota River, 31

Minot, Charles, 118

Missionary (passenger train), 192

Mississippi River, 24

Missouri Pacific Railroad, 46, *113*, 130

Missouri River, 25, 46, 61

Missouri Southern Railroad, 113–114

Mitchell, Thomas, 22

Mobile, Alabama, 38, 55, 109, 179

Model Railroader (magazine), 147

Model railroaders, 147

Mohawk Airlines, 216

Moingona, Iowa, 136

Monmouth (steamboat), 44

Monmouth, Illinois, 184

Monroe, James, 65–66

Montgomery, Alabama, 38, 109

Montrose, Iowa, 40

Montrose, Pennsylvania, 11

Morgan, David, 203

Morgan, J. P., Sr., 96

Morrow, Jeremiah, 71

Mostly Canallers (book), 92

Motor Bus Society, 180

Motor Carrier Act (1935), 157

Motor Coach Age (publication), 180

Motor Transit Company, 163

Motor Transit Lines, 169

Mount Carmel, Indiana, 88

Mount Taylor, New Mexico, 194

Moyer, W. U., 193

Murray, Charles, 15

Murray, David Christie, 55

Murry, Pauli, 177

Muscatine, Iowa, 16

Museum of Bus Transportation, 180

Napoleon, Arkansas, 42

Narragansett Bay, 54

Nashua, Iowa, 165

Nashua Junction, New Hampshire, 5

Nashville, Chattanooga & St. Louis Railway, 41, 136

Nashville, Tennessee, 41, 136

Nassau, Bahamas, 185

Natchez, Mississippi, 43

National Air and Space Museum, 217

National Air Lines, 196, 204, 210

National Association of Railroad Enthusiasts. *See* Railroads: Enthusiasts

National Gallery of Art, 61

National Labor Relations Board, 179

National Mississippi River Museum and Aquarium, 61

National Motor Bus Association, 180

National Park Service, 92

National Railroad Passenger Corporation, 111, 137, 162–163

National Railway Historical Society, 146

National Road, 4, 7, 12, 14

Neil, William, 5

Neoga, Iowa, 99

New Albany, Indiana, 101–102

New Albany & Salem Rail Road, 101–102

Newark, Ohio, 71

New Castle & Frenchtown Rail Road, 117

New England States (passenger train), 128

Newfane, Vermont, 100–101

New Hampshire Public Service Corporation, 153

New Haven Railroad. *See* New York, New Haven & Hartford Railroad

New Orleans (steamboat), 28

New Orleans, Louisiana, 38, 36, 42–43, 65, 109

Newport, Rhode Island, 185

Newport News, Virginia, 55

"News butchers," 111

New York, New Haven & Hartford Railroad, 96, 107

New York, New York, 2, 29, 34, 50, 53–56, 64, 70, 72, 87, 96, 105, 107, 110–111, 114, 119, 122, 132, 137, 146, 161–162, 170, 185, 187–188, 191, 197–199, 201–204, 210

New York & New Haven Railroad, 135

New York and Texas Steamship Company, 56

New York Central Railroad, 96, 105–106, 110, 114, 118–120, 122, 128, 132, 188. *See also* Lake Shore & Michigan Southern Railroad; Michigan Central Railroad

New York Express (passenger train), 135

New York State Barge Canal, 93

Niagara (canal boat), 77

Niagara Falls, 171

Nicaragua Route, 58

No. 999 (locomotive), 118, 231n

Norfolk, Nebraska, 165

Norfolk, Virginia, 55

North Central Airlines, 201

Northern Pacific (steamship), 59

Northern Pacific Railroad, 59, 129–130, 143

Northern Steamship Company, 51

Northland (steamboat), 51–52

Northland Transportation Company, 163

North West (steamboat), 51–52

Northwest Airlines, 206, 214

North Western Railway. *See* Chicago & North Western Railway

Northwest Steamship Company, 60

Oakland, California, 110

Oakland, Nebraska, *115*

Oatman Pass, Arizona, 166

Official Bus Schedule, *151*

Ohio & Erie Canal, 66–68, 70–71, 74, 76, 79, 81, 84, 88–90, 100

Ohio River, 26, 37, 39–40

Ohio Stage Company, 4

Ohio State Penitentiary, 68

Old Dominion Line, 55

Olympia, Washington, 206

Omaha, Nebraska, 96, 108, 187, 199

Omaha Road. *See* Chicago, St. Paul, Minneapolis & Omaha Railroad

Oregon Motor Stages, 163

Oriental Limited (passenger train), 132

Ottawa, Illinois, 71

Overland (automobile), 155

Overland Limited (passenger train), 126, 129

Owego, New York, *141*

Ozark Airlines, 201, 210

Pacific (steamship), 58

Pacific Airlines, 196

Pacific Bus Museum, 180

Pacific Coast Steamship Company, 56, 59

Pacific Greyhound Lines, 171

Pacific Rail Road, 4

Pacific Steamship Company, 59

Paducah, Kentucky, 160

Panama City, Panama, 58

Panama Railroad, 58

Pan-American (passenger train), 109

Pan American World Airways, 204

Paris, France, 187, 204

Parkhurst, Charlie, 220n
Patterson, Caldwell & Company
  Stage Line, 5
Pendleton, Oregon, 199
Penn Central Transportation
  Company, 96
Pennsylvania & Ohio Canal, 74, 76
Pennsylvania-Central Airlines, 215
Pennsylvania Limited (passenger
  train), 119–120
Pennsylvania Railroad, 96, 103, 106,
  110–111, 119, 120, 122, *124–125*,
  188, *189*, 191
Pennsylvania Special (passenger
  train), 119
Pennsylvania State Works, 65–66,
  78, 82, 100, 127
Pentagon, Washington, DC, 210
People's Express, 205–206
Peoria, Illinois, 153
Peter Pan Bus Lines, 164, 174
Philadelphia, Pennsylvania, 2, 111,
  137, 146, 202
Phoebe Snow (passenger train), *141*
Phoenix, Arizona, 5
Picknelly, Peter, 164
Pickwick Airways, 153
Pickwick Stages, 153, *154*, 163
Picolata, Florida, 14
Piedmont Airlines, 201, 213–214
Pierce, George Foster, 38–39
Pioneer (locomotive), *102*
Pioneer (sleeping car), *104*, 105
Pittsburgh (steamboat), 39
Pittsburgh, Pennsylvania, 26–28, 36,
  38, 74, 160–161
Plane Talk (magazine), 192
Plessy v. Ferguson (1896), 140
Polk, James K., 61
Portair, New Mexico, 192
Port Amboy, New Jersey, 2
Port Columbus, Ohio, 191, 193
Port Huron, Michigan, 51
Portland, Maine, 55
Portland, Oregon, 38, 59, 108, 199
Portsmouth, New Hampshire, 2
Portsmouth, Ohio, 88
Post House (restaurant), 168
Powell, William Norland, 181
PowerShips (magazine), 61
Prairie (steamboat), 43
Prescott, Arizona, 5
Priscilla (steamboat), 55
Procter & Gamble Company, 211
Promontory, Utah, 96

Providence (steamboat), 55
Providence, Rhode Island, 54, 122
PSA Airlines, 216
Pullman, George M., 104–105
Pullman Company, 105, 111, 122,
  126–127, 138
Putnam (steamboat), 38

Quannah, Acme & Pacific Railway,
  98
Quannah, Texas, 98
Queen of the Pacific (steamship), 58

Railroad Development Corporation,
  161–162
Railroad History (journal), 146
Railroad Museum of Pennsylvania,
  148
Railroads
  Accidents, 135, *136*, 137
  Construction openings, 100–102
  Early projects, 96
  Enthusiasts, *146*, 147
  Hobos and tramps, 132–134
  Mileage, 95–96
  Passenger rolling stock, 102–103,
    104, 105, *106*, 107, *108–109*,
    110–111, *121*, *123*, *128*, *130*
  Popularity of projects, 97–99
  Racial segregation, 140
  Regulatory commissions and
    public complaints, 141–143
  Sexual segregation, 139–140
  Speed records, 118–120, 122
  Streamliners, 127
  System building and expansion,
    96–97
  Track structure, 102, 106
  Train crews: brakemen, 115;
    conductors, 111–115; engineers,
    111, *112–113*, 114; firemen, *112*,
    114; Pullman porters, 105
  Train discontinuances, 143
  Train dispatchers, 116–117
  Travel displeasures, 117, 122, 127,
    134–141, 143–144
  Travel pleasures, 117–120, 122–132
  Station agents, *115*, *116*
  Weather disruptions, 137
Railroad State Historical Society,
  147
Railway & Locomotive Historical
  Society, 145
Raleigh & Augusta Railroad, 134
Range Rapid Transit Company, 149

Rapid City, South Dakota, *158*
Rathbone, John, 71
Rawlins, Wyoming, 12
Reading Railroad, 120, 143
Red Ball Transportation Company,
  165
Red Bird Line, 77, 87
Red Devil (airplane), 183
Red Oak, Iowa, 108
Red Oak & North Eastern Railway,
  108
Red River, 25
Red River of the North, 31
Reed Line (packet boat company),
  73, 81
Reedsville, Pennsylvania, *123*
Reno, Nevada, 187
Rensselaer & Saratoga Railway, 117
Rensselaer Polytechnic Institute,
  66
Rensselaer School, 89
*Report of the Secretary of the Treasury
  on the Subject of Roads and
  Canals* (US report), 65
Resort Air, 208
Richmond, Virginia, 55, 79
Ritter, Iowa, 142
Rochester, New York, 68, 81, 84, 87
Rockefeller, John D., 127
Rock Island Railroad. *See* Chicago,
  Rock Island & Pacific Railroad
Rockledge, Florida, 173
Rock Springs, Wyoming, 167
Rocky Mountain Rocket (passenger
  train), 107
Rodgers, Calbraith Perry, 183
Rogers, Charles "Buddy," 217
Rome Haul (book), 92
Royal Limited (passenger train), 120
Rumsey, James, 27
Russell, Sir Charles, 58
Russell, William, 5
Russellville, Indiana, 88

Saar, Henry, 99–100
Sacramento, California, 96, 148
Sacramento River, 26
Saint Augustine, Florida, 14
Saint Clair Junction, Ontario, 119
Saint Joseph, Missouri, 5
Saint Louis, Missouri, 4, 15, 21, 36,
  38, 42, 46, 132, 149, 153, 183, 187,
  191, 194, 211
Saint Mary's Falls Ship Canal, 23
Saint Paul, Minnesota, 38, 46, 87

Saint Petersburg-Tampa Airboat Line, 184

Salem, Oregon, 206

Salt Lake City, Utah, 21, 187, 199

San Antonio, Texas, 42, 168–169

San Diego, California, 58, 153, 163

Sandwich, New Hampshire, 5

Sandy & Beaver Canal, 89, 92

San Francisco, California, 4, 21, 58–59, 126, 139, 170, 179, 187, 192, 201, 218

San Francisco and Portland Steamship Company, 58–59

San Francisco National Historical Park, 61

Santa Ana, California, 163

Santa Cruz, California, 131

Santa Fe, New Mexico, 164

Santa Fe Railway. *See* Atchison, Topeka & Santa Fe Railway

Santa Fe Trail Transportation Company, 171

Santa Fe Trailways, 169

Santa Fe Transportation Company, 164, 171

Santee Canal, 67

Saratoga Springs, New York, 117

Savannah, Georgia, 3, 40, 55

Savannah River, 40

Schenectady, New York, 78, 81–82, 85–87

Science of Railways (book), 113

Scott, Walter "Death Valley Scotty," 119

Seaboard Air Line Railroad, 110

Seattle, Washington, 58–60, 153, 199

Seattle-Victoria Air Mail Line, 185

"Second Great Awakening," 89

Seeanbee (lake boat), 52

Separatist Society of Zoar, 68

Shaw, Ronald, 92–93

Short Way Lines, 171–172

Shreve, Henry, 29

Sioux City, Iowa, 140, 149, 165

Sioux Falls, South Dakota, 149

Sioux Falls Traction System, 149

Skagway, Alaska, 60

Smithsonian Institution, 217

Soo Line Railroad. *See* Minneapolis, St. Paul & Sault Ste. Marie Railroad

South Coast Pacific Railroad, 131

Southern Greyhound, 177

Southern Pacific Historical & Technical Society, 147

Southern Pacific Railroad, 42, 58–59, 96, 108, 110, 129–130, 188

Southern Railway, 106

Southern Railway Historical Society, 147

Southhampton, Long Island, 185

South Lawrence, Massachusetts, 118

South Londonderry, Vermont, 101

South Norwalk, Connecticut, 135

Southwest Airlines, 206, 216

Spalding & Rodgers Circus, 88

Spirit Airlines, 210

Spirit Fruit Society, 89

Spirit of St. Louis (Airplane), 187

Spokane, Portland & Seattle Railway, 59

Springfield (sleeping car), 104–105

Springfield, Illinois, 105, 153

Springfield, Massachusetts, 164

Stack, Robert, 218

Stagecoach (film), 22

Stagecoaches

  Descriptions, 2, 6–7, 18, 20–21

  Drivers, 8–10

  Horses and mules, 7–8

  Legacies, 21–22

  Origins and early development, 1–5

  Travel pleasures, 11–13

  Travel displeasures, 13–17, 19–21

Stansbury, Helen, 200

Statesmen (steamboat), 43

Steam Boat (steamboat), 27

Steamboat Disasters and Railroad Accidents in the United States (book), 54

Steamship Historical Society of America, 60–61

Steel City Flyer (bus), 161, 162–163

Stevenson, Robert Louis, 131–132, 135

St. Louis-San Francisco Railway, 98

Stockton, California, 176

Stonington, Rhode Island, 54

Stout Airlines, 153, 196, 214

Strasburg, Pennsylvania, 148

Stratoliners (airplanes), 202

Sultana (steamboat), 41, 223–224n

Superior (lake boat), 47

Surry, Illinois, 119

Swain, Davd, 14

Swan (steamboat), 40

Tacoma, Washington, 59

Talgo (passenger train), 110–111

Tauck, Arthur C., Sr., 164–165

Tauck Company, 164–165

Tennessee River, 24–25, 28

Terre Haute, Indiana, 65, 77, 88

Timber, Oregon, 108

Time and Tide (steamboat), 31

"Tin Goose." *See* Ford Tri-Motor

Tipton, Missouri, 4

Tip Top, Arizona, 5

Tise, Larry, 93

Toledo, Ohio, 47, 50, 51, 70, 77, 160

Toledo, St. Louis & Kansas City Railroad, 91

Tracy, California, 176–177

Trailways System, 157, 163, 173, 177. *See also* Burlington Trailways; Santa Fe Trailways

Trains (magazine), 147

Train X (passenger train), 111

Transcontinental Air Transport, 188, 189, 190, 191–194

Transcontinental & Western Air Lines, 193, 197, 214

Trans-Continental Passenger Association, 167

Transportation Act (1958), 95, 143

Transportation Security Administration, 210

Trans-World Airways, 193, 204–205, 208, 210

Trenton (sailboat), 44

Trevor, Claire, 22

Treynor, Iowa, 98–99

Troy, New York, 6, 84, 87, 89

Troy Stagecoach, 6

Tucson, Arizona, 4

Tulsa, Oklahoma, 167

TurboTrain (passenger train), 111

Turnpikes, 2–3, 5, 11

Twain, Mark, 8, 13, 61

Twentieth Century Limited (passenger train), 110, 119, 122

Twin City Zephyrs (passenger trains), 110, 120

Union, Illinois, 148

Union Pacific Railroad, 5, 96, 97, 106–110, 126, 129, 144, 188

Union Pacific Stages, 167

United Air Lines, 196–197, 199–200, 204, 208, 211, 214, 216

United Motor Coach Company, 174

Universal Air Lines, 194

Uppercu, Inglis, 185–187

US Air, 214

US Army, 187

US Army Air Corps, 212
US Department of Commerce, 187
US Department of Justice, 178
US Equal Employment Opportunity
    Commission, 216
US Military Academy, 66
US Navy, 186–187
US Office of Defense
    Transportation, 168
US Post Office Department, 185, 187
Utica, New York, 80, 85–86

Vanderbilt, Cornelius, 53–54
Vanderbilt, William H., 152–153
Varney Airlines, 196
Vermont Transit Bus Company, 152
Vincennes, Indiana, 88
Virginia (lake boat), *49*
Virginia, Minnesota, 149
Virginia & Truckee Railroad, 118
von Gerstner, Franz Anton Ritter,
    36, 46

Wabash & Erie Canal, 65, 70, 75–77,
    83, 85, 88
Wabash Railroad, 132
Wabash Railroad Historical Society,
    147
Wagner Palace Car Company, 105
Walhonding Canal, 69, 71
Walk-in-the-Water (lake boat), *46*
Warner's Ranch, California, 22
Warren (steamboat), *44*
Washington (steamboat), *29*
Washington, DC, 111, 137, 187, 195,
    202, 210, 217
Waterbury, Vermont, 22
Waterford, New York, 117

Waterloo, Iowa, 194
Waterways
    Canoes and pirogues, 26
    Coastal vessels, 53–55, 57;
        accidents, 54; travel
        experiences, 54–56, 57, 58–60
    Flatboats and keelboats, 26–27
    Geography, 23–24
    Great Lakes boats, 46–48, *49–51*,
        52, 53; accidents, 48, 50; crews,
        48; railroad competition, 50;
        travel experiences, 50, 52–53
    Legacy, 60–61
    River piracy, 27
    Snags and sawyers, 25–26, 41–42
    Steamboats, 24, 27–31; accidents,
        40–44; crews, 31–34;
        excursions, 45, 46; railroad
        competition, 46; travel
        experiences–negative, 37–44,
        46; travel experiences–positive,
        34–37
Wayne, John, 218
Waynoka, Oklahoma, 191–193
Webster City, Iowa, *146*
Weirs, New Hampshire, 5
Welland Canal, 23
Wells Fargo Museum, 21, 22
Western Air Lines, 193
Western Pacific Railroad, 110
Western Seaman's Friend Society, 75
Western Stage Company, 7
Western World (lake boat), *48*
Westerners International, 21
West Point, New York, 37
Whipple, Henry Benjamin, 14, 19,
    20, 56
White, Alice, 170

Wichita, Kansas, 191
Wilder, Laura Ingles, 135
Wiley, Dr. Harvey, 128–129
Willamette River, 28
Williamson, Ellen Douglas,
    126–127
Windsor, John B., 193
Windsor, Ontario, 119
Wings (film), 217
Winslow, Arizona, 192
Wisconsin Motor Bus Line,
    157–158
Wolf, Thomas, 160
Wolfschlager, Mrs. A. F., 130
Women Airforce Service Pilots
    (WASP), 213
Woodruff Sleeping Car Company,
    105
Worcester, Massachusetts, 138
World's Columbian Exposition, 118
World Trade Center, 210
Wrentham, Massachusetts, 13
Wright, Benjamin, 66
Wright, Orville, 183
Wright, Wilbur, 183

Yakin River, 93
Yale (steamship), 59
Yelloway Bus Company, 158, 166–167,
    174, 178
Yelverton, Theresa (Viscountess
    Avonmore), 139–140
York, Pennsylvania, 140
Yukon, Canada, 59
Yukon River, 59

Zanesville, Ohio, 38, 179
Zephyr (passenger train), *109*

H. ROGER GRANT is Kathryn and Calhoun Lemon Professor of History at Clemson University. He is author of numerous books, including *Visionary Railroader, John W. Barriger III, Railroaders without Borders: A History of the Railroad Development Corporation,* and *Railroads and the American People.*

www.ingramcontent.com/pod-product-compliance
Lightning Source LLC
Chambersburg PA
CBHW040844100426
42812CB00014B/2599